Enterprise Risk Management in Today's World, Part B

EMERALD STUDIES IN FINANCE, INSURANCE, AND RISK MANAGEMENT

Series Editor: Simon Grima

Books in this series collect quantitative and qualitative studies in areas relating to finance, insurance, and risk management. Subjects of interest may include banking, accounting, auditing, compliance, sustainability, behaviour, management, and business economics.

In the disruption of political upheaval, new technologies, climate change, and new regulations, it is more important than ever to understand risk in the financial industry. Providing high-quality academic research, this book series provides a platform for authors to explore, analyse and discuss current and new financial models and theories, and engage with innovative research on an international scale.

Previously published:

Uncertainty and Challenges in Contemporary Economic Behaviour
Ercan Özen and Simon Grima

New Challenges for Future Sustainability and Wellbeing
Ercan Özen, Simon Grima and Rebecca Dalli Gonzi

Insurance and Risk Management for Disruptions in Social, Economic and Environmental Systems: Decision and Control Allocations within New Domains of Risk
Simon Grima, Ercan Özen and Rebecca Dalli Gonzi

Public Sector Leadership in Assessing and Addressing Risk
Peter C. Young, Simon Grima and Rebecca Dalli Gonzi

Big Data Analytics in the Insurance Market
Kiran Sood, B. Balamurugan, Simon Grima and Pierpaolo Marano

Big Data: A Game Changer for Insurance Industry
Kiran Sood, Rajesh Kumar Dhanaraj, B. Balamurugan, Simon Grima and R. Uma Maheshwari

The Adoption and Effect of Artificial Intelligence on Human Resources Management, Part A
Pallavi Tyagi, Naveen Chilamkurti, Simon Grima, Kiran Sood and B. Balamurugan

The Adoption and Effect of Artificial Intelligence on Human Resources Management, Part B
Pallavi Tyagi, Naveen Chilamkurti, Simon Grima, Kiran Sood and B. Balamurugan

Contemporary Studies of Risks in Emerging Technology, Part A
Simon Grima, Kiran Sood and Ercan Özen

Contemporary Studies of Risks in Emerging Technology, Part B
Simon Grima, Kiran Sood and Ercan Özen

The Framework for Resilient Industry: A Holistic Approach for Developing Economies
Narinder Kumar, Kiran Sood, Ercan Özen and Simon Grima

VUCA and Other Analytics in Business Resilience, Part A
Deepmala Singh, Kiran Sood, Sandeep Kautish and Simon Grima

VUCA and Other Analytics in Business Resilience, Part B
Deepmala Singh, Kiran Sood, Sandeep Kautish and Simon Grima

Finance Analytics in Business: Perspectives on Enhancing Efficiency and Accuracy
Sanjay Taneja, Pawan Kumar, Kiran Sood, Ercan Özen and Simon Grima

Enterprise Risk Management in Today's World: Enterprise-Wide Risk Management and Strategy, Part A
Author: Jean-Paul Louisot; Editor: Simon Grima

Enterprise Risk Management in Today's World: A Current and Futuristic View of the Complexity, Resilience, Responsibility and Tools in ERM, Part B

BY

JEAN-PAUL LOUISOT
JPLA Consultants LLC, France

EDITED BY

SIMON GRIMA
University of Malta, Malta

emerald
PUBLISHING

United Kingdom – North America – Japan – India – Malaysia – China

Emerald Publishing Limited
Emerald Publishing, Floor 5, Northspring, 21-23 Wellington Street, Leeds LS1 4DL.

First edition 2024

British Library Cataloguing in Publication Data
A catalogue record for this book is available from the British Library

ISBN: 978-1-83608-393-1 (Print)
ISBN: 978-1-83608-392-4 (Online)
ISBN: 978-1-83608-394-8 (Epub)

Printed and bound by CPI Group (UK) Ltd, Croydon, CR0 4YY

INVESTOR IN PEOPLE

Epigraph

Whenever a theory appears to you as the only possible one, take this as a sign that you have neither understood the theory nor the problem which it was intended to solve.

The old scientific ideal of episteme – of absolutely certain, demonstrable knowledge – has proved to be an idol. The demand for scientific objectivity makes it inevitable that every scientific statement must remain tentative forever.

Karl Popper

You can't depend on your eyes when your imagination is out of focus.

Mark Twain

Our greatest glory is not in ever falling, but in rising every time we fall.

Confucius

The position and momentum of a particle cannot be simultaneously measured with arbitrarily high precision. There is a minimum for the product of the uncertainties of these two measurements. There is likewise a minimum for the product of the uncertainties of the energy and time.

Heisenberg, in *Uncertainty principle paper*, 1927

The world is changing. Networks without a specific branding strategy will be killed I envision a world of narrowly niche services and tightly run companies without room for all the overhead the established networks carry.

Barry Diller, press Tycoon

'If a nation expects to be ignorant and free in a state of civilization, it expects what was and never will be. The people cannot be free without information.'

Thomas Jefferson letter to Charles Yancy (1816)

Contents

Part 3: ERM, Governance & ESG

Part 4: ERM for Tomorrow

Part 5: ERM Specific Domains & Tools

List of Figures and Tables

Figures

Tables

About the Author

Prof Jean-Paul Louisot holds a PhD in Management Sciences (Université PARIS 1 Panthéon Sorbonne – 2014), a mining engineering degree, a Master in Economics, and an MBA from the Kellogg School of Management. Since 1993, he has been teaching and coaching post-graduate students and risk management professionals. After 9 years at Paris 1 Panthéon-Sorbonne University, and 10 years in postgraduate courses in Risk Management at the Institut Catholique de Lille, he has participated in the development of the European designation, Rimap, promoted by FERMA.

About the Editor

Prof Simon Grima is the Deputy Dean of the Faculty of Economics, Management and Accountancy, Associate Professor and the Head of the Department of Insurance and Risk Management. He is also a Professor at the University of Latvia, Faculty of Business, Management and Economics and a visiting Professor at UNICATT Milan.

Preface: Context for Linking ERM and Strategy

The complexity of the business context, combined with the intricacy and interconnections of risk and objectives – necessitates the organisation implement a strategic approach to business and operational resilience. Indeed, there is a growing focus on resilience exacerbated by the pandemic and ensuing geopolitical upheavals. Resilience is the capacity to recover quickly from difficulties/ruptures; the ability of a business to spring back from any disturbance. This is quite critical and many organisations rightfully merge risk management and business continuity management into what is ERM, sometimes defined as a resilience programme.

Any academic studying risk-management can only be surprised that at a time when the world is becoming more and more complex and volatile, most MBA programs are still resting on old scientific principles: they remain founded on Democritus' description of the atom, or at best Bohr's. To be specific, management principles are still anchored on classical physics that allows five-year planning exercises. If governments dropped this practice after the fall of the Soviet Union, how is it possible that so many firms are still indulging in it? Could it be that too many managers have failed to recognise that times are no longer such that a deterministic approach to the future is reasonable?

Traditional physics is founded on the principle that similar causes have similar consequences and proportional causes have proportional consequences. This was fundamentally challenged with advances of modern microphysics, which can be summarised in the uncertainty principle, also called the uncertainty relations, set out by Heisenberg. To some extent, it is this research that opened the path to chaos theory, which does not yet seem to have influenced strategic thinking in most organisations, even if some visionaries appear to be inspired by it, consciously or unconsciously.

Of course, the founders of Apple, Google, and other GAFA come to mind. However, there are also leaders of start-ups and SMEs that may be visionary in their own right like the founders of Air B&B, Uber, etc. SMEs are at the heart of jobs and value creation not only in developed countries but also in emerging countries.

To summarize, it seems reasonable to assess that the strategic processes currently implemented in most organizations are too rigid and sequential. Strategy still relies on the idea that the world's evolution is a series of steps that allow for controllable processes. Resting on periodic reviews of their internal and external contexts, the leaders of these organisations operate without the continuous scouting of the future that would allow them to decipher low-level noises or sentinel events that facilitate an efficient forecast of future evolutions and anticipation of revolutions so the organisation's relevance for its stakeholders' networks can be maintained at all times.

Major economic players, including nation states, have now the capacity to develop and implement models that are increasingly powerful and even include learning capabilities thanks to artificial intelligence (AI): 'Our systems learn by themselves from experience; however, we still choose their learning path. But we must always keep in mind that even the more complex games are more accessible to the computers than the general issues confronting the real world'.[1]

However, even AI specialists remain cautious when it comes to replacing human brains with machines in complex decision-making. As for Werner Heisenberg, reading his principle makes it clear that he questioned the use of the normal distribution, thus opening the possibility of extreme situations, rupture, or black and grey swans. Risk Management Professionals prefer the concept of artificially enhanced intelligence.

About quantum physics, Heisenberg stipulated that as the exact position of a particle cannot be known at a given point in time, the future cannot be determined. A specific trajectory does not lend itself to a precise computation, but only a range of possible trajectories can be determined (however, using Erwin Schrödinger's equation, it is possible to assign a probability to each trajectory).

Economists have yet to produce an equivalent of Schrödinger's equation, as the economic world cannot be described with a simple list of drivers. It is complex and necessitates factoring in the human dimension so interactions are volatile and will need to be approached with fuzzy logic integrations. Would it be reasonable to expect forecasting the future with precision, when even the present eludes the human brain?

For risk management professionals, the good news is that uncertainty and risk must be more and more at the centre of all decision-making, strategic, tactical, or operational; that does not result in the world of decision-making belonging to risk-managers. However, all professionals have understood that the issue of risk has become essential in any decision-making; and they are ready to occupy the field should the existing risk-management professionals not step up to the plate. Competition for the attention of the board for risk issues is open with:

- internal and external auditors with their three lines of defence;
- quality control managers *(whose legitimacy in tackling risk is reinforced by the ISO9000:2015 which includes a chapter on risks)*;
- security and safety specialists, economic intelligence consultants, and
- continuity managers *(another member of the risk professional community)*!

And the list is still open with resilience management as the newest entry. There is a growing list of risk-management in specialised branches but they can be gathered under one roof as they have common goals and use the same tools. With the proliferation of ISO standards dealing with specific risks, the erection of new silos can be feared.

[1]Denis Hassais, founder of DeepMind.

There is no doubt that risk-management has a bright future, especially after the pandemic and the geopolitical unrest, even if it might be shared by many, indeed by all practitioners. As far as the risk-manager's function in any organisation is concerned, even adorned with the title of CRO, a function that is still developing after over two decades of existence while the CIO is now widespread and involved in cyber-risk management, it will survive in this maelstrom only if the incumbents can acquire the talents and competencies needed to grasp what is at stake and manoeuvre to make it to the front of the pack!

The management of risk is a director's and officer's mission; there is not much debate about it now that the codes of governance worldwide tend to assign them direct responsibility and liability to develop and guide their organisations' policies with a clear understanding of and due consideration to the uncertainties and storms of the future. However, without proper gears and relays at all levels in the organisation and with its main partners, the extended enterprise, even the best-defined policy would have little effect on the well-being of the organisation, or society at large.

Managing risk is a core mission for all public and private actors. The survival of all depends on the vigilance of each one. This has a special echo for those individuals who have been trained for Special Forces or intervention units and those dealing with terrorist attacks!

Furthermore, the generalised explosion of social media, now a key player in all social debates, means that transparency in communication and consultation with key stakeholders has become essential; however, it may interfere with speedy decisions required at the early stages of a rupture when a dramatic strategic change may be called for.

Whatever the situation, any new strategy has a reasonable chance of success only if all those involved embrace the change, not only within the organisation but also beyond, i.e. both internal and external stakeholders. This is the reason why a continuous strategic process must be developed and implemented, provided it is informed by global and integrated risk-management and positioned in a change management effort where all can be heard and listened to.

In such a context, the question of democracy in the company, which was at the heart of the debates at the end of the sixties during the students' upheavals, seems to gain new momentum. However, it is unlikely that there will be a 'one size fits all' route to democracy. Sometimes it will surge from the base, others it will result from the will of top management, but success will require both to meet on a common course.

When it comes to change, top management must do it, but all those involved must then embrace it. There is no unique strategy to develop and implement the instruments and processes of resilience, and this is indeed the case for the guidelines proposed in the ISO 31000 standard: it is a toolbox where each artisan must find the most efficient way to use them in each organisation.

In a world evermore complex and volatile, it is not reasonable to build models on deterministic approaches or one man's vision; therefore ERM (Enterprise-wide Risk Management) becomes a key as it offers an approach in which uncertainty is at the centre of any decision. Furthermore, ERM top-bottom and bottom-up paths ensure that all adhere to permanent change, whereas change is what destabilises human beings in any society, as well as any organisation.

As far as democracy and equality are concerned, nobody (except for a few admirers of Proudhon) wants to stray from capitalism, but many want to see a return to the reduced levels of inequality that prevailed before the late eighties.[2]

Readers looking for simple solutions or checklists will be disappointed. The present book is not a cookbook with recipes but rather a book of questions, on all the challenges that any entrepreneur, director, officer, or elected official must meet if (s)he is to promote resilience and justice for the future in a very uncertain context, and to navigate safely through the high seas ahead. ERM does not set aside hazards but aims to optimise risk-taking: enhancing opportunities and curbing threats. ERM is therefore in essence at the core of any strategic exercise.

If climactic change is not heavily mentioned, it is because there are already many books offering experts' thoughts on the matter, from the likely causes to the prevention and protection measures that could be implemented not to mention the GIEC reports.

Furthermore, most of these solutions are beyond the domain of decision and strategy of individual actors, even if individual efforts should not be undervalued. There is also the nagging issue of artificial intelligence, already mentioned. OECD expects AI will become a major threat to humankind within twenty years, but investigations into this scenario seem still at an early stage despite recent developments like chatGPT. However, all organisations must consider these risks in their strategic process at the horizon of 2030/2050. As with other emerging risks, AI and climate change are sources of threats, but they also offer many opportunities for innovators, including transition risk.

[2]Atkinson, A. B. (2015, May). *Unequality – What can be done?* Harvard University Press. http://www.hup.harvard.edu/catalog.php?isbn=9780674504769&content=reviews.

Part 1

Theoretical Contributions to Risk Management

Chapter 1

Enterprise Risk Management: Cindynics Contribution

The capacity to estimate the total cost of accidents or disasters is an essential element in justifying the allocation of resources, particularly financial, for prevention, protection, risk engineering, and more generally risk management. Is it now an important factor in determining the budgets to be allocated to prevent or contain future pandemics or other natural or technological disasters? For the health sector, it is also a way to raise public awareness of its role in creating a safer society and to improve the perception of risk in the public domain, even in France the problem of white planes.

The strategic process begins with a description of the organisation's situation in its context. The situation emerges from a list of networks of actors concerned, stakeholders of sustainable development. While it is fundamental that the description be holistic, different models propose such an approach including:

1. Corporate functions approach:

It lists the 12 functions noted from R1 to R12, which are essential for the establishment of governance that is extended to the entire company:

→ R1: Human Resources;
→ R2: Finances;
→ R3: Marketing;
→ R4: R&D – Research & Development;
→ R5: IT – Information Systems;
→ R6: Strategy, Planning/Budget Control;
→ R7: Risk Management;
→ R8: Legal;
→ R9: Audit;
→ R10: Communication;
→ R11: Logistics;
→ R12: Purchasing/Supply.

Enterprise Risk Management in Today's World: A Current and Futuristic View of the Complexity, Resilience, Responsibility and Tools in ERM, Part B, 3–13

Published under exclusive licence by Emerald Publishing Limited
doi:10.1108/978-1-83608-392-420241001

2. *Resource classes approach:*

In Louisot's 2023 book on risk diagnosis,[1] an impact model has been developed in France to identify all the uncertainties that weigh on the future of an organisation thus allowing it to navigate in the best interests of its stakeholders and value creation in compliance with the values. The space of vulnerability uses three dimensions to achieve this goal and facilitates a complete diagnosis.

The five networks (or resource classes) of the vulnerability space are:

- H = Human: All persons linked to the organisation by employment contracts or mandates, and whose specific skills, training, and experiences make it a real asset for the company. Demographic data such as age, sex, and family status, which may have an impact on production capacity, should also be taken into account. In a nutshell, these are the elements considered, because it is traditional to call 'knowledge management', skills or talent management.
- T = Technical: Buildings, equipment, tools... in a word, all the physical assets within the organisation's direct scope of control. The legal nature of detention is secondary to direct control. Some belong to the organisation and are recorded in the assets of its balance sheet, some are at its disposal under a lease or leasing agreement, and others are on deposit and belong to third parties, including partners. There may be other situations that would take too long to fully identify here.
- I = Information: All the information flows that circulate within the organisation, that are transformed or stored, whatever the medium (computer, paper, or human). The resource also incorporates information about the organisation itself: the perception that others have, i.e. the organisation's stakeholders of the organisation. It can be summarised in the term 'reputation' among emerging risks. These are therefore all elements at the heart of the mission of economic intelligence.
- P = Partners (upstream, downstream, & lateral): All the support of the economic partners of the organisation, upstream (subcontractors and suppliers), downstream (customers), and lateral (co-contractors, known or not, in a global project) essential to the organisation to achieve its objectives or fulfil its missions. These are the partners, for the most part, who are under contract with the organisation and are therefore in a transaction with it, without forgetting their dependency networks.
- F = Financial: All financial flows through the organisation. They affect both short-term flows (cash, liquid, or near-liquid assets) and medium- and long-term flows (financing plan, equity and reserves, and long-term debt). In a nutshell, it's the strategic financial management of the organisation.

---

[1]Jean-Paul Louisot Comprendre et Mettre en Œuvre le diagnostic des risques (AFNOR Paris 2023).

However, the model would not be complete without a sixth network that represents non-contractual exchanges with the environment and externalities in the sense of the economy:

- G = 'Free' Resources:

→ Physical environment;
→ Political, legal, & social environment;
→ Competitive & benefits from third parties ENVIRONMENT.

These five networks plus one are a condensed version of the 12 functions of the previous model and allow for consideration of all the resources that are needed to develop and implement a strategy. In this model, vulnerability/exposure is characterised by the set of impacts on an organisation's objectives when an event occurs changing the amount of a resource.

For this framework, three factors define an exposure:

→ Risk object (or resource in risk);
→ Random event (peril or hazard); and
→ Potential impact (on the organisation's objectives).

Today, it is no longer enough to consider only financial impacts on an organisation; the consequences for stakeholders in the context of the ESG must also be considered, therefore damages are distinguished as follows:

→ Primary and secondary damages: those related to the organisation itself and its resources, including induced damages such as additional costs or operating losses.
→ Tertiary damages: those affecting third parties or the environment.

The analysis must also take into account the positive risk (see Fig. 1.1). Of course, it is important to keep in mind that threats to the organisation may offer opportunities for competitors. Furthermore, risk management's mission is to seek the optimal balance between positive and negative risks, i.e., enhancing opportunities and containing threats.

Alignment between risk management and strategy:

The concept of 'exposures portfolio' is a clear step in leading the integration of risk management into the design and implementation of the organisation's strategy. By enhancing opportunities and containing threats, not only before taking the road but also throughout the stages, risk management contributes to the path to excellence.

The resources can be linked to the multiple functions of the management team, i.e. Human Resources, Finance, Marketing, R&D (research & development), Information systems, Strategy, Planning/Budget Control, Risk management, Legal, Audit, Communication, Logistics, Purchasing, etc.

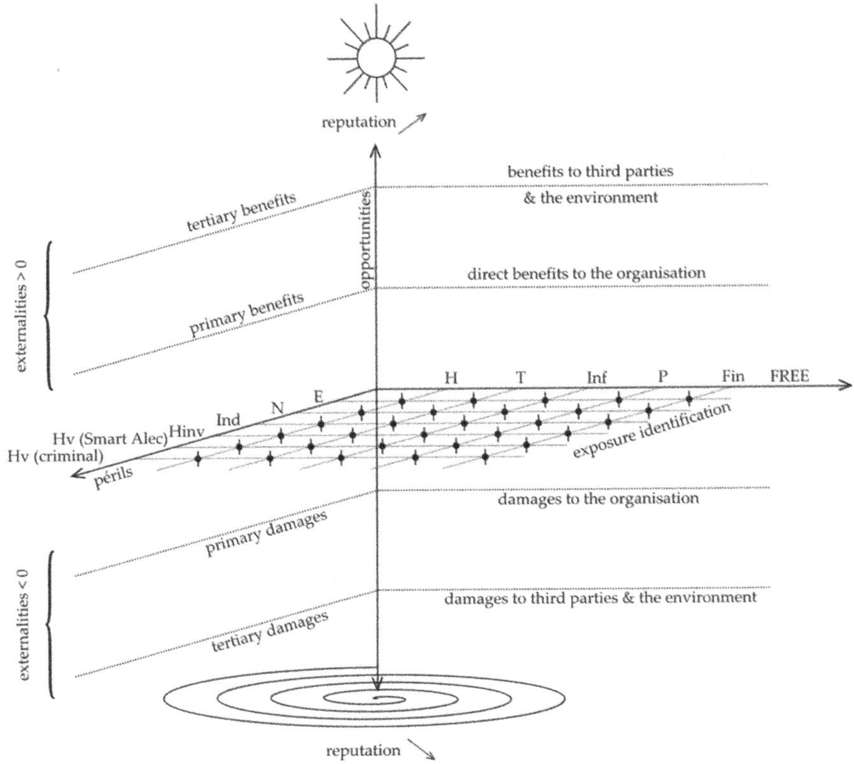

Fig. 1.1. Exposures Space. *Source*: Louisot (2023).

The representation of this process in a circle provides evidence for:

→ Strategy development (outside circle);
→ Multi-annual planning (central circle); and
→ Development of annual budgets and action plans (inner circle).

This approach incorporates two important mechanisms:

→ Truly holistic resource allocation and active attention from all professionals;
→ Alignment between annual budget decisions and strategic priorities (the divergence between the two 'time spaces' is often the main obstacle to a successful implementation of a strategy).

The interface between strategy and risk management induces the need for interaction between strategy manager and risk manager. The model supports cooperation as it aims to understand the chain of causality that leads to events and the chain of consequences of induced impacts. Managers could legitimately imagine merging the two functions to build flexible and adaptable strategies to adapt to changes in external and internal contexts during their implementation and to ensure greater consistency. A new definition for the job description of the CRO (Chief Risk Officer) might be needed as the scout of the uncertain.

- ***Bowtie model:***

The components of a systemic strategic plan taking into account all aspects of an integrated management approach are consolidated in a register. From a strategic perspective, risk has always been seen as positive, i.e. opportunities as cash flow generators, but too often it has ignored the negative, the threats. Conversely, in risk management, until the recent advent of what is now known as Enterprise-wide Risk Management (ERM), the risk manager was only in charge of negative risks, i.e. threats, that could compromise the achievement of 'the strategic vision' of leaders. This old model is still found in many except those with international stature.

Precisely, with its focus on objectives and/or missions of the organisation achievement, the model proposed here invites all risk owners to identify all vulnerabilities and to assess impacts, threats, and opportunities, any significant change in the level of an organism's resource by distinguishing direct impacts on the organism itself, primary impact, and those on its environment, including its partners, tertiary impact.

This approach coupled with the 'bow-tie' shown in Fig. 1.2, which provides a simplified version of the systemic analysis but also invites to ensure that a 'feedback', is in place for each systematic incident/accident. Of course, this does not remove the need for the scenario approach (for what has never happened) and the in-depth analysis thanks to the cindynic situation concept for complex systems with major sociological components (see below).

The model of the bowtie above lists the causes before the event (and the resources at the heart of the suggested device) and through a tree of causes can identify the chains of causality to be interrupted and analysed by the tree of consequences, right can define the consequences, positive or negative, on the organisation itself and all stakeholders.

Together the space of exposures and the bowtie should allow leaving unknown no major uncertainty. However, there are potentially promising or hazardous situations left out if a system is too complex to lend itself to the linearity of the

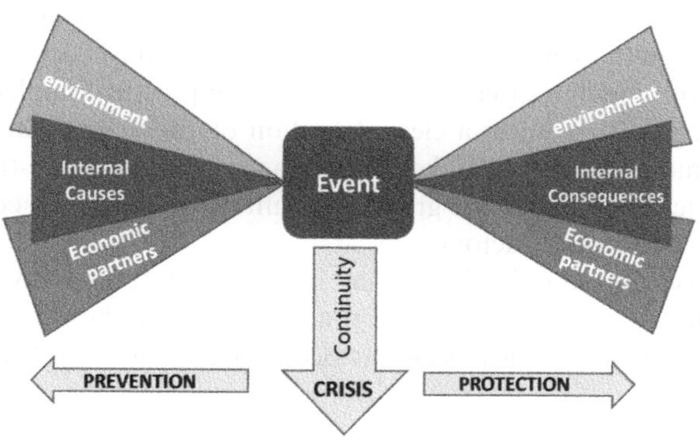

Fig. 1.2. Bowtie Revisited.

approach chains of causes or consequences. This is the case for systems in which the relationships between men and the socio-cultural context are essential. The root causes analysis using the cindynic model makes it possible to find the fracture lines of the system before any sign of rupture occurs.

Fig. 1.2 lends itself to further comments:

⇒ On the left side, the causal chains are identified around the poles that constitute the main functions of an enterprise and are recorded as R(J) while the exposures space model focuses on resource classes and affects their management only in a second step depending on the breakdown of the system into sub-systems called risk centres. The cooperation between the CRO and the CP (Corporate Planner) ensures the holistic management of threats and opportunities.

⇒ On the right side, the CP and CRO are working together to assess the cost/benefit implications of different solutions. However, if there is no reliable database of the past, then the Bayesian network approach (see below for risk quantification) makes it possible to rely on expert advice to initiate a recurrent process to build experience data. This is particularly the situation faced by institutions that implement operational risk management systems (like Basel 2 for banks and Solvency II for European insurers).

Other approaches are possible but we have taken the step of promoting those that combine conceptualisation and practice to be applicable in any organisation.

- ***A fundamental concept – the cindynic situation:***

'Cindynics', the term comes from the ancient Greek κίνδυνος (kindunos) which means 'hazard' (IMdR, n.d.). This discipline was officially founded at La Sorbonne on 8 December 1987, during a symposium on technological risk management bringing together industrialists, doctors, sociologists, insurers, etc.[2]

Cindynics includes all the sciences and techniques that study hazards, associated risks, and their prevention. It is a systemic approach based on different complementary disciplines – humanities and natural sciences: sociology, economics, chemistry, etc. – to allow the mapping of the global context of a situation

The object here is to provide the essential aspects of the Cindynic approach to better understand the synergy between the cindynic and the five resources models. The concept of cindynic situation is central to the practical implementation of cindynic concepts. It requires a clear definition of the actors who will be supported (internal and external stakeholders), as well as the space-time object of the study. In general, 'actors' are grouped by affinity over a set of common characteristics, i.e. networks of actors.

In the description, only functional fields or resources have been highlighted to find common features. The practical interface between strategy and risk management has already been stressed above reconciling the six resource

---

[2]The initiator that convened the conference was G-Y Kervern.

classes (HTIPF + G) and the 12 function registers – R(J), that is to say, the two descriptions of a company allowing to show the interactions between the internal stakeholders and the external stakeholders that accompany and condition its development.

Both descriptions are based on a specific glance. The glance is a set of aspects. For the strategy, these aspects are the essential parameters defining each function (we could mention the market share for marketing, for example) while for risk management, the cindynic approach retains five aspects: data, models, rules, values, and objectives. Based on these aspects, or hyperspace, the observer identifies absences (e.g. no database) and dissonances (conflicts between different networks or stakeholders). From there, it is possible to formalise vulnerability, in some way the dual variable of resilience, as a potential function of absences and dissonances.

The hyperspace of danger is in itself a representation, a model. A diagnostic tool, it commands to make decisions to reduce the cindynic potential.

In addition to the technical aspects, it is important to explore the interactions between the different actors in these situations. These interactions very often lead to undetectable hazards without this analysis. The aim is to assess the propensity of a natural, technological, or even computer disaster to occur to prevent it. By exploiting 'weak signals', Cindynics assess and prioritise likely consequences and preventive actions. This type of analysis also allows us to understand after the facts the gaps that are responsible for a disaster like the ones the world has experienced since the beginning of the century, especially the recent pandemic. Cindynics postulates that the danger lies essentially in cultural, organisational, or managerial deficits.

The cindynic analysis therefore consists of performing the following operations:

→ Develop a description of the system or organisation;
→ Define the cindynic situation;
→ Identify cindynogenic systemic deficits;
→ Develop and analyse hyperspaces associated with stakeholder networks;
→ Establish the deficit matrix;
→ Establish the dissonance matrix;
→ Identify deficit reduction actions and dissonances.

The cindynic analysis is the first step to establish a diagnosis, understand, and assess the potential of danger of the system or the organism considered on a technical, psychological, and sociological basis (Fig. 1.3). It must be followed by the establishment of a Project Leader Network (PLN), which will lead the transformation by reducing the deficits (application of the teleological space of PLN in the teleological spaces of all networks).

Measures designed to reduce them or to make them known (where the reduction is impossible in particular because of conflicting objectives) should be placed in the face of each deficit and each dissonance. These measures must be recorded in space and time. The aim here is to set up the 'programmatic' application of the PLN in all the time-space horizons of the networks.

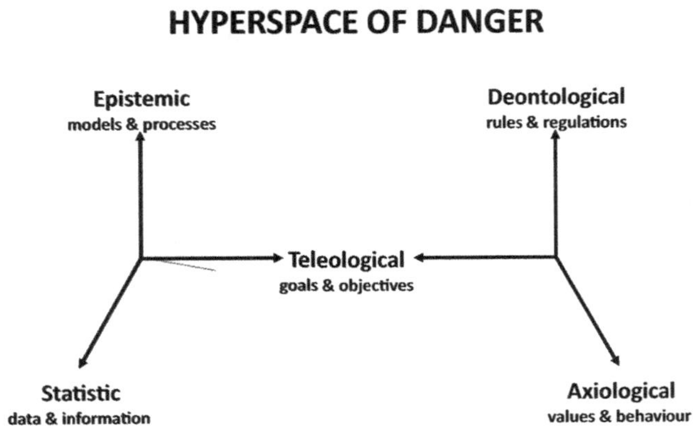

Fig. 1.3. Hyperspace of Danger. Original Source: GY Kervern (Adapted from Lombardi et al., 2019).

- ***For a multifaceted approach to risks/exposures:***

Quantum theory and the concepts of description illuminate the mystery of the Iceberg, which is really just a metaphor for revising the traditional interpretation of risk management to pragmatically ask:

> What frameworks or processes should the organisation develop to ensure a harmonious consolidation of strategy and risk management so that both sides of the risk, Opportunity and threat are taken into account for the design and execution of the strategy in accordance with the risk appetite defined by the Board of Directors?

It is the challenge of the paradigm known as ERM. In fact, it translates in practice into a comprehensive and integrated approach to managing uncertainties not only when the strategy is designed but throughout its execution to keep pace with evolving risks.

It is a joint effort of strategy and risk management to ensure that the submerged elements of the Iceberg are effectively taken into account through a systematic analysis of functions and resources throughout the life of the organism, in times of strategic decision-making, as in times of tactics and day-to-day operations.

For example, if the 'logistics' and 'communication' functions were not involved in the diagnosis and treatment process, then the risks involved are an entire 'risks' that could be 'orphaned' or unidentified.

However, specific concepts developed within the cindynic approach, provide leaders with powerful tools to discover the root causes, or roots, of risks in complex situations. To clarify, the concept of 'cindynic situation' defines the relationships between networks of actors located precisely in time and space from the 'hyperspace of hazards' defined for each of them. The gaze of the third-party observer, internal or external consultant, makes it possible to formalise these relations. But this tool is cumbersome to implement and must therefore be reserved for situations identified as particularly complex and volatile.

This implies that information on unmanageable risks in the field can be traced from the bottom up to the Executive Management and the Board of Directors. Specifically, the ERM model assigns to each operation the responsibility of identifying in the field the resources they need on the six resource classes such as a business manager, micro-enterprise, or cellular enterprise.

Of course, the field manager escalates along the chain of command what he cannot manage, and the principle of subsidiarity applies so that the transversal managers at the executive level receive the 'consolidated' mission in terms of impact risks 'potentially strategic'.

The Director of Environment or Sustainable Development is also responsible for the organisation's needs in this area and not only for ensuring that the company respects the environment. For the 'competitive' environment or the 'magnet factor' it is indeed the external ones to keep an eye open, both downstream and upstream. Legal monitoring and the Security Department have to deal with the 'anthropo/socio/legal' environment.

But again, under the ERM approach, the vulnerability space model expects each field manager (risk owner) to support the program by collecting vulnerabilities (opportunities as threats) at their level and managing what is within their jurisdiction. It is this combination of cindynic gaze that truly ensures the resilience of the organisation.

For example, for a healthcare institution, the exposure space model with the contribution of hyperspace of hazard can serve as a continuous training approach for all employees, caregivers or administrators, while inviting them to take into account essential stakeholders, patients, families, and supervisory authorities at all levels. In addition, this approach encourages dialogue between the various networks of caregivers, doctors, nurses, and administrative staff, without forgetting the people assigned to the household, even though it still seems too often difficult.

- ***Applying cindynic concepts to the COVID-19 pandemic:***

Dr Hansen, a disaster medicine and cindynics expert, explained the contribution of the cindynic approach to the 2019 coronavirus crisis early in the pandemic.

> Very little is known about the characteristics of this virus (tropism, virulence, contagiousness) and its short-, medium- and long-term clinical consequences. However, those responsible must make strategic decisions to ensure the best possible balance between protecting the health of the population and preserving socio-economic activity. It is these characteristics that allow us to model the behaviour of a given species of coronavirus. (Esanum, n.d.)

At that time, the 900 confirmed cases of infection by 2019-nCoV (as of 25 January 2020) were mostly located in China in the city of Wuhan. Isolated cases were found in other Chinese cities and a dozen countries (Thailand, Singapore, Japan, the Republic of Korea, Vietnam, Taiwan, the United States, Mexico, France, etc.).

The modelling of the virus behaviour had not been shared. It appears that its reproductive rate (RT) – the number of secondary cases generated from a contagious individual – had not yet been determined with certainty. Later the value of RT was found to be greater than 1, and in this case, each infected person is likely to contaminate several people. Otherwise, the epidemic will run out. This RT value varies over time, depending on the actions taken by the authorities or the immune status of the affected population. The flu rate varies from 4 to 5 depending on the episodes.

Covid tropism was also not perfectly defined. Which animal species, along with humans, are contaminated? What organs are affected? What are the target cells? To answer this question, immuno-histo-chemical markings of post-mortem samples on animals and deceased victims present at the Huanan South China Seafood Market were studied but in the fall of 2023, no definitive conclusions were published.

The issue of lethality is still not precisely determined. It seems that it is currently between 2% and 3% of symptomatic cases. However, the decline is not enough to be sure that this statistic is reliable. Finally, in January 2020, there were no cases of human-to-human contamination from 'imported' cases and therefore no autonomous secondary households outside China. What lesson can be learned about future pandemics?

- ***In such a context, cindynics has proven to be the art of asking the right questions:***

Cindynics study the evolution of situations to assess their propensity to move towards a more or less dangerous zone. They do not simply calculate a probability or the supposed severity of a situation, but they assess its 'teractivity' (which perceives, which perforates). To this end, they invite decision-makers, public or private, to evaluate their decisions through the five axes of issues related to the hyperspace of danger:

→ DATA: What facts decision-makers are ready to share?
→ MODELS: How do decision-makers think their plan can be organised and work what representations do they have of the implementation of this plan, and what representations do they want to transmit to their partners?
→ RULES: What do the decision-makers of an action plan choose to impose on all stakeholders?
→ GOALS & OBJECTIVES: What is the purpose of the information, instructions, recommendations, and instructions that are provided?
→ VALUES: What dictates decision-makers' actions? What guides the choice?

In the case of the pandemic, Dr Hansen suggested a list of the basic elements to be taken into consideration, the relevance of which only the future could uncover.

→ What will be the threshold of tolerance of the French population in the face of this epidemic, even if its overall mortality is ultimately three times lower? *(Knowing that she considers it 'normal' that influenza annually causes about 65,600 emergency department visits, 11,000 hospitalisations, 1,900 resuscitation admissions, and 290 deaths.)*
→ How many pandemic-induced cases of severe respiratory distress will the management of 5,700 resuscitation beds become problematic?
→ At what rate will hospitals be unable to cope with the usual influx of patients?

Chapter 2

Prospect Theory and Its Contribution to ERM

As a scientific discipline, economics is still in its teens since it was born practically at the end of the 16th century with the quantitative theory of money of Jean Bodin, if we leave aside the few mentions in the Bible, the right price, Aristotle, currency as a unit of account, a reserve of value and an intermediary of trade, and Saint Thomas Aquinas, usury. If the first economic writings date from the 16th century, with the mercantilists, it is in the 18th century that the economy is claimed as a new science by the physiocratic school, which, in France, includes the first liberals who designate it by 'political economy'. It is still under this name that the teaching was given at the university in the sixties and the academic books published by Raymond Barre had a name (McNally, 1990).

However, marginalism signifies a moment of rupture – we speak more often of a 'marginalist revolution' – in the history of economic thought, between 1870 and 1890, where an alternative to traditional economic thought is put in place; it is the marginalists who forged the term 'economic science' at the end of the 19th century but if it is today commonly used to qualify this discipline it became the norm only towards the end of the 20th century with the developments around econometrics.

The strong intuitions, working hypotheses, and guiding ideas of economists have thus been forged over the last four centuries. The relatively short history of economic thought is marked by the existence of currents of thought which differ both in the place they give to a particular question (money, value, social inequalities, balance, employment, income, finance, information,...) and the answers they provide. If some theories, such as mercantilism or physiocracy, have almost disappeared, others, which have been dominant, such as the classical school, or very influential, such as Marxism, are now dormant.

The second half of the 20th century was characterised by the professionalisation of economists and the contemporary appearance of behavioural economics which is mainly concerned with the limits of the rationality of economic agents. The contribution of mathematical sciences has gradually impacted all fields of the economy. In this movement, economists who want to make economics a

Enterprise Risk Management in Today's World: A Current and Futuristic View of the Complexity, Resilience, Responsibility and Tools in ERM, Part B, 15–25

doi:10.1108/978-1-83608-392-420241002

'neutral' science have joined forces in particular around the term econometrics and mathematicians who want to reaffirm their discipline as an axiomatic science and not a mere branch of engineering.

As the methodology of economic discipline becomes clearer, the contours of this same discipline become hazy since economists are now interested in all social phenomena. Economics would no longer be just the science of studying economic objects, but the discipline using the methods of economists to study the world. If at the same time, the discipline seems to have lost the adjective 'political', already omitted by the marginalists at the end of the 19th century, nevertheless, it must be kept in mind that the definition and evolution of economic 'methods' remains a power stake.

Today, macro-economists, micro-economists, and empiricists work together and the scientific process consists of a permanent back and forth between theory and empiricism. Economists now have access to microeconomic business data that allows them to micro-base macroeconomics and go beyond the representative agent model. Thus, growth models must take into account the heterogeneity of the behaviour of firms to solve the puzzles of growth, such as secular stagnation, the lack of convergence of some countries, or the effects of competition on growth. In the area of inequalities, it is important to vary the measures, put them in relation, and ask about the sources of inequalities (rent or innovation) to understand the dynamics of inequalities. The prospect theory has emerged in the context of behavioural economics.

What Does Prospect Theory Consist of?

Dominant economic thinking postulates that decisions are made rationally. Human beings are economic agents who act rationally according to the information made available to them to make their choices. Gary Becker's rational choice theory is a good example.

However, if human beings made rational choices, they would not smoke and they would not use drugs; they would not put their health or their life in danger for nothing. Human beings often make non-rational decisions because they are above all a being of impulses. The proof is provided by the purse where some will sink because they refuse to take their loss, their ego does not allow them to recognise that they made a bad decision; they cannot accept it in their mental structure, they will therefore resist the principle of reality.

In the early 1980s, two economists Daniel Kahneman and Amos Tversky put forward the prospect theory. They argue that people make decisions based on how they are presented with a choice to be made, not just on the criteria of potential outcomes and probability that are rational. It all depends on the framework in which each person makes a decision, and on the presentation that can be made of a situation (Barberis, 2013).

The prospect theory belongs to the subgroup of behavioural economics, describing how individuals choose between probabilistic alternatives where risk is involved and the probability of different outcomes is unknown. The authors of this theory felt that it was more psychologically accurate as to how decisions are made about the theory of mathematical expectation of utility.

Prospect theory deals with the description of preferences about the mathematical expectation of usefulness that a choice will give. The theory of utility dates back to 1738 and was developed by the Swiss mathematician and physicist Daniel Bernoulli. For a long time, this theory has been the dominant explanation for decisions whose results are uncertain. The chances and risks are not absolute, but relative to the situation.

All these theories deal in detail with risks. However, there is a distinction between risk and uncertainty where risk can be measured and uncertainty cannot be measured. Bernoulli indicated at the time that odds are assessed differently based on moral expectations. The prospect theory is also based on this and the example of a lottery is often cited in several theories.

Prospect theory differs from the theory of mathematical expectation of utility in that it-this assumes that individuals will choose the outcome that gives the maximum utility given the probability of the outcomes whereas the prospect theory takes into account the fact that individuals may choose a decision that does not necessarily maximise utility because that they place other considerations at the top of humans' choices.

The prospect theory focuses on how individuals conceive of situations and outcomes in their minds. Individuals can use the rules of thumb and status quo bias:

- Certainty effect: Individuals give more weight to certainty than to outcomes that are simply likely.
- Isolation effect: In terms of positive gains, individuals give greater weight to a certain small gain versus a larger likely gain. But, in terms of negative gains, individuals show risk-seeking behaviour – people prefer a likely loss to a certain small loss; this seems to contradict the desire for insurance, but it's for moderate losses, rather than catastrophic losses.

Prospect theory indicates that individuals will accept an investment when gains are presented as opposed to losses. In other words, investors give more value to potential gains than to potential losses. The following considerations can then be highlighted:

- What does prospect theory mean? Prospect theory indicates that investors value gains and losses differently. In other words, if an investor is presented with one investment option based on potential gains and another based on potential losses, the investor will choose an investment where potential gains are presented.
- Why is prospect theory important? It is useful for investors to understand their biases, where losses tend to have a greater emotional impact than the equivalent gain. Outlook theory helps describe how decisions are made by investors.
- What are the main components of prospect theory? It describes how individuals make decisions between alternatives where risk is involved and the likelihood of different outcomes is unknown. There is a certainty effect in the prospect theory, where people seek certain outcomes, only underestimating the likely outcomes.

- Who postulated the prospect theory? The prospect theory was introduced in 1979 by Amos Tversky and Daniel Kahneman, who later developed the idea in 1992. The couple said the prospect theory was better at accurately describing how decisions are made, compared to the theory of expected utility.
- What did Kahneman and Tversky do? They proposed that the losses have a greater emotional impact than a gain of the same amount. They said that, given the choices presented in two ways, when both offer the same result, one person will choose the option offering earnings received.

How the Prospect Theory Works and What Are Its Implementations?

Prospect theory proposes an approach to decision-making aiming to explain how people's decisions are influenced by their attitudes towards risk, uncertainty, loss, and gain. Thus, it states that people are influenced by a systematic inability to assess probabilities correctly and in most cases are motivated more by fear of loss than by the prospect of making the equivalent gain (American Psychological Association).

It has also been used to help explain a wide range of phenomena, including why people make suboptimal decisions, how they use mental (heuristic) shortcuts when making decisions, and how different cultures make decisions differently (Nickerson, 2023).

The prospect theory is based on three key assumptions about human decision-making:

- Individuals are more concerned about avoiding losses than making gains, so-called loss aversion.
- Individuals receive gains and losses from a reference point, which is usually their current situation. This means that people are more likely to take risks to avoid losses than to make gains.
- Individuals have difficulty accurately estimating probability and, in most cases, tend to overestimate the likelihood of low-probability events and underestimate the likelihood of high probability events.

In general, outlook theory predicts that people will be more reluctant to take risks when it comes to avoiding losses than when it comes to making gains. This means that people are more likely to take measures that minimise losses and avoid measures that could lead to losses.

The reference point is a key concept in the theory of prospects. It is the starting point for decisions on gains and losses. The reference point can be a real or imaginary starting point. The authors proposed that the reference point be determined by several factors, including:

- Past experiences;
- Present circumstances;
- Cultural norms;
- Individual preferences.

The authors also suggested that the reference point may change over time in response to new information or experiences.

Prospect theory assumes that people make decisions in two stages, i.e. editing and evaluation:

- At the editing stage, people simplify complex situations by ignoring certain information and using mental (heuristic) shortcuts.
- At the assessment stage, people use their attitudes towards risk and uncertainty to choose between different courses of action (Nickerson, 2023).

The prospect theory has been applied in many cases in political science, particularly in the field of international relations, and also in the field of comparative politics. In international relations, the theory has been used to try to explain decision-making that involves seemingly irrational risks, such as continuing to incur sunk costs. In this way, prospect theory was called upon to help explain the hostage rescue mission in Iran and the Cuban missile crisis, among others. In addition, comparative politics has been used to explain the nature of risk in the economic restructuring of Latin American countries.

The main criticisms of prospect theory in political science concern the inability to provide an adequate theory of framing that explains how and why actors generate, search, and use the frameworks they use. Additional concerns concern the external validity of the original experimental paradigm. This point would certainly find agreement among the original designers; Kahneman, at least, does not intend the work to be applied more broadly outside the narrow economic field in which it was initially studied.

More recent criticism within psychology has focused on how the prospect theory provided a limited representation of human emotional and emotional responses. Kahneman's more recent work has focused more on the more hedonistic aspects of human decision-making, with a focus on well-being and happiness.

Some work has attempted to compare the predictions offered by rational choice and the models of prospect theory to anticipate the outcome of real-world political events, such as the outcome of Good Friday peace agreements in Northern Ireland. Other recent studies have attempted to synthesise and integrate the more cognitive approach advocated by the prospect theory with a more evolutionary understanding of sources of risk differing preferences.

According to the theory of optimal nutrition sensitive to risk, subsistence objectives can be maximised by pursuing a strategy that gives priority to the search for risks under conditions of threat to survival in particular. Several assumptions are needed for any discussion on the concept of thought:

- ***Hypothesis of the existence of thought:*** If there were no proof of thought in the world, thought would have little or no meaning. Recognition of this fact throughout history explains the development of various theories of thought. It can be assumed that words such as 'thought' or 'think' cannot, because of their ambiguity, help define the sphere of thought.

But whatever the relationship between thought and perception, thought seems to involve more – for almost all observers – than simply receiving impressions from the outside. This seems to be the opinion of those who make thought a consequence of perception, as well as of those who regard the thought process as independent of meaning. For both, the thinking goes beyond detection, either as an elaboration of meaning materials or as an apprehension of objects that are totally out of the reach of the senses.

- ***Hypothesis, a root common to all conceptions of thought, is that of knowledge:*** This can be questioned on the ground that, if there were sensation without any form of thought, judgement, or reasoning, there would be at least a rudimentary form of knowledge, some degree of consciousness or consciousness through one thing or another. If one accepts the point of this objection, it nevertheless seems true that the distinction between truth and falsehood and the difference between knowledge, error, and ignorance or between knowledge, belief, and opinion do not apply to sensations in the total absence of thought.

Any understanding of knowledge that implies these distinctions seems to involve the mind for the same reason that it implies thought. There is another implication of thought in the fact of self-knowledge. Detection can be the consciousness of an object, and to this extent, it can be a kind of knowledge, but it has never been observed that the senses can feel or be conscious of them.

The thought seems to be not only thoughtful but thoughtful, that is, capable of considering itself, defining the nature of thought, and developing theories of thought. This fact of thought, its reflexivity, also seems to be a common element in all the meanings of the 'mind'. We sometimes speak of the 'reflexivity of the intellect', the 'reflexive power of understanding', and the 'ability to understand how to reflect on one's actions' or 'self-awareness'. Whatever the formulation, a world without self-awareness or self-awareness would be a world in which the traditional conception of thought probably would not have arisen (Britannica, 2024).

- ***Hypothesis of the existence of a goal or intention:*** There is the development of a plan of action with the prior knowledge of its goal or to work in any other way towards a desired and intended objective. As in the case of sensitivity, the phenomena of desire do not indicate, without any other qualification, the domain of thought. According to the theory of natural desire, for example, the natural tendencies of inanimate and insensitive things are expressions of desire. But it is not in this sense of desire that the hypothesis of purpose or intention is here taken as evidence of the existence of thought.

The factor called the direction of conduct towards future ends is either an element common to all the meanings of the 'mind' or at least one element associated with the mind. It is sometimes called the faculty of will, rational desire, or intellectual appetite. Sometimes it is treated as the act of wanting, which, with thought, is one of the two main activities of thought or understanding, and sometimes meaning is considered the very essence of mentality.

These hypotheses – thought, knowledge or self-knowledge, and purpose – seem common to all theories of thought. More than that, it seems that these are hypotheses that require the development of the design. The conflict of theories about what the human mind is, what structure it has, what parts belong to it, and what it belongs to does not include the full range of controversy on the subject.

Furthermore, enough elements are common to all theories of thought to allow some other questions to be formulated: How does thought work? How does he do his job, and with what intrinsic excellence or flaws? What is the relation of thought to matter, bodily organs, material conditions, or from one mind to another (see Mind-Body Dualism)? Is thought a common possession of humans and animals, or is what might be called thought in animals distinctly different from human thought? Are there thoughts or thoughts outside of man and the whole world of bodily life? What are the limitations of so-called artificial intelligence, the ability of machines to perform functions generally associated with the mind?

How Do Prospect Theory and Risk Management Intersect?

The survival of any living organism requires the ability to detect and avoid harmful conditions in the environment in which they operate. Survival is also facilitated by the ability to codify and learn from past experiences. Humans have the additional capacity to modify and respond to their environment.

Risk is a personal, occupational, and social burden. 'At what level of safety is safety satisfactory?' is the common factor in increasingly difficult decision-making in identifying acceptable risk in a precarious social environment.

Risk perception requires an assessment of the likelihood and ability to think intelligently and carefully about an unlikely but relevant emergency. Typically, a decision-maker assigns the probabilistic nature of the event, therefore assesses it as more or less likely, and makes risk management decisions accordingly.

It is through the importance of the perception of risk that the importance of prospect theory on the optimisation of choices in terms of risk management strategy is clearly shown by showing the limits of a purely rational approach to decisions based on the theory of optimisation of the mathematical expectation of utility. All the following remarks show the relevance of the study.

However, the process of risk perception is limited by an individual's mental and physical perception, since he can only treat the stimuli and cognitions he perceives. This is why risk perception is a very personal decision-making process based on a frame of reference that an individual has developed throughout his or her life. Therefore, the central issue in risk perception is the multidimensional understanding of the individual as a risk assessor, and how he thinks, feels, and acts on hazards, threats, and associated risks.

The results of psychological experiments show that an individual is not the best risk assessor, and that, facing uncertainty, he systematically violates the principles of rational decision-making. Therefore, risk management does not meet the basic requirements for being reasonable and consistent, as risk perception is primarily influenced by personal experience, foresight, thoughts, feelings, and desires.

The perception of risk is therefore rarely completely rational. Instead, an individual perceives risk using a mixture of cognitive skills (e.g. assessing evidence, using arguments and logic to conclude) and emotional assessment (intuition or imagination). The process is further compounded by an excess of confidence in the accuracy of one's judgement, in which an individual too often trusts one's judgement, especially those in charge of strategic decisions, even if they are wrong.

Such overconfidence is dangerous because it shows that too often decision-makers are unaware of how little they know about potential threats and risks, and how much additional information and interdisciplinary approach they would still need. This excessive self-esteem is also fuelled by the individual's desire for certainty, which often manifests as a negation of uncertainty. In this aspect, the asymmetry between gains and losses is also interesting; a person prefers to believe that he is playing a game with high gains, even if he may end up with nothing.

Risk perception is therefore a very complex process based more on theoretical analyses than on direct experience. The perception of risk contains at least two sources of uncertainty, namely the natural uncertainty variable (the uncertainty that must be assessed) and the uncertainty resulting from the risk assessor's lack of expertise, knowledge, and information. However, these two uncertainties are uniform and cannot be synthetically separated. However, compliance with some rules can improve and regulate the perception of risk. By anticipating what will happen, we can reduce pessimism. This approach affects feelings of fear and may lead to assessing the risk higher than it is. Because of the need for control, officials often feel they have more control over the situation than they do. This 'control illusion' leads us to perceive risk as a lesser threat (Bertoncelj, 2019).

- *Fear of change*: The risks that are not yet perceived lead individuals to consider them more, and therefore to assess them as riskier (see also change management).
- *The choice between several alternatives*: Choosing between two equally risky events may result in the risk being perceived as being lower than it is, allowing choosing.
- *Media Awareness:* While risk attracts a lot of public attention, especially through social media, it is considered more important than it is by heuristic availability.
- *Personal Exposure to Hazard:* If personally exposed, the decision-maker ranks it higher.
- *Risk Levelling Due to Benefits:* If opportunities and threats are interconnected and a given choice could result in gains, the decision-maker may perceive the actual risk to be lower than it is.
- *Stakeholders' confidence:* When risk involves the actions of others, how the decision-maker accesses risk will have a significant impact on the extent of trust of the parties involved.
- *Time horizon:* The system of perception of a person's risk is established unconsciously and quickly by his mind (the amygdala or fear centre of the brain) even before acquiring the real facts. This 'blinking' instinct can help avoid

simple and immediate hazards, but it is not the most thoughtful way to determine what to do about complex future threats.

- *Optimism about unclear situations:* You can be too optimistic when the details are unclear. Try to imagine that the threats are more difficult and imminent.
- *Compromise:* Always keep in mind that there may be intermediate solutions to imagine from a limited number of apparent choices (Bertoncelj, 2019).

Some say that risk management is too subjective. How true is that statement and what are the implications for event organisers? It is, therefore, necessary to critically analyse whether risk management within the event industry, in particular, is too subjective and whether subjectivity influences positively or negatively the effectiveness of decision-making.

In today's global high-risk society, event organisers find themselves in an environment of varied and dynamic risks, ranging from domestic violent extremism, cyber threats, cancellations of events due to severe weather conditions, and a saturated market that offers locals and visitors a variety of competing events to choose from. Due to the serious impacts of these issues and incidents, event organisers should consider risk management as a fundamental responsibility for planning and delivering secure events. In addition, a rational and structured approach to risk management will enhance the ability of event organisers to make appropriate decisions in dynamic, complex, and uncertain environments. Risk management is also subject to subjectivity, bias, and error, resulting in exaggeration, overestimation, or underestimation.

Event organisers need to understand the interconnected concepts of risk management, uncertainty, and subjectivity to determine whether risk management is rational and objective or, on the contrary, subjective. Next, it is important to explore how these sociocultural perspectives can influence the effectiveness of a rational or subjective approach to risk management for event organisers. There is a need for critical analysis to determine whether the effectiveness and credibility of risk-based decisions are influenced positively or negatively by the organisers' perception of risk and organisational culture.

Finally, the issue is to determine how event organisers identify with and respond to risks in today's global risk society. However, despite gaps in evidence and documentation on event risk management, the risk management approach taken by event organisers appears to be primarily subjective; however, this approach does not negatively impact their ability to make decisions under ambiguous conditions.

The artificial comparison between a rational assessment on the part of professionals and an irrational conception on the part of laypeople has not only masked the limits and values of the two approaches but also highlighted constraints on an effective risk management approach.

The professional calculation of risk should be an essential component of the decision-making process concerning acceptability and risk management. However, no one wants to substitute scientific knowledge for intuition. For professional evaluations, the only criteria for judging the 'acceptability' or 'desirability' of a technology or a risk management policy, should lead policymakers to design public policies in line with shared social values.

What Could Be the Prospect Theory Contribution to the Evolution of Risk Management?

With the introduction of cognitive psychology, the problem of behavioural decision-making, derived from the paradox of the theory of mathematical hope of utility, opened a new way of research. Now countless researchers are wandering in the behavioural decision related to the prospect theory, it is worth mentioning it is thanks to the prospect theory that Daniel Kahneman was awarded the Nobel Prize for Economics in 2002. This award recognises his significant contribution to university research (The Nobel Prize, n.d.).

By examining the emergence and development of prospect theory, we can see that the framework of the prospect theory has been formed and that it has a better explanatory power to these phenomena which cannot be explained by the theory of mathematical expectation of effectiveness. From the point of view of existing research, the main focus is on the value function, the specific shape of the weight function, and the determination of parameters. Relative gains and losses based on benchmarks are also applied in many areas. However, as can be seen from the literature review, the prospect theory may have limitations in two aspects.

First, the value function and the weight function need to be studied further. The existing theoretical model of perspective still has some phenomena incompatible with empirical evidence. The main reason is that the value function and the weight function have some subjectivity in shape selection, and there is no uniform and standard method for adjusting function parameters.

Second, prospect theory is also one of the main foundations of behavioural finance, but current research is essentially in the risk category, and most research methods use experimental data adjustment or discrete model simulation construction. There is not a lot of research on the behavioural decision-making of companies in the market environment. If the research model relevant to the uncertainty of the natural environment can be adapted to the internal and external environment of companies, the prospect theory can also be developed. It aims to integrate the results of psychological studies, sociological and cultural, and presents key social science findings that seem relevant for a deeper understanding of risk and the role of risk perception in risk management.

To integrate risk assessment and perception, it is necessary to analyse the strengths and weaknesses of each risk analysis approach and highlight the potential contributions that technical and social sciences can make to risk management. Technical assessments provide the best estimate to assess the average likelihood of an adverse effect related to an object or activity:

- First, public perception should govern the selection criteria on which the acceptability or 'tolerance' of risk should be assessed;
- Second, public participation is necessary to determine trade-offs between criteria; and
- Third, public preferences are needed to design resilient strategies to address remaining uncertainties.

This is why a model needs to take into account the stakeholders, which promises an integration of analytical knowledge and a deliberative process involving stakeholders who will be affected by the respective risks.

The scope of the prospect theory is still expanding, but its disciplinary applicability is not sufficient. The prospect theory is above all a model of decision-making under risk. As such, the most obvious areas to look for applications are those of finance and insurance, and more generally of ERM (Enterprise-wide Risk Management) where risk attitudes play a key role.

Chapter 3

Circular Economy and Sustainability

Natural capital is declining around the world, despite improved resource efficiency. In this overall scenario, the major importing countries of all types of raw materials, such as Italy to give an example within the EU itself, are more dependent on foreign markets and, as a result, a significant risk to the competitiveness of SMEs and, more generally, their domestic industry.

As a result, to remain competitive, these countries need to adopt alternative resource models that can truly support their production networks and competitiveness by improving resource efficiency. A possible alternative to the above scenario of chronic dependence of their economy on foreign markets is represented by the circular economy (CE) which, over the last two years, has become the central element of the European Green Deal, and the post-European 'Green Economic Recovery' COVID-19.

It has become very clear just about everywhere that the world is going to have to get used to waves of disruption and, therefore, a constant battle. One could describe the current situation as one where we have gone from all-out war to hunting to a dangerous criminal who appears in many different forms; such situation forces officials to take different measures depending on where they occur, and does not disappear without action.

Since the beginning of this century, sustainability has become one of the cornerstones of Corporate Social Responsibility (CSR) risks, to be convinced, it is enough to quote the definition of the European Union: CSR also known as CSR is defined by the European Commission as the voluntary integration by companies of social and environmental concerns into their business activities and their relationships with stakeholders. In other words, 'CSR is the contribution of companies to sustainable development issues.'

In these circumstances, it is not surprising that the Enterprise-wide Risk Management (ERM) programmes developed within the organisations also have sustainable development at the heart of their objectives but at the same time there is more talk of a CE; thus it is logical to ask the question of the link between sustainability and the CE.

The CE aims to change the paradigm that founded the linear economy, by limiting the impact on the environment and the waste of resources, as well as increasing

Enterprise Risk Management in Today's World: A Current and Futuristic View of the Complexity, Resilience, Responsibility and Tools in ERM, Part B, 27–40

Published under exclusive licence by Emerald Publishing Limited
doi:10.1108/978-1-83608-392-420241003

efficiency at all stages of the product economy. Recent warnings about waste pollution and the limits of natural resources are encouraging the development of the CE. What is the definition of the CE, and what are its advantages and solutions?

Companies and authorities around the world are increasingly working together to ensure that more sustainable economic, environmental, and social measures are adopted and implemented. The CE model based on sharing, leasing, reusing, repairing, refuelling, and recycling existing materials and products for as long as possible is the cornerstone of sustainability.

Circular Economy Definitions, Advantages, and Solutions Within the European Union[1]

The CE is a model of production and consumption, which involves sharing, renting, reusing, repairing, refurbishing, and recycling existing materials and products for as long as possible. In this way, the product life cycle is extended. This represents a stark deviation from the traditional linear economic model, which is based on a take-away consumption model. This model is based on large quantities of cheap and easily accessible materials and energy. Another part of this model is planned obsolescence when a product has been designed to have a limited lifespan to encourage consumers to buy it again. The European Parliament has called for measures to combat this practice.

Measures such as waste control, eco-design, and reuse could generate savings for European companies while reducing total annual greenhouse gas emissions. Currently, the production of materials we use every day accounts for 45% of CO_2 emissions. The transition to a more CE could bring benefits such as reducing pressure on the environment, improving the security of raw material supplies, increasing competitiveness, stimulating innovation, strengthening economic growth (an additional 0.5% of gross domestic product), creating jobs (700,000 jobs in the EU alone by 2030). Consumers will also receive more sustainable and innovative products that will improve their quality of life and save them money in the long term.

In March 2020, the European Commission presented the Circular Economy Action Plan, which announces initiatives throughout the product life cycle and aims to promote more sustainable product design, to reduce waste, and to empower consumers, for example by creating a right to repair. It therefore encourages sustainable consumption and ensures that waste is avoided and that the resources used are conserved for as long as possible in the EU economy. The focus is on resource-intensive sectors such as electronics and ICT, plastics, textiles, and construction. It introduces legislative and non-legislative measures targeting areas where action at the EU level brings real added value.

In February 2021, Parliament adopted a resolution on the new CE action plan calling for additional measures to achieve a carbon-neutral, environmentally sustainable CE, free of toxicity and fully circular by 2050, including stricter recycling

---

[1]See Economy. (2022, April 26). *Circular economy: Definition, importance, and benefits*. https://www.europarl.europa.eu/news/en/headlines/economy/20151201STO05603/circular-economy-definition-importance-and-benefits

rules and binding targets for the use and consumption of materials by 2030 (EU Monitor, n.d.). In March 2022, the Commission released the first phase of measures to accelerate the transition to a CE as part of the CE action plan. Proposals include promoting sustainable products, empowering consumers for the green transition, revising the regulation of construction products, and creating a sustainable textiles strategy.

The transition to a more CE is a source of many opportunities such as reducing pressure on the environment, increasing the security of supply of raw materials and competitiveness, and increasing innovation, growth, and jobs. However, challenges to finance, key economic enablers, skills, consumer behaviour, business development models, and multi-level governance should not be underestimated.

Cognitive Economy: A New Hope for a Sustainable Economic System[2]

Economic and environmental crises come from the same source and reinforce each other because of the current economic model that favours short-term benefits without considering longer-term benefits to ecosystems as rare assets or to the environment and society.

In response to current problems, a new trend is emerging in the economy, the green economy, which has undoubtedly been favoured by the difficulties encountered by the dominant economic paradigm due to the crisis and market failures that have been generated during the first two decades of the 21st century, in particular the financial and economic crisis of 2008.

This new evolution in economic thinking seeks strategies to resolve the various crises that have hindered the development of global society since the beginning of the 21st century. The consequences of climate change, the food crisis, the recent economic and financial crisis, and low poverty reduction rates have been important factors in the definition of the concept, to which the United Nations has contributed through the environment program – UNEP.

Innovation and scientific and technological advances have improved industrial productivity and competitiveness, as well as standards and quality of life. While the potential of a strategy based on 'knowledge, learning and innovation' to achieve 'sustainable development' is taken into account and solves many problems, these same factors have been the source of the current instability and even create new problems. Their resolution requires complex expertise and more expensive technology. However, it is difficult to imagine an effective strategy to protect the environment and achieve sustainable development without making full use of knowledge and innovation.

Much of our money, resources, energy, and creativity are devoted to problem-solving rather than to the development of the human soul, which is our most

[2]Norouzi, N. (2022). Learning economy: A new hope to achieve a sustainable economic system. *Circular Economy and Sustainability*, *2*, 535–555. https://link.springer.com/paper/10.1007/s43615-021-00107-z.

precious resource. But the existence of a crisis is also an opportunity to change the way of thinking and acting.

The United Nations has announced a new concept of a SDG. This concept is the first multi-criteria economic development framework, which simultaneously takes into account many other aspects, such as cultural, social, economic, political, and environmental aspects. This concept aims to maintain every interconnected aspect of human society at an optimal equilibrium point.

This concept revised the materialisation of nature, which occurred within the framework of green economic development and considered each aspect unique but dependent on other aspects. This uniqueness means that each aspect is valuable and necessary, but the change in each parameter has consequences in other aspects due to dependence. For example, economic growth requires more resources and results in environmental degradation; in this case, the traditional economy prescribes the indefinite importance of economic growth without taking into account the environment.

The sustainable economy becomes a model that promotes growth, income, and job creation, 'sustainable jobs', which aims to change the interaction between economic progress and environmental sustainability, especially if wealth is measured by taking into account natural assets and not just productivity. The above also makes a substantial contribution to reducing social inequalities between countries and eradicating global poverty.

To achieve the objectives proposed by the sustainable economy, the proposed alternatives must be accepted and implemented both by developed and developing countries by allocating the necessary economic resources, greater rigour in environmental regulation, creation of grants, friendly activities with the environment, and optimisation of land planning processes (Norouzi, 2021).

The amount of resources used and wasted, and the environmental impacts caused by eutrophication and greenhouse gas emissions are enormous in this context. This is why the Joint Venture (JV) should be accepted as a catalyst for sustainability and therefore also a catalyst for the transformation of some major university programs. Now is the time to make structural changes to higher education to address the need for a 'Build Back Better' strategy for the expected recovery from the decade ahead and to prevent potential shocks of magnitude caused by the latest pandemic.

CE, Sustainability, and Waste Management[3]

Since the beginning of the industrialisation era in the 19th century, the linear model of production and consumption in which raw materials are transformed into goods, and value is added to the raw material was established. Once used,

---

[3]See *Disentangling circular economy, sustainability and waste management principles.* https://www.bakerinstitute.org/research/disentangling-circular-economy-sustainability-and-waste-management-principles; *How a circular economy could help businesses turn waste into resources.* https://topicinsights.com/sustainability/circular-economy-economic-model/.

the residue becomes waste and is usually treated unconsciously or discarded. The model was based on an implicit assumption of the existence of infinite resources on the earth.

In contrast, CE is a model for an economy that integrates regenerative design thinking and ways to improve the performance of resources that were once discarded as waste. The JV is an economic model that is gaining popularity for its waste reduction potential by providing companies with a new framework for sustainable production and manufacturing. Could the CE be the new way of thinking needed to reverse the harmful effects of climate change?

With the introduction of CE principles in major regions of the world, interest in the concept has increased considerably in recent years. It is growing in the political, economic, and scientific fields and is gaining popularity in corporate strategies. Local and national governments – including China, Japan, the United Kingdom, France, Germany, Canada, the Netherlands, Sweden, and Finland – also adhere to the principles of lifelong learning.

In a traditional linear economy, resources are extracted to make a product. Once the life cycle of this product is complete, it is discarded. In contrast, a CE provides a more sustainable economic model in which the flow of resources forms a loop rather than a line. The ultimate goal of CE is therefore to move from the current linear arrangement to a regenerative circular system where the societal value of products, materials, and resources is maximised over time.

Sustainability is intrinsically linked to decarbonisation, energy transition, and waste control, which is arguably the most misinterpreted descriptor of the decade and often used in conjunction or association with the JV. Circularity and Sustainability – these terms are very often used together and somewhat interchangeably, but are they the same? Is CE always sustainable?

Sustainability is about the environment, the economy, and society – while the main beneficiaries of the CE appear to be the economic actors implementing the system. There is also a difference in the agency, which influences the understanding of the agents who should influence system changes. While the agency is diffuse in the case of sustainability… As priorities must be defined by all stakeholders, the CE has a clear focus on governments and businesses.

The CE focuses on improving environmental performance rather than on a holistic view of the three dimensions of sustainability. For the CE, these are primarily individual economic benefits from reduced inputs, efficiencies, and waste avoidance, with relatively immediate results relative to sustainability (Collectivegreen, n.d.). So while there is a relationship between sustainability and EC, these two concepts are very distinct.

- ***Sustainability: a system's approach***

Sustainability in its most authentic form is a systems approach that takes into account a wide range of environmental, social, and economic factors associated with a process or product and assesses their interaction. For example, it assesses geopolitics, impacts on Indigenous communities, socio-technical capacities, and other sub-domains. The most commonly accepted definition aims to reconcile economic development with the protection of society and the environment by 'development that meets the needs of the present without compromising the ability of future generations to meet their own needs'.

In theory, sustainability is not the intrinsic property of a component. Insulated components cannot be sustainable (paper straws, solar panels, electric vehicles, etc.). Sustainability is a feature of a system as a whole, not a focus on a subset or component. It embodies how the parties intersect to enable effective overall outcomes.

The relationship between a complete system and its environment is what gives rise to a large-scale balance and, through this understanding, avoids risks and unintended consequences. From a sustainability point of view, individual parts cannot be optimised without optimising the whole. For example, an electric vehicle is unsustainable if you take into account the non-quantified and unaccounted social and environmental impacts that span the lifecycle of the lithium-ion battery that powers the vehicle – from mining, processing, merging, trade, and transportation across the network supply chain with no recycling and reuse options for end-of-life batteries.

When assessing something as complex as an entire economy or a global supply network, it becomes even more critical to understand how the components synchronise and integrate into the overall network. Focusing only on individual parts invariably shifts risks elsewhere in the system, resulting in unsustainable and undesirable outcomes.

- ***Interaction between sustainability and CE:***

CE provides the economic system with an alternative flow model that is cyclical and regenerative by design and builds resilience against future disturbances – such as pandemics, extreme and one-time weather events, or the impacts of a changing climate. Sustainability, fostered by innovation, can enable CE, and CE can be a means or a stepping stone towards alignment between the three dimensions of sustainability.

However, circularity in itself does not guarantee positive social, economic, and environmental performance. Although there has been a proliferation of concepts, themes, and circular frameworks, there is no method or combination of methods that quantify the impacts of circular strategies to measure innovations brought by the CE, it is necessary to develop multidimensional circularity indicators to measure the CE as a whole.

After careful consideration of the range of sustainability factors, an institution may decide that a CE program may not be the most prudent path in the short to medium term, especially if it contravenes the waste management hierarchy and sustainability goals. It is important to understand this relationship and its differentiation. It may be difficult, if not impossible, to set dynamic and simultaneous goals for circularity and sustainability, if they are directly misaligned, if there are limited means of measuring impacts, and if there are no strategic or practical ways of achieving these objectives.

- ***CE, waste hierarchy, and sustainability principles***

The traditional hierarchy of waste treatment has been the foundation of waste management policy for more than 30 years, and its origin was born from the desire to divert waste from landfills. It indicates that waste management options are relatively desirable, but one of the main blind spots is that it does not indicate trade-offs and the social, environmental, and economic impacts on the local economy. Therefore, from a sustainability perspective, the optimal environmental outcome within the hierarchy is not guaranteed.

For example, recycling is expensive and can be a high-energy and resource-intensive process that produces higher overall impacts throughout its life cycle than other methods. In areas of the world that don't have the capacity, skills, technology, and resources for recycling, the preferred sustainable option, and perhaps the lowest carbon, maybe energy recovery or waste management in a safe and licenced landfill.

When it was designed, the hierarchy did not envision a future scenario that would involve circularity, advanced innovations, or a systemic design of sustainability that challenges the archaic preferential order of waste management. As the company has grown, practitioners and policy-makers who interpret and apply waste hierarchy principles have failed to adapt policies to emerging and disruptive technologies that can create circulars, and potentially more sustainable ones, the results that the limits of the hierarchy.

- ***How to build connectivity to balance the system?***

Ensuring a successful transition to sustainable EC requires a common understanding and approach to circularity, recognition of the circularity relationship and contributions to sustainability and long-term waste management principles, and the ability to measure and report consistently at the micro level (single enterprise, single product or single process), and at the macro level (an entire company; local, regional or national government; or even a global system). In addition, systemic thinking needs to be integrated into new policies, and joining forces across the value chain can minimise the impacts of supply and extraction and can improve recycling and waste management.

The practice of quantitatively comparing the impacts of circular systems on sustainability with their linear counterparts is emerging. Analysis of the feasibility and integration of several well-defined and standardised methods – such as life cycle assessments, material flow analysis, system dynamics, etc. – can provide a more holistic view that forms the basis for assessing a range of impacts of a product, service, process, or technology. This analysis can also help clarify the relationship and potential conflicts between sustainability, CE, and waste management principles and provide important tools to identify risks, understand trade-offs, and avoid unexpected externalities.

In summary, the current CE model is an intentionally designed human construction, anchored in the techno-sphere with a clear focus on governments and businesses. Sustainability, on the other hand, aims to favour the environment, the economy, and society in general; responsibilities are shared by all but are not clearly defined.

Position of the International Research Society for Sustainable Development 2020 Conference (ISDRS)[4]

The 26th annual ISDRS conference provided a forum for interdisciplinary discussion on sustainability research, facilitating an exchange of ideas between various aspects of the field. The CE has taken an important place at the conference in recent years, bringing a long presence of fundamental fields such as industrial ecology, industrial symbiosis, life cycle analysis, cleaner production, and their implications. Resource efficiency themes were presented at each ISDRS conference. As the titles progressed, the path of innovation and resource efficiency impacts has produced many journals' special issues over the years.

The implementation of CE is widely recognised as involving input from multiple organisations, including businesses, business associations, governmental organisations, and potentially third-party sector organisations.

The papers gathered by ISDRS provide important evidence and arguments for the development of CE approaches, as the concept matures from a level of ambitious aspiration to an approach that must be asserted in practice. In the process and analysis of the implementation attempt, the concept itself is likely to undergo some adjustment.

The empirical contributions here point out that while the idea of CE has indeed taken shape in recent years, there is a lack of understanding and prioritisation shared by the various stakeholders involved. Businesses are becoming more familiar with CE practices, and business associations/networks play a role. However, the public sector case study remains focused on end-of-life, although overshadowed by purchasing problems.

There still appears to be a gap in training and education in the broader, non-environmental aspects of the CE, i.e. how and even why, from a stakeholder perspective, these aspects could be implemented.

Interactions Between Risk Management and Sustainability[5]

As the COVID-19 crisis has demonstrated, decision-making has become more difficult in an environment of rapid change, increasing uncertainty and volatility. The speed of change is inevitably faster than our understanding of the consequences, particularly concerning risks and emerging shocks.

---

[4]See Deutz, P., Cecchin, A., & Salomone, R. *Circular economy and sustainability: View from the International Sustainable Development Research Society 2020 Conference*. https://gtmhub.com/esg-strategy-create-measurable-results-in-sustainability-whitepaper?utm_term=sustainable%20economy&utm_campaign=lead-tofu-esg-whitepaper-emea-apac-search-bing&utm_source=bing&utm_medium=cpc&ppcp_platform=bing&msclkid=d8ff6988e4fc12ca79d90aacc97a6a37.

[5]See Boult, M. (2022, July 14). *Where risk meets sustainability*. https://www.strategic-risk-europe.com/home/where-risk-meets-sustainability/1441768.paper?utm_source=adestra&utm_term=Read%20more&utm_medium=email&utm_campaign=26149.

Traditional and emerging risks are accelerating and amplified in so many different directions that the risk manager, who is supposed to always keep an eye on the future, will be too busy reacting. None of this will be easier, especially as the challenges facing the world, including climate change, are fundamental and long-term. Risk and sustainability management must be integrated into the way organisations operate to achieve sustainable success. This is why it is legitimate to ask: Is risk management strategic when it is too reactive and too compliance-oriented?

Decision-makers must adapt to be more focused on future opportunities and needs. Good results will be a consequence of doing the right thing. Regardless of the position occupied in the world, men seek to gain insight into the future to help them develop and formulate a vision, establish a strategy, and implement an effective and efficient system to achieve personal and/or organisational objectives.

But increasingly, these objectives are insufficient and the aim must be to meet the needs of a wider group of stakeholders. The current resonance of the industry after COP26 is 'It is not enough! Targets are set at a low level!' So what is the role of risk management when these macro-trends are taken into account, and in its current form, is it still relevant to the objective?

- ***Integrating sustainability at the heart of all objectives:***

When leaders are asked about 'what is most important for an organisation to succeed sustainably', a theme dominates the responses: the need to integrate sustainability at the heart of each organisation's goal. From a risk management perspective, this is the key 'control' – or perhaps the 'catalyst' – to succeed sustainably, or to adopt a stakeholder capitalism model.

An organisation should therefore have as its mission, generally expressed by a permanent objective, a vision, and equivalent values or declarations, which embrace sustainability.

While sustainability is a fundamental factor at the heart of the mission, it is naturally integrated into strategic, tactical, and operational objectives; and, ultimately, into how the organisation operates: its behaviour, systems, and operations.

- ***Establishing the context:***

When leaders are asked about 'what is most important for an organisation to succeed sustainably', a theme dominates the responses: the need to integrate sustainability at the heart of each organisation's goal. From a risk management perspective, this is the key 'control' – or perhaps the 'catalyst' – to succeed sustainably, or to adopt a stakeholder capitalism model.

An organisation should therefore have as its mission, generally expressed by a permanent objective, a vision, and equivalent values or declarations, which embrace sustainability.

While sustainability is a fundamental factor at the heart of the mission, it is naturally integrated into strategic, tactical, and operational objectives; and, ultimately, into how the organisation operates: its behaviour, systems, and operations. Therefore, all strategies and activities should be (in addition) evaluated and monitored against sustainability objectives.

Understanding the context is an approach that all organisations seek to undertake in one way or another. This can take the form of an informal discussion between the heads of an SME to discuss what they hear from their clients, suppliers, newspapers, etc., or large organisations that conduct surveys, collect and analyse trends, conduct formal interviews with stakeholders, etc.

In risk management, setting the context is the first key step in the risk management process defined by ISO 31000:2018. It provides a solid foundation for risk identification (including sustainability risks), informing an organisation's risk management strategy. Although separate functions (risk, sustainability, operations, business, finance, etc.) may develop their descriptions of the context with various objectives, grouping them can provide a more holistic view.

In summary, from a sustainability risk perspective, there are two main reasons why understanding the organisation's context is necessary as it allows the organisation to:

→ Understand the sustainable development risk for itself, its stakeholders, and society as a whole, and inform its objectives and strategy.
→ Create a strong foundation to determine how to manage sustainability risks from its operations.

- ***Adopting a risk-based sustainability approach:***

Sustainability is an extremely broad discipline, as evidenced by the number and diversity of the UN SDGs mentioned above. In a paper, Kris Clements wrote: 'Previously, the goal was to help the company achieve its strategic objectives, as these other [sustainability] elements were considered less important. But that is no longer the case.'

Until recently, risk management has focused on a limited number of areas with significant impacts, such as people, the environment, assets (including economic and financial aspects), and reputation. Additional categories covering all UN SDGs may be considered impractical, but their impacts on sustainability must be taken into account, at least those that are important to the organisation and its operations.

It is common in sustainability functions to undertake 'materiality assessments' that help the organisation understand, organise, and prioritise areas where it has an impact on sustainability so that its strategy can focus on areas where it can have the greatest impact.

Discussions with risk and sustainability experts have revealed that these assessments can help an organisation ensure that its risk management activities effectively address sustainability. Here are some key recommendations:

→ Involve the sustainability and risk functions in the materiality assessments of the organisation.
→ Consider both 'issues' and 'sustainability risks':
  - Issues – Where the activities of organisations currently have an impact on sustainability (CO_2 emissions, use of raw materials and society, etc.).

   ○ Risks – Where an event/incident could occur in the organisation's operations, which would then impact sustainability (a clothing company contracts with a new supplier without indicating that it uses child labour, or that a mine dam breaks down, resulting in environmental pollution, ecosystem damage and impacts on the health of local communities, etc.).

→ Consider the global enterprise, that is, the entire supply network, from raw materials to the use of the organisation's products and services by its clients (not just those of its own operations).

GRI[6] [Global Reporting Initiative] model is a useful tool, which can be used to improve understanding of your organisation's context and the sustainability issues and risks an organisation faces.

- ***Sustainability in decision-making:***

It's clear to people who are interested in risk and sustainability that when you identify potential risks. It is important to consider all the possible ripple effects of what you do to determine what unintended consequences may occur. These issues can then be addressed in the plans and communicated to decision-makers so that they have as complete a picture as possible of their decisions. Another challenge arises when it comes to making decisions among other options when their sustainability impacts and/or risks affect different aspects of sustainability.

For example, you may have options to choose where one is better for poverty (UN SDG 1) and worse for climate action (UN SDG 13) and the other is better for responsible consumption and production (UN SDG 12) and worse for clean water (UN SDG 6).

Based on discussions with experts in this area, it appears that, to date, assessments have generally been qualitative and focused more on sustainability impacts than risks. While the people consulted do not have a silver bullet to solve this problem, current risk approaches can be used effectively to assess different types of consequences.

Sustainability risk can be quantitatively considered by assessing its impact on business value using the traditional EBITDA-based financial reporting too.

- ***The importance of managing 'sustainability risk':***

It is interesting to report on an organisation's sustainability objectives, activities, and performance. An organisation can demonstrate its commitment to what it and its stakeholders' value, as well as its achievements. This has a positive impact, ranging from better staff morale and financing to increased customer and sales loyalty.

---

[6]La Global Reporting Initiative (GRI) est un organisme international indépendant de normalisation qui aide les entreprises, les gouvernements et d'autres organismes à comprendre et à communiquer leurs impacts sur des questions telles que les changements climatiques, les droits de l'homme et la corruption. GRI fournit les normes de reporting de durabilité les plus utilisées au monde (les normes GRI) – voir: https://www.esgtoday.com/gri-launches-major-update-to-sustainability-reporting-standards/.

Organisations are faced with an increasing number of regulatory reporting requirements, contractual reporting requirements, and good practices. Many risk professionals will have heard of reporting frameworks, a real alphabetic soup that includes GRI, IIRC, SASB, TCFD, etc. This introduces the risks of sustainability reporting and conduct, or what's called 'greening'. For example:

→ Not commit to sustainability following stakeholder expectations.
→ Commit and then show that it was broken.
→ Omit items in reports/lack of openness and transparency.
→ Misrepresenting sustainability performance
→ Lack of clarity in sustainability reports.

While the typical causes of these risks are more likely, to be honest mistakes, blind spots, or misjudgements of those within an organisation, rather than deliberate intentions to hide and deceive, all may have negative impacts; reputational and brand damage, reduced sales, increased financial costs, and even litigation and/or regulatory action.

A key point is that the communication on sustainability is not just an annual exercise for the official report on corporate sustainability. This may include marketing claims, posters, and similar materials used to communicate desired behavioural changes, and communications with suppliers and customers. All this needs to be carefully managed. Taking an open and honest approach promotes responsibility, trust, and reputation.

In summary, integrating sustainability criteria into risk management and risk-based decision-making begins with understanding the context of the organisation. It is then possible to determine which SDGs are important to the organisation, and how best to manage and report on them and avoid clinging to a comfort zone that would not allow to build organisational and societal resilience to an uncertain and more volatile risk environment.

Supply Networks: Security at the Heart of Resilience

The concept of a new circular and sustainable economy is not new; it has roots in post-war environmental movements. Sustainability is recognised by economic agents and decision-makers as a promising approach to jointly achieve environmental improvements and economic growth. Circularity is a more sustainable term whose aim is to extend the life of resources by keeping them in the economy, facilitating their replacement cycle, by making waste a new source of energy rather than a disposable material.

The shift of economic agents towards sustainability implies fundamental changes in ecosystems and a systematic overhaul of production and consumption behaviour. Linear economies have only been able to work so far because the Earth and future generations have paid a portion of the cost of each product that is manufactured. Producers have always made unsustainable products that create waste because it allows businesses and consumers to contain costs and prices.

But this economic model is only profitable because we continue to ignore the true environmental cost of our consumption. It is only cheaper for manufacturers

> In a world of ongoing disruption, governments, businesses, and societies must build resilience to ensure a sustainable and inclusive future for all. Success will depend on how leaders respond to key challenges. Combating health inequalities, preparing for the future of work, moving beyond skills and education for all, and investing in subsistence wages around the world are among the top priorities for the public and private sectors. How to deploy new tools, policies, and approaches to build resilience toward inclusive, equitable, and sustainable economies and societies?

Fig. 3.1. Building Resilient Economies and Societies.

to produce a virgin plastic water bottle because its environmental impact is spread across society and future generations. Climate change has drifted far beyond the point where small incremental changes will save the world from the consequences of human choices. Humans need to rethink how they consume all goods and services, and a CE could serve as a model in this regard (Fig. 3.1).

In particular, SMEs/SMIs and midcaps must therefore prepare for the latter challenge, as they are the natural partners in the CE. In this respect, it should be noted that many of them have already developed related activities based on their visions of the future.

The words 'ecological' or 'environmentally sensitive' have a fairly similar but not so broad meaning and description of something that benefits the environment and is not harmful to the environment, respectively. The CE does not necessarily have a link to sustainability. The concept presents some ideas that can help sustainability, but always evaluate whether they can be applied in terms of sustainability.

Crop production for bio-fuels could include intensive agriculture, and subsequent fertiliser use, degrading terrestrial habitats and freshwater ecosystems, and bio-composting plastics often require industrial heating at a temperature high enough for microbes to decompose.

Companies like to use terms like 'circular', 'sustainable', 'green' or 'green' for 'eco-bleaching', and in most cases, it's just 'blanket demands with no action to support them'. There is no environmentally friendly product and, for the moment, the best solution is to be an environmentally conscious consumer, to explore ideas for sustainable living, and to make transitions in everyday practices and spaces.

Among the potential pitfalls that executives and executives may fall into is thinking that the next phase would be 'a return to what I had before' rather than seeing it as an opportunity to ask the right questions: 'Can I reset or reinvent my organisation?' Indeed, the most fruitful exchanges with CEOs must revolve around this issue: 'How can I reframe my organisation for this speed based on design rather than adrenaline?'

The transition to the 'new normal' will involve developing new management practices and technological solutions to improve resource utilisation and make processes more sustainable; reduce food waste and loss; turn waste and by-products into resources; integrate consumers in supporting circularity; and implement traceability systems.

Move from a linear 'take-do-eliminate' management model to 'reduce, reuse, recycle', a more complex and circular resource coordination system will also depend on the availability of many numerical data concerning the characteristics and origin of materials, the conditions of supply, packaging systems, shipping systems, social requirements, Circularity and Environmental Sustainability Index.

Chapter 4

Complexity, Systems and Risk

How Can Complex Systems Be Managed?

William Black has formulated four principles that can help risk professionals apply systemic thinking to their environment which are the four fundamental principles of complex systemic thinking (IRM India, 2022).

- ***First principle: Top management must recognise that the system in question is advanced and complex.***

For Black, this is often the main barrier, as once managers recognise this reality, they also accept that conventional project and risk management approaches will not work as well, so we need to think about and develop new approaches.

Formally recognising that existing methods are context-altered and therefore new advanced levels of thought and practice are required is often the most difficult step in solving complex problems.

- ***Second principle: Focus more on the connected system as a whole rather than on each of its components.***

In risk management, individual components are often placed on a thermal map and separate controls are assigned that are prioritised based on impact and likelihood.

When a number of components are connected for a common objective, like an organisation, they constitute a system of co-dependent risks. When facing risks in a complex environment, it is necessary to manage the entire system, not just individual contributors.

This is why it is critical to learn about global macroeconomic threats, such as growing economic vulnerability, increased COVID-19 disruptions, geopolitical tensions, and climate change. They cannot be individually on a risk register because they affect many parts of the organisation in unpredictable ways. They are all connected and must be managed as a co-dependent connected system because they conduct and influence each other.

Enterprise Risk Management in Today's World: A Current and Futuristic View of the Complexity, Resilience, Responsibility and Tools in ERM, Part B, 41–47

doi:10.1108/978-1-83608-392-420241004

- ***Third principle: Recognise that because complex system behaviours are influenced by signals and feedback, they respond to changes in the environment and the behaviour of other elements in the system.***

For Black, regardless of the complexity of the system, its behaviour is normally determined by only a handful of leading contributing agents.

Risk managers have to choose who the major contributing agents are – and if you can influence, say, these three to five agents, the signals and feedback they will produce will be in the direction of what you want. There may never be total control, so he will do exactly what you want him to do, but if you influence him positively, you will most often get positive risk outcomes.

- ***Fourth principle: Recognise that all truly complex systems will evolve through different states and orders as they evolve and evolve naturally.***

With each new state or order, new phenomena and behaviours specific to this order will emerge. For this reason, standardised and 'universal' approaches to management control are extremely limited when addressing complex issues.

What Are Multiple Scales?

For Black, to meet this multi-faceted change challenge, Snowden developed a framework in the 1980s, still relevant today (Cynefin Framework, 2021). It shows how complex states move between different levels of organisation. A phenomenon can go from complicated to chaotic very quickly, or from complex to obvious. Black people's favourite example is the conflict in Palestine: one day it is complex, the next chaotic as the situation in the fall of 2023 – but it is rarely simple or orderly. In essence, each complex environment has multiple scales, and for each scale or order, new phenomena and, more importantly, new rules emerge.

This is something that risk management has yet to achieve because each of the four scales of the same phenomenon needs four different risk strategies. The more complex a system becomes and risks chaos, the more relevant the approach to the resilience of natural systems and complex systems thinking becomes.

Furthermore, controls and processes that operate in one environment are not guaranteed to operate in another, so organisations may need to build a whole new risk strategy for each complex system. Therefore, risk managers need to ask themselves how they can help their organisations build their natural resilience so they don't need to specifically predict crises because they have the right systems in place to deal with events as they happen.

Defining Complexity Risk in a Few Words?[1]

In a few words, complexity risk is the type of risk that arises from and is unique to complex systems. However, before identifying and managing complexity risk,

[1]See Miller, G., & Bartlett, M. *Harnessing complexity*. file:///d:/Users/LOUISOT/Downloads/Enterprise%20Risk%20-%20Autumn%202022.pdf.

one must understand the characteristics of complex systems. It is useful to contrast complicated, complex, and chaotic systems. Complicated systems are rich in details, while complex systems are rich in structure. A good example of a complicated system is a car engine. It contains many parts that work together for a common purpose.

However, the conduct engine can be designed, predicted, and controlled accurately. This is not the case for complex systems, such as forest ecosystems or countries' economies, which develop, adapt, and evolve according to external conditions and the behaviour of the stakeholders. Although these examples of complex systems are very different, they share common features that distinguish them from simply complicated systems (see Common Features of Complex Systems). Because of the listed characteristics of complex systems, the behaviour cannot be explained by the simple sum of parts.

This critical determinant of a complex system is called emergent behaviour. A good example of emergent behaviour is the property of consciousness arising from the interaction of neurons in the brain. There is nothing in the individual neurons or the simple rules by which they are governed to suggest that consciousness will emerge. The science of the analysis of the behaviour of individual neurons is very different from the analysis of human consciousness and its resulting behaviour. This comparison can be expanded to show how laws governing elementary components at the micro level limit behaviour at the macro level.

When sensitivity to initial conditions in a complex system becomes more pronounced, chaotic systems are produced in which we have even less ability to predict results. This is illustrated by the famous analogy of the butterfly effect put forward by Edward Lorenz in 1963, where the flapping of a butterfly's wings could eventually lead to a tornado. While immediate inputs and outputs are not random in isolation, the number of variables and their sensitivity to initial conditions means that they appear random when the analyses are repeated. This makes chaotic systems extremely difficult to predict to a certain point, beyond which it becomes impossible.

What Is the Meaning of the Concept of 'Nested Systems'?

Complex systems themselves often consist of several complex systems. Just like Russian dolls, a global company could be made up of regional offices containing each of the departments and teams. Each of these self-organised components will have the characteristics of a complex system. They are of course composed of people, each of whom is a complex system of cells that function as independent agents and organise themselves to form a multi-cellular being.

Complex systems therefore do not operate in isolation, but interact with others, both inside and outside the nested system. These may involve interactions with complex external physical, technical, environmental, economic, and socio-political systems. The risk of complexity therefore comes with additional concerns and considerations due to a high degree of interdependence and emerging behaviour, root causes/roots, and subsequent impacts of risk.

Complex systems have distributed rather than centralised control, where decisions and actions are taken without structured coordination. While efforts to exert top-down influence have some of the desired results, it must be taken into account that much of the control rests with the agents in the system. But, if used correctly, the distributed control function of complex systems can promote the effective deployment of people's skills and expertise in contemporary organisations.

How Can Different Levels of Complexity Be Taken Into Account?

Organisations often fail to appreciate the levels of complexity inherent in their structures and interactions with the outside world. With multi-level supply networks employing just-in-time, methods, rigid hierarchical management structures, and increased public and regulatory pressures to address social and environmental impacts in operations, there have never been so many factors to consider in risk management.

From a series of articles published in recent years comes a consensus on the need to move away from our traditional methods or, at the very least, to improve them to cope with our new hyper-connected world, including risk analysis in the metaverse.

If they maintained a narrow and siloed approach to risk management, organisations would be ignoring the complex reality. Dividing an organisation into small pieces makes sense from a management perspective, but as noted above, it should be kept in mind that this creates barriers to effective risk information transfer. This applies not only internally, but to the broader enterprise, including suppliers, contractual partners, customers, shareholders, and more generally stakeholders and the broader public network.

Complex organisations produce large amounts of valuable data with their daily activities. Often, however, these data are not collected and used meaningfully. Data capture and analysis are critical to managing risk in highly unpredictable complex systems. By identifying recurring themes in the data, lessons can be learned from actual events. This is the best defence against uncertainty in complex systems; it supports the development of reduction measures that can be applied repeatedly, while the organisation continues to learn from its successes and its failures.

The influence of human factors such as bias and heuristics in the identification, assessment, management, and communication of complexity risk is often underestimated. The perception of an individual risk can vary considerably depending on the views and experiences of the person examining it. In addition, individuals acting as agents in an organisation's complex system, and their interactions with each other will produce emerging behaviours and create additional risks.

How Can Complexity Risk Be Assessed?

The first step in managing complexity risks is to recognise that they exist and will require additional controls to manage them. A change of mentality is needed not only at the level of risk managers and those directly involved in the risk management process but also at the level of the board of directors. A comprehensive assessment of the organisation and its components is required to identify, assess, and understand the nature of the complexity within that specific organisation.

At the outset, tried and tested techniques already mentioned above such as political, economic, sociological, technological, legal, and environmental analyses (PESTLE) and volatility, uncertainty, complexity, and ambiguity (VUCA) can be valuable in framing the organisation's structure and identifying key areas of complexity.

Factors such as the volume, the uniqueness of the components, the uniqueness of the environment, the novelty of the products or services offered, the capacity of the organisation to provide them, and the network of stakeholders, should be taken into account. Once these factors have been identified and assessed, the linkages between them should be mapped at a high level before going into detail. Particular attention should be paid to silos, which can represent complex systems in their own right. This includes various risk management functions such as supply network risk, operational risk, and project risk. The key is to open channels of communication between all these different parties to capitalise on their combined effort.

It is important to understand that complexity is not something that could or should be eliminated; rather it must be understood and accepted. While it poses challenges for those seeking to manage related threats, it creates opportunities for those who are open to it. Complex systems rely on diversity. The more sources of information, perspectives, and innovations in a complex system, the more opportunities there are for innovation within an organisation and its broader industrial sector. On the other hand, it is essential to ensure that lessons are learned and that knowledge is transmitted as and when.

To initiate the site, risk professionals are likely to face barriers in the early stages of preparing for complexity risk management. Changing the mindset of the board of directors to deal with complexity is no small feat, as it runs counter to the management effectiveness agenda that prevails in many long-standing organisations. However, this is an essential first step in the process of delivering the message. In addition, not only is the support of the board of directors essential, but it is also likely, at least initially, that additional or redeployed resources are needed to begin with.

It will take time and effort to understand the organisation's culture, behaviours, current trends, and the connections between them. Cascading the findings and resulting changes will also require resources, including cash. This is also true if we need to procure software that can capture and model the risk of complexity by recognising that it is connected.

While reflecting on Listening and Learning, Stephen Sidebottom[2] also notes that risk professionals need to have a set of compelling 'performance competencies' to support effective risk management. These skills will be used to promote the benefits of managing complexity risk to the board of directors. However, it is not difficult to sell to the board.

The understanding and effectiveness of mapping and complexity risk management will result in cost savings in all aspects of the organisation. While any initial expenditure is likely to be viewed with scepticism, the return on investment will

[2]Stephen Sidebottom MA MBA Chartered FCIPD FRSA is non-executive chairman of the IRM since June 2021.

speak for itself. As part of a support presentation, the plans should be detailed. Setting out a step-by-step process to achieve the objectives is likely to allay reservations.

It will also be useful to demonstrate where similar approaches have been successfully undertaken elsewhere. Doing something of this nature alone is always more difficult. Maintaining relationships with cross-sector networks, including MRI, academic institutions, and research organisations such as the Santa Fe Institute, and leveraging their work will help keep the transformation on track based on the most recent knowledge.

How Do Complexity and System Design Intersect?[3]

Systems are generally made up of a multitude of elements interacting with their accessories, which is why they are usually complex systems. In terms of risk management, these are in principle socio-economic systems; for example, we can think of an online social platform or a network of companies that jointly develop patents.

At the same time, systems are integrated into an environment with which they are connected through exchange processes. This distinction between what is an element and what is the environment versus the system defines what is to be understood by the respective system, especially when it comes to the extended enterprise including its partner networks. As systems may contain subsystems and at the same time be part of super-systems, there is no clear definition. Rather, different perspectives on a system must be taken into account.

The key question concerns the inherent dynamics of systems, in other words, their behaviour before actors exert a targeted influence on them. It is only when this self-dynamics is well understood, captured in the model, and reproduced, that it is possible to formulate requirements for systems design in the first place. Two characteristics must be considered:

- ***Self-organisation:*** Complex systems can self-organise, because they are capable of producing new structures of order and collective dynamics, provided certain critical conditions are met. This transition to a new system state usually occurs by leaps and it is called emergence.

Some emerging properties are desirable, such as the conductivity of metals or consciousness in the brain; others are undesirable, such as traffic congestion on the highway or massive panic during a rock concert. It is difficult to specifically influence these self-organising processes, as collective characteristics cannot be reduced to individual system elements.

- ***Adaptability:*** Complex systems are also adaptive systems that constantly monitor changes. These may include external changes to the system, such as a change in the corporate tax rate resulting in the arrival or departure of businesses, but also internal changes, such as the loss of an employee resulting in a redistribution of duties.

[3]See Schweitzer, F. *The bigger picture: Complexity meets systems design.*

Various scientific disciplines, such as macroeconomics or social psychology, have done important preliminary work, especially on top-down access. The purpose of system design is to use these approaches to develop an even more complete picture of the dynamics of these systems. Feedback between different levels of the system, for example between the economy and the environment, is particularly important.

This feedback loop also plays a major role in the spread of risks, which initially seem rather limited. Failures affect one level, for example in energy supply, and can lead to a systemic collapse at a completely different level, for example in telecommunications.

The modelling of these meta-systems, systems of systems, is becoming increasingly important with growing integration. Globalisation, resulting in the interdependence of separate economic activities in space, is only one of the drivers of this development. Another is the vertical integration of different systems within the framework of digitalisation.

Modelling such systems has long ceased to be a task for individual disciplines, it requires an interdisciplinarity approach; this is what makes system design tasks so difficult. The sum of individual scientific results does not allow an understanding of systems. Who should develop such systems models?

Will the pioneers of research in the discipline suddenly generate a systemic perspective? Or should we invent a systemic science in the best sense of the word, capable of integrating disciplinary approaches while developing our methodology? What are the elements that help decision-makers to understand and model not only special economic systems but also socio-technical, urban, or ecological systems in a global approach?

A degree in economics, biology, or another traditional scientific discipline is no longer enough. Where are the educational programs that allow interdisciplinary studies? Where are the journals that publish such publications? Where are the positions of professors with such a profile displayed? With these questions, we are suddenly no longer dealing with methodological and technical aspects of system modelling, but rather with the profile of universities and scientific policy.

Ecology, which has always been a pioneer of systemic thinking, has provided enough examples of how seemingly positive interventions have led to negative consequences. It is by preventing small forest fires that large uncontrollable forest fires become possible. Only the extermination of the 'evil' wolves led to the disappearance of whole species and a radical change in the landscape.

Of course, these negative consequences were unintended, precisely because the interrelations within the overall system were not understood. Better system models make this understanding possible. Yet the hope of designing systems without negative consequences is misleading. It is the tension between desirable and undesirable changes that ultimately drives the development of all systems.

And even breakdowns are part of the dynamics of the system because they create space to imagine something new. Their systematic prevention also means that innovations cannot be asserted. Instead of dreaming of eternally stable systems without errors and disadvantages, humanity should see system design as a way to better understand the link between costs and benefits.

Chapter 5

Risk Management and Modelling

The range of risks that organisations need to consider is so broad that practitioners and academics have sought a risk management (RM) approach that can reflect the potential interdependencies between risks and facilitate decision-makers examining the likely effects of all types of risks on their organisational processes, products, and services, among other things. In this regard, Enterprise-wide Risk Management's (ERM's) comprehensive and integrated approach combines all RM activities into a single framework that facilitates the identification of these interdependencies.

ERM is more efficient than traditional approaches because of the consideration of interdependencies between different risks. While equities on each risk reduce the volatility of results from a single source, the ERM reduces overall volatility by limiting the aggregation of risks between the different sources; but it is still necessary to be able to model the future to 'create likelihood alleys in the fog of the future'.

In this context, what is the purpose of a strategy 'model' when all possible models are so clearly wrong? And what is the use of the necessary model simplifications? Perhaps strategists should recognise and deal with complexity more directly, thinking creatively about the problem, and avoiding using models that are necessarily false.

No strategic model is a perfect representation of the world, but some, those who provide frameworks for systematic thinking or create powerful and sticky images for communication, offer valuable ideas that justify their costs. What are the most powerful models and metaphors? And what are the consequences of using one model over another?

In principle, risk modelling allows for a better measure of the rate of occurrence of certain events but does not make it possible to predict the occurrence accurately. In this risk modelling work, the choice of methods and techniques allowing the construction of the model, the choice of the estimation method, and even the choice of data directly and significantly influence the responses obtained and, therefore, despite the appearance of rigour, these choices are not neutral.

The issue of modelling dependence is also important when it comes to properly measuring risks. Finally, a fundamental question arises: who is responsible for financial crises: buyers, financial institutions, control bodies, etc.?

Enterprise Risk Management in Today's World: A Current and Futuristic View of the Complexity, Resilience, Responsibility and Tools in ERM, Part B, 49–63

Published under exclusive licence by Emerald Publishing Limited
doi:10.1108/978-1-83608-392-420241005

However, it is not possible to eliminate uncertainty, since it is impossible to predict the future with certainty and the modelling itself is not of absolute precision. But it is possible to tame chance, to identify it, to control its harmful effects. Modelling allows decision-makers to deal with uncertainties.

It is never possible to tame chance to the point of submitting it, so all must learn to deal with uncertainty and complexity. Whatever the quality of a model, it does not provide decision-makers with a crystal ball.

Predictive Modelling for RM: Myth or Reality?

Predictive modelling plays an increasing role in improving organisations' safety, specifically for the shipping industry. This approach may seem limited, but shipping is an important component of any company's logistics networks, making their analysis relevant to most economic operators around the world. Moreover, the limitations of modelling in the sea world are found in many sectors.

Even those who don't know exactly what predictive modelling covers have probably already crossed paths with at least one company that uses predictive modelling to project potential risks to its fleets. While predictive modelling allows companies to obtain early warning of their key risks, it is not a modern method of prediction. It doesn't allow anybody to see the future, and it doesn't provide a crystal ball.

On the other hand, predictive modelling is much simpler than many imagine – it is a combination of mathematics and statistics used to calculate the potential risks from the companies' data. Done correctly, predictive modelling has proven to eliminate preventable incidents, save lives at sea, and prevent damage to ships, the environment, and the bottom line of businesses. When predictive modelling is ineffective, it is a missed opportunity for everyone in the industry.

Predictive modelling treats data differently, therefore it signals problems not observed when using other systems. In this example, it gives the shipping industry a better chance of predicting problems, and avoiding disasters for safer seas for all.

- ***Predictive modelling in different industrial sectors:***

Companies around the world share their data for predictive modelling and benefit from customised risk reports that report the most likely threats to their crew. Predictive modelling has also proven effective in many other areas.

For example, in the United States, the use of predictive modelling has been extremely effective in reducing crime and improving safety in cities. For example, the Richmond Police Service in Virginia used historical data to predict when firearms would be used on New Year's Eve 2003. They used the forecasts to plan their surveillance routes and found a 47% decrease in fire.

- ***Changing attitudes make seas safer:***

The marine industry benefits from effective data sharing, unprecedented in the past. Historically, data sharing in the marine industry has always been reactive. The industry as a whole would have access to the basic details of an incident when it was already too late, through headlines or investigations. This meant that shared data was extremely basic and that industries in general had little opportunity to learn information. This method also meant that by the time the information was available, it was unfortunately too late to avoid an incident at sea.

Historically, shipping companies have been reluctant to share their data, fearing fallout from their mistakes and loss of market share in a competitive environment. As attitudes change and companies accept the idea of sharing their data for the common good, predictive modelling is gradually becoming more robust and accurate for all those who rely on it to ensure the safety of their crews at sea, and the faculties of their clients.

- ***What can grow wrong with predictive modelling:***

Predictive modelling is only as good as the data on which it is based. The traditional GIGO (garbage in – garbage out) applies here. If the data are incorrect, predictive modelling will not be able to identify the events most likely to endanger a vessel or its crew.

To work well, predictive modelling requires internal data that goes beyond what is available in the company's incident management system. It is essential to collect internal data from each data set, allowing the process to analyse all possible risks within an organisation. Effective predictive modelling requires information collected from each data set, source, and business owner.

- ***Success factors of predictive modelling:***

For predictive modelling to be effective, small events or near misses can be leading indicators and must be taken into account; data from different sources and from each data set cross-analysed. Also, sharing data from each dataset allows for accurate analysis of all possible situations to make it much easier to identify key incidents that would otherwise be missed until an incident occurs.

The more companies that share their data for predictive modelling, the more it's possible to get a full picture of exactly what's happening in the marine industry, providing an overview for RM firms conducting predictive modelling. This unique perspective means that greater accuracy can be achieved when assessing risk and safer seas assured for all.

What Do Data Analytics Contribute to RM?

Today, data availability is limitless, technology is becoming increasingly 'smart' and business dynamics are more challenging than ever. With the complexity of increasingly rapid change, it has become imperative to leverage the power of an effective RM process to ensure an organisation's long-term strategic success. Traditional RM approaches, based primarily on individual subjectivity and perceptions, are not sufficient to address the new risk environment.

This is why organisations need to move from traditional RM to risk-based performance management (RBPM). With RBPM, the focus is on mapping business drivers critical to achieving objectives and assisting operational stakeholders to identify relevant emerging trends and risk measures to ensure effective oversight which lies in the granularity of operational factors into key strategies and tasks, from a macroeconomic perspective.

Therefore, data analysis must be integrated with RM, i.e. integrate these technologies throughout the process, from identification to assessment, mitigation, and monitoring. Each step of the RM process allows us to make the most of the power of analytics, namely:

- ***Risk identification:***

For organisations, the risk may have internal sources *(inadequate processes and controls, business portfolio, lack of funding, etc.)* and/or external sources *(macroeconomic changes, political environment, regulation, climate change, etc.)*. Industries and economies around the world are increasingly large and complex. This is how new databases were created in terms of speed, volume, and variety. With the emergence of Big Data, it is possible to integrate internal and external data points to identify emerging risks, even latent ones *(relevant tools and assets – web scrappers, data ingestion tools, and 'analytics' tool and visualisation platform)*.

- ***Risk analysis, evaluation, and prioritisation:***

Leaders need to focus on critical sectors. Organisations need to extend their understanding of the risk landscape to easily accessible data associated with strategic risks, down to the operational and functional levels. By aligning the data with risk profiles and indicators, a risk profile integrating impact and probability can be developed and thus analytical models can be developed to detect potential risks, fully assess their financial and related impacts, and create an analytical framework to balance financial and strategic impacts against investment through efficient RM *(relevant tools and assets – data ingestion tools, data models, analytics tool and visualisation platform)*.

- ***Risk treatment – reduction:***

Effective risk treatment involves assessing the various options available, not only to select the best alternative but also to consider the impact of the chosen option. It must also monitor the effectiveness of the response to correct the incident promptly. Various risk modelling techniques can be adopted to simulate hypothetical scenarios (based on past risk occurrences and future forecasts) by integrating various data elements, this helps to decide on the most optimal intervention strategy.

Data analysis can also be used to track the effectiveness of implementation of implemented mitigation plans. This could be particularly useful to alert the mitigation lead in case the implementation schedule is not on track and requires a new visit/focus *(relevant tools and assets – AI/ML models, scenario models, workflow tool, analysis tool, and visualisation platform)*.

- ***Risk monitoring and review:***

Rigorous and timely risk monitoring is vital in today's dynamic environment. The identification of key risk indicators for each risk is important to measure trends and changes in risk data parameters. It is important to identify lead and delay indicators and determine the most appropriate and relevant data source to monitor these parameters. Risk analysis has an important role to play. Effective workflow technology includes automated alerts and reminders *(linking to the data source platform)*, allowing operational stakeholders to take timely action *(relevant tools and assets – workflow tool, analytics tool and visualisation platform)*.

- ***Risk reporting:***

Timely and relevant risk reporting by integrating the entire RM cycle into an integrated technology platform is a steering instrument. They provide a real-time view of the risks and keep track of past lessons. Data analytics can be effectively deployed and integrated into a platform and serves as a data feed strain for each step of the RM process *(relevant tools and assets – workflow tool, analytics tool, and visualisation platform)*.

Migration to a RBPM approach and harnessing the power of cutting-edge technology and data analytics can give organisations a competitive edge and ensure their long-term resilience.

How to Measure the Critical Elements of Risk to Make Better Decisions?

In the case of projects, RM processes are used by organisations to determine their specific project risk tolerances, the myriad of risks and threats associated with the project, and the best ways to reduce risk exposure. Unfortunately, organisations are held back when it comes to risk assessment because they have either a poor understanding of risk or erroneous, non-scientific methodologies, or even fall victim to paralysing misconceptions about measurement and quantification that trip even experienced statisticians.

To avoid pitfalls that can lead to bad decisions – or worse, sometimes no decisions – Hubbard Decision Research uses a unique modelling methodology that provides a better understanding of uncertainty, a better way to quantify and measure risk and other 'intangibles', and more concrete information to help decision-makers improve decision-making for all initiatives.

- ***Identify issues with current RM practices:***

Poor decisions often come from poor data or misinterpretation of data, especially in the area of risk. Managers, risk consultants, and senior managers are often victims of misconceptions about RM. These misconceptions include:

→ Believing that the risk is 'intangible' and not measurable;
→ Relying on methods not based on statistics or decision science;
→ Feel that risk measures are insufficient due to small sample sizes or lack of data;
→ Use subjective judgements (such as 'weighted rating' techniques);
→ Relying too much on experience and instinct to assess risk rather than quantitative analysis.

Non-scientific methods have led to disasters as there are many risks that can harm an organisation – and perhaps the most dangerous is a flawed RM approach.

- ***Explore the fundamentals of effective risk control:***

Even strong ERM programs never eliminate risk, but the right approach helps determine how to manage the current risk and allocate resources to the best choice in the future; it helps to take risk efficiently providing quantitative methods to scientifically measure and analyse each component of risk and potential loss.

A scientific approach is a question of using statistics and probabilistic risk models in conjunction with a methodology based on the science of decisions and supported by research objectively and impartially, not dependent on human factors (intuition, opinion, or experience) that too often mislead decision-makers.

Uncertainty remains to be defined as the foundation of risk; by understanding and measuring uncertainty, an organisation can obtain valuable data to inform decisions, which can then enable decision-makers to:

→ Choose to invest in more and often different data;
→ Assess the likelihood of an event or loss occurring;
→ Seek cost-effective ways to mitigate these risks;
→ Consider risk tolerance and degree of uncertainty.

A scientific process eliminates or mitigates human prejudices.

- ***Using a proven management approach – applied information economy:***

Applied Information Economics (AIE)[1] is a framework combining economics, actuarial science, and other mathematical methods to provide better risk analysis. Using the IEA, Hubbard Decision Research can define the decisions being considered, model what we know now, measure what really matters, and then use these measurements and analyses to help decision-makers make better decisions.

The advantage of Applied Information Economics (AIE) over many of the most popular RM methods is that it gives results. With AIE, an organisation can put a number on risk and uncertainty, including the likelihood of internal and external risks occurring, the likelihood of losses resulting from those risks, and the value of more information. Based on verifiable scientific data, this information brings greater confidence, less risk exposure, and better corporate performance through a statistically validated risk reduction plan and decision-making process.

How to Understand the Role of Threat Modelling in RM?[2]

With increasing new security threats, breaches, and regulations, the challenge is to establish a strategy to identify and prioritise new threats before malicious entities use them to their advantage.

---

[1]AIE is a synthesis of techniques of economics, actuarial science, and other mathematical methods. The AIE uses methods proven by a large number of peer-reviewed academic research and empirical data on improving human expert judgements.

[2]See Abouki, Y. (2018, February 28). *Understanding the role of threat modelling in risk management*. https://resources.infosecinstitute.com/topic/understanding-role-threat-modelling-risk-management/.

- ***What is threat modelling?***

Within information security, threat modelling is a structured approach and process for analysing the security of an application. The process begins with the identification of all ports of entry and follows with the enumeration and prioritisation of all potential threats associated with each asset or port of entry. The ultimate goal is to reduce all these threats and prevent future attacks.

Organisations have also begun to integrate threat modelling into their security software to ensure that their applications are developed with integrated security measures.

- ***What is the role of threat modelling in RM?***

The security of information systems (ISS) is one of the concerns underlying the strategy of large companies, including the risk of non-compliance, data breaches, infrastructure failures, legal penalties, and more.

Information security rules are now stricter than ever. They are strongly focused on RM and the implementation of controls to prevent potential threats; as a reminder, this is the General Data Protection Regulation (GDPR) at the level of the European Union. Non-compliant organisations may face massive fines. This is where threat modelling comes in to address all the underlying threats and root causes of high-level threats.

Threat modelling, combined with RM, cannot answer the question of who will attack systems or where the attack will come from. But threat modelling provides valuable information on the IS risks faced by organisations, and describes the necessary measures and controls to stop the threat before it becomes effective.

- ***What are the different threat modelling methods?***

Threat modelling is a structured process that follows a certain set of rules, the most popular of which include:

1. **STRIDE:** It is a threat model originally developed by Microsoft in 1999. Classification focuses more on the attacker's objectives, including:
   - Impersonation of the user;
   - Alteration;
   - Repudiation;
   - Disclosure of information;
   - Denial of service;
   - Privilege elevation.

2. **PASTA**: This threat analysis and attack simulation process is a risk-based methodology that attempts to link business objectives and technical requirements. The PASTA methodology is a seven-step process to provide a dynamic process from identification, enumeration to scoring.
3. **TRIKE**: This method is frequently used as a RM tool during security audits. The TRIKE framework is based on the Requirements Model which defines the acceptable level of risk for stakeholder feedback. The resulting threat model generally contains all the listed threats, as well as risk ratings.

TRIKE is also used to describe the security features of a given system from its high-level to low-level architecture.

4. **VAST:** Visual, agile, and simple threat modelling, the current VAST methodology has been highlighted primarily to address the limitations and gaps of other threat methods. The principle of the VAST methodology is the importance of adapting the threat modelling process to the entire infrastructure and ISS, and ensuring seamless integration into an agile software development methodology. VAST aims to provide useful and actionable information to various stakeholders, including senior managers, developers, and security professionals.

- ***What are data flow diagrams?***

The information collected during the process will be modelled using data flow diagrams (DFDs). These should provide a better overview, or visual presentation, of the application as a whole, as well as how the data is processed and moved. These diagrams are hierarchically structured to break down the application into subsystems. DFD uses a number of conventional representations and symbols in threat modelling as explained below:

→ External Entity: Used to represent external entities that interact with the application via an entry point.
→ Process: Refers to a task that processes data in the application. The task can process data or perform data-based action.
→ Multiple Processes: Used to present a set of sub-processes.
→ Data Store: Used to represent locations where data are stored.
→ Data Flow: Represents the movement of data whose direction is represented by the arrow.
→ Privilege Limit: Used to represent the change in privilege levels as data flows through the application.

Process flow diagrams (PFDs) provide a visualisation that is more focused on how a user flows through different features of the application rather than how the data flow. Process diagrams consist of breaking the application down into various functionality or use cases (e.g. login, registration, post articles, post comments, etc.) and defining all communication protocols (HTTP, HTTPS, etc.) that allow users to browse functions. Therefore, the identification of potential threats and the appropriate security controls needed to address them should be an easy process since the model was built from a user interaction perspective.

- ***What are some popular threat modelling tools?***

Several tools can be used during a threat modelling assignment, among them:

→ ***Microsoft threat modelling:*** This tool is widely used in threat modelling. Its interface should allow non-safety experts to still build models. The tool provides guidance while designing models, and supports integration of Stride methodology, reports, etc. The tool is more software and design-analysis oriented than assets.

→ ***Threat modeller:*** It is enterprise threat modelling software based on Visual, Agile, Simple, Threat (VAST) modelling methodology. It offers collaborative modelling functionality involving all stakeholders, as well as an intuitive and easy-to-use interface that allows security and non-security experts to build threat models.
→ ***Irius risk***: This is another tool with an integrated console to manage application security threats across the ISS.
→ ***SD elements***: It is a software security requirements management platform that provides exclusively automated threat modelling capabilities.

Ultimately, it is important to overcome a widespread misconception that information security is primarily a network problem. The fact is that over 70% of security vulnerabilities exist at the application level, hence the importance of regular threat modelling and security tests.

What Is Modelling Risk and How Can It Be Managed?[3]

A model is a quantitative and mathematical system or approach used in the processing of input data; it processes input into quantitative estimates. It is built on a set of assumptions and variable data for inputs, processes, outputs, and scenarios. It applies mathematical, statistical, financial, and economic data and techniques in a model. A model contains three main components:

→ Inputs: Model data and assumptions;
→ Process: Processes that transform inputs into quantitative estimates;
→ Reports: Expression of estimates into useful management information.

Model risks have become significant and very concerning as a result of the use of sophisticated quantitative models to process applications in large disciplines. Risk arises primarily from potential model errors and appropriate use and implementation of the model. Errors and inaccuracies can result in significant monetary losses, poor organisational decisions and damage to institutional reputation. Hence, model risk arises primarily from two sources:

→ fundamental inaccuracies in the model that would produce erroneous results for its intended use;
→ incorrect or inappropriate use of the model.

---

[3]See *Risk management and modelling – Measure what matters, make better decisions.* https://hubbardresearch.com/risk-management-modelling/ and Bonfiglioli, E. (2021 April 6). *What is model risk management?* https://www.yields.io/blog/what-is-model-risk-management/.

Model Risk Management (MRM) refers to the oversight of risks defined by the potential negative consequences of decisions based on incorrect or misused models. The purpose of MRM is to use techniques, practices, or behaviours that will identify, measure, and mitigate model risks – the potential for model error or misuse of the model.

In summary, while model risk and its management are essentially a problem for financial institutions, the fact remains that all organisations are affected in their exchanges with them. In addition, the considerations apply to any risk modelling regardless of the sector concerned.

- ***Risk Management Model Framework (RMMF)***

A good Risk Management Framework (RMF) model should be developed based on industry best practices and be consistent with regulatory guidelines. For the United States, the US Federal Reserve's Supervisory Guidance on Model Risk Management (SR 11-07) is a good reference for the Grievance Redress Mechanism (GRM) framework that should include the following processes in its life cycle:

1. ***Modelling risk standards:*** Standards should include standards for data quality, model changes, model use, expert judgement, model methodology, model validation, documentation, external model data, model reporting, etc.
2. ***Risk appetite for modelling:*** The level of risk appetite associated with the model will depend on its objectives. Model risk appetite should be expressed in terms of risk tolerance and various relevant measures such as overall quantitative risk exposure, number of high-risk models, etc.
3. ***Modelling risk identification:*** An inventory of existing models should be drawn up to identify the main model changes. The following characteristics are classified *(among others)*:
   → Model Name;
   → Description of the purpose of the model;
   → Use of the model;
   → Frequency of its use;
   → Model assumptions or inputs.
4. ***Modelling risk analysis and evaluation:*** Model risk quantification uses various model risk measurement approaches, or they may use operational risk model approaches. There are three main techniques for quantifying risk, including:
   → Sensitivity Analysis – Changes in model assumptions and parameters and monitoring of changes in results;
   → Validate the model in the past – Test a model using historical data and comparing results to previous results;
   → Validate the model by comparison – Comparing the results of one model with the results of another model using the same data.A quantitative assessment will measure and collate each separate quantifiable model risk assessment using appropriate correlation factors. The result will indicate the robustness of the model, which will impact the risk rating of the model.

In contrast, a qualitative assessment considers the use of qualitative parameters to measure risk in a model – including compliance with standards, cumulative model errors, the degree of risk assessment of the model, and other qualitative factors.

5. ***Risk treatment modelling:*** Potential risk reduction strategies may include:
   - → Modify the model development process;
   - → Conduct additional model validation taking into account changes in the nature and structure of existing risks and the emergence of new risks to which the organism is exposed;
   - → Use independent expert judgements on the interpretation of model results due to model uncertainties;
   - → Follow model and applicability to new risk regulations;
   - → Model efficiency and applicability improvements to reduce risks, such as additional capital and mitigate risks.
6. ***Modelling risk monitoring and reporting:*** The model's risk monitoring and reporting function aims to identify the following issues:
   - → Monitor compliance with the Model Risk Policy and Risk Appetite as per the Policy. The process will recommend if management intervention is required in the event of a discrepancy;
   - → Establish an inventory of material models should be conducted for each model to determine if it is being used following the GRM policy framework;
   - → Analyse the results of model risk assessment and validation and take corrective action to address identified weaknesses;
   - → Provide an overview of emerging trends in MRM and any other relevant issues.

The effectiveness of the overall RM framework depends on its implementation and the quality of the staff who use it. Therefore, an organisation should cultivate a good risk culture. The potential value of sophisticated or mature MRMs far exceeds the issue of regulatory compliance.

What Role for Bayesian Networks for Risk Modelling?[4]

As risks are not directly observable, the approach to trying to understand the future rests on observing and modelling past events, and this is essentially unsuitable for understanding and considering risks rationally. The decomposition of risks into mechanisms generating events and consequences was much more fruitful than simple statistical modelling, which of course remains essential in some cases. The mechanisms underlying the occurrence and deployment of risks can be described by random causal sequences, which are well represented by Bayesian networks.

---

[4]See Naim, P. (2022, May 12). *Les réseaux Bayésiens pour la modélisation du risque.* Risques. https://variances.eu/?p=6672.

Inadequate perception of potential events or future difficulties can lead to unrealistic targets. Risk perception should guide the definition of objectives and strategy. If ISO 31000 defines risk as 'a deviation from what is expected', this definition can be reworded in mathematical terms as 'risk is the variance of the objective around its expected value'. It is not necessarily a financial objective as the objective can be defined as income or profit but also as safety, impact on the environment, reputation, etc.

To rank uncertainty, we can refer to the taxonomy 'Known/Unknown', popularised by Donald Rumsfeld then Secretary of Defence of the United States:

→ 'Known Known' are certainties, and therefore out of the realm of uncertainty;
→ 'Known Unknown', or things we know we don't know about. Some of the known unknowns can be treated with probabilities. These are identified variables or events for which we can characterise our uncertainty. This is uncertainty due to a lack of knowledge;
→ 'Unknown Known' may seem contradictory, but 'things we don't know we know about' could refer to knowledge that is accessible to us. but for which we must engage in some work to make it explicit – it is the uncertainty due to laziness; and
→ 'Unknown Unknown' or 'things we don't know we don't know about' are events that are not even identified, such as technological disruptions, geopolitical changes, etc. We could now call them emerging risks.

There is a similar, though not equivalent, distinction proposed by some authors that refers to measurable uncertainty by the term risk and retains the term 'uncertainty' for non-measurable uncertainty. According to Knight, profit is the result of real uncertainty (Knight, 1921), whereas measurable RM only results in a form of salary linked to the exploitation of the structure of chance, as in insurance. Profit is born from the inherent and absolute unpredictability of things, from the crude fact that the results of human activity cannot be anticipated, to the extent that even a calculation of probability concerning them is impossible and meaningless.

To the extent that risk is defined as the effect of uncertainty on objectives, we can either (1) use statistical approaches to assess dispersion around the objective or (2) try to identify all possible events that could have an impact on the achievement of this objective and evaluate their consequences.

This applies, for example, to project risk: a project leader will try to identify, measure, and mitigate all the risks of his or her project, while a program manager, responsible for a portfolio of projects, will prefer to use a statistical approach for each project. In the banking sector, the same applies to credit risk. Since the default of borrowers is not directly manageable by the bank, the probability of default will be assessed statistically. But the risk level of the global portfolio can be managed by a rational allocation, taking into account the different probabilities of default, and correlations between defaults.

A purely statistical measurement approach is appropriate if the risk is measured for an entity considered to be beyond the control of the risk manager. When the Risk Manager effectively manages the risks – of a company, project, asset portfolio, or project portfolio – the appropriate approach is the analytical approach.

Through formalising the intuitive link between 'information' and 'probability', or in other words between 'knowledge' and 'uncertainty', Bayes thus lays the foundations for any decision theory. A rational decision-maker seeks all available information – making informed decisions.

Created by Judea Pearl in the 1980s, Bayesian networks are probabilistic causal models. A Bayesian network consists of a graph deriving causal dependencies between variables and a probability distribution describing the residual uncertainty of this dependence. The graph thus represents the structure of knowledge, and the probabilities represent the uncertain part of the domain (Heckerman, 2008).

What is a Framework for AI RM?[5]

Remarkable breakthroughs in artificial intelligence (AI) capabilities have led to a wide range of innovations that can benefit almost every aspect of our society and economy – from trade and health care to transportation and cyber security. AI systems are used for tasks such as informing and advising individuals and taking action when they can have a beneficial impact, such as security and housing.

AI systems sometimes do not function as intended because they make inferences based on trends in the data rather than a true understanding of what causes these trends. Ensuring that these inferences are useful and not harmful in specific use cases – especially when the inferences are rapidly scaled and amplified – is critical for AI to be reliable.

A voluntary framework provides a flexible, structured and measurable process to address AI risks throughout the AI life cycle, providing guidance for the development and use of a reliable and accountable AI. It aims to improve understanding and help organisations manage corporate and societal risks related to the development, deployment, and use of AI systems. Adoption of the AI RMF can help organisations, industrial sectors, and society understand and determine their acceptable risk levels.

A RM framework should provide a structured but flexible approach to managing enterprise and societal risks arising from the integration of AI systems into products, processes, organisations, systems, and companies. Organisations that manage a company's AI risk must also pay attention to AI considerations and risks in the company. If a RM framework can help effectively manage AI risks and negative impacts, it can lead to more reliable AI systems.

Why Models are Critical to Managing Tomorrow's Risks?

ERM is not a one-size-fits-all solution, and it cannot be reduced to basic elements that can simply be reassembled in a different context and result in an identical result.

---

[5]See *AI risk management framework: Initial draft* – March 17, 2022. https://www.nist.gov/system/files/documents/2022/03/17/AI-RMF-1stdraft.pdf.

In each case, senior management must decide on the content and configuration of an ERM solution based on environmental parameters, such as industry and the competitive environment, and internal parameters, such as the organisation's objectives and strategy.

Ultimately, there is no single RM framework that meets the objectives of each organisation. Organisations need to be honest about their risk thresholds, uses of models, and organisational realities. More importantly, they should not do too much too soon. Focusing on the basics is critical to creating an effective MRM framework that can be sustained over the long term.

The implementation of a RM strategy consists of three stages: evaluation, formalisation, and operation. This process will allow us to anticipate risks that could compromise the company's strategy but also highlight new opportunities.

- ***Risk assessment and prioritisation:*** The prioritisation of all risk factors is a way to highlight events that could influence the organisation's activity.

The second objective will be to evaluate the impact of these events on the body. Whether it is negative or positive, it will determine their significance and establish a risk classification. This assessment must not be based solely on financial impacts, but on all the elements that make up the company.

- ***Risk formalisation:*** Risk modelling consists in putting in place strategies that will eliminate or reduce the impact of these risks. The process of modelling a risk must therefore be as complete as possible, where appropriate, the conclusions drawn could be biased.

Risk modelling will necessarily have to go through a stage of identification of all the factors that create it, which will ultimately lead to a more global view of the situation. The formalisation stage involves budgeting and the implementation of a RM strategy. Indeed, it is important to evaluate financial and human investments to anticipate the budgetary constraints related to the resolution of a risk.

- ***Exploitation of risk:*** The operating phase must allow companies that have implemented a RM strategy to gain a competitive advantage by exploiting the risks they face, avoiding them, reducing them, by sharing or accepting them.

Model-based RM continues to grow as technology, compliance, and stakeholder expectations evolve. This is particularly true in the insurance sector, which has become more dependent on models in recent years for everything from strategic planning to generally accepted accounting principles and statutory valuation.

Good model governance requires the establishment of a holistic MRM framework that is tailored to the unique needs of each organisation. To gain stakeholder confidence, companies need to slow down to move fast. When Ethics, Society and Governance (ESG) is integrated into all aspects of the business, there is a need for willingness and rigour. It is not a simple marketing or public relations game; it must be an essential part of the overall strategy.

ESG factors are an important framework that all boards need to understand to minimise risk and meet the immediate needs of shareholders, clients, and employees. In addition, boards now need to focus on the climate challenge affecting sectors and industries and require system thinkers in every boardroom.

The challenge is to understand the changes that occur around the organisation, and to think and plan. The key is to ask the tough questions – what could go wrong that would prevent us from achieving our goals and what needs to go well for us to succeed?

Part 2

ERM & Resilience

Chapter 6

ERM and ESG: Risk Management as the Cornerstone of Resilience

Risk management has become a global and integrated approach and takes into account the interests and expectations of all stakeholders and the societal challenges. Until recently, Corporate Social Responsibility (CSR) has rarely been associated with risk management. It made sense as long as risk management was essentially about ensuring that an organisation knew and understood the threats to which it was exposed, identifying them through a clear and structured approach, and putting in place a mechanism to prevent or at least reduce the impact of disasters, and ultimately to finance the associated costs.

CSR, for its part, aims at the resilience of companies in a sustainable society through the 'citizen' behaviour of companies. The main economic and financial experts agree that CSR has become not only useful in this decade, that is to say, value-creating, but essential because stakeholders, starting with business partners, consumers, customers, suppliers, and even investors, expect it, or even demand it. CSR contributes to building brand capital; CSR attracts and retains talent; CSR makes financial sense; and it could even be argued that CSR is one of the responses to the crisis of the end of the second decade of the century. However, reference has been made to CSR mainly in terms of issues or challenges, or even methods, as proposed by the ISO 26000 standard on social and societal responsibility.

As CSR made it to the TOP 10 of major corporate risks, this is indeed interesting news, as risk management is clearly in the managers' field of thought. The disadvantage is that it is then considered a further compliance and not a standalone activity. But it justifies the risk management methods applied to CSR which is, de facto, integrated as a decisive element to protect long-term value creation.

Risk managers are still battling with their insurers with whom they thought they had built strong relationships, the war for tariffs, the war for traditional risk coverages, and what about emerging risks? If weariness is also gaining ground in the community of risk management professionals, it is because they have worked like never before to help their organisations through the pandemic and a new economic crisis. Then, as the world slowly emerged from the pandemic, the war in Ukraine once again toppled the table.

Enterprise Risk Management in Today's World: A Current and Futuristic View of the Complexity, Resilience, Responsibility and Tools in ERM, Part B, 67–79

Published under exclusive licence by Emerald Publishing Limited
doi:10.1108/978-1-83608-392-420241006

As for the insurance markets they have also experienced difficulties for several years, and it does not seem to be on the way to an improvement. Insurers continue to claim that they have not reached sustainable levels in all branches, while risk managers are increasingly being questioned by their boards of directors on the appropriateness of purchasing insurance coverage in the future. At the same time, faced with push-button increases and the revision of covers, they wonder about the value of the relationships they thought they had established over the years, sometimes decades.

The issue of stakeholders' trust, particularly in the ability of organisations to contain threats and seize opportunities, is at the heart of building true personal, organisational, and societal resilience.

What Motivates Managers' Interest in CSR Risks?

Communication and consultation with stakeholders is another point of 'contact' between CSR and ERM, as it has become essential for their effectiveness as there are still doubts about the organisations' commitment to Environmental, Societal and Governance (ESG) risks.

Perhaps one of the most relevant criticisms against organisations is one developed by philosopher and sociologist Anne Salmon, a university professor and author of *Moralising Capitalism, Is It Possible?* In her book, Anne Salmon seems to doubt that the phenomenon of the 'production of values' and 'ethical offers' of companies can be able to moralise capitalism. Would it not be, she asks, rather a barely disguised attempt to found a 'saving' of ethics, to transform it into a simple management tool and managerial guidance aimed at restoring the confidence and motivation of both employees and consumers in a context of crisis, loss of meaning, and moral scandal?

In this case, what would be the meaning of the everywhere-heard assertion that we must 'put human beings at the centre of the economy'? Its importance is stressed by the Nobel Prize-winning economist, Joseph Stiglitz, suggestion to replace GDP (Gross Domestic Product), the GIH (Gross Individual Happiness)?

Clearly, as part of an ERM approach, risk management must be an integral part of the strategy's development and execution, and to the extent that the creation of value is essentially achieved through reputation, that is, the trust of stakeholders, it must ensure that it remains in line with their expectations through communication and consultations.

Building Societal Resilience[1]

The world has no other choice than 'adapt' as it has failed to implement the necessary measures to prevent global warming effectively. Today, the challenge of adaptation,

---

[1]See *Préparer la 'résilience sociétale'* inspiré du chapitre 'Prospective' du volume 'Benchmarking Working Europe 2021' de l'ETUI – Philippe Pochet, directeur général de l'ETUI consacré aux inégalités en Europe. https://www.alternatives-economiques.fr/christophe-degryse/preparer-resilience-societale/00101626.

made even more urgent by the fallout from the wars in Ukraine, and in the Middle East, is becoming as central as that of reducing greenhouse gas emissions.

In addition to the data presented in the Recovery and Resilience Dashboard on common milestones, targets, disbursements, and indicators, the European Commission provides a series of thematic analyses of the measures included in the recovery and resilience plans to illustrate the progress made in implementing the Recovery and Resilience Dashboard (RRD) under the six policy pillars:

- Sustainable mobility;
- Digital competencies and education;
- Research and innovation;
- Culture and creative industries;
- Social protection;
- Rule of law.

The entry of the word resilience into the vocabulary of climate transition reflects the observation that it will be a shock, and not a long, quiet river. If the word resilience is inspired by physical mechanics as the ability of a metal to regain its original state after a shock, the word transition means the passage from one state to another.

So the transitions will not bring the world back to its original state, and it's not just a matter of 'withstanding' a shock, but the world must prepare for a new state, i.e. other economic models and other societies.

- ***Radical transformations***

Several EU Commission documents, in particular the Recovery and Resilience Facility (RRF), reflect faith in technologies to resolve climate, environmental, health, and economic issues. Such faith can be perceived by some as excessive, even demobilising: to paraphrase Mozorov, to solve all these problems, just click a button… Big Techs are the first to maintain the myth of global technological solutions.

But the two dimensions of transition – investments and technologies – should not overshadow a third fundamental dimension: active preparation of our societies that is, of men and women, for the radical transformations that await them. Transitions will affect social cohesion, create new inequalities, and call for increased protection against extreme weather events for housing, work, and health.

Yet human experience has so far ill-equipped us to deal with such radical transformations and unprecedented uncertainties. How to prepare for it? A research project led by the University of Auckland for the International Network for Government Science Advice (INGSA) is trying to provide answers.

This project proposes to redefine the concept of resilience by adding the term 'societal' to designate

> the ability of a society or an organisation to adapt or transform positively in response to transitions or significant threats to its well-being. Social cohesion is an essential element of the broader concept of societal resilience, which can be defined in concrete

> societal and political terms as the willingness of members of a society, to accept their diversity, to cooperate to succeed and prosper. The five key considerations are belonging, inclusion, participation, recognition, and legitimacy

which open the following questions:

→ How to shape education systems to prepare young generations for transitions?
→ How can we involve and involve citizens in the transformations that await us?
→ How can social protection systems be adapted to ensure that they play their full role in transitions?
→ How can we build a broad consensus on measures to increase their effectiveness and encourage people to embrace the values of a post-transition society?
→ How can we ensure that the costs and benefits of transitions are shared in a spirit of social justice to strengthen cohesion?

Investments and technological innovations are needed, but they will not be enough to create a just and equitable society on their own. This is why we need to add to the policies designed in terms of societal resilience, which must become a compass in the implementation of transitions. At the risk of succeeding the latter but by producing dislocated companies, a beautiful project for the community of risk management professionals as a whole.

Crisis Management as a Building Block of Resilience[2]

To continue to protect people's lives and livelihoods, the crisis management community could re-evaluate the roles and responsibilities of key stakeholders, including government organisations, as well as communities, individuals, and private sector institutions. In light of these considerations, the crisis management community can collectively answer five questions to ensure success over the next two decades:

- ***Question 1: How can different governmental organisations coordinate and collaborate to foster management?***

Clarifying roles can improve coordination and collaboration between national, regional, and local actors. In the midst of recovery and disaster response, it can be difficult to determine which entity is responsible for a particular task and how best to communicate with other stakeholders.

Long-term recovery efforts could improve coordination. The Budget Office should target long-term recovery as an area where coordination issues are

[2]See: D'Emidio, T., Fox, Z., Spaner, J., & Usher, O. *Building resilience: The history and future of US crisis management*. https://www.mckinsey.com/business-functions/risk-and-resilience/our-insights/building-resilience-the-history-and-future-of-us-crisis-management

particularly acute largely due to complex documentation requirements that slow down partner efforts locally. Streamlining requirements and developing better frameworks for long-term coordination of recovery could be a particularly successful area for improving efficiency over the next two decades.

- ***Question 2: What role could the private sector play in reducing, preparing, responding, and restarting?***

The private sector can play a leading role in formulating disaster-related incentive structures, including through insurance markets that influence risk-related behaviours and approaches. For example, without private sector engagement, the United States will not reach full resilience potential.

In the United States, successful approaches to preparedness, recovery, and response have often involved the private sector and several companies have made significant efforts to highlight the importance of disaster management and contribute to recovery efforts. Home renovation retailer Home Depot, for example, is partnering with Federal Emergency Management Agency (FEMA) to deliver readiness workshops, supply checklists, and guides to help people prepare for extreme weather conditions while Walmart uses its website to promote employee readiness and provide advice on preparation and other disaster information.

However, the private sector could play an even greater role in disaster management. In many cases, investments in resilience are more profitable than investments in disaster relief and recovery.

- ***Question 3: How can the professional community encourage more citizens to participate in crisis management?***

Individuals can also play an active role in reduction, preparation, intervention, and restart. To date, much of the community effort at the individual level has been focused on intervention. However, the crisis management community has the potential to play a more active role in helping people prepare, which is probably where they could play the biggest role.

Individuals sometimes aggravate disasters by not investing in the resilience of their homes in risk areas, not clearing property in wildfire-prone areas or failing to develop reasonable natural disaster preparedness plans.

Over the next two decades, the crisis management community could encourage public participation in crisis management by examining the effectiveness of existing programmes. Organisations could partner with not-for-profit corporations and associations to provide more information on how owners and small businesses could improve their preparedness efforts.

- ***Question 4: What investments are needed for crisis management?***

In addition to determining the right level and mix of investments needed to support response and restart, the crisis management community needs to understand what is necessary to build resilience.

To determine the appropriate mix of investments in reduction, prevention, preparedness, response, and restart, crisis managers could consider new frameworks and approaches, especially in the area of reduction, to determine the efficiency of investments in crisis management portfolios. The Risk Return on Investment (RROI), which has recently been supported by various stakeholders,[3] is a promising measure.

The expected RROI calculation for various crisis management activities could be a powerful tool to clarify trade-offs and help prioritise investments in disaster management.

The widespread use of an IRR methodology (internal rate of return) to assess investments in disaster management could encourage stakeholders to gather data that will help refine and improve IRR calculations over time with a better account of risk.

- ***Question 5: How equitable restart could be considered in crisis management thinking?***

Underprivileged communities are disproportionately affected by natural disasters, in part because they have less access to response resources. Limited resources, in turn, can impede long-term recovery.

In the future, equity can be integrated into all aspects of crisis management, and the community should identify the causes of inequalities and work diligently to eliminate them. The causes of inequity in crisis management are many but include requirements for documenting claims, replacement policies, and the manual processes required at the local level to obtain compensation. In restarting, for example, a barrier for underprivileged communities may be the requirement for verification such as property titles.

Decision makers, and insurers, could consider these factors when designing funding formulas for recovery assistance to achieve more equitable outcomes across communities. Finally, the distribution of funding still depends heavily on those affected to act. In France, funds can be made available to those affected by the state of disaster declared by the Interior Department (Fig. 6.1).

Crisis management is often divided into four stages:

- Reduction measures: Measures taken to prevent or reduce the consequences of disasters.
- Preparedness: Planning and training for disasters that cannot be avoided.
- Response: Assistance to affected populations immediately following a disaster.
- Restart: Recovery efforts, usually in the aftermath of a disaster.

Fig. 6.1. The Stages of Disaster Management.[4]

[3]Resilience Shift is a partnership between Lloyd's Register and the Arup Group.
[4]Definitions derived from the FEMA glossary.

Comprehensive and Integrated Management of ESG Risk[5]

Organisations are being forced to engage in a profound change to create greater accountability, transparency, and sustainability at all levels of their operations. In particular, emphasis is placed on the implementation of ESG risk management programmes in all organisations.

The implementation process for the management of ESG risk remains somewhat unclear to date. This gap persists because there is little information available to guide risk managers on how to conduct their organisation in managing ESG risks; this is why they should be integrated into the ERM programme, thus including the systematic and holistic approach to ESG risk management as part of the overall corporate risk portfolio.

- ***The benefits of taking into account ESG risk:***

The increased focus on principles and practices in conjunction with the ESG can provide organisations with a framework to understand the organisation's sustainability issues with the following benefits:

→ ***Gain a competitive advantage:*** Adapt to and benefit from changing environmental and socio-economic conditions through strategic growth and cost reductions that help the organisation differentiate itself from its competitors;
→ ***Driving culture change:*** Attracting and retaining top talent in times of scarcity – people, especially millennials, choose to work for organisations that adhere to strong ESG principles, where they can contribute to the common good;
→ ***Build reputation:*** Raise awareness of ESG and demonstrate commitment to embed it in the organisation's business practices to build stakeholder confidence;
→ ***Improve risk management:*** Adapt risk strategies to improve the organisation's position in the face of current and emerging ESG risks.

As organisations include ESG risks in their operational, tactical, and strategic decision-making, the adoption of an integrated management approach for ESG risk, including within their procurement network, becomes essential to their success and the establishment of effective channels for communicating ESG activities to their main stakeholders.

- ***Adopt an ERM perspective:***

ERM provides an organisation with a holistic and systematic approach to managing its risk portfolio and can make a significant contribution to these complex long-term issues. It allows them to systematically identify, assess, and monitor potential exposures to real and emerging risks. In turn, identified risk exposures and associated treatment and reduction plans inform organisation-wide planning, and risk-informed decision-making, and provide information on key operational activities.

---

[5]See: Angkaw, J. P. (2022, August 1). *Applying ERM to ESG.* https://www.rmmagazine.com/articles/article/2022/08/01/applying-erm-to-esg

Using an ERM approach to address ESG risks within the broader risk portfolio allows organisations to engage and empower internal and external stakeholders and make improvements in the following areas:

→ ***Risk culture:*** Foster risk-based dialogue and decision-making at all levels of the organisation to foster an integrated approach to ESG risk management.
→ ***Risk awareness:*** Improve awareness of ESG risks to improve the organisation's ability to manage current risks and proactively identify emerging risks.
→ ***Resource allocation:*** Identify risk exposures to determine how and where to invest resources that will have a direct and lasting impact on improving ESG risk management.
→ ***Risk acumen:*** Advancing risk information to enhance organisational expertise through professional development to effectively manage ESG risks across the organisation.
→ ***Risk integration:*** Implement risk management controls within core business practices to strengthen the first layer of ESG risk protection.

- ***Integrate ESG risk into an ERM programme:***

Risk professionals can take five specific steps to integrate and manage ESG risks into an existing ERM programme:

1. Early engagement of ESG leads

Organisations need to appoint leads to guide the implementation of the ESG strategy and support efforts to develop initiatives and achieve specific objectives. To maximise efficiency, these efforts need to be aligned and integrated into the organisation's MRA programme. Risk professionals should contact ESG leaders to discuss how to manage ESG risks across the organisation.

After consultation with ESG leaders and the Corporate Risk Management Committee, risk managers must ensure that the strategy is implemented by the appropriate managers. These individuals will become the owners of each of the specific ESG risks.

2. ESG risk approach based on the ESG strategy

An ESG strategy should describe specific objectives and initiatives, and communicate the concrete actions the organisation is taking to achieve the desired outcomes.

Once ESG risks are aligned with the ESG strategy, objectives, and initiatives, risk professionals can work with the team to validate and document the risk statement and volatility scenarios.

3. Definition of risk appetite in the matter of ESG risk

Organisations often manage their risk profile within the parameters of their risk appetite. As the risk appetite concisely expresses the risk-taking attitude across the organisation, it should apply to ESG risks so that all stakeholders have a clear understanding of the level of exposure the organisation is willing to accept.

Once the risk appetite statement is aligned with ESG risks, risk professionals should consider providing tangible upper and lower limits to communicate the scenarios to their various stakeholders.

4. Adoption of a holistic approach to ESG risk

Organisations that have an ERM programme in place should avoid reinventing the wheel when it comes to managing ESG risks. Rather, organisations need to leverage established ERM programmes to provide a systematic and holistic approach to ESG risk management.

An effective ERM programme will be composed of different components (e.g. governance, framework, policies, and procedures), and these components must be modified to reflect ESG risks. Risk professionals should pay particular attention to the following:

→ Risk identification: Integrate ESG risks into risk diagnostic processes and have respondents assess these risks based on likelihood, impact, and speed.
→ Risk assessment: Adapt the probability, impact and velocity scales for risk assessment to ESG risks.
→ Risk reduction: Adapt risk response plans to ensure a comprehensive approach to ESG risk management, including risk avoidance, prevention, transfer, and protection.
→ Risk interdependencies: Integrate ESG risk dependencies, such as drivers and impacts, to demonstrate correlation with other risks and activities within the organisation.

Once the ERM programme is extended to ESG risks, risk professionals should briefly summarise the changes and inform ESG risk managers and the risk committee. Risk professionals must also clearly document ESG risks and risk responses, as well as any dependencies across the organisation.

5. Use of data to assess ESG risk

In any ERM programme in place, data are essential to track risk exposure and risk treatment plans and to assess whether the organisation is effectively managing its risk profile. Existing MRA programmes must rely on well-selected data to inform dialogue and informed risk decision-making.

Part of this process involves determining whether the organisation has sufficient and quality data. This may also justify a dialogue with operational managers who oversee data and information systems.

Once there is consensus on key risk indicators and data sources, risk professionals should document the agreed-upon indicator and the rationale for their choice. In some cases, the risk professional will need to document how the indicator data is extracted as this may impact the quality of the databases.

How to Integrate ESG into the Organisation's Strategy and Culture[6]

Ordinary citizens and administrators around the world share a deep belief in the importance of environmental, social, and governance (ESG) issues. Recent events demonstrate that humanity has reason to be concerned. Most countries are still lagging behind the Paris Conference commitments on the environment and progress towards gender equality appears to be slowing; furthermore, innovation is necessary to fight against warming without resorting to a systematic decline?

Public confidence in organisations of all types in their ESG commitments remains low, and in democratic countries, as elections approach, confidence in politicians remains low. While discontent is widespread, views on critical issues and recommended solutions vary widely. They reflect the diversity of humanity and the breadth of ESG issues. The benefits of an integrated ESG approach include:

- → Improve ESG performance and reporting;
- → Improve efficiency and compliance;
- → Build reputation and trust;
- → Increasing competitiveness and differentiation;
- → Attract new talent and engage employees;
- → Create better harmonisation and inter-functional collaboration;
- → Increase organisational resilience over the long term.

Integrating ESG risks across the organisation amplifies its impact and enhances its maturity, which helps meet external expectations; the three key links that are at the heart of effective integration of ESG risks are:

- → ***Objective:*** Link ESG to the organisation's culture and strategy.
- → ***Human resources:*** Link functions to stakeholders for collaboration.
- → ***Process:*** Linking data and insights to inform ESG actions at all levels.

A good understanding of the contribution of ESG risks to the organisation's overall strategy is essential to translate into detailed plans, metrics, and Key Performance Indicators (KPIs). If the Board and Officers do not establish these foundations, ESG risks will likely only be an exercise of ticking boxes on a printout.

Addressing ESG issues cannot be limited to a one-way conversation, listening directly to stakeholder concerns to hear concerns that would otherwise not be heard if management filters information. The diversity of views provides valuable information to help develop the strategy and set priorities. These views bring action to life, support action, and facilitate more effective consultation. These exchanges also help maintain momentum as progress is made. Stakeholders remain sceptical about eco-laundering. Organisations that fail to convert their stated goals into measurable progress are at risk of tarnishing their reputation in the long term.

---

[6]See Diligent. *Down to Earth ESG – Three ways for organisations to take an integrated approach*. https://www.diligent.com/en-au/insights/white-paper/down-to-earth-esg-report/.

The mission of the board of directors in setting the tone at the top is now well known by the very rules of governance, but directors need to step outside their comfort zone to have the greatest impact. The imperative to make balanced decisions is conditioned by increasing uncertainty. The volume of data increases, but it does not yet provide all the answers.

ESG risks are a moving target that requires continued efforts to keep pace with competitors and community expectations. The integration of ESG at the strategic level underscores its importance as an integral part of the organisation. Thus, updated ESG targets are part of the landscape, as are ambitious financial performance targets.

- ***Human resources – Connect functions and stakeholders to foster collaboration***

As organisations grow, sharing information can be more difficult and time-consuming. Silos can develop, which hinders monitoring and alignment. Without clear ownership and shared access to data, ESG teams can become the hub that connects functions, units, and sites. Their time is absorbed in responding to requests for information, moving them away from activities that drive progress.

A coordinated approach to ESG risks is also essential to identify gaps in the data population and reduce potential overlap. It is important to monitor local changes and global trends to monitor the changing ESG context. This is particularly relevant for organisations working in regions that have additional needs or are competing for international investment capital. It can also be beneficial to look at what other organisations are doing. ESG teams need regular and reliable sources of information.

While ESG risks are increasingly recognised as an essential component of the corporate landscape, they are still in their infancy compared to many other functions.

- ***Process – Linking data and information to guide ESG actions at each stage***

ESG risks involve the people and data of each function. Collecting data to track progress and produce reports can quickly move to an ongoing cycle of project management and information updates. Add to this the pressure of regulatory developments and team changes and frustration increases.

Small organisations, such as SMEs/SMIs, face a double challenge. Without a data integration system, they must collect data from separate systems such as accounting and production, as well as manual records, including travel and energy consumption. Resource and time constraints complicate this challenge. Integrated ESG systems can reduce the time spent on routine data collection and reporting, allowing people to focus on high-level projects. The framework in Fig. 6.2 gives the main characteristics of an integrated ESG system.

Organisations are subject to a range of ESG obligations based on their size, industry, location, and ownership. They need flexibility to structure processes and reports according to their particular circumstances. Implementing an ESG system that does not support this aspect can be as cumbersome as continuing manual processes.

Integrated ESG systems can help people avoid getting bogged down in details and focus on key areas of action. Delays in identifying trends can result in missed opportunities or deterioration of problems before they are identified. Benchmarking puts progress in a broader context, revealing relative strengths and areas for improvement.

- Simplified links with other systems to automate data collection.
- Customised reports at multiple levels, including across the organisation and by business unit, region, entity, and site.
- Project management capabilities to monitor the progress of activities and report completion.
- Advanced analytics capabilities to identify trends and anomalies and quickly detect emerging risks.
- Support multiple ESG frameworks simultaneously, such as Task Force on Climate-related Financial Disclosures (TCFD) GRI, and UN SDG, with regular updates to reflect changes.
- Integrate benchmarking against organisations, industries, indices, and best practices.
- Have an extensive library of metrics and indicators and the ability to add custom KPIs.
- Integrations of calculations and conversions to ensure consistency and compliance.
- Verification of data quality and validation to identify gaps or potential errors.
- Automate workflows to assign actions and drive effective review, approval and follow-up.
- Control customisable access to protect sensitive information while supporting cross-functional collaboration.
- Clear audit trail for reasonable audit and assurance.

Fig. 6.2. Key Features of Integrated ESG Systems.

Projecting into the Next Decade and Beyond

ESG practices can help organisations become more resilient by preparing them for the impact of new issues. Recent developments in key ESG markets, trends and reporting requirements, as well as best practices to address these issues, and cover various topics: ESG governance, risk management, key performance indicators, target setting, reporting, and assurance. Forward-thinking companies now have the opportunity to capitalise on their initial positions freed from short-term chains and obtain multiples on the stock market that make them attractive targets for medium- and long-term investors.

Some interpret ESG as an investment philosophy, while others might intuitively refer to ESG as a substitute for 'good risk management' and alignment with core values. In a risk environment, these ESG factors represent the underlying causes of risk considered not only by investors and in the risk assessment strategies embedded in investment decisions and risk management processes but also by the expectations of public and private stakeholders.

When developing an ESG strategy, ESG risk definitions add difficulty as they are moving targets. Today, the US ESG taxonomy is largely borrowed from the EU and drawn from political commitments, such as the Paris

Agreement on Climate Change. The Global Reporting Initiative and the Sustainability Accounting Standards Board play a role in updating terminology and methodology.

Many of the top-rated companies for their ESG management are also members of the Dow Jones Sustainability Index. In particular, risk is minimised for investors, who invest in companies that are more responsible and more likely to succeed in the long term, and for organisations that consider their supply networks, third-party policies, workforce strategies, and CSR monitoring.

As climate risk disclosure or carbon neutrality campaigns become a priority, best practices in ESG transformation strengthen personal, organisational, and societal resilience.

Chapter 7

Managing Intercultural Risk

Intercultural, multicultural, and transcultural are terms used more and more since the beginning of the century to qualify practices (professional or not) of the transfer of one language into another to solve the social and political problems defined as intrinsic to contact with people and/or groups said to be of 'different cultures'.

Intercultural management is a recent discipline in the academic world and the practice of organisations. The growing interest in this subject is a consequence of the phenomenon of globalisation in companies that dates from the last decade of the 20th century and has consolidated in recent years. Culture[1] is one of the key levers that managers can use to drive organisational effectiveness. To create effective distributed teams, people managers need to navigate and adapt their operations, organisational models, and even the language used in daily work interactions with varying (and sometimes invisible) cultural nuances of their team.

In an interconnected and global world, successfully leading and managing across cultures has multiple benefits. First, the risk of conflict between team members is limited. Understanding and managing different social norms minimises the risk of misunderstanding, mistrust, and accidental disrespect. This is accompanied by better communication between colleagues, increased confidence, increased respect, and, in the long run, success for all in the workplace.

Teams with a high degree of cultural awareness tend to be more competitive. The overall approach to culture within the organisation also influences how employees treat partners, customers, and suppliers. They are more empathetic and can respond more quickly and satisfactorily to the expectations of upstream and downstream partners. This translates into stronger ties and loyalty among all partners.

[1] *The key to managing across cultures in 2022 and beyond.* https://www.oysterhr.com/library/the-key-to-managing-across-cultures-in-2022-and-beyond.

Enterprise Risk Management in Today's World: A Current and Futuristic View of the Complexity, Resilience, Responsibility and Tools in ERM, Part B, 81–94

Published under exclusive licence by Emerald Publishing Limited
doi:10.1108/978-1-83608-392-420241007

What Are the Challenges and Solutions for Intercultural Management?[2]

Cross-cultural management can be challenging and the main barriers that managers face when leading a multicultural team are:

- ***Different styles of communication:***

Communication is a major challenge for multicultural teams that could result from language barriers, where some team members cannot speak the company's language. In this case, team members have difficulty communicating their ideas or getting their message across. In extreme cases, colleagues do not take them seriously because of their lack of language skills.

Even in unilingual companies, some social groups have different communication styles and familiar words, phrases, or slang forms. In particular, under the English umbrella, there are important differences between Great Britain, the United States, Canada, Australia, and New Zealand, and even in the United Kingdom, England, Wales, Scotland, and Ireland. And what about English-speaking Africa, a kaleidoscope of different ethnic groups!

- ***Different ways of working:***

Differences in work styles are probably the most important challenge facing intercultural managers. Culture often dictates a person's work style. This impacts their approach to decision-making *(does the team make decisions collectively or differs from the team leader?)* and authority *(how much deference and respect do individuals contribute to status?)*.

Most of these cultural nuances are deeply rooted in the psyche of the individual and leaders should not expect to overcome them with only superficial cross-cultural awareness training.

- ***Recognise different motivators:***

Human resource professionals can make the mistake of defining incentives and motivational techniques based on the company's original or current national identity. Whereas enterprise-wide incentive or recognition programmes are excellent and easy to implement, they can be limiting and, in some cases, generate demotivation for not taking into account cultural differences within the company. Poor management of a multicultural team's recognition and reward system can lead to reduced staff productivity and attrition.

- ***Accept different attitudes towards showing emotions:***

Each culture has a specific attitude towards showing emotions, sources of misunderstanding, or conflict. The following questions may seem natural to some but intrusive to other team members:

→ What was the cause or your role in the conflict?
→ Could you tell me a little more about yourself?

---

[2]*The key to managing across cultures in 2022 and beyond.* https://www.oysterhr.com/library/the-key-to-managing-across-cultures-in-2022-and-beyond.

To overcome these challenges, there are proven methods that can promote effective intercultural management, including:

- ***Promote open communication:***

To achieve this, direct lines of communication must be created. When planning a virtual team meeting, the agenda should be sent to each team member in advance with a clear solicitation of their opinion. In this way, they feel free to express themselves during the meeting and will not feel dominated or belittled.

- ***Stay tuned:***

Making assumptions and falling into cultural prejudices of any kind, must be avoided as this can destroy trust between team members. A good leader should understand why team members in some locations may also fall into this trap and promote listening to each other on all sites.

- ***Promote flexibility:***

Working with people from different cultures requires flexibility. Rigid schedules could only cause frustration both for team members and management.

Thanks to understanding the cultural motivations and priorities of each team members, a leader learns flexibility and takes into account the differences of each team member, but this flexibility must extend to each team member.

- ***Get to know and understand each team member:***

Take the time to get to know each team member, make individual calls with each team member, and learn more about their professional path and personal history. It is thus possible to understand the personality of each team member and to guide them better while encouraging them to know each other better to ensure team cohesion.

- ***Develop intercultural awareness programmes:***

These programmes are a great way to help team members learn how to interact effectively with each other. They may cover aspects such as etiquette, greetings, communication styles, etc.

They help to eliminate prejudices that cultural differences could generate. Also, team members must be informed about the different cultural styles and strengths of other team members.

- ***Act rapidly when a conflict arises:***

In the event of a conflict, it must be addressed decisively. This means carefully navigating the different cultural perspectives involved and finding common ground. Any intercultural manager needs to become a cultural bridge between team members.

- ***Respect team differences and work together:***

One key to effective intercultural management is to understand and appreciate the cultural frame of reference of each team member. Once this is achieved, it becomes much easier to promote competitive and effective cross-cultural teams.

Performance optimisation can only be achieved if the organisational culture aims to encourage employees to develop their talents and skills, regardless of their race or nationality. Good cultural management will ensure a competitive advantage for the company and increase the efficiency of the team, resulting in better job performance.

However, when cultural diversity is not well managed, it can be a source of conflict for many employees who would feel threatened by working with people from different cultural backgrounds. This insecurity would eventually affect the company's overall productivity.

Specific Issues & Approaches to Overcome Cultural Barriers in the Workplace[3]

In a multicultural context, there may be cultural and linguistic barriers between employees. Work etiquette is a term that can be used to describe social behaviour at work. Employees interact with each other according to their cultural norms. In daily operations, difficulties arise that must be overcome and the main ones are:

- ***Employees from some cultures may have difficulty sharing their ideas:***

During a brainstorming session with a multicultural team, some employees will feel uncomfortable speaking out while others will be happy to participate and share their thoughts. Speaking depends on the personality, but also on the cultural models of each.

In contrast, employees in hierarchical cultures, such as Japan, India, and the Middle East, are accustomed to expressing their thoughts in descending order. Speaking rules are also important in Singapore, during meetings with clients, only senior managers are allowed to speak, while junior employees can only listen.

- ***Employees perceive personal space differently across cultures:***

During an exchange with colleagues, it is better not to stand too close to not invade their privacy. But how close depends on cultural norms. A study published in the *Washington Post* shows that people in Argentina and other South American countries require less personal space than people in Asian countries. In Romania, foreigners must keep their distance. When it comes to Japanese or Brazilians, one can stay close to a Brazilian colleague without making him uncomfortable; whereas the culture of Japanese colleagues calls for not standing too close to them.

- ***Employees in some cultures are less likely to disagree:***

It's because they believe that disagreements can lead to conflict, which disrupts the harmony of the group. Other cultures value having a 'good fight' and claim

---

[3]For this development, see Fisic, I. (2022, March 28). *How to overcome cultural and language barriers in the workplace* – https://clockify.me/blog/managing-teams/cultural-and-language-barriers-at-work/.

that it is a sign of trust within the group. For example, employees from Latin and Middle Eastern cultures usually raise their voices to express their arguments. However, workers in Asia and Scandinavia disagree by remaining silent and body language. In addition, Danes are generally not afraid to disagree with their line managers.

- ***Employees negotiation methods vary according to their culture:***

For Erin Meyer, author of *The Culture Map* (2014), when negotiating with partners from other cultures, one needs to know the rules of negotiation, and first, the rules of disagreement.

→ ***Open disagreement can be interpreted as positive or negative, depending on the culture:*** Even people from emotionally expressive cultures, such as Brazil, Mexico, and Saudi Arabia, are not very eager to get negative feedback. However, for employees in Germany, Denmark, and the Netherlands, open disagreements are considered positive if quietly expressed.

→ ***Building trust between two parties to the negotiations also depends on the culture:*** There are two types of trust, cognitive, based on skills, achievements, and reliability, and emotional, based on the emotional connection with the other person. During negotiations, in the American culture, separating cognitive and emotional trust is a must as mixing these two areas of trust is not professional, whereas Chinese are more likely to establish personal relationships with business partners.

→ ***Avoiding 'yes' and 'no' questions where possible:*** In many cultures, such as Indonesia, it is rude to say 'no' in face-to-face conversations. So they can say yes, but later on they can e-mail the other party and say no. At the same time, in French culture, it is acceptable to say 'no' in-person meetings. In their culture, this is part of the debate before the agreement is signed.

→ ***Signing the contract:*** In the American culture, signing the contract is a crucial part of any negotiations. Once both parties have agreed on the terms, the Americans confirm the agreement with the signing of a legally binding contract. But in cultures like Nigeria, offering a contract is a sign of mistrust. Nigerians rely heavily on relationships, so having a written contract is not important to them. Here's why: In countries like Nigeria, China, and Indonesia, business people prefer to be flexible. For them, a contract is only the beginning of a relationship and it can be modified in case of changes in the parties.

- ***Employee evaluation varies across cultures:***

While individualistic cultures promote immediate feedback, even in public, hierarchical cultures prefer to give and receive feedback in a more private setting, such as individual meetings, and even in an informal environment, such as outside the workplace. In these cultures, praising a person rather than an entire team can be embarrassing for that person. Thus, giving positive feedback to a group can decrease employees' performance.

How to React to These Specific Cultural Barriers in the Workplace?

Here are some methods to overcome specific cultural barriers in a multicultural team:

- ***Defining acceptable cultural behaviours for a job and workplace:***

  Not all culture-specific behaviours impact negatively an employee's performance. But showing up late for work or meetings should not be tolerated, regardless of cultural background. If this is the case for employees in a company, they should be made aware that, even if their culture is respected, punctuality is the company's policy.

- ***To be willing to adapt:***

  In some cultures, disagreement with colleagues, especially line managers, is forbidden in the workplace, but acceptable in a non-professional environment. However, some cultures are not used to direct feedback. Therefore, the team leader must learn more about the distinct cultural norms of employees so that coaching can adapt. This will ease communication between leaders and their teams and individual initiative will not violate cultural norms.

- ***Organising an intercultural education programme:***

  The goal of an intercultural training programme is to educate leaders on how to successfully lead their multicultural teams. But, all employees can also benefit from this training programme as it helps workers learn to act when uncomfortable or accidentally make a co-worker uncomfortable.

Specific Issues & Approaches to Overcome Linguistic Barriers in the Workplace

In a famous metaphor, Claude Lévi-Strauss, the French anthropologist, establishes a link between myths and the communication process, or myths and language. For him, those who participate in a communication process are like members of an orchestra. Even if each of them plays a different instrument, they all use the same score to produce a soothing melody.

However, when it comes to intercultural communication, musicians in the orchestra play on the base of not one but several musical scores. This results in an unusual melody or even cacophony. Understanding what each team culture 'plays' requires acknowledging language barriers.

- ***What are linguistic barriers?***

  It's 'the inability to communicate using a language'. Due to language barriers, people misunderstand or misinterpret messages.

  A recent research study on the impact of the language barrier and communication style in organisational culture shows that 65% of companies had language barriers between managers and managers and employees. Concerning poor communication, 67% of respondents said it had led to inefficiency. In addition, 40% of respondents had difficulty collaborating due to poor communication.

- ***Taxonomy of workplace language barriers:***

  The following are the most common language barriers at work:

→ ***Employees cannot understand each other completely because of a lack of communication skills***: It can happen even when two employees speak the same language. There can still easily be a misunderstanding between the sender and the recipient of different social and educational backgrounds.

→ ***Employees who speak a foreign language may have difficulty expressing their thoughts or understanding others:*** For example, if the official language of work is English, employees who do not speak English even with a good command of the language, do not always understand idiomatic expressions.

For instance, during a conference call between American and Israeli managers, the Israeli manager mentioned that his company's R&D staff 'did not care' about particular changes. Naturally, American leaders were offended by this statement, whereas the Israeli manager meant that these changes would not disturb his R&D staff; this manager was supposed to say 'would not mind' rather than 'didn't care'.

→ ***Employees from certain cultures prefer a direct style of communication:*** In some countries, when a person is too direct, they are considered rude. This behaviour is particularly discouraged when communicating with line managers. This must be kept in mind when speaking with business partners from other countries and cultures.

→ ***Employees cannot understand each other because of dialect differences:*** In some situations, employees speaking the same language will not understand each other because of dialect differences.

For example, in India, there are 22 main languages (the official languages are Hindi and English), but there are more than 720 dialects, then employees misunderstand each other when using slang and jargon; in Cameroon where there are less than 25 Million inhabitants, there are more than 200 local languages.

Slang also includes 'not only words, but words used in a particular way in a certain social context'; slang, jargon, or certain symbols that are unique to a certain site tend to add to people's confusion.

How to React to Specific Linguistic Barriers?

The following tips will help to overcome the language barriers between employees:

- ***Use an interpreter:***

An interpreter is invaluable during one-on-one meetings when giving feedback to an employee or instructions to a group of employees. The message should be well understood, and an employee having difficulty expressing his/her opinion could do so through the interpreter.

- ***Translate all relevant documents in the involved employees' maternal language:***

It may also be useful to have bilingual documents. The documents should include the official language of the company, as well as the employee's mother tongue. Of course, not all documents need to be translated, but, at the very least, employment contracts, internal rules and regulations and similar documents should be translated.

- ***Offer language courses for the concerned employees:***

Ideally, all company's employees should be fluent in the company's official language. For those who do not, the company should organise language courses. For example, if the official language of a company is German. It will be beneficial for them to learn particular expressions, the terminology used in the company, or some common expressions. Finally, they will feel more comfortable working in such an environment.

- ***Use visual aids:***

When workstations require special training and instructions, ensure that all written documents also contain visual explanations. In general, it will be easier for employees to learn new skills when they see graphics and images, regardless of their vernacular language.

- ***Learn the mother tongue of concerned employees:***

The best way to show employees' appreciation and cultural diversity is to learn their mother tongue. Team members from different cultures should be allowed to speak their language. They can write several words and phrases with their meanings.

In short to overcome cultural differences and establish effective communication within the team, one must be willing to adapt and learn through intercultural training and language courses.

Ten Myths About Hiring International Employees[4]

The world is increasingly using distance work, barriers to hire employees globally are gradually disappearing and yet many companies remain reluctant to hiring international employees. Old ideas and beliefs about international hiring remain despite globalisation and technological advances that have gained businesses new insights. Hiring employees globally poses several challenges, but disinformation should not be part of it.

- ***Myth 1: There is no need to hire employees globally***

Why deny an organisation's access to the best talent? With the communication technologies that exist today to connect teams across continents, there is

---

[4]Pour cette partie voir: *True or false? 10 myths about hiring global employees*–https://www.oysterhr.com/library/myths-about-hiring-global-employees?utm_campaign=22-06-14%20CD%20Global%20Employment%20Report&utm_medium=email&_hsmi=216755048&_hsenc=p2ANqtz-_IQU474JUhcWxXyg6z19eUVRNZaV9SRGYf-pJ5p0haMpt6HT9Tt2ShoPKDerAmMZtx1IqKTzlVhPkZKacoHNtE1jIAaqw&utm_content=216755048&utm_source=hs_automation.

no reason why we can't or need to expand the geographic scope of an organisation's hiring efforts. A company will also benefit from the diversity of perspectives offered by foreign employees, including cultural sensitivity. This is even more important for companies that want to conquer international markets.

- ***Myth 2: Hiring international employees is difficult***

International legal and regulatory contexts can be intimidating, but there are providers to help managers navigate the various requirements for confident hiring. Some global employment platforms can help hire and integrate team members across borders.

- ***Myth 3: The process of hiring international employees is slow and costly***

Depending on the desired skill set for a future hire, it may prove to be faster to search the global market. For example, if the need involves someone who can quickly communicate with foreign manufacturers or someone with particular experience in science, technology, and engineering, it may be possible to fill a vacancy more quickly by recruiting from abroad. Global hiring can often be the best response to local labour shortages.

- ***Myth 4: Local employees more likely to succeed in the workplace***

When hiring, many employers look for candidates they can integrate quickly and they believe that additional challenges of assimilation will negatively impact a foreign employee's chances of success.

Workplaces that provide appropriate support, an inclusive culture, and development tools can help any employee thrive. Employee success must primarily be determined by the alignment of skills and tasks, ambition, and level of experience. In reality, the country of origin of an employee is not an important factor for the success of the integration process.

- ***Myth 5: Global employees' unique backgrounds and experiences can generate challenges within the team***

The diversity of a team's backgrounds provides more opportunities for creative thinking, thoughtful collaboration, and new perspectives. Differences that were once seen as a challenge can be viewed as cross-learning opportunities within diverse teams.

- ***Myth 6: Only large companies should hire employees globally***

While some companies hire entire teams – for example, by outsourcing their entire customer support services division – global hiring can take many different forms, taking advantage of hybrid work to fill gaps in all the functions of the company itself within SMEs that can benefit from cultural diversity.

The truth is that the size of the company is not the essential factor for international hiring. The focus should be on recruiting the best talent, without geographical concern. With digital resources available today, even small businesses can recruit internationally.

- ***Myth 7: Global hiring is only suitable for non-administrative positions***

Global hiring for leadership and management positions allows a company to strategically address the cultural differences and nuances your audience is aware of. Diversity within management acts as a magnet for various employees and partners, suppliers and customers.

Consumers also tend to be attracted to businesses that reflect their values. Similarly, diverse job seekers will look for companies where they can authentically present themselves and still succeed. The best way for a company to demonstrate its commitment to creating an inclusive environment is through diversity at all levels of the organisation.

When there is a shortage of talent with the kind of leadership experience a company needs, don't hesitate to look beyond its borders for the best leadership talent.

- ***Myth 8: International employees hire local talents***

Hiring abroad does not necessarily mean taking jobs away from local or national employees. Often, companies look abroad when they cannot find the necessary skills locally or face a small pool of qualified candidates for an important role.

Hiring international employees allows companies to benefit from the expertise, experience, and knowledge of highly qualified global talent. With the right talent, companies can thrive and create even more job opportunities for domestic and international employees. International employees should not be feared but rather embraced by countries looking to expand their industries.

- ***Myth 9: There is no need to change recruitment strategies when hiring globally***

Global hiring requires companies to adopt thoughtful and intentional hiring practices. To reach a global audience, we need to expand recruitment methods, promote a proactive diversity and inclusion policy, and change the job offer for inclusion.

By adopting hiring processes that take into account various cultural factors, an organisation can find the best candidates for any position while demonstrating its ability to adapt to international markets. Any company should research to understand local economies and networks, identify the best sources of candidates, and write appropriate job descriptions including basic salary and benefits.

- ***Myth 10: Current employees are already ready to integrate new employees globally***

When hiring abroad for the first time, the team in place must be prepared to mobilise to integrate the new team member(s). Dispersed teams may require additional support and preparation to overcome the communication challenges inherent in working remotely. There are many cultural training programmes to promote intercultural communication and specialised consultants offer courses to prepare a team by improving how everyone works together.

In summary, hiring internationally requires efforts and dedication, but the benefits of diverse perspectives, skills, and knowledge sharing in inclusive workplaces make this a fruitful activity. If some challenges remain, resources are available to help a company of any size to hire employees in the global labour market with a reasonable amount of resources.

Intercultural Risk Management Is a Strategic Challenge for Companies[5]

Understanding the culture of each country, even of each region, must be a major strategic challenge for businesses. Disillusionment can be great when a negotiation is not successful for cultural 'clumsiness'. For UNESCO – in its broadest sense, culture can today be considered as the set of distinctive, spiritual, material, intellectual, and emotional traits that characterise a society or social group. It encompasses, in addition to the arts, letters and sciences, lifestyles, laws, value systems, traditions, and beliefs (UIS, 2010).

It is therefore the cement of the social life of a country, linking it with human relations while being evolutionary both in its forms and in time. It is therefore legitimate to question three distinct phenomena, linked to the risks induced by a negation of the culture of the other, whether he is an employee, a customer, a supplier, or a manager.

- ***Management through the lens of multiculturalism***

Multiculturalism is a major challenge for many companies. Managers can be confronted with multiculturalism in several ways, during an expatriation or directly within their company as part of team management.

When a manager is going to be posted abroad, a period of acculturation is necessary. He/she must acquire a good knowledge of the political-social context, demographics, behaviours and also investigate on management practices of the country concerned. Efficient management in the company's home country may prove inappropriate in another country. This is not a guarantee of success, but it helps to adapt the management style to the practices of the country and to promote local workers.

Then, the manager has to create a synergy between employees from different cultures to achieve a company-specific culture. However, a multicultural team can pose a risk of internal dysfunction that can be overcome with specific training in intercultural management.

- ***The cultural factor in a negotiation***

Negotiation is an art; its mastery is difficult and involves many factors. The process consists of a series of steps and discussions aiming to find an agreement. But there is no universal method of negotiation and international negotiation has to adapt to the cultures of the countries involved.

An agreement that would be very favourable for all stakeholders can fail due to a negotiation style that is not compatible with the other party's. The two basic types of negotiations are:

→ Integrative: promotes problem-solving and compromise.
→ Distributive: which promotes a competitive win/lose negotiation.

---

[5]For this development, see Landini, M. *La gestion des risques interculturels: un enjeu stratégique pour les entreprises.* https://portail-ie.fr/analysis/2082/jdr-la-gestion-des-risques-interculturels-un-enjeu-strategique-pour-les-entreprises.

Here are five situations to illustrate how uncontrolled risks result from not knowing each other:

→ In Asian culture, like in Japan and China, it is inconceivable to enter into a lose/win confrontation. No stakeholder should lose face and all parties should emerge from the negotiation with the best compromise. Also, corresponds to a privileged moment to build bonds of trust. The 'guanxi' (the network) thus created allows for new professional relationships.
→ The Anglo-Saxons – just like the French – are considered aggressive; they prefer to defend their interests rather than find a win-win agreement.
→ Americans are characterised by their professionalism but lack intercultural knowledge.
→ The French are focused on rational negotiation as an exchange of arguments where the best win.
→ In the Middle East, the human relationship woven with the interlocutor is essential. It must be sincere, a relationship of friendship, and trust is to be sought. Also, it would be a mistake to neglect the intermediaries.

During a negotiation, reflection precedes movement and this movement is the result of different cognitive approaches depending on cultures.

- ***Examples of failed relocations abroad***

After three years of presence in India, Renault sells its remaining footprint to its Indian partner Mahindra. The bitter failure of LOGAN in this developing country may at first seem incomprehensible; the Indian market seemed made for the low-cost French car, which was also elsewhere a resounding success.

Renault, despite a partnership with a local manufacturer, did not take into account the geopolitical, economic, and cultural context. Here are the major mistakes committed by Renault:

→ The Logan was marketed during an economic crisis;
→ Renault did not modify its model to take into account a tax measure by the Indian government that penalised cars that were too long, including the Logan;
→ The study of the Indian market shows that it was suitable for small cars. 'TATA' understood this with the commercialisation of its NANO car, the world's cheapest compact vehicle;
→ Indian people expected a somewhat more luxurious car to reflect the French builder's image, which LOGAN did not;
→ The advertising campaign launched for the marketing of the Logan proved to be an aberration as it ignored the Indian culture.

Other car manufacturers such as Toyota, Suzuki, and Ford have well understood the requirements of the Indian market; they produce locally for the local market and do not import simple replicas of their European or Japanese models.

The example of IKEA's development in South Korea is quite striking, as the Scandinavian blue and yellow mark was expected by local consumers. A reference for years in the world of furniture and interior design, IKEA has successfully developed in China and Japan since the late 1990s and early 2000s.

The furniture and decorative goods market is virtually absent from South Korea, so much so that expatriates had a hard time equipping their homes. While all the indicators were green for the implementation of the Swedish giant, what mistakes could have been made to close the fiasco?

First of all, IKEA, in a quasi-monopoly position, took the liberty of applying much higher prices than in other countries, which did not fail to raise future customers' eyebrows. The Korean government launched an investigation into IKEA's tariff policy.

Another mistake is that of having named the sea that borders South Korea 'the Sea of Japan' on a decorative poster that appears in their catalogue, while South Korea has taken steps internationally to re-baptise this sea 'East Sea'. This 'bad-buzz' before opening did not discourage the clientele.

The names of the products offered have not been adapted to the Korean market, which makes the purchase all the more problematic, as well as the offer of free services that Koreans are accustomed to, which becomes 'to assemble themselves...'. IKEA's presence in South Korea, despite its misgivings due to lack of knowledge and consideration of cultural risk, has come to an end thanks to its unique position in this market.

International interactions are daily and can occur at all levels, employees, suppliers, customers, partners, etc. If neglecting cultural factors companies take the risk of predictable failure.

The Role of Intercultural Risk in Future Risk Management

Command of a language is not sufficient to understand a culture especially when the same language is used by different cultures and social organisations, as is the case for English, French, Spanish, or Portuguese when considering only languages of European origin.

Cultural differences between two or more groups need to be identified and addressed head-on. If left unchecked, they pose unnecessary threats to the success of the project. The issues that need to be managed and how to do it effectively should be identified at the beginning of a cross-cultural project and the cost, time, and effort to address issues should be included in the execution plan.

Cultural differences are a key factor in globalisation. National values in different countries are more evidenced in the way people dress, speak, and act socially, and in their religious practices. Most junior employees can be recruited to the country where the subsidiary is incorporated. Top management positions are generally native from the company's origin, so cross-cultural concerns are inevitable. These positions put additional demands on managers' skills in managing employees of different orientations and cultures.

Organisational culture varies from company to company and can influence a company's performance. According to Griffin and Moorhead (2007), the three elements of organisational management culture are:

→ Leverage existing culture;
→ Teach organisational culture;
→ Changing the organisational culture.

Top management and staff may face a problem of integration if the leader comes from the headquarters' country while middle and lower management and staff come from another country. This becomes more urgent as the organisation becomes more geographically diverse and culturally complex. This requires a higher level of integration to make cultural issues more visible.

However, when organisations adapt systems to increase integration, other complications may occur. In this case, executives and staff should be aware of how to be flexible in meeting the needs of mid-level and lower-level staff in the organisation. The branch should be given the authority to accommodate different levels of tolerance for ambiguity and complexity.

Employee training and motivation can address pressing cultural issues that go well beyond human resources alone; creating and maintaining a well-motivated sales force is a difficult task. The trust and motivation of sellers are constantly exhausted by the inevitable rejections they experience from customers. Employees should be trained in the art of selling with motivation.

The resilience of supply networks also requires understanding the different cultures in which suppliers and subcontractors operate and the commercial development of the understanding of consumer expectations. Finally, reputation and the 'social licence to operate' are not universal and must be built with each community with respect to its cultural specificity.

Chapter 8

ERM, Crisis and Continuity

Organisations around the world are increasingly focusing on crisis management (CM). This focus is driven by the global perception that the frequency of crises and their impact is growing exponentially. This perception is based on the fact that 80% of organisations worldwide have had to mobilise their CM teams at least once in the past two years.

In addition, crises may be now the result of simple incidents exacerbated by social media coverage of organisations' failures. An organisation's reputation can be threatened as information continues to spread around the world at an incredible speed. With the increasing frequency and growing impact of crises, organisations need to be able to prevent crises whenever possible and operate with agility should they occur.

An appropriate ERM programme should examine potential impacts on the organisation in concentric circles from its centre. The circle closest to the centre focuses on the balance sheet, income statement, and income based on the origin of the crisis, like Russia and Ukraine for the current war in Europe, and neighbouring countries. If an organisation has operations that can have a significant impact on revenues in these countries, they may need to be moved to mitigate the risk to operations and revenues. The middle circle looks at supply network operations or inputs in the surrounding countries beyond Russia and Ukraine for the current crisis.

The outside circle would examine the impact that the economic challenges brought about by the crisis will have on an organisation. This includes inflation, the effects of interest rates, and the availability of capital. The crisis could also dampen economic enthusiasm, with the ensuing reduction in spending that could lead to another slowdown; for some businesses, the biggest risk could be an economic downturn.

Any organisation should identify and assess changes that can have a significant impact on business strategy and objectives and ensure continuous adjustment to the changes in the external context. An organisation's risk landscape evolves as the environment changes; the events that led to the crisis between 2020 and 2022 confirmed the need to constantly be prepared for emerging risks as an

Enterprise Risk Management in Today's World: A Current and Futuristic View of the Complexity, Resilience, Responsibility and Tools in ERM, Part B, 95–104

Published under exclusive licence by Emerald Publishing Limited
doi:10.1108/978-1-83608-392-420241008

organisation seeks to optimise its performance. Monitoring of the ERM process, continuous and proactive, allows an organisation to update its strategy quickly and effectively.

When it comes to the Ukrainian situation, an effective ERM process should have recognised the build-up of troops at the Ukrainian border and helped an organisation prepare for potential disruptions that could be associated with an invasion. There would have been risks to fuel availability and prices, supply chain challenges related to food and precious metals, and cyber risks.

There is therefore an intrinsic link between risk management and CM, with the issue of continuity at the heart of the system; the entire uncertainty and disruption management program has a growing focus on building individual, organisational, and societal resilience.

Why Has Research Concluded That Organisations Need a Mature ERM?[1]

In the event of a crisis, top management must remain calm under pressure, listens to the advice of their staff, and has a high awareness of the situation; however, it is difficult to anticipate individuals' reactions before a crisis occurs. To help leaders prepare their organisations to fend off crises, it is necessary to:

→ Design and communicate a management structure for CM;
→ Provide tools and techniques to assist leaders in a crisis;
→ Understand, improve, and counterbalance leaders' trends and styles.

Between the challenges of the global economy and those related to supply networks, geopolitical events, cyber-threats, and other disruptions of all kinds, risk management remains a complex and difficult effort for public and private organisations in all activities.

As an example, when analysing the 13 risk status reports from the North Carolina State University and American Institute for Certified Public Accountants (AICPA), it appears that, for the last two years, Executives have assessed the level of risk and complexity at their highest levels in over a decade. The report presents its findings in several areas to compare respondents' ERM practices on the following factors:

- ***Drivers for strengthening risk management:***

Organisations planning to improve their ERM programme have identified two main motivations:

→ ***Operational resilience***: Organisations planning to improve their ERM programme have indicated two motivations so to do: resilience and performance.

[1]See Quantitative. (2022, July 22). *The state of ERM: Research reveals need for risk management maturity*. https://quantivate.com/erm-risk-management-maturity-benchmarks/.

For financial services, the increasing focus on resilience is linked to an increase in 'significant operational surprises' in sectors that started in 2020, with the upward trend continuing in 2022. The financial services sector reported the largest increase in unexpected risk events from 2019 to 2020. Due to these high levels of disruption, 75% of financial services organisations believe there will be significant changes in their current approach to business continuity planning and CM:

→ ***Risk intelligence***: Increased pressure from stakeholders to provide information that allows the organisation to prepare for and manage emerging risks is another incentive to improve risk management. External and internal demands from regulators, boards of directors, and management teams to improve risk oversight remain strong, particularly for public companies and financial services companies.

For financial services, 40% of financial institutions report increasing expectations from regulators for senior management involvement in risk oversight.

- ***Strategic value of risk management:***

Many organisations struggle to see risk management as a value creation proposition. Research suggests some common gaps in ERM programmes that prevent organisations from obtaining strategic information and making risk-based decisions (Quantivate, 2022):

→ ***Insufficient focus on emerging strategic, market, or sector risks:*** Less than half (45%) of respondents indicated that their organisation focuses 'primarily' or 'largely' on identification, formal assessment, and response to these emerging risks.
→ ***Limited consideration of risk exposure:*** Less than (47%) of organisations 'primarily' or 'largely' consider risk exposure when assessing new policy initiatives.
→ ***Lack of definition of risk appetite or tolerance:*** Only one-third of surveyed organisations express 'primarily' or 'broadly' risk appetite or tolerance in the context of strategic planning.

- ***Risk management maturity:***

Although ERM implementation has increased over the past decade, programme maturity has been limited in recent years, based on reports on the state of risk monitoring.

Here are the results for financial services organisations about the full sample of respondents when asked to select the statements that best describe their level of maturity:

→ The process is systematic, robust, and repeatable, with regular reporting on the most serious risks to the Board of Directors – Financial Services 52%, Full Sample 39%.
→ The process is mostly informal and unstructured, with ad hoc reports on overall risk exposure to the Board of Directors – Financial Services 28%, Full Sample 28%.

→ Risks are tracked based on individual risk silos, with a minimum of reporting on the highest risks to the Board of Directors – Financial Services: 12%, Full Sample: 18%.
→ No structured process in place to identify and report key risks to the Board of Directors – Financial Services: 8%, Full Sample: 15% (Quantivate, 2022).

Most leaders consider their organisation to be mature for crisis preparedness, but only a small percentage has tested it through simulations. For example, 88% of organisations responded that they were confident they could respond effectively to a corporate scandal, but only 17% conducted a simulation exercise to verify their readiness. This trend has manifested itself in all types of crisis scenarios identified by organisations.

To close this gap between perception and reality, it is recommended to simply perform simulations for all possible crises. Organisations should include simulations in their CM and these simulations should be comprehensive in their design. All employees who would be involved in a real crisis must participate in the simulation tests of that specific crisis.

Here are four questions to begin the process of assessing the organisation's risk management capabilities in the current environment:

1. What are the positive elements of the organisation's RM approach?
2. What elements of the organisation's RM approach need to be improved?
3. What are the key actions to strengthen the integration of risk information into strategic decision-making for the organisation?
4. What should be priority number 1?

If they are aware of the need to accelerate the maturity of their enterprise risk management programme, leaders should rely on capabilities such as risk integration, automated management processes, and streamlined reporting, consider investing in risk management technology, as needed, using external skills.

What Are the Complementarities and Differences Between Risk and CM?[2]

By continually identifying potential vulnerabilities within an organisation, RM professionals can mitigate the possibility of a crisis occurring. Various organisations and sectors will face different risks, and it is important to be aware of those that are relevant to a given organisation.

Many problems can cause disruptions. A key supplier may be late in delivering a key piece of equipment, or a craft labour supplier may get hooked on another

[2]See *Risk management versus crisis management explained*. https://pm-alliance.com/risk-management-versus-crisis-management-explained/; *Risk & crisis management*. https://tuckerhall.com/specialties/risk-management-crisis-management/; and *Difference between crisis management and risk management*. www.differencebetween.com.

job, resulting in implementing a restart plan unexpectedly. Success in the face of challenges is not so much about the type of challenges to be met, but rather how they are met. The response will either allow overcoming the situation and continuing to achieve objectives on time or delay, reduce quality, or increase expenditures to keep the organisation on track. Then, where lays the main the difference between CM and risk management?

- ***What is CM?***

A situation escalates into a crisis due to a lack of preparation, which is the opposite of proactive management. Crisis teams waste time reacting to problems. They must develop their response on the fly, leaving little room for good decision-making. Valuable resources are spent – not just time, but money – to solve problems, often at the last minute. If a critical piece of machinery is delayed, for example, a team in crisis mode will not have an emergency plan to fall back on. Instead, they will be forced to reschedule activities into the project schedule or spend additional dollars to expedite shipping. They can even sacrifice quality to buy an item with fewer features or less capacity.

- ***How is risk management different?***

Risk management allows the organisation to address the same types of risk challenges, but RM managers take now a proactive approach rather than a reactive one. Potential risk areas are identified during the planning phase and can range from workforce concerns to concerns about adverse weather conditions that create scheduling conflicts.

It may also include determining if there are bottlenecks in the production or supply system that could affect the ability to purchase equipment or other materials or if a lack of stakeholder enthusiasm may negatively impact the development.

For each actual risk, strategies to mitigate them are developed including contingency plans that can be implemented quickly, such as identifying backup suppliers for labour and specific missions, or critical materials.

Contingency funds may also be set aside to cover expenses associated with these alternatives. This reduces the time the team must spend seeking approval for additional funding and also ensures that the project does not exceed its main budget.

By understanding how to move away from CM and instead adopt a robust risk management approach to project planning and delivery, organisations will be able to avoid problems of continuous existence in crisis mode and benefit from a methodology that supports reproducible success.

- ***What are the essential elements of CM:***

Three elements are necessary for an effective management of a crisis should such a disruption occur:

→ ***Have a plan ready to be activated:***

The plan should define the chain of command/communication in a crisis, establish the tasks and responsibilities of the CM team, and establish a process and prioritisation for various scenarios. The first step in dealing with a crisis is to ensure that all key parties are aware of what happened and that they have all the relevant information available. Once all key participants, including members of the CM team, are informed, it is possible to start implementing the plan, knowing that it needs to be prepared and repeated in advance.

→ ***Communicate and be transparent:***

Even if the organisation has a pre-established CM plan, it is essential to communicate honestly and openly because circumstances are inherently unique. The public will look to the organisation for information. If they are not informed of what is going on by the people in charge of the organisation, someone else will do so, which can spread contradictory information, even false news, and result in confusion that is not conducive to maintaining trust. Honest and open communication can help reduce the flow of misinformation and enable more effective action to address the issue while protecting the organisation's reputation.

→ ***Continue to work to resolve the issue:***

Regardless of the details of communicating to the public, media, and team about the developments, the organisation must continue to work to improve or resolve the issue. When necessary actions are taken, all stakeholders need to be informed and made aware of what the organisation is doing, why, and what leaders hope to achieve. It may prove useful to hire experienced consultants before any event to enable them to properly support the organisation in times of crisis.

If a CM plan is properly maintained, the financial impact of a crisis will be substantially reduced. A CM plan is more effective when directors and officers are involved and participate in CM testing as it leads to better engagement of all operational functions to help manage an emerging crisis. To get them on board, it is important to take care of the board's top risks in the CM plan. Furthermore, some crisis scenarios require the board's involvement, and having a board prepared to deal with crises can make a significant difference to the continuity and survival of the business.

Integrating Crisis and Continuity Management[3]

Too many organisations treat CM and Business Continuity Management (BCM) as separate disciplines with separate reporting lines. As a result, they often lose the ability to take advantage of the inherent interaction of these two disciplines when managing a disruptive event that threatens an organisation's reputation or ongoing activities.

In such organisations, the challenge stems from dissonant responses to the same event coming from different perspectives. For example, a severe computer disruption is generally treated, at least initially, as a purely technical event with its language and taxonomy, i.e. a traditional technical incident management process

---

[3]See *Integrating crisis management & business continuity for a successful response.* https://www.thebci.org/news/integrating-crisis-management-business-continuity-for-a-successful-response.html.

is activated where business continuity may have little or no role. Better integration between CM and Business Continuity Plan (BCP) can improve responses by reducing the risk of delays, conflicting priorities, and poor communication.

→ BCM is defined as a holistic management process that identifies potential impacts of threats and develops response plans. The ultimate goal is to minimise the impact of disturbances by increasing the speed of recovery.
→ CM is the overall coordination of an organisation's response to a crisis, to avoid or minimise damage to its profitability, reputation, or operational capacity.

CM and continuity management can collectively be described as two sides of the same tool, each with its purpose, but working in symbiosis to strengthen the outcome.

CM is a tool in the risk management toolkit and it can be implemented at the tactical level by a management team, perhaps at the divisional level. This will depend on the size of the organisation and the nature of the disruptive event. The two levels of implementation will allow the operational team to act at its own level. The nature of the event and its impact will determine the level of activation required.

It is then handled at the tactical level by the management team when the division's CM plan is implemented within the overall ERM programme. Branches are kept informed of the impact of the incident and the status of the resolution. Should this event have a greater impact on the institution by beginning to impact other services, such as payments and client services. It will be forwarded to headquarters for corporate decisions to reduce the impact on regulatory compliance and reputation (BCI, n.d.).

What are the benefits of integrating CM and business continuity?

The six main benefits are the following:

→ Ensure a transparent response from all levels of the organisation as roles, responsibilities, and expected actions are clearly defined and understood in the business continuity and CM functions. This allows the organisation to focus on recovery in a shorter timeframe.
→ Incorporate business continuity representatives into action and allow the organisation to identify operational issues and their strategic implications more quickly. It also accelerates de-escalation, resolutions, and recovery.
→ Give the impression that everything is under control. The disruptive event is managed by appropriate and competent teams, which helps protect the reputation and interests of stakeholders.
→ Improve communication channels. The change management function collects relevant information from all three levels and disseminates it to stakeholders.
→ Ensure cohesion between the teams. When change management and BCM work together on a disruptive event, a sense of interdependence is formed, which helps the organisation better achieve the objective – business continuity.
→ Improve transparency and ensure end-to-end incident reporting, allowing for an overview of the event, as well as identifying areas for improvement and lessons learned (BCI, n.d.).

- ***How to integrate CM and business continuity?***

Integration of CM and continuity takes place during the implementation phase of the continuity management life cycle, as described in the Good Practice Guidelines and ISO 22301:2018. There are also other phases of the continuity life cycle that contribute to this integration process. Business impact analysis (BIA) – where critical services for the recovery strategy are identified – is one of them.

The reboot program will then guide the content for the integration of these two functions as the strategic actions to manage an event will be outlined in the CM plan and operational recovery measures in the business continuity plans. Therefore, it is very important to devote sufficient time to the BIA and reboot phases to obtain the practical content of the CM and business continuity plans. The CM plan cannot be efficient if there is no knowledge of the impacts that have to be reduced to a tolerable level within a specified timeframe.

The business continuity plan and change management plan must refer to each other. It can be represented as a hierarchy of plans with the CM and crisis communication plan at the top and the business continuity plans as an underlying support to the CM plan with up and down arrows on the side to indicate bi-directional activation and escalations.

Business continuity plans are implemented based on the decision-making processes within the change management team. Only then can the reboot teams implement the appropriate actions at the right level.

Integration is necessary to enable organisations to respond effectively to any disruptive event. Whether at the division level or the head office level, having an integrated system ensures a coherent response to achieve a single objective during a crisis – that is, to resume operations as quickly as possible, at acceptable and tolerable levels with limited financial, regulatory, and reputational impact.

As the frequency and impact of crises continue to rise, organisations must boost their CM capacity. Organisational leaders should be familiar with CM policies and procedures and related soft skills. Well-designed and implemented stress tests are a key way to bring confidence in crisis preparedness. Finally, organisations should analyse how third parties can cause or be affected by crises and should work with them to effectively manage these threats. Integration of crisis and continuity is essential within an ERM effort.

Integration of Risk Management and Business Continuity[4]

Business continuity has been developed as a risk management tool to help reach a key objective of ERM. If an organisation's risk management framework exists, the evidence is to use it in business continuity planning by ensuring that the risk register includes for each risk an assessment of the business consequences to be taken into account as part of the business continuity plan.

[4]See Deloitte. *Tying the knot: Integrating ERM and BCM to improve resiliency*. https://www2.deloitte.com/id/en/pages/risk/articles/integrating-erm-bcm.html.

The existing risk register is the starting point. However, some business continuity plans may apply to risks that have a lower overall impact but are vital to top management or production units. However, in risk management, which is mainly committed to optimising risk-taking, business continuity is more concerned with developing an action plan to react in the worst-case scenario.

BCM is a tool activated in the event of a business disruption, while enterprise risk management is a strategic tool used by management to achieve its business objectives. However, BCM contributes to action plans aimed at achieving operational objectives, for example, the resumption of activities within a maximum time compatible with the overall performance.

So, business continuity is both a tool and a key objective of ERM, and it's in information security risk management or health and safety risk management. BIA flows from the organisation's risk management process, and the business continuity plan is a series of emergency measures.

Business continuity specialists, part of the risk management team, assist the operational staff in preparing the business continuity, but they do not manage directly; it is indeed necessary that the operatives independently manage the continuity on the ground in case of disruption without waiting for the arrival of specialists.

Conducting a specific business continuity risk assessment helps to take into account the various resources and associated risks; this activity has already been mentioned earlier under the acronym BIA. BIA also helps validate current controls in place and assess additional controls that could be put in place.

Nowadays, ERM integrates BCM into a strategic approach that envisions all uncertainties that may impact the organisation's objectives. Business continuity risk assessments will focus on tactical-level risks to resources impacting processes and the delivery of products and services (such as space-related risk loss).

Finally, continuity management is an essential component of an organisation's operational resilience whereas ERM is more focused on strategy with an interest in difficulties at the level of operational entities that would have repercussions on the whole of the organisation with a questioning of strategic objectives. Risk interdependencies within the 'extended enterprise' require considering different scenarios to develop pragmatic solutions to contain threats and size opportunities.

Combining of Risk, Crisis, & Continuity Management in the Future

Going through a crisis can prompt an organisation to take a closer look at its methods of crisis prevention and detection. Organisations that have faced a crisis have identified several areas to improve their CM, the top five include:

→ Optimising early warning and detection systems;
→ investing more in prevention;
→ Improving the identification of potential crisis scenarios;
→ Defining precisely the chain of command for specific scenarios;
→ Communicating more effectively with employees, and stakeholders.

Table 8.1. Risk & Crisis Management.

CM is the process of responding to an unplanned event that could harm or threaten commercial operations or individuals	Risk management is the identification and acceptance or compensation of risks that may have an impact (negative or positive) on an organisation
Nature	
CM is reactive *(when activated)*	Risk management is proactive
Main Objective	
Reduce tensions during severe disturbances	Identify and assess risks *(threats & opportunities)*
Commitment	
Make or react with practical sense	Know the goods and services and their interactions with stakeholders

In addition, CM, continuity, and risk management are interdependent and provide strong support for better governance within an organisation, ensuring the stability of the company in a competitive environment. These three approaches are essential to a sound governance structure. The main difference between crisis, continuity and risk management lies in the limits of their nature and the commitment procedures (Table 8.1).

Cyber-risks require special attention as all organisations become more dependent on their IT systems. While each organisation is specific in terms of the complexity of the infrastructure and the types of systems used, they are all subject to the key emerging trends and threats, i.e.:

→ ***Internet:*** Internet-connected devices in employee homes – including thermostats and baby monitors – all have specific operating systems that are ready to be exploited by hackers because they are rarely updated. Depending on the VPN configuration, it is easy for hackers to access employees' home networks and, from there, the organisation's network.

→ ***Phishing:*** Criminals take advantage of people's fears and current headlines to steal employee IDs and throw ransomware.

→ ***Internal threats:*** Working remotely has resulted in the temporary relaxation of many internal controls. While organisations try to circumvent the fact that they do not have the resources to share data securely (e.g., through the use of USB keys and external file sharing), there are many unintended data leaks.

→ ***Supply network risk:*** Layoffs and lockdowns also affect service providers, including the level of service they provide, impacting the strength and quality of any organisation's network security.

Chapter 9

Managing Risk to Reputation

Already at the end of the 18th century, Benjamin Franklin wrote 'It takes many good deeds to build a good reputation, and only one bad one to lose it' (Sue, 2010). He was much later echoed by Warren Buffett's much more publicised comment: 'It takes 20 years to build a reputation and five minutes to ruin it. If you think about that you'll do things differently' (Berman, 2014). Since the beginning of the 21st century, managing risks to reputation has become a real preoccupation for private, public, and not-for-profit organisations.

Due to many corporate catastrophes that happened in the first two decades of this century, organisations' context has become more complex and more volatile. More specifically, regulations and corporate governance have been significantly strengthened and regulators' powers expanded. Furthermore, pressure groups activism and rising stakeholders' expectations dictate to have a robust approach to brand and reputation management. The explosion of social media with the advent of real-time global telecommunications serves as a magnifying glass so that even a minor incident in a company's local operation can drift into a major crisis as the information snowballs internationally.

A good reputation is an intangible asset bringing many returns including the continuing loyalty of customers, investors, suppliers, regulators, staff, and other stakeholders, and a competitive advantage. In contrast, a poor reputation can cause loss of customers; difficulties with suppliers; staff demotivation; and shareholder dissatisfaction, and could lead to the organisation's failure in the end.

Whereas they can prove unexpectedly resilient during well-managed major events, hard-earned reputations can be tarnished or irrevocably damaged because of a moment's lapse of judgement or an unfortunate remark. Therefore, it is vital to manage risks to reputation systematically within the ERM programme and to develop reliable metrics allowing external stakeholders to assess the quality of the management and ultimately to reinforce its resilience.

Enterprise Risk Management in Today's World: A Current and Futuristic View of the Complexity, Resilience, Responsibility and Tools in ERM, Part B, 105–115

Published under exclusive licence by Emerald Publishing Limited
doi:10.1108/978-1-83608-392-420241009

Reputation: An Intangible Asset at Risk

The concept is summarised in the following reputation equation (Soudi & Mokhlis, 2021):

reputation = experiences − expectations

Stakeholder expectations are shaped by their beliefs about what an organisation is and what it does. These beliefs are influenced both by what the business says about itself and by what others say about it. Stakeholders then evaluate their experience of their interactions with the organisation and compare it with their expectations. A good reputation is gained through the congruence between an organisation's purpose, goals, and values (see mission statement), and its daily conduct and actions (what it does in practice). Then, stakeholders' experiences exceed their expectations. Therefore, maintaining a good reputation requires managing emerging gaps, i.e. risk, between experiences and expectations of the various stakeholders.

- ***Reputation as a valuable intangible asset***

Although reputation is not a separate item on a business balance sheet, some see it as the most important factor in the surplus of market value over book value. As total intangibles may account for 75% or more of market value, for many organisations, reputation is their single most valuable asset.

Beyond an organisation's 'social licence to operate', a strong reputation opens the door to expansion, new partnerships, and additional income streams, as it can secure preferred partner status on future projects, or enable premium pricing for products and services. Reputation is also a potential source of competitive advantage and the foundation for future business success and a critical business differentiator.

Furthermore, a 'good' reputation allows the organisation to build up a reserve of goodwill (often called 'reputational capital' or 'reputational equity') that helps it sail through future shocks and crises. This reputational capital, built on stakeholders' trust and confidence, serves as a 'fire retardant' when a crisis occurs as stakeholders grant the organisation the benefit of the doubt and a second chance. However, reputational capital never provides an absolute shield.

For example, Northern Rock's reputation at the start of its crisis was in the middle of the range for banks, but the shock was too severe and had too immediate an effect on customers for the enterprise to weather the storm on the other hand British Petroleum's (BP's) reputation was strong and it took three crises to shake is severely (Alaska pipeline leak, Texas refinery explosion, and Deep Water explosion in the Gulf of Mexico).

- ***Stakeholders' perspective***

Since the secret of a good reputation is meeting stakeholders' expectations, it is vital to prioritise stakeholders to identify the strategic ones and find out their expectations and current perceptions of the organisation. Thus, gaps can be unearthed and work begins on filling them. The starting point consists in listing and prioritising stakeholders with a direct link to the organisation, both internal (staff) and external (shareholders, investors, suppliers, customers, regulators, analysts, insurers, regulators, government, etc.). For heavily regulated sectors such as financial services, and food and pharmaceutical industries, the regulator is likely to be a key stakeholder. Opening the range of stakeholders considered is essential to ensure no major interest group is neglected; a single omission may generate an unidentified killer risk.

Once the main characteristics of the context for the stakeholders have been identified, the main focus should be on key players: with those critical stakeholders it is vital to establish an active two-way dialogue so that what they expect of the organisation and think of it, and this dialogue must be continuously monitored. This is how an organisation identifies risks associated with reputation, both threats and opportunities, to secure a competitive advantage.

- ***Risk to reputation: threat or opportunity?***

Reputation is intrinsically an asset, therefore, reputational risk is not the best way to name 'risks to reputation' as it designates all ways by which the reputation can be enhanced or damaged. Some specialists also use 'reputational risk' as a convenient catch-all for all those events that can impact reputation, whatever their sources. As an example, the source could be legal non-compliance, data security lapse, unexpected profit warnings, unethical behaviour in the boardroom, etc.

Managing risk to reputation requires an organisation to assess all potential reputational impact resulting from all the risks or exposures in the risk register and thus ensures that risks to reputation are fully integrated into the core ERM framework. Reputational risks cannot be neatly packaged and handed to the public relations (PR) department for action, nevertheless, PR involvement is required to make sure relevant messages are sent by the organisation and received by targeted stakeholders.

When discussing reputational risk, many boards consider only the downside, i.e. potential damages to the organisation's reputation. However, uncertainty can have positive outcomes and entails business opportunities that can be a source of competitive advantage and create value. Climate change is a threat now asserted, yet many companies have seen the underlying opportunity to build a competitive advantage through Ethics, Society and Governance (ESG) engagement like developing or using green technologies, thus standing as environmental leaders in their industry.

Aligned with the ISO 31000:2018 definition of risks, risks to reputation can be defined as:

> **'Any uncertain action, event or situation that could adversely or beneficially impact an organisation's reputation.'**

- ***Key sources of risk to reputation***

As a result of the definition above, a crucial step in managing risk to reputation is identifying the factors that could impact reputation, either positively or negatively. But the range of risk to reputation is so wide that a robust framework

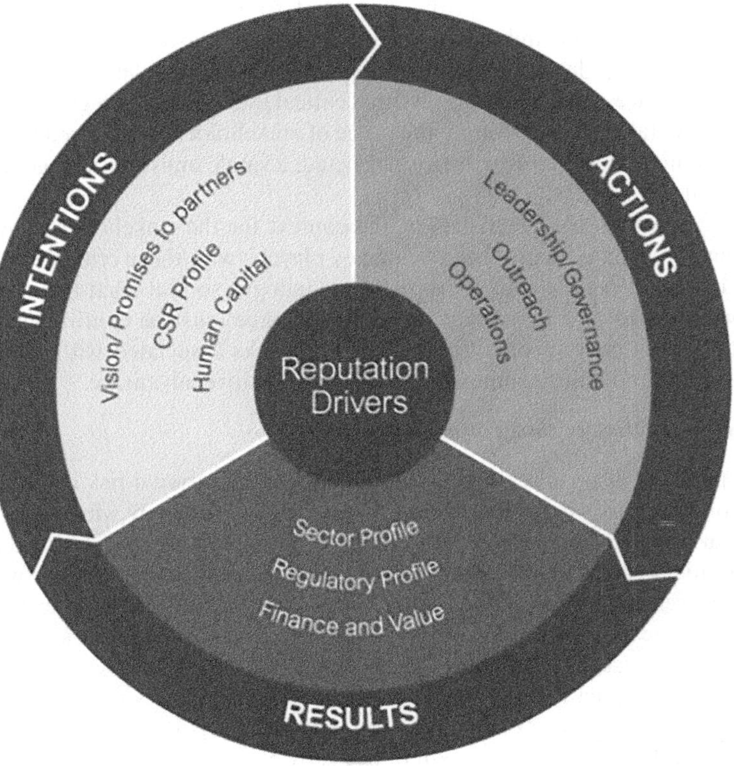

Fig. 9.1. The Nine Drivers' Model for Risk to Reputation (*Source*: JP. Louisot & Ch. Girardet).

is needed to try to be exhaustive. One such framework is the nine key drivers of reputation resulting from several well-respected reputation surveys around the world[1] as the most fertile sources of risk to reputation. These are split into nine drivers[2] of reputation and sources of risk to reputation risk in Fig. 9.1.

[1]These include: *Fortune* Magazine's annual Most Admired Companies survey; the *Financial Times* World's most respected companies survey; and the Reputation Institute's Global Pulse study on the world's most respected companies. No financial institutions appeared in the world's top 10 most reputable companies in 2021 according to this last study and the podium is Lego, Rolex, Ferrari – https://www.reptrak.com/news/2021-global-reptrak-100-corporate-reputations-esg-brand/.

[2]In this model, all seven drivers initially developed by Jenny Rayner and the New York-based Reputation Institute and two more are added:

- **Operations:** to reflect how the organisation's practical implementation in its production sites or offices is perceived about its promises and stakeholders' expectations, and

A useful question to unravel risks to reputation is: *'What newspaper headline would the board least like to see about the organisation? And what event or situation could trigger it?'* Of course today, the board would worry even more about a topic on social media!

Managing Tune in the Middle[3]

An effective ERM strategy takes into account middle management, a crucial source to ensure a culture of risk management and compliance permeates throughout the organisation. The concept of 'tone at the top' is commonly used; it refers to the important role of executive and board leadership in setting ethical and cultural values for the organisation. But, an effective ERM strategy considers the middle of the organisation – those who are responsible for managing employees and initiatives – a crucial source to ensure a culture of risk management and compliance permeates throughout the enterprise, and this is particularly true when it comes to risk to reputation.

- ***Key Insights on Managing Tone in the Middle***
  - → **Culture starts with tone at the top**. It must be built into the company's vision, mission, and values – and the executive team and the board must commit to those values.
  - → **Managing tone in the middle of the organisation is crucial, but also hard**. It is necessary to help employees understand the value of risk management across the entire organisation, including their roles. The challenge is tailoring the message and approach to the middle management, who may have a shorter-term, operational focus.
  - → **Shift the focus**. Instead of only focusing on audit, compliance, or 'fixing past issues,' related to risk management; the focus must be shifted towards proactive thinking and early risk identification.

- ***Three Practical Tactics to Manage Tone in the Middle***
  - → **Monthly themes:** To build awareness of risk management issues across the company, creating a monthly theme may prove useful. 'Storm Preparedness Month' is one such example. Every part of the world is impacted by some type of weather event. During this theme month, for instance, employees explore the potential impact of proactive planning for major weather events.

- **Sector**: to take into account the potential systemic risk (threats and opportunities) due to the specific branch in which the organisation operates.

[3]Ferrell, C. *Managing tune in the middle*. https://erm.ncsu.edu/library/article/managing-tone-in-the-middle?utm_campaign=ERM%20Monthly%20Insights%20%7C%20 2023&utm_medium=email&_hsmi=252459716&_hsenc=p2ANqts-9_fB50Ywk3D-37nigvBclYbPRxO7Df7gOMjcoQRuMR1jKcTOLu9oWyyKdHEjLy46fMc14hVS-eGRi_AV_0XdOKhlcZJBHQ&utm_content=252459716&utm_source=hs_email.

→ **Knowledge boosters:** Education and information must be offered systematically to all employees on key topics, such as the importance of risk identification or monitoring third-party service providers.
→ **Business risk champions**. It is important to establish business 'risk champions' — liaisons embedded throughout the business who act as risk 'culture carriers.' They tend to have more influence with their peer group because they are not part of executive leadership.

Five Risk to Reputation Considerations Linked with Money Laundering[4]

In a survey of the state of financial crime in 2023, more than one in three French compliance professionals cited reputational risk as the most likely factor to drive change within their organisation. If this issue is of prime importance for financial institutions, organisations in all sectors dealing with foreign accounts should be aware of it. However, being aware of the potential impact of fraud and money laundering on a company's risk to reputation is not enough, developing a proactive strategy to mitigate these risks and identify emerging threats is essential. Five factors must be considered:

- ***Economic volatility***: To effectively manage reputable risks related to economic volatility, companies need to be proactive and improve their ability to assess customer risks. It will also improve the ability of compliance teams to detect unusual behavioural patterns in existing customers.

  The challenge for compliance teams is twofold. If companies adapt their risk management policies too much, they risk frustrating existing customers and affecting their growth, which will make it difficult to start a relationship with new customers.

- ***Ransomware***: Ransomware has become the biggest cyber-security threat facing organisations around the world today. Many organisations are aware of the need to ensure that their cyber defences, data hygiene, and training programs are continually reviewed to ensure they can adapt quickly and effectively to changing threats.

  Knowledge of the latest behaviours and any specific form of ransomware targeting their industry will be essential to protect customers and a company's reputation. As ransomware and crypto-currencies intersect, companies need to pay particular attention to training and risk management practices related to crypto-ransomware attacks.

- ***Environmental crimes***: International concerns about environmental crimes and wildlife trafficking skyrocketed since the beginning of the decade, reflecting the threat to food security, political stability, conflict, and forced migration.

---

[4]https://complyadvantage.com/fr/insights/risques-reputation-2023/

Some of the recent growth in environmental and wildlife crimes can be attributed to the easing of pandemic restrictions, which has facilitated activities such as poaching. This coincides with a growing public awareness of the importance of preserving the environment and the desire to work with ethical brands that reflect their values.

To mitigate this risk, companies should consider improving their transaction monitoring scenarios and rules in light of their growing understanding of how environmental crimes intersect with other types of crimes. Furthermore, global policy-makers and regulators are likely to act to curb this crime epidemic.

- ***Crowd-funding***: Specialists report having noted an increase in the use of crowd-funding platforms to finance extremism. Events such as the 2022 protests in Ottawa and at the US–Canada border crossings fuelled this growing concern.

  Relevant to crowd-funding platforms, banks, and other financial institutions that support them, the risk factors associated with the challenge platforms must be managed through robust Know Your Customer (KYC) measures, such as enhanced due diligence (EDD). Compliance teams must also ensure that they are informed of emerging regulations in the crypto-currency space and crowd-funding to ensure that they have adequate financial crime control solutions, efficient and scalable.

- ***Data***: Amid challenges with customer data management, growing regulatory expectations, and competitive pressure, companies are increasingly focusing on data and organisational transformations. Beyond the increase in data breaches, there is also a correlation with growing concerns about existing systems, as good data hygiene is only possible if systems can support it.

  Considering the high percentage of companies that focus on updating their legacy systems, companies that have not yet done it risk building up a backlog of alerts that could impede their ability to act quickly in the event of suspicious activity. This could lead to enforcement action by regulators. Organisations are also at risk of slowing down customer relationships and hindering their ability to transact and manage their accounts effectively.

In the case of a cyber-security breach at a company, as illustrated by recent events, they all follow the same trajectory: the organisation suffers a huge financial loss and reputational damage; then it is likely to experience a drop-in customers' following and even stock value, causing further financial harm. Therefore, beyond money laundering, reputation and managing cyber risk are inextricably linked. And, with the fourth industrial revolution showing no sign of abating, the impact that cyber-security issues have on reputation will only explode.

Intangible Asset but Tangible Threat

While corporations, boardrooms, and risk managers worry about the things that are visible, like buildings, fires, faulty products, or HR issues, too little consideration is given to less obvious risks. Over the past few decades, intangible assets have become more valuable than physical assets, and 'intellectual capital' is the leading global asset class today. The nature of intangible asset risks is such that they are regarded as either not important at all, or important but not urgent. But when things go wrong, they become catastrophic quite quickly.

Age-old accounting approaches are not equipped to value intangible assets, with much of a company's value buried in 'goodwill'. Accounting standards suggest to ignore the intangible assets on the balance sheet, they just get lost until IAIS starts retackling this issue. So far, it is largely deemed unimportant because accountants can't measure it. Furthermore, there is an innate cognitive bias. Humans prefer physical things over intangible assets. Every risk manager understands the danger of a house burning down, or a car being stolen, but there is less understanding of intangible. There's a big issue around understanding intangible assets and how to deal with them.

How should risk managers address the issue of new forms of risk? The single most important thing is to recognise these assets exist. You can't manage it otherwise. Directors and officers get sued if they fail their fiduciary duty to manage tangible asset risks. If a factory is not insured against fire or theft, top management would be rightly sued by shareholders; a spate of lawsuits can be expected over the next decade as people realise this, and directors will be on the hook for what amounts to negligence, for failing to take care of these assets, and this is particularly true of risk to reputation as it is from far the bulk of 'intangible assets' in many organisations.

As bearers of the reputation, customers, employees, political actors, supervisors, and investors all want to understand a company's purpose and values. Thus, recognising the importance of diversity, equity, and inclusion, and clearly communicating that importance to those stakeholders, is a critical element to building trust and a strong reputation. ESG has become a hot topic for businesses over the past few years. While in the past the focus has tended to lie with the environmental issues of ESG, social and governance issues are increasingly emerging into the foreground and have become a key factor in making – or breaking – a company's reputation.

When operating in a legal environment, the organisations' leaders know the legal and regulatory boundaries. But, in this area of risk to reputation, things are not as clearly defined which makes it very difficult. One person's morals and ethics are different from another's, and one might object to something done by an organisation whereas others might not.

At another level, innovation is a key factor in reputation management in many industries; one of the lesser-known facts about innovative organisations is that they are relentlessly debating, re-defining, tinkering, iterating, and experimenting to take the seed of a big idea and make it into something that resonates with customers and meaningfully changes their customer experience over a long period.

Reputation appears at the top of many companies' lists of concerns because, often, it makes the difference between success and failure. To mitigate reputational damage, businesses need to take a proactive approach that is informed by risk intelligence. To solve these complex global challenges, data-led solutions for stakeholders' strategy and engagement are needed. Risk intelligence drives strategic results for ESG, Policy, Risk, Media, Brand, and Reputation.

Reputation Risks Accelerate and Amplify

In today's hyper-connected world dominated by mobile devices, social media, and evolving expectations from society, information can spread like wildfire. This convergence of mobile devices and social media is intensifying the impact of risks to reputation for organisations and is driving them to fundamentally rethink their approaches to risk management and proactively address these accelerated amplified risks.

- ***What forces are driving this trend?***
  - → Social media is creating a more connected, networked world where information is rapidly amplified;
  - → Disruptive mobile technologies are ushering in a new era of hyper-availability in which people are always available and connected;
  - → An upsurge of socially conscious consumers, and growing consumer activism, are putting pressure on businesses to be socially responsible and transparent;
  - → New multichannel marketing strategies built on social platforms allow for greater interactivity for consumers and less control for brands;
  - → Globally distributed business models are increasingly dependent on third parties and other stakeholders.
- ***What are the opportunities?***
  - → Develop new capabilities for proactive brand-related crisis management;
  - → Scan continually media sources with technology-enabled intelligence capabilities to monitor reputation risk;
  - → Initiate targeted campaigns and develop an external ambassador programme to nurture external brand advocates;
  - → Foster a more risk-intelligent culture with tools, resources, and training opportunities to help employees see the reputation implications of their actions.
- ***What are potential threats and pitfalls?***
  - → Personal online activity of employees can cause reputational damage to the organisation;
  - → Organisations may be forced to respond to risk events in haste without fully investigating the situation.

Managing Risk to Reputation – A Key Component of an ERM Programme

The cost of reputational attacks against companies has increased by more than 500% over the past six years, fuelled by an angry public, weaponised social media and influencers; managing risk to reputation requires companies to develop an ultra-fast reaction to macro movements. Organisations need to get maximum utility from their technology and data to accelerate their reaction time.

Beyond ERM, no doubt more years are still needed to reinvent business intelligence systems to provide the 'reasonable assurance' that the information received, transformed, and released to all parties is of the highest quality. Although misinformation has been around for centuries, social media's growing influence and presence in all lives have brought it into the foreground. Through channels like these, a small story can gain traction in a very short time and even if it is later proved to be false, the reputational damage it causes is already done.

Analysis of real-time sentiment is an increasingly important tool for monitoring developments in the global economy, it can be crucial in identifying turning points such as the recent pandemic. The data show real-time indicators of where the current recession will hit, and which countries will battle declines in consumer confidence and therefore spending. Armed with this insight, the different economies will be able to prepare the right roadmap forward.

Now that reputation importance is recognised, non-executive board members will feel the need to gain the competencies to do a good job at monitoring risk management activities in their organisations; with the legal and regulatory evolution, the responsibility of the board and the executives for managing risks has increased: for top management, the issue is long-term sustainable growth for which reputation is a key factor.

As stated above, to achieve a sound level of resilience, any business needs to enjoy the trust and confidence of all its major stakeholders; that can be achieved only when its actions are in harmony with its words. In practice, that requires integrating into the overall strategy the key elements of trust building: corporate governance, risk management, corporate social responsibility, and reputation management.

Whereas all practitioners, directors, and officers have become aware of the need for a global corporate risk management strategy, there seems to be a mushrooming of new 'silos' in risk management such as sustainable development risk management, procurement risk management, marketing risk management, etc.

Trust can be gained, preserved, and enhanced only through transparency and ethical behaviour; this is why, reputation risk management is becoming the cornerstone to the desired risk management integration (ERM). Executives and board members must keep in mind that a reputation must be built both 'inside-out' and 'outside-in'.

Ethical conduct is the core ingredient of trust, hence of reputation. However, as important as ethics are, we have seen there are many drivers to reputation and many stakeholders whose confidence has to be nurtured and simple common sense would not allow them to make sound decisions in such complex networks of intertwined relationships.

The nine drivers' model presented here will equip the board of directors, or governing body, with the toolbox that will allow them to best utilise their talent for the benefit of the organisation as the optimal solution provided will rely heavily on their specific competencies and insight. This will require an ongoing effort for the organisation to manage the index defined in the model.

The reputation index at a given point in time is less important than its evolution through time and this is precisely why it provides a tool to monitor investments in reputation at the strategic decision level. Therefore, there is no doubt that this index monitoring process will represent an ongoing cost if the optimal return on the initial investment is sought to strengthen reputation as a competitive advantage and resilience as a gage of long-term thriving survival.

Individual board members need not grasp the complex relationship between the different drivers as it is the model itself that will generate them. It provides additional information through the aggregation processes, contrary to what would happen with a weighted arithmetic mean that would destroy information. The expertise of the board will be enhanced by the model but they will still have to make decisions but with a better insight.

Chapter 10

How to Use Captives in the Post-COVID World?

After almost two decades of low premiums and extended cover, the insurance market woke up again at the beginning of the decade, with higher premiums, restricted cover, and a new interest in ESG risk.[1] In this context, it is not surprising that more companies are increasing their risk retention rates and turning to captives to reduce the cost of risk and fill gaps in their coverage. The collision of growing economic and geopolitical risks with a challenging commercial insurance market forces organisations to fund and manage more risks themselves.

Effectively, retention through a captive (re)insurance company can help businesses limit rising insurance costs. And it can fill the gaps in coverage left by the current insurance market, where premiums and deductibles are increasing and organisations are retaining more risk on their balance sheets. A captive can also be used to build reserves to cover risks that might otherwise be difficult to transfer, especially emerging risks that are not well modelled and where loss data are less available. Captives are therefore a complement, but in most cases do not replace commercial insurance. Generally, a captive consolidates the risks of various units or subsidiaries and uses the internal effects of risk diversification as a means of reducing the total cost of risk.

Captives are no longer reserved for large companies, as more innovative new products, such as virtual captives and protected cell captives (PCCS), are offering medium-sized businesses vehicles to access the world of captives:

→ A virtual captive is a multi-year contract with a licenced insurance company. It reproduces the financial mechanism of a traditional captive without the need to set up a regulated (re)insurance company. The client will fund most

[1] *McKinsey report tells insurers it is time to act to maintain relevance.* https://www.commercialriskonline.com/mckinsey-report-tells-insurers-it-is-time-to-act-to-maintain-relevance/?utm_source=feedotter&utm_medium=email&utm_campaign=FO-02-16-2022&utm_content=httpswwwcommercialriskonlinecommckinseyreporttellsinsurersitistimetoacttomaintainrelevance&mkt_tok=NDMyLUZYRS01NDcAAAGCoUU3QVvbDQx31kleHWU4gb6ejP31joh-2JNgbg_V-97txjqLK3nIH9gwrVThm0ev-4mOoKYhBqgafGkqCkMoN7_ccWVY4S1gh1drS0Q.

Enterprise Risk Management in Today's World: A Current and Futuristic View of the Complexity, Resilience, Responsibility and Tools in ERM, Part B, 117–128

Published under exclusive licence by Emerald Publishing Limited
doi:10.1108/978-1-83608-392-420241010

of the risk himself, while the remainder of the peak and tail risk will be transferred to the insurer. The insurer, in turn, collects a risk premium and fees to cover the costs of providing the balance sheet and managing the programme.

→ In the context of insurance and risk management, Protected Cell Companies (PCC) provide a legal structure allowing a single company to establish multiple cells, each with its own assets and liabilities, under a common umbrella. This structure is beneficial for creating Protected Cell Captives (PCCS), which are individual cells used by different organizations to finance their own risk while maintaining legal separation from other cells within the same company.

Any organisation should answer a simple question: *'Does it make sense to fund risk internally?'*

How Do European Captives Cope with the Reinsurance Market and Transition Risks?[2]

Since the beginning of the tightening of the insurance market, there has been an increase in the use and importance of captives to facilitate their owners' navigation through the insurance cycle and access to insurance at a time when market capacity is contracting.

Despite generally higher retention rates, even captives with a good claim history had to accept new premium increases for their reinsurance programmes on renewals for 2023. The rating agency also indicates in its latest industry report that a captive's approach to ESG is often closely linked to that of its parent company(s); therefore, transition risk management could lead to increased use of these important vehicles.

However, since 2021, insurance premium rate increases have begun to slow down; as pricing moves closer to market balance, competitive pressure is increasing. However, some covers still see very strong rate increases like the cyber market still experiencing a difficult stage of the cycle.

Luxembourg, Guernsey, and the Isle of Man are the main captive domiciles in Europe in terms of the number of captives. These three homes totalled 483 captives at the end of 2021, compared to 489 the previous year, according to a recent survey conducted by Business Insurance.

ESG-based changes affecting a number of companies will have a ripple effect on captives. Since 2018, AM Best's methodology has included ESG factors that

[2]See Ladbury, A. (2022, November 22). *Evolving European captives face up to hardening reinsurance market and transition risks*. https://www.commercialriskonline.com/evolving-european-captives-face-up-to-hardening-reinsurance-market-and-transition-risks/?utm_source=feedotter&utm_medium=email&utm_campaign=FO-11-22-2022&utm_content=httpswwwcommercialriskonlinecomevolvingeuropeancaptivesfaceuptohardeningreinsurancemarketandtransitionrisks&mkt_tok=NDMyLUZYRS01NDcAAAGIPiD_he9_UUnFujlcjqVrvMfddpF8gol6q53OZZ5sITbMHLKrUm2OqQ4hvNr-C6lB1CIgHZ0KAdl_asY8j8ZXhrBEZ8R6FCJ4eRjGmJw.

influence the core elements considered in its rating process, i.e. strength of the balance sheet, the operational return, the business profile, and business risk management. To a large extent, the ESG factors of captives generally reflect the risk profile and the ESG strategy adopted by their parent company. They can vary considerably from one industry to another.

Transition risk – financial exposure that could result from significant policy changes, legal, technological, and market as the world moves from a high-carbon global economy to a low-carbon global economy – is another area that captives may want to monitor closely.

Companies with clear and credible plans to manage their transition risk should be able to maintain good access to commercial (re)insurance markets. This access would allow their captives to continue to use fronting companies or reinsurers to manage the overall group retention.

How to Use Captive Arrangements to Cover New and Emerging Risks?

The hardening of the commercial insurance market[3] has led to a significant expansion in captive use while owners increasingly using vehicles to cover risks that were previously excluded. In particular, potentially catastrophic risks are increasingly covered, and owners with favourable losses divert more liability premiums to their captives. As a result, captive owners structure their captive covers in other ways, such as providing an over-coverage line or using quota shares to take a percentage of a line.

In this context,[4] interest in shared captives, and particularly protected cell companies (PCC), is growing rapidly as more and more organisations are turning to these schemes to finance non-traditional risks. PCC are not new, but they are experiencing a huge growth to subscribe different lines of cover. Indeed, cyber is another risk that organisations seek to manage through their captive insurer. After the recent ransomware attacks, companies are looking to use their captives to improve their finances and 'protect the company'.

---

[3]See Souter, G. (2022, February 16). *Risk managers turn to captives for cat risk as coverages expand in hard market*. https://www.commercialriskonline.com/risk-managers-turn-to-captives-for-cat-risk-as-coverages-expand-in-hard-market/?utm_source=feedotter&utm_medium=email&utm_campaign=FO-02-16-2022&utm_content=httpswwwcommercialriskonlinecomriskmanagersturntocaptivesforcatriskascoveragesexpandinhardmarket&mkt_tok=NDMyLUZYRS01NDcAAAGCoUU3QWoO4pIprRr5XKdqxcXJ_MEukdoZAl7yF0DMCC6EDkyqNGbXq3bR5mrml8xu-2uLTQtPEPLLpOGGtFRjUgXFiSXWfswuP_8MMfA.

[4]See Wilkinson, C. (2022, February 16). *Non-traditional risks increasingly addressed in cell captives*. https://www.commercialriskonline.com/non-traditional-risks-increasingly-addressed-in-cell-captives/?utm_source=feedotter&utm_medium=email&utm_campaign=FO-02-16-2022&utm_content=httpswwwcommercialriskonlinecomnontraditionalrisksincreasinglyaddressedincellcaptives&mkt_tok=NDMyLUZYRS01NDcAAAGCoUU3QVGXZi8ifMfsCn8Al2vLpNTk8MtFEMn71XQ67_qyusRtOSt-BECc8MggBNoSlXBSZOAjq4A4qZJyJRlCPK6yXpGQmlMkp5DCAcg.

Captive domiciles[5] are seeing growing interest to underwrite cyber liability covers in captives under increasingly challenging market conditions. As cybercrime rates have increased and terms have become more restrictive, business insurance buyers are looking for other ways to finance cyber risk.

Most environmental coverage contracts also have exclusions for communicable diseases or bacteria. Some contracts, however, may have favourable language that could be interpreted as claiming coverage for pandemic losses, and brokers advise their clients to submit claims for these contracts, even if the wording has not been fully verified as to whether it provides coverage.

During the pandemic, for a time most captive insurance owners and key service providers continued to operate as usual. Some claims are still being processed, financial reports are being issued, renewals are being negotiated, etc. Meanwhile, regulators are practical and flexible.

Some captives suffer the impact of the volatility of investment markets on their balance sheets. This impact depends on investment policies and asset allocation in the captive balance sheet. Catering industry captives saw a significant drop in workers' compensation claims because they had no guests in their restaurants while they are closed. On the other hand, workers' compensation exposure is on the rise for captives in nursing homes and hospitals, as is occupational liability exposure. Captive owners should work closely with actuaries to analyse and price risk, develop appropriate documentation, and conduct stress tests to satisfy regulators.

Solvency II Evolution as It Applies to Captives?[6]

In Europe, the issue of captives' domiciles within the EU rests on the evolution of legislation on the solvency of insurers. Three generations of EU directives applicable since the 1970s have paved the way for an insurance market based on freedom of establishment and freedom to provide services within the European Union. Over time, the regulatory framework seemed increasingly ill-suited to overseeing the industry.

The Solvency II Directive (Directive 2009/138/EC [recast]) was adopted in November 2009 and amended by Directive 2014/51/EU of the European Parliament and of the Council of 16 April 2014 (the so-called 'Omnibus II' Directive). On 10 October 2014, the European Commission (EC) adopted the Delegated Regulation (EU Delegated Regulation (EU) 2015/35) containing the implementing

[5]See Wilkinson, C. (2022, February 7). *Cyber captives experiencing a boom, say regulators*. https://www.commercialriskonline.com/cyber-captives-experiencing-a-boom-say-regulators/?utm_source=feedotter&utm_medium=email&utm_campaign=FO-02-17-2022&utm_content=httpswwwcommercialriskonlinecomcybercaptivesexperiencingaboomsayregulators&mkt_tok=NDMyLUZYRS01NDcAAAGCppTMYkzRu2vYfQp2w6royn8G4tUh4Ydfns1J6KO2R3xwQRHcaZ_9VlP2AY7ToiIN2AMl09vfAQBY42-sthbL54ZdNqk5ze9uh60ooA.

[6]See *Captives presented opportunity for greater proportionality under Solvency II*. https://www.airmic.com/news/guest-stories/captives-presented-opportunity-greater-proportionality-under-solvency-ii.

rules for Solvency II. The Delegated Rules were published in the official journal on 17 January 2015.

The first Solvency II Implementing Regulation laying down the technical implementing standards for prudential approval procedures for enterprise-specific parameters, ancillary own funds, counterpart adjustment, special vehicles, internal models, and a joint decision on the group's internal models was adopted in March 2015. The second implementing regulation was adopted later in 2015.

Since the implementation of Solvency II throughout the EU on 1 January 2016, captive insurers are subject to the same regulatory and reporting requirements as large commercial carriers. The captive market has long advocated for broader and more consistent application of the principle of proportionality but has been largely disappointed by the response of EIOPA and regulators across the continent.

EIOPA's 2020 Solvency II review opinion includes suggestions on how to apply greater proportionality, including limits on the scope of reporting in areas such as investments and derivatives, assets and liabilities by currency, and analysis of changes. It also recommends that the Own Risk and Solvency Assessment (ORSA) for captives be submitted every two years rather than annually, while credit and financial reporting may be withdrawn for captives and not required to be publicly available.

For the revision process introduced in 2020, EIOPA consulted with the users, and captive solution owners, at the initiative of FERMA, and simplifications were suggested in its report through the principle of proportionality but for a very restrictive definition of strictly closed captives, which is not in agreement with market opinion. The proposals still have to be approved by the EC and then implemented in the various states and will probably not enter into force before 2025, but captive owners have welcomed this development.[7]

In France, AMRAE assesses that although only 8 French groups have domiciled their captives in France, 50 French companies are waiting for more attractive domiciliation conditions to take an initiative. A commission organised by French Public authorities lasted for more than three years to collect information on captives before the legislation was enacted with the budget law 2023. AMRAE announced the creation of a specific association: the 'Fédération Française des Captives d'Entreprise' with the mission to support the creation and deployment of these tools in France, aiming to ensure an efficient implementation of the new French legislation.

The United Kingdom has left the European Union so the problem of the evolution of Solvency II does not directly concern the operators of this country but they also wonder about the evolution of the regulatory context of captive schemes in this country. Since the UK has a large financial services ecosystem it should be an

[7]For more development see: *European Captives – Analytical Review of Solvency II Reports* (2022, November). https://www.scor.com/en/download/file?token=def5020-0528813e3c33b50cb2c3508c2c8b258e9effaa3767914b5ed69ddfe8457c7c70c9d4fa9d8671dac0a652bcd58bbd54876f756877ea7e6da8c70ef4703d2a3785d8838670e6cb-cf0f4007d06c5ceebd12bc5cc841c797d1183d98693a20c0e8e65cc643f03a991181a447e-01a8efdcea0516fff8467b46bbb5610210ab8d20ae9f82.

ideal home for captives but the UK is not seen as a viable place for captive insurance vehicles due to regulatory restrictions. AIRMIC is currently working on changes with the FCA. Guernsey and the Isle of Man are the most common captive jurisdictions for UK-based companies and public sector organisations. Ireland, Malta, Bermuda, the Cayman Islands, and Vermont (USA) are also used.

In addition, the insurance industry has criticised the UK Insurance Linked Security (ILS) legislation (Evans, 2023). In April 2022, the Treasury Secretary stated in an investigation into the regulation of insurance and commercial reinsurance that efforts to develop a captive and ILS market in the United Kingdom had limited success. Regulations were adopted in 2017 to encourage ILS growth, but only eight ILS operations have been launched in the UK in the last five years.

What About PCC?[8]

Guernsey was the first domicile to introduce PCC legislation in 1997 and other domiciles followed shortly thereafter, including the Cayman Islands, Bermuda, Gibraltar, and Malta. More recently, segregation has been introduced in many US states, the UK, Ireland (Dublin), and Luxembourg. Transactions in protected cells are now taking place in many countries.

Protected Cell Company legislation has been adopted primarily to encourage the growth of the captive insurance and reinsurance industry by bringing captive promoters under one entity but allowing the separation of assets between them to satisfy third-party claims and limiting their liability accordingly.

In the case of Malta, whose law was promulgated in 2004, with nearly two decades of experience in cell company structures, supervisors are well aware of this segment. Malta has also developed the concept of cell enterprise and put on the market different cell enterprise structures, including the Incorporated Cell Company. Both structures allow companies to write risks using cells within a primary company and offer companies a cost-effective alternative to creating a stand-alone insurance company.

Investors who pursue a bona fide business activity have sought to benefit from the capital protection laws under the 'CCP Act'; in the same manner as they would have done if they had decided to conduct their affairs through an ordinary limited partnership or limited partnership; then, why should they, and all creditors who have dealt with the PCC in the hope that their rights will be determined by the laws on PCC, be deprived of such protection by the court?

The PCC Act provides a protection of capital and creditors rule like any other. For a foreign court to decide otherwise would be contrary to the very principles on which international trade has developed since the 18th century, namely, the double principle of limited liability for those who put capital at risk and acceptance that, in a global economy, countries must recognise other trade laws.

[8] *Pour ce développement voir Protected Cell Companies: Untangling the cellular knot.* https://www.gibraltarlaw.com/insights/protected-cell-companies/.

The Impact of the Pandemic on Integrated Management Centres[9]

As already mentioned, the protection from business disruptions related to the COVID-19 pandemic has resulted in many litigation cases between insured and insurers in the developed world in particular. Many organisations have discovered that their BI insurance contracts do not cover pandemics, and many have taken legal action and pressured legislators to pass legislation retroactively forcing insurers to cover it.

Typically, captives operate where the traditional insurance market has failed. This trend has gained momentum when business leaders realised the gap in their traditional covers and wished they had had a captive when the pandemic hit.

Many professionals believe that captive scheme owners will be in a better position after the COVID-19 pandemic. Captives have become once again a necessity as a result of the pandemic; it is reinforcing their main benefits. Current market conditions are precisely similar to those for which they were originally formed. Owners that have persevered with their captives through the bear cycle in recent years reap now the benefits of their choice. Captives belong to long-term strategy and captive owners are better positioned to address the challenges facing insurance buyers today.

Many organisations have developed global innovation, and captive management centres (CMCs) in India and other countries to provide a range of IT services, business processing, analytics, digital, and cloud across the enterprise. These organisations prefer to rely on their staff to develop the core of their IT systems and thus retain essential data and expertise internally. CMCs have provided these organisations with agility, alignment, and integration benefits, as well as cost savings.

The global pandemic, a 'Black Swan' event, is likely to have a major impact on CMCs and the fundamental questions are:

- ***What initiatives have CMCs taken to manage the impacts of the pandemic?***
  - Infrastructure:
    - → Ensure the availability of the underlying infrastructure and upgrade it to increase capacity, speed, and reliability;
    - → Provide reliable laptops, desktops, mobile devices, and Wi-Fi hotspots for remote connectivity.
  - Security:
    - → Implement security measures and protocols (including for dedicated VPN and VDI secure networks) to prevent unauthorised access, transmission, or loss of sensitive data;
    - → Upgrade cyber security and updated antivirus software for all devices connected to the network.

---

[9] *Pour ce développement voir: COVID-19-transforming offshore captives/global innovation centers.* https://www.jdsupra.com/legalnews/covid-19-transforming-offshore-captives-62699/.

  - Staff:
    - → Further support employees working remotely to improve efficiency and collaboration;
    - → Communicate regularly with employees to improve morale and provide timely information;
    - → Communicate regularly with partners (customers and suppliers) to build trust in business operations and security.

- ***How have CMCs re-opened facilities when lockdown restrictions have been lifted?***
  - Gradual Return to Work: Phase 1 – 'Essential'; Phase 2 – 'Auxiliary Essential'; and Phase 3 – 'The Rest';
  - Priority for hygiene and cleanliness, including the use of disinfectants, masks, and other PPE, on-site medical screening before entry;
  - Temporary measures including visitor control, temperature control, hands-free access, food delivery to individuals (instead of cafeterias), and staggered entrances and exits;
  - Different use and configuration of facilities, including use of space for collaboration or engagement activities and conversion of space to allow social distancing;
  - Implementation of local health and safety regulations, which will continue to evolve globally in the coming years. Compliance measures will take into account the costs, values, and culture of the company;
  - Retention of existing headquarters where significant investments have been made; creative use of offices for brainstorming, product design, or team engagement activities; Move away from non-essential seating to create space for social distancing.

- ***How will CMCs evolve and will organisations prefer certain domiciles?***
  - Re-evaluate employees' productivity in the office and at home, including re-examining assumptions about remote staffing (and the amount of office space required);
  - Focus on key roles within the GC (rather than corporate functions) to support and create more in-depth critical areas of expertise;
  - Offer measured response to government pressures to preserve local employment and avoid layoffs (e.g. US, UK, Australia);
  - Prefer established locations with talent and infrastructure, including India, Philippines, Eastern Europe, and Mexico, versus emerging locations that will be considered riskier;
  - Prefer established service providers and partners with a strong track record; there will be a 'flight to quality';
  - Develop geographic diversity to ensure business continuity and disaster recovery.

- ***Has the pandemic changed the perception of CMC appeal versus outsourcing?***

Three categories of organisations will review their external, internal, or shared procurement strategies:

  - ***Organisations in heavily affected sectors***, such as retail, hospitality, and aviation, will focus on survival and the need to immediately reduce expenditures and the total cost of operations. They may consider selling their CMC or partnering with vendors for managed services. *(With the possibility of retaking control of the CMC in the future.)*
  - ***Organisations in moderately affected sectors,*** such as banks, consumer durables, and electronics, will also want to preserve and optimise their liquidity. They will be able to explore a range of options, including joint ventures to receive an injection of funds or develop service offerings to transform the CMC or generate new sources of revenue.
  - ***Organisations in the least impacted sectors*** such as food, pharmaceuticals, IT collaborators, and the Cloud will seek to grow their CMCs in established locations using an operational excellence model; they may consider partnering with suppliers that will transform the CMC to increase the organisation's flexibility and resilience.

For each category of organisation, final decisions will include an assessment of procurement options to balance costs, risks, business continuity, security, agility, and access to global talent and capabilities; Established CMCs may be assessed differently from relatively new CMCs.

- ***How has the pandemic affected CMCs' ability to retain and attract talent?***
  - Organisations in the least affected sectors will have the advantage of being more likely to retain and attract top talent.
  - Talent will focus more attention on the organisation's financial situation, brand image, industry (and pandemic impacts), and future career opportunities.
  - In the short to medium term, rising unemployment and underemployment could make the most talented people more available to CMCs at lower pay.

- ***What will be the long-term impact of the pandemic on CMCs?***
  - ***Pioneer users***: Organisations that have a remote working culture and invest in collaboration tools and cloud, including seamless connectivity and 24/7 availability and support, 7 days a week, proactively reaching out to their employees and customers. Pioneers will look to upgrade their infrastructure and deepen the transformation with their CMCs.
  - ***Mainstream users***: Organisations with an on-site work culture (but some remote employee experience) and limited investments in collaboration tools

and the cloud took longer to communicate with their employees and customers and required more assistance from partners. Intermediary firms will seek to partner with suppliers (and their infrastructure), optimise costs, and achieve economies of scale and scope.

- ***Late users:*** Organisations with little or no experience working remotely and negligible investments in collaboration tools and the cloud and have taken much longer to address challenges and are now heavily reliant on suppliers (as well as their infrastructure and capabilities).
- ***Recent users:*** They will look to reduce their operating margin or get a down payment to resolve cash flow issues by separating from their CMC.

Implementing a CMC requires thoughtful execution and planning to address legal and compliance considerations, including issues related to international trade, corporations, taxation, business, HR, real estate, and transactions under the laws applicable to the organisation and the CMC.

How to Use Parametric Cover in a Captive?[10]

With the prospect of a new normal accompanied by an explosion of emerging risks for which the appetite of traditional insurers remains to be assessed, one of the solutions for some of these catastrophic risks is probably the use of parametric cover that can be implemented in a captive.

Parametric insurance is growing rapidly worldwide and is hailed as an attractive alternative to some traditional insurance programmes. While it may seem somewhat complex, parametric insurance (or event insurance) is simpler than traditional cover. Compared to a typical insurance claim that compensates for damage or loss, parametric insurance country a pre-agreed amount based on a 'triggered' event using objective datasets that neither the insurer nor the client can control.

The rise of natural disaster risks is combined with changing market dynamics to create a complex environment for risk managers. Insurance prices go up, while coverage often goes down. In this context, we have seen increasing interest and adoption of parametric products.

Parametric covers indemnify based on natural parameters, such as wind speed, for example, and can offer a useful exclusion solution from your real estate programme for specific catnat risks. The added benefit is that payments are immediate if a predetermined threshold is reached, providing much-needed

---

[10]Swiss Re Corporate Solutions. (2022, October 9). *Four things captive owners should know about parametric solutions*. https://www.commercialriskonline.com/four-things-captive-owners-should-know-about-parametric-solutions/?utm_source=feedotter&utm_medium=email&utm_campaign=FO-10-18-2022&utm_content=httpswwwcommercialriskonlinecomfourthingscaptiveownersshouldknowaboutparametricsolutions&mkt_tok=NDMyLUZYRS01NDcAAAGHiilysf-mWquVglDIfiPwpECXTf9AS0u4K-bvNDj3SsWqdQAuyCE8liEdrSvHwxs4rVHhUs7UIg1H4e-Cg1FxMIJd0dsrsK30-j_9HA.

post-disaster liquidity. Here are four considerations for risk managers before considering the possibility:

- ***Defining basic risk appetite:***

Housing parametric covers in a captive can be a complicated process. Parametric insurance leaves the insured with a so-called basic risk. This is the risk of the parent company incurring a loss when the cover is not triggered.

Then, can the captive pass on this risk to the insured? If so, the cover of policyholders simply reflects the basic risk that comes from the parametric coverage they purchase from the market.

However, although in principle this works for captives and parametric contracts, in practice it is often a stumbling block for captives when it comes to purchasing parametric (re)insurance.

- ***Beware of using a jackhammer to break a nut:***

Essentially, parametric cover is considered a cumbersome process mainly because presently parametric insurance providers are a small number in the marketplace, and the whole concept remains a niche in the huge market for commercial insurance based on compensation.

For such a solution, the broker could go to 10 insurers to get a quote for a solution, for example, that pays $100 million for a category 5 hurricane. And the buyer can choose the cheapest offer. However, the basic risk for this type of product necessarily remains high due to its lack of sophistication. Thus, today's compromise is customisation versus receiving a satisfactory number of comparable quotes.

- ***Is it possible to 'sell' a more customised solution internally?***

When choosing a parametric solution for a captive, risk and insurance managers usually have to meet with their CFO and show them several proposals. As a result, the ability to choose a more customised product with the lowest basic risk is inhibited, and therefore this solution becomes undesirable for some because it is more difficult to 'sell' internally.

This may exclude more suitable parametric products such as STORM[11] by Swiss Re, which looks at wind speed exactly where a customer specifies. Payments are not only based on which category hurricane category, but rather on the exact wind speed at each covered location.

Thanks to this mechanism, STORM offers a very low base risk; because of the small number of insurers offering this product, a customer cannot directly compare several quotes.

---

[11]*STORM: A tropical cyclone, hurricane, and parametric storm insurance solution* – An index-based hurricane & storm insurance solution that helps you recover faster after a tropical cyclone. https://corporatesolutions.swissre.com/innovative-risk-solutions/parametric-solutions/storm.html.

- ***Is the organisation ready to become a parametric innovator?***

Because captives have a better understanding of their parent company's risk profile, they are in the best position to implement more personalised parametric insurance solutions, with the added benefit of a much lower base risk.

As the parametric insurance market grows and matures, there is a real opportunity for captive owners to strengthen the function of their risk retention vehicle while analysing and using available data to improve their understanding of how parameters can complement the range of traditional covers in the captive with a wider range of risks thanks to parametric pricing.

Part 3

ERM, Governance & ESG

Chapter 11

Risk Management from the Top: An Executive Approach to Risk

When directors and officers turn to their staff for risk information, they are often disappointed by what they get. Too many non-financial businesses are still in the early stages of implementing a comprehensive and integrated risk management (ERM) programme, providing insufficient or poorly structured information on the main risks facing the company. Others have implemented a comprehensive ERM programme but it consists in bureaucratic risk management processes that create little value.

ERM requires a risk management framework, which typically involves identifying specific events or circumstances relevant to the organisation's objectives, threats, and opportunities, assessing them in terms of likelihood and severity, and identifying a response strategy and monitoring process. By proactively identifying and managing risks, threats and opportunities, organisations protect and create value for their stakeholders, including shareholders, employees, customers, regulators, and society.

Developing a sustainable competitive advantage is the main challenge facing officers and directors in the third decade. In this complex and volatile world, organisations must anticipate risks in their internal and external contexts to seize opportunities or contain threats within their risk appetite and risk tolerance.

Risk Management and Top Management's Expectations in Time of a Crisis

In times of a crisis, the treasurer and the finance director are often called upon to answer the strategic questions of the CEO and the Board of Directors and finally help pull the organisation out of the storm.

As they seek to weight strategy changes while assessing news and data in uncertain times, it is up to the treasurer to focus on business continuity, activating cash, and reducing disruptions in the global supply network.

Top management needs quick answers to questions by the directors and investors about the company's financial situation: Does it have the cash to get through next

Enterprise Risk Management in Today's World: A Current and Futuristic View of the Complexity, Resilience, Responsibility and Tools in ERM, Part B, 131–138

Published under exclusive licence by Emerald Publishing Limited
doi:10.1108/978-1-83608-392-420241011

week's deadlines, next month? How confident are they in cash flow forecasting? Is it a fraud case? How can the company withstand disruptions to the supply network?

- ***Expectations of Directors and Officers concerning Finance:***

During a crisis, the focus is on people first, with a priority on employees' safety while ensuring that customers have what they need. Once these concerns are addressed, managers focus on the company, asking if they have access to the right data, ensuring that there is enough money, and determining the main risks they face and how to treat them.

Finally, there are eight key risks that top management strives to address; Treasury and Finance are in charge of managing and mitigating those risks: human resources, internal processes and tools, volatility in treasury, fraud, foreign exchange and interest rates, debt and counterparty, volatility in turnover, and disruption in the supply network.

- ***The eight major risks exacerbated in times of a crisis and how to manage them:***

Here is the list and the way to treat them:

→ ***Human resources***: A major concern for top management is the potential loss of key people. Investors wonder what will happen if part of the employees in the finance and treasury function are sick, hospitalised, or caring for their loved ones. What would happen in case of dismissal? Are employees able to perform all their daily tasks from home?

Today, it is increasingly important to adopt automation and technology. Working with software-as-a-service (SaaS) solutions allows employees to access the data they need and perform daily tasks wherever they are and automation of manual processes to mitigate some of the key risks to employees and reduce errors.

→ ***Deficiencies in internal processes and tools***: As businesses adopt new processes and mandates, business continuity issues will arise. Business Continuity Plans (BCP) that have not been designed to be sustainable will show, over time, gaps in processes and systems that can become increasingly dangerous to the business, especially when it depends on manual processes and spreadsheets.

Increased use of business continuity can exacerbate gaps, but investing in systems to promote automation, business continuity, and extended connectivity with other systems can help identify and close those gaps, facilitate disaster recovery, and improve the visibility of cash, liquidity, and financial exposures.

→ ***Cash volatility***: In times of economic crisis, businesses often face fundraising delays and uncertain revenues. Customers can pay late or renegotiate payment terms to amortise cash reserves and remain solvent, or they can delay purchasing decisions until conditions stabilise.

Companies can stabilise their cash position by forecasting cash flows and setting limits. Forecasting cash flows with scenarios allows companies to better understand their international liquidity needs. In addition, stress tests allow for determining what happens if customers pay late, do not pay at all, or if expected revenues do not materialise: automation of limit management for counterparties can help mitigate cash instability.

→ ***Fraud***: When normal processes are disrupted due to a crisis, there is often an increased risk of fraud, especially if approval processes are circumvented to continue operations. There was a six-fold increase in the number of phishing emails reported from February and March 2020, as fraudsters sought to exploit the global disruptions resulting from the COVID-19 pandemic. Disrupted normal processes offer ideal conditions for fraudsters; if a business relies on spreadsheets, there is an increased risk of financial fraud, not only for cash but for the organisation as a whole.

The simplest way to improve controls and combat fraud and cybercrime is to digitise payment flows and automate fraud protection and detection. This approach standardises payment controls to comply with internal payment policies, approval procedures, and limits so that only authorised payments are executed. Real-time fraud detection filters payments against government sanctions lists, corporate payment policies, and historical data models to automatically quarantine suspicious and non-compliant payments for threat assessment purposes.

→ ***Exchange rates and interest rates***: The fiscal strength of individual countries and their timing for recovery can have a significant impact on exchange rates. Hedges can be asymmetric and unreliable and currency exchange rates can cause unexpected losses. In addition, inaccurate forecasts can divert attention from cash flow hedging to balance sheet protection.

The best way to manage currency risk is to have an overview of all the company's foreign exchange exposures that can be mitigated by hedging or eliminating the internal exposure. Having a sense of how currencies are impacting financial results at all times is necessary to manage foreign currency exposure efficiently and avoid unnecessary impacts on the company's financial results.

→ ***Debt and counterparty risk***: An increase in debt and counterparty risk is common when normal operations are disrupted. Debt can be increased or managed differently, which could increase unforeseen costs. Concerning counterparty risk, some banks in some regions may present an increased risk of insolvency, which raises concerns on committees and boards of directors.

Companies must demonstrate their ability to increase leverage responsibly, refinance debt where appropriate, reaffirm compliance with commitments, and automatically manage board compliance limits for all counterparties.

→ ***Turnover volatility***: Income volatility can have a fatal impact on the structure of fixed costs but adapting to the cost structure can save a business.

Cost reduction is the key to managing revenue volatility. This can be done by reducing bank fees, and businesses can save up to 80% on banking connectivity, allowing them to allocate staff for better use. In addition, cash flow forecasting allows companies to manage revenues and ancillary revenues, and ensure that deficits are covered and surpluses are allocated to achieve return on excess cash.

→ ***Risk of disruption in the supply network***: Supply bottlenecks and suppliers' failure are common concerns, especially in times of crisis. To stay afloat, suppliers can request an advance payment to amortise cash reserves and remain solvent.

In such cases, the treasury must explore alternatives in the supply network and for working capital. By implementing working capital optimisation programmes such as supply chain financing and dynamic discounting, companies can reduce the cash conversion cycle/procurement cash flow, provide financial support to suppliers with internal or external funding, secure preferred buyer status, and support the procurement and diversification of other supply chains.

→ ***One technology provider, four solutions***: Treasury teams can improve their preparation for temporary and longer-term scenarios by implementing business continuity and pro-active liquidity strategy, thus pre-emptively managing these risks.

Treasurers who excel in each of these areas will not only support the top management but also emerge as valuable strategic advisors, creating additional opportunities to influence and drive success. Through automation to mitigate risks related to human skills and reduce costs, a unique control and risk offering for crisis management, and the best business intelligence and business continuity guaranteed, treasury and finance will always be equipped with the tools they need to cope with any crisis through SaaS solutions.

Transforming Risk Management into Risk Intelligence[1]

Leading consulting firms have undertaken to transform risk management into risk intelligence to improve information available to top management tables and decision-making processes. In the past, all kinds of assessments, whether it's a risk assessment, a control assessment, or compliance issues, landed on management desks in Excel forms or some sort of hard-to-use corporate software.

This means that to be accurate and of good quality, the front line must be equipped with tools that look like consumer apps. So the way to achieve this is to develop software with a so-called code-free platform, rather than the hard coding that allows us to tailor the platform to the exact needs of that client. However, customised solutions can prove costly and inefficient, as they are updated with iterations required by a changing environment. However, with customer-centric service companies, the cost drift can be avoided. This allows the user to connect a risk to the things they care about, whether it's a process, goal, decision, or project in an agile manner.

- ***Key trends in risk management during and after the pandemic:***

There is more interest in business continuity in Europe now, although this may not last, as interest has already declined as the world seems to be gradually returning to a new normal state. Europe is also an important driver of incident management as there are stronger incident management requirements in Canada and the EU.

---

[1]See *Transforming risk management into risk intelligence*. https://globalriskcommunity.com/profiles/blogs/transforming-risk-management-into-risk-intelligence.

In addition, there is also a continuous trend towards greater integration. Therefore, officials should verify controls that must be rigorous in areas of high risk. There is a lot of integration, particularly on the European side, and the topic of cyber security is also at the top of the leader's agenda. For a technology company, this is particularly crucial because their main risk is cyber security. Any major incident could mean a shutdown.

In other sectors, of course, this is one of several risks; it is important that companies and decision-making bodies also focus on topics such as legal risk or security risk – in particular, taking into account the challenges of the pandemic.

- ***The role of technology in risk management today:***

There are a lot of emerging technologies like artificial intelligence, and machine learning, and everybody talks about it in all industries. The issue is whether they will be implemented or not; most likely, but they are not without risks. For example, in terms of ERM deployment, they were deployed more on the incident side because there were complaints about the narratives.

For a good implementation of AI, it is necessary to be able to go through a block of text and identify people, organisations, dates, times, places, and this kind of information, and to transform it into usable labels.

- ***Risk management cantered on the organisation's objectives:***

There's no point in assessing risk against something that doesn't matter, and what matters at the end of the day are the objectives of the organisation. And to be relevant to a branch, you still have to speak your language and respond to your concerns. Often now, the term risk management is used to refer to ERM, i.e. comprehensive and integrated risk management, but it implies a completely different dimension. It's not just a question of assessing risk to assess risk; it's like a box-checking exercise that wouldn't be very helpful.

Flexibility is required to implement specially designed modelling solutions. And if one focuses on the fact that everything has to be quantified and everything has to be modelled, the danger is not to grasp certain nuances that do not lend themselves to modelling. However, quantification is always very important, and we should try to quantify as much as possible. However, keep in mind that there are a lot of things in the world that don't lend themselves to modelling and excessive focus on modelling could miss important qualitative factors.

- ***Important considerations:***

Two important aspects must also be taken into account:

→ ***Consumption and focus on the front line*** – Without reliable data, there is no point in focusing on reporting and everything else. If the data is not good or obtained late, we are in trouble. COVID-19 is a great example as almost no one had a pandemic in their risk management plan in January 2020.

Most organisations that had identified the pandemic risk had not planned any treatment considering him highly unlikely. And if we were to do a quarterly update, in April the world would have been out of whack. While this is an extreme example, this type of high-velocity risk occurs regularly. So, it's important to integrate with the front line to make it easier for them to do that.

→ ***Integration*** – Today, there is a shift towards integration and the purchase of compartmentalised systems for SOX (Sarbanes-Oxley Act in the USA), ERM, compliance, and IT risk no longer makes much sense. They may have more red flags, but we gain more by asking for a global evaluation instead of asking employees to do the same thing in different systems and then trying to assemble them.

A Strategic Vision for Modelled Risk Management[2]

Although McKinsey's report is primarily aimed at financial institutions, most of the messages and challenges identified apply to all sectors and only need to be adapted to the specific context in which a given organisation operates.

In 2020, McKinsey held several risk management forums for financial institutions around the world. These professionals exchanged their views on the challenges and emerging themes of modelled risk management. We sent out a questionnaire to which over 150 professionals from 100 institutions responded. Three priority areas emerged from this: the impact of COVID-19 on risk management, changes in models, and the challenges of using AI and machine learning.

The COVID-19 pandemic has impacted the performance of models globally, including traditional financial risk models such as credit risk, as well as non-financial risk models and fraud management. Banks have responded with short-term measures. Responses included more frequent monitoring to identify risk models, compensatory controls such as model overlays, and substitutions using other existing models. Some of these short-term measures (such as overlaps) did not have adequate controls, so appropriate governance had to be developed.

Major institutions are also implementing longer-term solutions, improving their Modelled Risk Management (MRM) functions to adapt to new conditions. Their goal is to take MRM to a new level, defined by meaningful collaboration between the first and second lines of defence. Institutions will need to integrate the MRM culture throughout the model life cycle. This entails changing not only the processes and procedures but also how people think and act in the model life cycle.

The MRM function should establish the governance of overlays covering business as usual and regulatory models. Transparency of all overlaps is essential as banks are exploring more systematic and reactive approaches to address overlaps across all segments (consumers, small- and medium-sized businesses, businesses).

The crisis highlighted the value of MRM and heightened the importance of the function as a strategic risk partner. The maturity of MRM varies by region, partly due to different regulatory guidelines. McKinsey found that the number of models requiring validation and risk reviews is increasing and that the scope of MRM is also expanding rapidly – into models for automatic decision-making, for example.

---

[2]See Laurent, M.-P., Raggl, A., Rougeaux, C., & Tejada, M. *A strategic vision for model risk management*. McKinsey Global Publishing.

The next level of maturity in the MRM pathway is defined by more advanced capabilities, which go beyond the validation-centric approach. The focus shifts from a review of the technical model to the perspective of a risk manager who assesses risks beyond the model methodology. The entire model portfolio is managed, including extended inventory beyond credit and market risk models, including non-financial and business models. Reporting becomes meaningful as senior managers gain a comprehensive view of model risk beyond the technical aspects, a view that presents real risk.

To keep pace with these artificial intelligence (AI) and advanced analytics (AA) developments, MRM needs to set standards and provide end-to-end management for new models. Most MRM functions do not have comprehensive standards tailored to AI and AA. They are needed to address specific challenges, including the detection of bias, ethical issues, and clarification. Other exposures result from a lack of appropriate AI and AA tools and infrastructure. The biggest challenge, however, is in the area of knowledge. Most MRM teams lack AI and AA talent. In addition, model submissions are often incomplete, as many owners of the new models do not adequately understand the responsibilities of a model owner and do not have a sufficient understanding of the risks associated with the model.

Risk from the Perspective of Top Management in the Post-Covid Era

The importance of modelled risk management was already fast developing before the COVID-19 crisis. In response to increasing levels of risk and the need for more sophisticated modelling, organisations have begun to develop AI and AA models to manage their overall financial and non-financial risks. The crisis has accelerated digital transformations, especially in the financial sector, which has been an important driver of the new generation of models.

The current context is therefore particularly propitious for developing the capabilities of risk management models. The strategic importance of the function is even more evident in a complex and volatile environment, in these times of Covid and post-Covid. The level of functionality of MRM increases proportionally, requiring greater efficiency of MRM. Organisations in any sector need a less validation-oriented function, one that can strategically prioritise model redesign and adjustment. A more comprehensive MRM approach, beyond validation, will help ensure a model life cycle better suited to the AI and AA models.

All leaders should assess their organisation's risk readiness, which they could do by asking themselves these four questions:

1. How would the organisation's management team describe the overall maturity of the organisation's risk management processes? How would the directors' vision differ from that of top management?
2. What has the organisation done to invest more time, attention, and resources to explicitly identify, analyse, and manage risks across the extended organisation?
3. Could the risk management approach within the organisation be described as explicit, structured, coordinated, or more implicit, ad hoc, or informal?

4. To what extent is risk management a siloed activity that exists within different business functions and has little coordination and aggregation of risk information at the corporate level?

This inside vision must be completed by an outside vision. So, the fifth question would be to get information on what the organisation's key stakeholders think about its risk management practices and its CSR policy.

When 'adverse' events such as threat materialisation occur, they can often significantly harm an entity's reputation and brand. More rigorous risk management processes should help top management and board members monitor risk and adopt proactive rather than reactive management. The core mission of an effective ERM programme is to help inform promptly top management and the board of directors of events that could emerge and impact reputation and brands.

While all executives name reputation as their main asset when asked about the extent to which they use their ERM programme to identify and manage significant risks that could harm the organisation's reputation and brand, the lack of precision in their answers is striking.

It is important to note that there are several barriers to the improvement of risk management within organisations. The perception that investing in risk management is a priority relative to other organisational initiatives or the perception that risk management does not create value is still present in many top management and boards of directors. Middle management is an essential relay often reluctant to get 'distracted' from their operational duties. This way of thinking reflects a lack of understanding of how effective risk monitoring can improve the organisation's ability to proactively manage all risks, particularly emerging risks.

Several resources are available to directors, officers, and senior managers to help them understand their responsibilities for risk monitoring and find effective tools and techniques to assist them in these activities. Professional associations of risk managers offer information and education that professionals can use and provide to their leaders, among them AMRAE and SoFGRES in France, FERMA at the level of the European continent, and user associations like CLUSIF in France for risks related to cyber-security.

As expectations for more effective risk monitoring across the organisation continue, it will be important for officers and directors whose personal responsibility is involved to continue to monitor changes in risk monitoring procedures to ensure the resilience and performance of the organisation as they are responsible for the future.

Chapter 12

ERM and the Board of Directors

Increasingly stringent regulations are requiring directors to ensure that risk management, as well as change management and talent issues, are regularly on the board's agenda, and even at the top of the agenda. In addition, the board should demonstrate its interest in the organisation's future through questions asked or not asked and items that make it to the top of the agenda. This is the best way to send strong signals to the organisation's top management and stakeholders.

In any organisation that takes charge of the changes and challenges of the future, the momentum is generated at the board level that must be actively involved in risk management issues from a resilience perspective.

The mission of the directors has become increasingly important since the enactment of the Sarbanes-Oxley Act in the United States in 2002 and the legal and regulatory context worldwide has increased the duties of the directors; here are the main milestones:

- The governance rules of the New York Stock Exchange require, at a minimum, that risk oversight be part of the Board's audit committee;
- The legislation adopted in the United States after the 2008–2009 financial crisis (known as Dodd-Frank) requires large financial institutions to have an official risk committee at the board level;
- An organisation's risk control process is one of the main risk criteria that major rating organisations consider before assigning a credit rating.

Board Risk Committee's Missions[1]

Directors have a key role to play which is also confirmed by law and regulation in many countries and the matrix below in Table 12.1 gives an idea of the main tasks of the board of directors' delegate to the risk committee.

---

[1]See Xilu. (2021, January 7). *Risk management committee: Role and responsibility assignment matrix*. https://tmqresearch.com/risk-management-committee-role-and-responsibility-assignment-matrix/.

Enterprise Risk Management in Today's World: A Current and Futuristic View of the Complexity, Resilience, Responsibility and Tools in ERM, Part B, 139–151

Published under exclusive licence by Emerald Publishing Limited
doi:10.1108/978-1-83608-392-420241012

Table 12.1. Risk Committee: Mission Matrix.

Mission	Risk-Manger Project	Compliance & Legal	Initial Risk Owner	Risk Management Support Group
Risk project planning	L	C	C	S
Risk identification	L	R	I	S
Risk analysis	L	R	I	S
Quantitative risk analysis	L	R	I	S
Response planning & action development	L	R	I	S
Risk monitoring & control	L/R	R/C	C	S
Feedback documentation	C	C	C	S

Note: L = Legally responsible; R = responsible for implementation; S = support; I = informed; C = consulted.

ERM & Risk Governance[2]

ERM supports an organisation's vision, mission, objectives, and strategies; this mission is the prime objective of any ERM. This is why ERM must take into account all the risks associated with all the projects in an organisation's portfolio. A 'risk governance framework' must be set up at the corporate level and a governance board oversees ERM and its framework, but what exactly is governance and what are its components?

The purpose of governance is to ensure that the entity is managed appropriately. Governance can exist at various levels: global, portfolio, programmes, or projects:

→ Organisational governance is a structured way to ensure governance at the corporate level. The objective is to achieve the organisation's strategic and operational objectives;
→ Portfolio, programme, or project (PPP) governance refers to the framework, functions, and processes that guide portfolio, programme, or project management activities, respectively.

In this context, they will be known as governance or governance framework respectively. So, the governance framework is part of the governance. Key components of an organisation's governance that interact include:

→ The Governing Body is a group of temporary or permanent members with responsibilities and powers. This agency provides the necessary direction and decision-making for portfolios, programmes, and projects. In principle it is the executive committee with a mirror committee on the board of directors;

[2]See Donaire, N. (2019, February 26). *Enterprise Risk Management (ERM) and the board: What you need to know*. https://www.diligent.com/au/enterprise-risk-management-erm-and-the-board-what-you-need-to-know/.

→ The governance framework contains governance areas with functions, processes, and activities for projects, programmes, and portfolios. Governance and governance performance communications are examples of such areas;
→ Governance is a group of functions performed by an individual, group, or organisation to address a particular area of concern. For example, the area of communications on governance focuses on the dissemination of information;
→ Governance functions are a group of related processes executed to support portfolio, programmes, and project governance.

Governance informs on the 'what' while management informs on the 'how'. The 'what' aspects concern the decision, the orientation provides the guarantee of the management of the PPP. 'How' affects the organisation and execution of work. Table 12.2 summarises the missions.

Here are the key points of risk governance:

→ Risk governance is created and the risk governance framework is also developed (the governance framework is a component of governance);
→ Within this framework, risks are identified at each level, that is, at the level of the enterprise/organisation or the PPP;
→ The identified risks are analysed qualitatively and quantitatively. Then the best level of governance can be chosen. This can be the portfolio governance layer, the programme governance layer, or the project governance;
→ It is possible that at each level of PPP governance, there may be a risk governance model, part of the governance of the corresponding P. For example, within the framework of project governance, we can have project risk governance;
→ The respective level of governance decides on the risks raised and what to do with them. Enterprise risks can be transferred to the appropriate level, at which they can be managed efficiently;
→ Risk governance, at the chosen level, provides:
  ✓ Guidance in the identification and appointment of risk managers. Risks can be escalated to the appropriate level if they can be managed at that level. There may be a two-way movement of risks within an organisation;
  ✓ Guidance on risk response strategies and risk response measures, which are associated with response strategies;
  ✓ Decision on the continuation or termination of a PPP.

Table 12.2. Governance Versus Management.

Level	Governance (What)	Management (How)
1	Governance develops and approves the governance framework	Management documents and monitors the governance framework
2	Governance approves charts, plans, and/or business plans	Management develops charts, plans, and/or business plans
3	Governance provides resources, including financial	Management establishes the need for resources, including financial

Then it is the risk manager's responsibility to delegate the risk management measures to the respective risk management managers.

Relationship Between CEO and Board, and Between Board Members[3]

The quality of the relationship between the Board of Directors and the Executive Director is critical to the success of the organisation. For a quality relationship, the CEO must develop insight into the role, expectations, and limitations of each of the parties. The wisdom is that the more the board avoids getting involved in day-to-day management and functions as an independent supervisory board, the better the financial performance of the organisation.

Although the ideal relationship between the Board of Directors and the CEO rests on the principle that each party fulfils its respective obligations without incursion into the territory of the other, recent history is full of examples of violations of this principle. Following the corporate scandals of the early 21st century, regulations were adopted to broaden the requirements on boards of directors, management, and accounting firms operating as auditors.

These new regulatory frameworks were designed to ensure the independence of the board, extend its oversight function, and place limits on management's response capabilities. These regulations were intended to protect against management abuses that generated scandals in the early 2000s; they maintain an operations and execution-oriented management while the Board exercises effective oversight and monitoring.

For their part, board members must have a strong sense of self-awareness and self-knowledge and a deep understanding of their strengths and weaknesses. With this knowledge, board members can lead, speak, and collaborate more effectively on relevant issues, as well as observe, learn, and defer to others, as appropriate. This creates strong and constant communication between board members and CEOs about facts and ideas, which ultimately ensures that board members learn from each other and that the best ideas are implemented.

ERM, Board, and Risk Appetite[4]

Boards that embrace ERM want a strategic vision of their organisation and its risks. In particular, the Board of Directors must fulfil one of its essential

[3]See Boyden Executive Monitor. (2018). *Regulation and the role of the board* (No. 14). https://www.boyden.com/media/regulation-and-the-role-of-boards-5441813/regulation-and-the-role-of-boards.pdf.

[4]See *Principles for an effective risk appetite framework*. Financial Stability Board. https://www.fsb.org/wp-content/uploads/r_131118.pdf – Although they are developed for financial institutions, the principles are relevant for all types of organisations.

missions: define a risk appetite for the entire organisation. First, it is necessary to define a framework for risk appetite (FRA). This risk appetite framework should take into account the risk capacity, risk appetite, risk limits, and risk profile for the different businesses and legal entities, where applicable, and within the group.

The elements of FRA must therefore be applied at the business and/or legal entity level in a manner proportionate to the size of the vulnerabilities, the complexity, and the importance of the risk. Establishing an effective FRA helps to strengthen a strong risk culture in the organisations involved, which is essential to sound risk management. A strong risk culture creates an environment for recognition, timely escalation, and management of emerging risks that will have a significant impact on an organisation and any risk-taking activity beyond the organisation's risk appetite.

The second step is to develop a risk appetite statement that should be easy to communicate and therefore easy to understand for all stakeholders. Appetite metrics can be expressed in terms of earnings, equity, cash flow, risk, or other appropriate indicators.

For risk appetite purposes, at the operational level, risk limits are the allocation or distribution of the overall risk appetite statement of the organisation to each business line, or at the corporate level, to specific risk categories, concentrations, and, where appropriate, other levels. To facilitate effective monitoring and reporting, risk limits should be specific and sensitive to the form of actual, measurable, frequency-based, reportable, and forward-looking portfolios or projects.

Stress tests should be conducted at the corporate level as well as for specific legal entities and risks. The number of limits chosen should balance the trade-off between completeness and cost and effectiveness of monitoring.

As far as the Board of Directors is concerned, it is up to it to establish the reference FRA and to approve the risk appetite statement, the board's obligations can be summarised as follows:

a. Approve the Corporate FRA, developed in collaboration with the CEO, the Risk Directorate, and the Finance Directorate, and ensure that it remains consistent with the organisation's short- and long-term strategy, financial programmes, asset management, risk capacity, and compensation programmes;
b. Hold the CEO and other members of management accountable for the integrity of the FRA, including the timely identification, management, and escalation of breaches of risk limits and material risk exposures;
c. Ensure that annual business plans are in line with the approved risk appetite and that incentives/disincentives are included in compensation programmes to facilitate compliance with the risk appetite;
d. Include an assessment of risk appetite in strategic discussions within the board, including decisions on mergers, acquisitions, and growth of business lines or products;
e. Review and monitor regularly the actual risk profile and risk limits against agreed levels (by business, legal entity, product, risk category), including qualitative measures of behavioural risk;

f. Discuss and monitor to ensure appropriate action is taken regarding 'violations' of risk limits;
g. Ask the branch about activities that are not part of the risk appetite statement approved by the Board of Directors, when applicable;
h. Obtain an independent assessment (through internal evaluators, third parties, or both) of the design and effectiveness of the FRA and its alignment with audit experience;
i. Ensure that mechanisms are in place to ensure that the branch can act promptly manner to effectively manage and, if necessary, mitigate significant exposures to risk; in particular those that are close to or exceed the approved risk appetite statement or approved risk limits;
j. Consult with the external audit, or control bodies that could intervene based on the activities of the organisation, decisions regarding the organisation, and the ongoing monitoring of risk appetite as well as significant changes in current levels of risk appetite or any regulatory expectations regarding risk appetite;
k. Ensure that adequate resources and expertise are dedicated to risk management and internal audit to provide independent assurance to the board and top management that they are operating within the approved FRA; including, where appropriate, the use of service providers to supplement existing resources;
l. Ensure that risk management is supported by adequate and robust information systems to enable rigorous and timely risk identification, measurement, assessment, and reporting.

ERM, Governance, & Culture

Even before initiating discussions with the directors, risk managers must ensure that they have good relations and good contacts with top management and that they participate in the decision-making from the outset. Too often, risk teams are only consulted and even implemented once the strategy is finalised, which means the role becomes more reactive than proactive. Reactive risk management creates value, but it does not go far enough to ensure positive governance and eliminate risk behaviours driven by poorly designed KPIs.

While experts are divided on the value of these tools in day-to-day risk management, most agree that the jargon and level of detail do not match the expectations of leaders, which means any risk professional who wants access to the board has to take a different approach. There are several barriers to advancing an organisation's risk management programme, with the belief that 'risks are managed in ways other than ERM' dominating the list.

There may be a lack of risk management skills, between desired and actual, as the majority of organisations describe their risk culture as 'strongly risk averse' versus 'risk averse' even though only a minority of managers dare to describe their risk management processes as 'mature' or 'robust'.

The organisational culture and the commitment of top management and the board have a direct impact on the level of risk management involvement in the strategic decision-making process. Each organisation should engage in introspection to understand the maturity of its risk management culture, which is articulated around the following five questions:

1. Based on the views and opinions expressed by the organisation's branches, could there not be a lack of support from the top down to participate in more robust risk management activities?
2. What are the common points of resistance encountered in attempts to involve different managers and heads of departments in discussions on risk management?
3. How does the organisation's overall culture impact risk management?
4. To what extent have the organisation's board members had the opportunity to learn about ERM and how it should be integrated into strategic decision-making?
5. Is the reluctance of managers at all levels to participate in ERM programmes due to a lack of appreciation of the strategic value of more proactive rather than reactive risk management?

Understanding the Board's Expectations on ERM Programmes[5]

Many organisations have difficulty providing their boards easily assimilated information; whereas COSO states that there is *'no single correct method of communication with the Board'*, the most important top management and risk managers' obligation is to communicate risk information to the board in a way that board members can understand.

For the board to be able to play an active role in risk management and strategic decision-making of the agency assigned to it by the regulations, parameters must be established to identify the issues that are ultimately brought to its attention. Managers tend to keep things at a high level so as not to burden the board with too much detail, but too high means that directors do not ultimately receive valuable and actionable information.

Interviews with the board or the risk committee must be prepared carefully; however, risk managers must keep in mind that board members are likely to lead the conversation in various directions; therefore, they must always be prepared to adapt to the issues and the circumstances. Three fundamental questions should find their way into the conversation:

Question 1: *What is your vision for the organisation and how do you think ERM will contribute to achieving this vision?*

Answers to this question may include increased market share, more streamlined operations, better collaboration within the organisation, a more fluid product

---

[5]See Williams, C. *3 Easy to use tips to understanding why executives want ERM*. https://www.erminsightsbycarol.com/understanding-why-executives-want-erm/; Williams, C. *3 Factors to consider before escalating risk issues to the board*. https://www.erminsightsbycarol.com/escalating-risk-issues-board/; Williams, C. *5 Tips to making board risk reports meaningful tools for decision-making*. https://www.erminsightsbycarol.com/board-risk-reports/.

development cycle, etc. Perhaps a colleague told them that adopting ERM helped them achieve their goals much faster or that they read a success story about ERM in a professional journal. In the case of a board member, he/she may have had experience in another organisation where he/she is also on duty.

Question 2*: What do you expect from ERM?*

This question is similar to the previous one, but formulated in a slightly different way and it can provide answers with different details. This question can be used to identify expectations of ERM team members, in practices or programme.

Question 3*: What do you expect to gain practically from ERM?*

It is not necessarily a matter of listing deliverables at this stage. Instead of a concrete organisational goal such as a 5% growth in market share, executives can say 'better communication between departments' or 'better customer service assessments' or another intangible objective.

However, some questions will be specific to the organisation and its business sector. However, based on the principle of 'starting with purpose' and 'seeking to understand first and then to be understood', it is possible to better understand the motivation of leaders for ERM and, therefore, adopt a course of action that will give them the benefits they expect. Of course, this step should allow the risk manager to be selective about the risks he/she chooses to bring to the attention of the directors and it is possible to formulate three factors that justify drawing the attention of the directors to a given risk:

1. Risk, both threats and opportunities, must be approached in a cross-functional manner when it is just an issue within a single function, like Marketing or Finance; therefore, it should be dealt with by the management. However, if the risk is pervasive and generalised, the board may need to speak out, requesting more global information to help make a decision or provide guidance.
2. Managing the risk will require significant time, human or financial resources. Again, if this is an issue that can be resolved in a matter of minutes and without any financial commitment, it is clear that the board does not need to be informed. The board may need to speak out if the problem requires the organisation to divert resources from other priorities, especially if it impacts strategic objectives.
3. The risk or issue could have a significant impact on the reputation of the organisation from an outsider's perspective.

To be useful to board members, the information provided should cover the following:

→ A description of the risk or problem;
→ The facts currently known about the risk or problem (not mere assumptions);
→ The unknowns to take into account;
→ Description of potential or actual impacts on the organisation;
→ The possible solutions.

The above list is, of course, just a general framework that should be tailored to the needs of a given organisation and the history of the BOD, preferred communication styles, etc.

If there is not a single model applicable in all situations, there are five general tips for developing effective risk reporting for boards, including:

1. **Writing High-Level Reports** – Board risk reports should be general and include only key risks impacting objectives but with practical bias avoiding overviews.
2. **Avoid Copying and Pasting Key Risk Reports** – A danger to organisations would be to simply share information contained in the World Economic Forum, US, or industry-specific risk reports. It is acceptable to refer to reports such as this, but the risk committee and the board must get information that is most directly relevant to the organisation.
3. **Describe measures that are already in place** – Taking into account relevant risks, a high-level discussion about what the organisation is already doing, and how it compares to similar organisations, competitors, or partners. This benchmarking activity helps the Audit Committee (AC) understand the organisation's current position and what to focus on.
4. **Highlight priorities for the future** – Benchmarking activity helps the board to see where the organisation is at, but will still need information on actions and priorities to manage key risks (threats and opportunities). If the experience of the organisation is similar to that of its peers, the priorities will be the same, but if the experience is more specific, and unique, the priorities will, of course, be different.
5. **Use visual presentations** – Slide information is easier to read, use visuals where possible. But be careful not to overload a slide with as much text as possible, it is better to prepare more slides if this helps the public to better understand and faster information.

Board, ERM, and Value Creation[6]

When ERM implementation is efficient, it can provide the board with the information it needs to monitor and mitigate risks to the organisation and its key stakeholders. As a result, board members who have a good understanding of the ERM framework and associated concepts will be better equipped to maximise the use of ERM for risk monitoring and creating value.

Effective risk oversight is the foundation of prudent governance and decision-making provided by board members:

→ Ask the necessary questions to establish and/or supervise ERM programmes;
→ Determine the organisation's risk tolerance and risk appetite;
→ Monitor ERM implementation,

A risk-conscious culture recognises that the future is unpredictable and that outcomes cannot be predicted with certainty. Each project or initiative has a

[6]See ASHRM. *Enterprise risk management for boards and trustees: Leveraging the value.* https://www.ashrm.org/sites/default/files/ashrm/ERM-for-Boards-and-Trustees.pdf.

range of potential inputs: cost, resources, mission objective, and outputs: performance, revenue, and mission delivery with various risks that impact each potential outcome. A risk-conscious culture aims to:

→ Quantify the potential variability of inputs and outputs when evaluating and prioritising alternative projects, initiatives, and strategic directions;
→ Identify the sources of this variability, known as key risk indicators (KRIs);
→ Measure the expected positive and negative consequences of this variability;
→ Develop mitigation strategies to reduce the impact and/or likelihood of negative consequences;
→ Develop contingency plans to address negative consequences if mitigation strategies fail or are not available.

Risk-adjusted decision-making represents a more sophisticated approach to decision-making than typical cost-benefit or return-on-investment (ROI) analyses. Boards promoting ERM see value from two perspectives:

→ ERM optimises organisations' decision-making by identifying the best strategies to reduce risks relative to those that are simply sufficient, and this aspect of ERM helps organisations maximise the value they derive from the decisions they make. When the risk is considered negative, a threat only, the goal is to reduce or eliminate the risk and minimise its impact;
→ ERM views risk as uncertainty, which means it can also lead to positive outcomes, and represent an opportunity that improves revenue, reputation, and value. There are many approaches to consider, among them SWOT analysis.

Boards should ask the following questions about the maturity of the organisation and its maturity before implementing an ERM initiative:

1. What are ERM needs today? *(Has a risk champion been identified?)*
2. What level of risk management competence does the board want to achieve across the organisation? *(Does the current state of the organisation's culture and environment support the adoption of ERM?)*
3. How will the board fully support the MRA process? *(Does the organisational culture –behaviours, beliefs, and values – encourage appropriate risk-taking?)*
4. Where will enhanced risk management activities provide the greatest value? *(Do employees have sufficient internal and external resources to support the adoption of ERM?)*
5. How will the implementation of ERM affect the operations of the organisation and how should it be managed? *(To what extent will information technology be used effectively to support the organisation's risk and control framework?)*
6. How will risks and controls be identified, assessed, monitored, and improved? *(Is there relevant expertise and experience within the organisation to implement an ERM framework?)*
7. Have the organisation's risk appetite and tolerance limits been defined, agreed upon, communicated, and understood? *(What communication will be required for internal and external stakeholders to encourage buy-in to the ERM framework?)*

8. What existing operations can be leveraged to integrate ERM across the organisation? (Is there a mechanism for continuous improvement of the framework?)
9. What will be the level of monitoring of risks and controls? *(How will the success and value of the ERM framework be measured and monitored?)*
10. Are risk management functions effectively aligned and coordinated to manage risks? *(Is risk awareness integrated into the organisation's strategic plan?)*

ERM contributes to value creation by enabling top management to effectively manage future uncertainty and respond in a way that reduces the likelihood of losses and enhances the likelihood of gains. That is why boards must ensure that there is alignment between what their organisations say and what it does to reinforce trust in stakeholders.

Good risk governance means that an organisation has a framework in place to continuously assess its obligations to all stakeholders and to make changes where necessary to preserve and enhance its 'reputation capital'.

Efficient Partnership Between Board Chair and Risk Manager[7]

CEOs can trust a good risk manager and rely on her/him to ensure the proper functioning of the organisation, but there is often a natural distance between the two roles due to differences in mentality. CEOs have many issues to address outside of the intricacies of risk and compliance and focus more on generating growth and shareholder value, which can be considered a cross-objective with risk management.

- ***Risk manager's role in supporting the chairperson and the CEO:***

A chairperson and/or CEO approaches the organisation as an explorer, with a focus on cutting edge and promoting the business, while the risk manager is more of a preservative, inward-oriented towards organisational orientation, control, and stability. Organisations need ambidextrous skills to adopt both mindsets simultaneously to drive innovation, not only internally, but also for clients and other stakeholders.

A balance can be achieved if both parties discuss and agree on three key points:

→ A shared vision of the organisation's vision, mission, and values;
→ An understanding of their respective roles and how they need to help each other;
→ Regular communication to avoid hitches.

- ***The qualities of a good risk manager for the chairperson and CEO:***

These qualities are the following:

→ ***Understanding actionable data and metrics:*** The organisation needs a leader who can provide statistical and operational information to advise the chair and CEO on data and how to move forward with a risk management strategy.

[7]Dowd, B. (2021, September 23). *Ensuring an effective CEO-risk manager partnership.* http://www.rmmagazine.com/articles/article/2021/09/23/ensuring-an-effective-ceo-risk-manager-partnership.

→ ***Stay ahead of technological trends:*** Organisations that proactively build advanced risk management capabilities to keep pace with continuous change can gain significant competitive advantages. With the constant emergence of new technologies and tools, it is essential to stay abreast of the latest trends for effective risk management.

→ ***Have symbiotic perspectives:*** Chair, CEOs, and risk managers should work to build trust and mutual understanding. When this cooperation works effectively, it can provide a creative space for innovation, supported by reliable and secure business operations.

→ ***Effective reporting for the Chair/CEO:*** In some cases, organisations do not have an appropriate reporting system. Some use spreadsheets; others have a risk register, while others use email to inform the appropriate internal stakeholders. Often these reports are not seized on the spot so that the chair and/or CEO can consult them later.

→ ***Being able to imagine the future and revisit certainties:*** The pandemic has shown why it is essential that risk mangers be flexible and at the forefront of progress, especially in areas such as exchange rates, retail trade, and healthcare. A good risk manager should know if the organisation is ready for a major disruption in its operations and what type of tools and technologies the organisation should adopt to ensure its security and resilience.

Sustainability and Resilience – An Utmost Duty for Directors

Environmental, societal, and governance (ESG) performance is now part of the assessment process for almost all institutional investors. In this context, sustainability, which takes into account ESG issues, is increasingly appearing at the top of the agendas of board meetings. While some leaders do not yet see it at such an urgent level, sustainability is now at the heart of any organisation's competitiveness as well as maintaining its 'social licence to operate'.

With increasing investors' interest in sustainability, there is often a greater focus on the governance element (the 'G') of ESG and the fiduciary obligation of the board of directors to oversee the strategy, risk, and capital allocation of an enterprise. Enterprise-wide risk management (ERM) is at the heart of any organisation's efforts to deepen the consideration of environmental and societal risks taking into account changing stakeholder expectations; they are increasingly active, thus these risks impact an organisation's ability to achieve its strategic objectives is increasing.

The systematic integration of ESG risks within the ERM programme promotes measurement and disclosure of meaningful ESG information and enables top management and the board of directors to assess overall resource requirements and allocate capital more efficiently. However, there is no single, standardised approach to formally integrating ESG considerations into board strategy and risk discussions to date.

All directors have a fiduciary responsibility within an organisation; they are challenged by investors and other stakeholders. They must be proactive in assessing competitive threats and understanding disruptive market trends, which include environmental and societal concerns. Board oversight is essential to investor confidence in an organisation's future performance.

Many boards feel they do not have access to the sustainability information they need, and they do not necessarily understand how sustainability is linked to business value. This is an opportunity for the board to work with management to define the broader universe of risks and critical stakeholders and determine what needs to be measured and communicated.

Ultimately, the main objective of the ERM is to support economic growth and societal progress that meet the needs of the present without compromising the opportunities for future generations, which is precisely the commitment to sustainability. So, sustainability is the ultimate mission of the ERM to ensure organisational and societal resilience.

Chapter 13

Board and ERM, Leading in the Future

The world is still experiencing new shocks, like the war in the Middle East, superimposed on previous shocks, a deadly global pandemic, disruptions to supply networks, the return of inflation and the war in Ukraine. These events have aggravated and accelerated major trends towards change and rupture, such as climate drift, digitalisation, and sustainability. In this context, two types of entrepreneurs are emerging:

- **The first type takes a cautious and defensive approach to volatility and uncertainty:** These leaders are bowing down and focusing on immediate threats. Their main concerns are scenario planning, resilience preparation, balance sheet management, short-term efficiency measures, and careful inflation monitoring. These leaders are in a state of waiting and strategic oversight as conditions change. The majority of executives fall into this category.
- **The second type takes all necessary defensive measures:** While accepting volatility, using it as a catalyst to galvanise action to seize new opportunities. The current disruption has strengthened the willingness of these leaders to boldly move forward, and they are revisiting elements of their strategy that may have been left fallow. These leaders play both on offence and defence.

Research dealing with corporate resilience shows that whereas purely defensive attitudes tend to produce median performances, offensive attitudes lead to a cocktail of occasional successes and catastrophic failures. Leaders and top performers combine both, cautious in managing recessions while aggressively pursuing rebounds.

The increase in ESG (environmental, societal, and governance) reporting regulation, such as the EU's proposed Directive on Business Sustainability Reporting, will make it easier to challenge board members on ESG issues and increase compliance risks. Risk managers are likely to face new challenges related to investors' and clients' ESG expectations.

Insurers are beginning to consider ESG issues in D&O underwriting decisions as risk increases. So, this is an area that directors are going to have to grapple with the foreseeable future.

Enterprise Risk Management in Today's World: A Current and Futuristic View of the Complexity, Resilience, Responsibility and Tools in ERM, Part B, 153–162

Published under exclusive licence by Emerald Publishing Limited
doi:10.1108/978-1-83608-392-420241013

Key Trends and Issues in Risk Management for the Foreseeable Future[1]

As the world moves along in the third decade of this century, it is essential to act on the lessons learned from the COVID-19 pandemic and the war in Ukraine. Globally, many organisations have already modified their operational approach, and some are considering changing again as new threats and opportunities are likely to emerge during this decade and beyond. Some of the trends and priorities that leaders need to adapt to address future risk factors are the following:

- **Mitigate the profound impacts of recent supply network disruptions:**

While there remains a degree of collective optimism about a recovery over the decade, risk managers in both the public and private sectors should continue to prioritise business continuity in the years ahead. In the professional community, there is increased sensitivity to supply network challenges, such as longer lead times, reduced capacity, or search for new suppliers, while requiring proactive solutions and ongoing management.

Despite all these projections and efforts, organisations cannot regain their former momentum unless they develop better strategies to meet new challenges of cumulative disruptions.

- ***Promote security and resilience:***

A new working environment has developed, working from home. As people and organisations have started to operate virtually using digital technology, threats to the cyber system are increasing everywhere. With advances in cloud technology, physical presence has become less important. However, this cloud-based technology is not free of threats and opportunities.

Cyber security in the online procurement network can be strengthened by managing an integrated and secure procurement system.

- ***Adopt full access to risk management:***

The increased use of cloud technology has brought to light a universally recognised fact that organisations, including SMEs, business units, and production services, can work well together. Now, managers have become aware that to do virtual business, they need to focus on cyber security and plans to manage the business successfully.

ESG factors involve elements that can be harmful and beneficial simultaneously. Success will be for organisations learning to manage these factors and take initiatives to face ESG challenges.

- ***Generating and using necessary data to analyse and manage risk:***

The success of an organisation in this decade will rest on good forecasting and planning. It is essential to review previous failures, to negotiate new commercial

[1]See *Risk management primary issues & trends for 2022*. https://www2.erm-academy.org/publication/risk-management-article/risk-management-primary-issues-trends-for-2022/.

conditions to sustain the pace of development of the organisation. But for forecasting and risk management, better technology and the digital marketplace will prove necessary. Investigating and collecting relevant content has become a much-needed ingredient in today's cyber world.

- ***Use predictive analytics to reduce event damage costs:***

To manage more efficiently online traffic, analysis in the field of predictive analysis has taken on a major importance. These analyses manage risk based on a variety of factors, such as data mining and statistics on systemic algorithms. The importance of predictive analysis is a key in predicting risk portfolios.

In a risk management strategy using predictive analysis, scientific techniques have been of paramount importance to date. Modern predictive data analytics can be developed using faster digital and virtual techniques, e.g. by inserting an integrated language for conversations.

The adoption of AI (Artificial Intelligence) is currently accelerating in organisations, particularly in supply networks. AI can mitigate the impact of disruptions of all kinds on the supply chain. In addition, greater elasticity of entrepreneurs can also advance the business in the medium term. In addition to the use of cloud technology, leveraging artificial intelligence and scientific techniques would mitigate the impact of future crises on businesses.

More Accountable, Transparent, and Strategic: Meet Board Members of the Future[2]

The Board of Directors of the future will be strongly focused on business resilience following a global pandemic, discussions on flexible work will have an impact on the boardroom strategy, and transparency between the board and branch will be at the forefront.

And strategic thinking will be essential for the tomorrow's director, according to a major report released today by the Governance Institute of Australia. The report on the board's future is based on a survey of 550 non-executive directors, CEOs and senior executives, company secretaries and senior managers in governance or risk management as well as a working group of senior executives and industry leaders.

- ***ESG and board accountability:***

Board responsibilities are expected to continue to increase, and the report shows that social licence will be the main ethical challenge (or culture of conduct)

[2]See *More accountable, transparent, and strategic: Meet the board of the future*. https://www.governanceinstitute.com.au/news-media/news/2021/nov/more-accountable-transparent-and-strategic-meet-the-board-of-the-future/?_cldee=anBsb3Vpc290QGFvbC5jb20%3d&recipientid=contact-3a2ccb17d497e61180ec020050d00007-8462cce044424690ad9bec186149da04&utm_source=ClickDimensions&utm_medium=email&utm_campaign=CDES042902%C2%A0-%20%20&esid=d90b8216-a030-ec11-b6e6-00224810e5f4.

for directors in 2025. ESG programs are being developed, and boards must ensure that they are engaged, accountable, and responsive to the non-financial risks that impact and impact their organisations.

- ***Strategic impact risks on the horizon*[3]*:***

Among emerging risks, inflation has become a medium-term concern. According to McKinsey, leaders need to take ownership and manage elements such as how the company 'can design products, services and experiences to deliver value'.

This would involve stabilising supply networks that can be broken, controlling costs, paying staff, and re-evaluating, among other tasks. Ultimately, it's about crisis management, says Sally Llewellyn, EMEA Regional Director of Security for International SOS:

> In the past, crisis teams were often activated for short-term crises, but COVID-19 has completely changed due to the ever-changing nature of the pandemic, government interventions, and other restrictions. In addition to COVID-19, other geopolitical issues, such as military conflicts, coups, terrorism, and other disruptions, have also led to the activation of crisis management teams.

- ***The importance of human capital for resilience*[4]*:***

At the heart of human capital management (HCM) is an organisation's efforts to motivate and invest in its workforce. HCM recognises that human capital is a critical asset in generating long-term value and that there is a clear correlation between HCM and asset performance. Just capital found that when companies pay their workers a decent wage, they get higher returns in the long run. In addition, during the recent Nasdaq Governance Solutions Board Engagement Team discussions with Officers and Directors, attraction, development, and retention of talent was identified as a top priority and a key risk to be managed.

Companies have historically organised their values around customer expectations. But today, with a younger and more diverse workforce, a larger clientele, investors, and other stakeholders, expectations are evolving and companies must evolve with them and take into account all stakeholders' expectations. As the

---

[3]See Parker, S. (2022, May 3). *Riding out the perfect storm.* https://www.strategic-risk-europe.com/home/riding-out-the-perfect-ztorm/1441041.article?utm_source=adestra&utm_term=Read%20more&utm_medium=email&utm_campaign=2579.

[4]See Nasdaq Governance Solutions. (2021, January 11). *Strength and resilience – Why human capital management matters.* https://www.governanceinstitute.com.au/news-media/news/2021/nov/strength-and-resilience-why-human-capital-management-matters/?_cldee=anBsb3Vpc290QGFvbC5jb20%3d&recipientid=contact-3a2ccb17d497e61180ec020050d00007-8462cce044424690ad9bec186149da04&utm_source=ClickDimensions&utm_medium=email&utm_campaign=CDES042902%C2%A0-%20%20&esid=d90b8216-a030-ec11-b6e6-00224810e5f4.

economic recovery stalls as a result of geopolitical instability and the induced energy crisis, many CEOs believe the time is right to re-evaluate their vision, mission, and purpose, how they will pursue a fair and inclusive strategy, and the legacy they want to leave the world.

- ***Diversity on the board:***

Given the recent significant advances in diversity, particularly at the gender level, attention is now turning to the diversity of skills, experience, and attributes of directors, highlighted as the most important for diversity and inclusion on boards, when gender and ethnicity seem less urgent.

- ***Tomorrow's board of directors in a glance:***

The main challenges for boards of directors in the decade will be:

→ Internally: The sustainability of the company is a priority.
→ Externally: Climate change, COVID-19 impacts, economic instability, technological disruption, and cyber security risk.

And the factors to take into account when recruiting a board:

→ *Three key competencies*: Strategic expertise, leadership and management, and technological know-how.
→ *Three main talents*: Strategic thinking, critical thinking, values, and ethics.
→ *The main ethical challenges are*: 'social licence to operate', conduct in the workplace, and culture.
→ *Preventing organisational failure*: Focus on ethics and values, culture, and financial management.
→ *Drivers of board-management dynamics*: A culture of transparency, trust, and respect between the board and management.
→ *Key technology disruptors*: Cyber Security and Data Protection, Understanding New Technology Risks, Governance and Compliance.

- ***What should be expected of the board in the future[5]:***

The risk governance role of directors in a complex and volatile world should be based on the following considerations, to which the essential elements must be added:

→ Explore and model the future of board and business meetings and join a community of pioneering companies.
→ Engage with stakeholders and engage employees, customers, suppliers, or local communities in conversations about how the company could evolve to meet the challenges its employees face.
→ Explore to learn – inspire the Board and teams with new skills and insights to help employees meet the challenges they face.

[5]*How can a Boardroom 2030 meeting benefit your business?* https://boardroom2030.org/

For the Board of Directors to fulfil these tasks it is necessary:

1. To redirect the purpose of an existing meeting, modify the agenda to ensure a direction to 2030, or invite different people to join you,
2. To schedule an extension of an existing meeting (30–60 minutes) to discuss 2030 plans, if agenda items are already scheduled for future meetings,
3. To organise the '2030' board room activation as part of a strategy session or 'in-the-field' seminar day with the current board,
4. To organise '2030' board activation outside of existing Board meetings. It may be composed and chaired by the next generation of organisation leaders and/or youth from the community, or other stakeholders.

The Long-Term Effects of the Pandemic on Health Risk Governance[6]

A critical consequence of the situation is that legislation, business stakeholders and public policy will now expect boards of directors to respond proactively to changing circumstances. As a result, boards of directors, particularly in health facilities, will be called upon to assess the impact on the governance of pandemic-specific lessons and experiences, and to implement changes deemed appropriate under the circumstances.

This does not mean that all corporate governance principles will be irrevocably changed by the pandemic. However, some key principles, including those related to board/management dynamics, levels of director engagement, and oversight of specific management functions, are likely to be significantly modified. The 10 components must appear on the agenda of the boards of directors of health institutions and be taken to the body by the administrators of all organisations:

- ***Dynamics between top management and board:***

The board and top management should be aware of the need to clarify the boundaries of their respective responsibilities. The ability of both management bodies to perform their functions in times of crisis requires a common understanding of the fundamental distinctions between governance and management roles. This is all the more the case as both seek to satisfy the increased expectations of their conduct created by the crisis.

- ***Increased board engagement:***

In the foreseeable future, boards of directors, especially in healthcare facilities will likely continue to have an increased level of commitment to governance and management responsibilities.

---

[6]See Peregrine, M. W., DeJong, R., & DiVarco, S. (July 16, 2020). *The long-term impact of the pandemic on corporate governance*. McDermott Will & Emery LLP. https://corpgov.law.harvard.edu/2020/07/16/the-long-term-impact-of-the-pandemic-on-corporate-governance/.

Disasters, such as the pandemic, require board involvement beyond the core governance principles. The pandemic presents challenges so fundamental to business stability that the organisational response cannot be delegated to senior management as it would normally be, or even in more traditional crises.

- ***Monitoring resilience:***

Business resilience is a critical component of the board's risk oversight function. It is based on the requirement to periodically review management plans to recover from a disaster, including tasks such as business continuity, physical security, cyber security, and crisis management.

- ***Special consideration to potentially catastrophic events:***

COVID-19 has confirmed the vital need for a robust ERM function. More significant is the extent to which it has confirmed that cataclysmic disasters can indeed occur and that they can now be taken more into account in the process of identifying the risks of ERM. These factors, in turn, will support a close evaluation of the effectiveness of the current ERM programme.

- ***Quality of care and patient's safety:***

In the past, boards may have considered 'operational' topics such as quality of care, infection control, and changes in regulatory compliance as the sole competence of management and staff. Going forward, the effects of the national health emergency and its lasting influence on healthcare operations indicate that these areas are appropriate for board review and decision-making. Monitoring and analysis to ensure that healthcare management and leaders have tested their plans and considered the impact on the organisation as a whole is the responsibility of the Board of Directors.

For example, pandemic demands and the resulting stresses due to a lack of healthcare equipment, personnel, and resources have highlighted complex issues such as rationing care and developing 'crisis care standards'. The involvement of the Board of Directors in the approval and adoption of care protocols or priorities developed by the organisation is important, as the potential legal, ethical, and reputational risks are entirely the responsibility of the institution.

- ***Executives' compensation:***

Compensation committees (and CEOs) will focus on greater discretionary power in executive compensation schemes and on finding a new balance between salary and performance.

Indeed, the lessons learned from the pandemic suggest that the compensation committee will need to address a variety of important and sometimes unique compensation concepts that could lead to a long-term expansion of its program.

Long-standing executive compensation or benefits schemes should be removed from the Automotive Pilot Program and given a new appearance. This includes reviewing additional retirement plans to understand all costs in a broader range of financial scenarios, assessing long-term feasibility, and adding discretion to suspend new benefits in the event of a crisis.

- ***Scenario-based technology planning:***

In the long run, there will be more rigorous monitoring of access to new technology, equipment, and treatments. The healthcare economy has long been based on the availability and efficiency of the technology and the technicians who use and maintain it. The pandemic and its collateral impacts on the adaptability of technology have shaken this dependency, which has had a significant impact on risk for similar physician groups, providers, and healthcare companies.

Based on lessons learned, the board should exercise rigorous oversight of management planning (including participation in 'simulated technology outages') to help ensure plant readiness.

- ***Monitoring employees' culture:***

When businesses have reopened their offices, cultural issues affecting the health, safety, and morale of the workforce have arisen. Employees' concerns in this regard, and general awareness of workplace safety, are likely to remain well after the widespread application of a vaccine or other anti-virus treatment. The success of the post-pandemic plant management model depends in part on the sensitivity of employees to virus concerns.

- ***Monitoring compliance:***

Boards can adjust the compliance function, and their oversight of this function, to include new risks and seek efficiency gains.

- ***Succession plans:***

Succession planning for executives and department heads will require much more attention from the board.

For many organisations, succession policies and procedures within management are too inadequate or informal to address the magnitude of succession challenges resulting from the pandemic that has exacerbated the demographic reality. Going forward, boards are expected to pay formal attention to succession issues which is a value driver for the organisation.

In a post-pandemic world, health facilities are evolving out of the disaster of a generation for which their organisations have borne a particularly painful burden. In many ways, their boards have been called upon to exercise an unprecedented level of commitment to support their organisations. What more can we ask them?

Changes the COVID-19 Generated on Boards and Governance[7]

As early as January 2020, the Global Preparedness Monitoring Board (GPMB) commended countries and the World Health Organisation (WHO) for the

[7]See Richard, B. (2020, October). *The effects of Covid-19 on boards and governance.* https://www.spencerstuart.com/research-and-insight/the-effects-of-covid-19-on-boards-and-governance.

speed of response so far, China's transparency in sharing information and genomic sequence of the virus, as well as the strong collaboration between China and affected countries and with the WHO. However, the council was concerned that many countries were still unprepared and urged the leaders of all countries to take the following immediate steps to ensure that they had the necessary capacity:

1. Countries, institutions, communities, and partners must ensure that all relevant information about the outbreak is shared openly and promptly to support the response by the International Health Regulations (IHR, 2005);
2. All countries and local governments, including those that have not yet been affected, must urgently devote resources to strengthening their essential preparedness capacities (as described in the IHR, 2005) to prevent, detect, inform, and respond to outbreaks, strengthen their health systems and are encouraged to follow WHO technical guidance for control measures by IHR (2005);
3. The research and development community must urgently accelerate the coordinated development of vaccines, diagnostics, and therapies for the coronavirus. The private sector and Coalition for Epidemic Preparedness Innovations (CEPI) initiatives should use vaccine research they support for other coronaviruses, such as MERS-CoV, to explore the development of 2019-nCoV vaccines. To ensure timely access to discoveries, all peer-reviewed research publications relevant to the outbreak should be made available immediately, and research relevant to the outbreak should be communicated promptly to the WHO. The international community should better understand the potential trajectories of the epidemic and its socio-economic impact;
4. All donors, including governments, the World Bank, regional development banks, GFATM, and the vaccine alliance (GAVI) should provide financial support to low-resource countries, including using the Pandemic Emergency Mechanism and other existing channels. Donors and development partners should give priority to financial and technical support to low- and middle-income at-risk countries/communities to help them build these capacities, in particular, to improve early detection and control of the virus, limit the risk of transmission, and their ability to respond;
5. Countries, institutions, the media, and WHO should communicate regularly and pro-actively factual information on the epidemic, on how to prepare for and prevent infection, in a transparent, timely, accurate, and open manner, and should find ways to mobilise local organisations and communities at all stages of planning and implementing response activities.

If the PMB's recommendations are addressed directly to state policymakers, they are at the level of each economic operator and it is up to the directors to ensure that their organisation learns from the previous pandemic to strengthen its resilience in the face of future disruptions, pandemics, or other.

Increasing Boards' Involvement in Risk Management[8]

For the first time since the seventies, the world is confronted with an energy crisis, with some energy-intensive industries facing an almost 50% production cost increase, according to the latest IMF calculations. The energy shock may be here to stay. Even if the international situation was to improve, most forecasters expect commodity prices to remain high for at least the next two years.

While recent years have seen disruptions in the political, legal, and economic spheres, they have also experienced a continuous evolution as technological changes accelerate. Innovation, new business models, rapidly changing markets and technologies transform the competitive and industrial landscape and impact companies' strategic plans and prospects for long-term sustainable value creation. Tax reform has also created new opportunities and challenges for businesses.

Organisations risk-taking and risk governance remain a priority for boards, investors, legislators, and the media. Key institutional shareholders and consulting firms are increasingly taking risk governance issues seriously when considering their votes in directors' selections and regularly holding organisations to account on issues risk-related.

Risk management is no longer simply an operational responsibility of management. It has also become a matter of governance that falls directly under the supervisory responsibility of the board of directors. Several issues have remained critical over the years and provide an update to reflect new and recent developments including:

→ the distinction between risk oversight and risk management;
→ the high concern of institutional investors for risk issues;
→ tone at the top and corporate culture;
→ fiduciary obligations, legal, and regulatory frameworks, and third-party advice on best practices;
→ specific recommendations to improve risk monitoring;
→ legal compliance programmes;
→ special considerations regarding cyber security issues;
→ specific environmental, social, and governance (ESG) risk considerations;
→ forecasting of future risks.

While avoiding involvement in the day-to-day management of risk, the board will need to be aware of the type and extent of the organisation's key risks and require the CEO and senior management to be fully engaged in risk management. Through its oversight role, the board can send a message to management and employees that Global Risk Management is not an impediment to doing business or simply a complement to a company's overall compliance program. Rather, it is integral to strategy, culture, and business operations.

---

[8]Lipton, M., Niles, S. V., & Miller, M. L. (2018, March 20). *Risk management and the board of directors*. Wachtell Lipton Rosen & Katz. https://corpgov.law.harvard.edu/2018/03/20/risk-management-and-the-board-of-directors-5/.

Chapter 14

ERM and Companies' Failure

How Bankruptcy Risk Can Be Mitigated with Innovation & Efficient and Integrated Risk Management

Trust is at the heart of any organisation's resilience. In a complex and uncertain economic and social context with heightened competition, an organisation can only survive and grow by developing and strengthening trust in all its key stakeholders, starting with its economic partners but also the communities in which it operates.

The capital providers' community is a key stakeholders' community, both investors and banking institutions that must be reassured about the quality of governance and compliance with laws, regulations, and ethics in the entire organisation, starting with directors and officers. Trust, the cornerstone of reputation, is the only guarantee of the organisation's sustainability.

This is why strategic, tactical, and operational choices and decisions must focus on building trust in the organisation. The trust of internal and external stakeholders is therefore an essential component of the intangible capital of any organisation, i.e. its reputation.

In some difficult situations, such as those that could result from a still feared economic collapse as a result of prolonged lockdowns and the sounds of boots around the world. Some organisations may be forced to resort to collective proceedings, which, given the context, could be an appropriate decision. Legally, the risk is a harmful event whose occurrence is uncertain. In an uncertain context, the risk of bankruptcy must be constantly anticipated.

The acceptance of the difficulties of the enterprise and their anticipation by the use of collective procedures therefore remain paramount in the face of the risk of bankruptcy. Reconciliation with the trust of stakeholders and employees should also be considered. However, even in a difficult environment, the risk of bankruptcy results mainly from a lack of anticipation and ultimately results from deficiencies in risk management at all levels within the organisation. This is why the establishment of a robust and mature ERM programme is the ultimate insurance against bankruptcy as the main factor in strengthening stakeholders' trust.

Enterprise Risk Management in Today's World: A Current and Futuristic View of the Complexity, Resilience, Responsibility and Tools in ERM, Part B, 163–169

Published under exclusive licence by Emerald Publishing Limited
doi:10.1108/978-1-83608-392-420241014

Risk Appetite & Tolerance – The Role of Board Members[1]

It is important to understand the distinction between appetite and tolerance because these are two concepts too often confused. According to the Institute of Internal Auditors (IIA), 'risk appetite' and 'risk tolerance' set limits on the risk an entity is willing to accept. However, there are some important differences between risk appetite and risk tolerance.

- → Risk appetite is a statement that takes into account the levels of risk-taking that executives consider acceptable. Risk tolerance is more narrowly defined and establishes an acceptable level of variation in performance objectives to achieve strategic objectives.
- → Risk tolerance, on the other hand, is the overall degree of deviation from its risk appetite that the organisation is willing to tolerate.

In the aftermath of the financial crisis of 2008–2010, companies and their boards of directors faced new communication requirements on risk monitoring by boards of directors in the USA, Canada, and Europe. Unfortunately, many organisations implemented ERM to improve their risk management capabilities.

Focusing on multiple workshops organised for participants to identify potentially harmful events, assess their likelihood and consequences, record identified risks in 'risk registers' and record them on 'Heat maps' of risks coded by colour to facilitate the board's assessment of the top 10, 20, or 100 risks, or 'killer' risks.

In most ERM programmes, the diagnostic exercise is repeated at least annually and the results after updating the risk register are communicated to the risk board or committee. This ERM approach has been found, at best, to be sub-optimal, and even 'deadly' when companies have completely missed the risks that threaten them, because of a sequential approach that does not meet the needs in an ever-changing world.

Most of these initiatives did not target the core mission of risk management: increase the certainty that strategic and value-creating objectives, as well as fundamental objectives such as compliance and the production of reliable financial statements, will be achieved within the risk tolerance of the organisation.

While the primary purpose of ERM programmes is to identify, measure, and report on key corporate risks, internal audit departments too often continue to use traditional evaluation approaches, developing 'risk-based' audit plans and providing subjective opinions on 'control effectiveness'

This approach addresses only a very small portion of the risk universe that boards of directors should focus on annually. Currently, few internal audit services use generally accepted risk assessment methods in their audits, taking into account the full range of 'risk treatments', including the sharing of contractual

[1]See Tonello, M. (2012, December 17). *Board oversight of management's risk appetite and tolerance. The Conference Board, on Monday*. https://corpgov.law.harvard.edu/2012/12/17/board-oversight-of-managements-risk-appetite-and-tolerance/.

risk insurance and risk avoidance. This is why they do not provide administrators with the necessary information to make informed decisions.

While risk governance objectives may vary from company to company, following its risk governance responsibility, each board should ensure that:

1. Risk appetite implicit in the business model, strategy, and execution of the business is appropriate;
2. Expected risks are proportional to expected rewards;
3. Management has implemented a system to manage, monitor, and mitigate risks and this system is appropriate given the business model and strategy of the company;
4. Risk management systems inform the Board of Directors of the main risks faced by the company;
5. An appropriate risk awareness culture exists across the organisation;
6. Risk management is recognised as critical to the successful execution of the strategy.

During the company's annual planning cycle, the Board of Directors should require management to identify critical strategic objectives and targets with the highest compound achievement uncertainty, including the specific risks for a given objective and associated estimates of the likelihood and consequences that threaten the achievement of these objectives, particularly in terms of return on capital.

In addition, the board should plan the time required to discuss the organisation's risk appetite and risk tolerance, including risk-taking decisions that could lead to erosion of working capital as was the case for the 2008 financial crisis, and the negative consequences that can result from regulatory violations of all kinds.

Gaps in ERM – Impacts and Remedies[2]

Poor risk management can have serious consequences for an organisation. Whether it's delays in projects or the lack of measures necessary to contain threats – one way or another, no organisation of any nature or mission can afford the ultimate risk of bankruptcy and in any case compromise its resilience.

Below is a summary of the main impacts of poor risk management and how to address them:

- ***First Impact:*** Poor risk management ends up delaying projects and possibly leading to failure: waste of time, an incomplete project, and even in case of completion, loss of value. Ultimately, this generates a loss of resources.

Action required: Implement risk management strategies in projects. This will help identify and prevent risks that could cause the entire project to fail. At the

---

[2]See Finance GAB. (2018, November 19). *The impacts of poor risk management? What can you do about it?* https://www.financegab.com/personal-finance/the-impacts-of-poor-risk-management-what-can-you-do-about-it/.

same time, robust methods should also be integrated so that the project team knows what to do when a hazard is detected and who is in charge of decisions to take appropriate action.

- ***Second Impact:*** Generally, customers do not want to engage in high-risk actions. They want to keep abreast of what is happening and what is being done to mitigate threats to the company.

Action required: Customers must be considered in risk management strategies so that they are aware of the measures taken to protect them and their investments. They must be kept informed of the current scenario and how risks are tracked.

- ***Third Impact:*** Risk management requires financial resources. If the risk turns out to be a real problem for the business, then the cost of dealing with it is much more than you ever thought. When the risk is not identified, the budget is overspent. In a project, the team tries to find funding before the project stops.

Action required: Always develop budgets and include items that are directly related to the project risk. If there are management activities in the Emergency Fund, they should be cancelled and this will help keep the project budget on track and not use it for other activities.

- ***Fourth Impact:*** All employees must follow a process, use tools, and stick to ideal methodologies, in other words, take ownership of risk management. If the administrators do not comply then there will be poor results and increased costs of risk management.

User adaptation is an issue that happens because the process is too intrusive which pushes employees to find shortcuts to follow their method. When techniques are not effective enough, managers must find alternative solutions to ensure sufficient control is maintained.

Action required: Communication is the answer to clarify to the employees how they work, still, it is necessary to ensure that the process put in place reflects the cultural environment and is feasible. If there is a legal issue, it is best to have a lawyer provide advice in difficult situations.

- ***Fifth Impact***: If there are too many threats, the company's opportunities will be lost, or the inefficient and slow management process will reduce all the expected benefits.

Action required: Ensure that risk management efforts are sufficient across the enterprise. Best practices that fit seamlessly into the culture of the organisation must be adapted and employees should not be involved in unnecessarily complicated processes.

- ***Sixth Impact***: Unforeseen risks can significantly slow down the project since it takes a long time to understand and assess them. Then, create management plans to identify and address risks.

The delay is also due to time spent on risk management activities, resulting in other scheduled tasks being on hold.

Action required: As delays tend to occur due to undiagnosed adverse risks, it is essential to identify them early. Workshops are required throughout the project. In addition, sufficient time is required for risk management activities and additional time for high-risk projects.

- ***Seventh Impact***: Regardless of the nature of the organisation, reputation is a key asset. Clients, and all stakeholders, must have confidence in the organisation and its ability to adequately address risks. Partners, especially clients, maybe the main risk to the organisation. Poor diagnosis can affect or even destroy the productivity of the body.

Action required: A robust risk assessment process strengthens the organisation's reputation. It is also crucial to maintain good communication/consultation with key stakeholders.

- ***Eighth Impact***: Poor risk management also has a huge impact on human costs. Threats and opportunities will cause anxiety, impacting operational decisions. Poor risk management causes anxiety among employees. Lack of confidence and inability to cope with risks could lead to misunderstandings between different levels of employees.

Action required: It is essential to hold specific sessions for employees who are responsible for risks. This will help them to open up and communicate the problem, but we still need to ensure that someone who understands human psychology leads the session.

Risk management must be efficient, that is, based on good practices, and encouraged by employees who can keep their heads cold and make rational decisions even in stressful situations. Failing this, the organisation could face many challenges but they could be addressed through suggested actions to strengthen the resilience of the organisation, even in a complex, volatile, and highly uncertain world.

- *ERM, Innovation, and Reduction of the Risk of Bankruptcy* [3]

Employees' culture and experience in innovation are closely linked to an organisation's overall success in innovation. Fear is a constant for almost all practitioners, but there are wide disparities in the nature and intensity of this fear, as well as in how companies mitigate its negative impact.

The innovation imperative for survival is accompanied by the need for a comprehensive and integrated approach to risk to anticipate the risks that will emerge from these innovations. For this reason, the conclusions and recommendations of

[3]See Zwen, A. A., Al-daamee, W. A. J., & Hindee, A. H. *The role of risk management in reducing organizational collapse – Analytical study at Iraqi Southern Cement Company.* University of Kufa College of Administration & Economics Business Administration Department. https://www.researchgate.net/publication/330656289_The_Role_of_Risk_Management_in_Reducing_Organizational_Collapse_Analytical_study_at_Iraqi_Southern_Cement_Company.

the study cited above go far beyond the scope of the company analysed and can serve as a basis for feedback for any manager concerned with setting up an efficient ERM programme to the risk of bankruptcy of the organisation for which he/she is responsible in particular as part of an innovation strategy.

- ***Main Conclusions:***

1. Failure of certain organisations, in particular industrial sectors, is due to the absence or deficiencies of independent risk management that carries out its activities labelled as risk, risk analysis, risk assessment, risk treatment, risk reduction and control, risk context analysis, and other processes.
2. Any organisation needs a scientific risk management methodology in the absence of a major system to deal with crises it may face, including financial crises.
3. Descriptive statistical results showed high levels, reflecting the attention and understanding of the sample of the risk management variable and the paragraph, which provides for the company to clarify the threat, the opportunity, or attitudes that give rise to the actual risks.
4. Research has revealed the importance of employee skills, which can be acquired through increased training, learning, delegation of authority, clear definition of responsibilities, and building trust.
5. Many organisations struggle to develop the creative capacity of their staff to think, analyse and interpret information.
6. An analysis of the failure of companies, particularly companies in Iraq, reveals the root cause of this failure in the absence of an integrated risk management system by these companies to counter the threat they face.
7. The instability of the business environment, particularly in Iraq, and the growing uncertainty that businesses must prepare for these cases are negatively affected.

The results of the statistical analysis showed that there is a statistically acceptable and negative correlation and relationship between the risk management variable and the regulatory collapse. The results of the statistical analysis showed a statistically significant impact related to the risk management variable in the organisational collapse variable.

- ***Recommendations:***

The organisation:

1. Should seek to increase the skill level of the working groups through increased training and learning, delegation of authority, definition of responsibilities, and building trust among its staff.
2. Needs to develop a scientific risk management methodology that helps it prepare for crises facing organisations, including current financial crises in the country.
3. Must address past crisis experiences to build a culture of learning from crises.

4. Must draw on the company's expertise and expertise from the company's administrators and consultants and experts to address crises affecting industrial companies.
5. Have leaders who provide the technology and potential to help each employee acquire the knowledge needed to work.
6. Have leaders who deploy an effective information system to understand and act on the company's competitive future.

Finally, directors need to pay close attention to the innovation programs of the companies. They ensure that a culture of risk management does not inhibit but encourages innovation initiatives by facilitating them through a climate of serenity despite the violence and the ruptures of the world.

Part 4

ERM for Tomorrow

Chapter 15

Managing Risk in the Metaverse*

The term 'Metaverse' is credited to author Neal Stephenson of his science fiction novel *Snow Crash* in 1992. The novel imagined the next iteration of the Internet where realistic virtual avatars connect through environments of virtual reality (VR) and realistic 3D buildings. Since then, advances in technology have allowed the development of the metaverse with a combination of computers, portable technologies, and machines, such as VR headsets, augmented reality (AR) glasses, sensor movement, and game consoles where users can 'live' in a universe digital.

Today's Internet experience is a two-dimensional scrolling and browsing experience on a screen. On the other hand, the metaverse is in 3D, which makes it possible to 'walk' through both worlds intertwined using connected glasses or headphones that result in the construction or participation in any desired universe in the digital world. In more simple terms, instead of browsing through a clothing store or online store, the website is transformed into a three-dimensional shopping centre or a building where users can interact as in-game characters or avatars.

The concept has been embraced by technology enthusiasts but insofar as it satisfies a desire for a decentralised virtual world and offers a place that is aligned with the physical world, the metaverse has now begun to penetrate the mainstream landscape.

The core of the Metaverse, also known as Web 3.0, is the evolution and generation that tracks the current Internet, including how users control their online identities and their digital assets through blockchain and crypto-currencies.

In the metaverse, each user has his avatar, analogous to his physical self, to experience an alternative life in a virtual world that is a metaphor for the real world. To achieve this duality, the development of the metaverse must go through three sequence stages, namely (I) the digital twins, (II) the digital natives, and finally (III) the coexistence of physical–VR or surreality.

*Metaverse combines the prefix 'meta' (meaning transcendental) with the word 'universe', used to describe a synthetic and hypothetical world linked to the physical or real world.

Enterprise Risk Management in Today's World: A Current and Futuristic View of the Complexity, Resilience, Responsibility and Tools in ERM, Part B, 173–184

Published under exclusive licence by Emerald Publishing Limited
doi:10.1108/978-1-83608-392-420241015

How to See Trust in the Metaverse?[1]

When an organisation decides to enter the metaverse, it could face a major new challenge: The old rules for gaining trust in your transactions, assets, data, and experience of brand and above may not apply. This challenge was born because the metaverse is evolving to become a new three-dimensional digital world, unbound by geography and currently without clear rules and regulations. In this world, the organisation and its stakeholders will be able to interact in new ways: buy and sell, recruit and train, collect and monetise data, sign contracts and enforce them, sponsor events, monetise virtual products, and more.

The following guidelines can help move forward with confidence in an immersive digital world, where it might be possible soon to conduct many real-life business activities, and some new too.

- ***The economy of the metaverse: building new modes of verification***

Most metaverse platforms encourage the use of crypto-currencies, tokens non-fungible assets (TNT), and other digital assets, which could soon become the main metaverse form of value exchange. It can also pose a trust challenge. Traditional intermediaries (such as banks and clearing houses) may not be affected.

Regulators may not have a good idea of these transactions and do not have a clear jurisdiction over them and the exchanges that represent them. Like the value is stored in crypto wallets, and that digital asset pools are traded and managed under smart contracts, hackers could potentially siphon assets by exploiting flaws in infrastructure or code software.

Risk postures may need to be revised, improving all three lines of defence (activities, risk management, and internal audit) with the necessary skills to verify transactions and regulatory compliance for digital assets. As for transactions in traditional financial services, these new transactions will require trusted third parties for additional control and verification.

- ***Navigate an interoperable metaverse: update data strategies:***

The ultimate goal of the metaverse is to become fully interoperable: customers and employees will likely be able to take their identities, assets, experiences, and data from one platform to another one day. Although nothing is certain at this time, it is expected that they can shop anywhere, browse social networks, and attend any meeting. The idea is that the current system of 'walled gardens', where each supplier of the platform controls the data and sets the rules, disappears.

Even a movement partial towards a relaxation of the transitions between the platforms can create new trust challenges. Without walled gardens, an organisation and its partners risk losing data control. Thus, it may be necessary to consider a new approach in data collection, governance, analysis, and security – an approach

[1]For this development, see *Trust and risks in the metaverse: 6 key considerations*. https://www.pwc.com/us/en/tech-effect/emerging-tech/metaverse-trust-and-risk-considerations.html.

that can follow stakeholders wherever they go, while protecting their privacy and inspiring trust that encourages data sharing.

- ***Governance in the metaverse: rethinking security***

The metaverse will need rules to govern security, user interactions, tax collection, data governance, regulatory compliance, and more. These rules are not yet established, but already, metaverse platforms can pose new governance and security challenges.

A new, less centralised digital world will offer new avenues of attack for malicious actors, including on connection devices such as portable devices. Three-dimensional experiences could make some cyber-attacks deeply traumatic. New metaverse-specific crime types are also emerging, such as 'pump and dump' ETFs and other investments fraudulent in the metaverse involving project-specific cryptographic tokens.

Suppliers and partners will need to be reassessed. Platform providers and cyber security companies may not have updated their security guide for the metaverse. Consideration should also be given to working with regulators to help shape the metaverse rules that follow. Need to update on Decentralised Autonomous Organisations (DAOs) – built on rules voluntarily agreed upon by a computer program that runs on a blockchain – which will likely play an increasing role in metaverse governance.[2]

- ***Who's who in the metaverse: understanding and shaping identity***

In the metaverse, users are expected to own their digital identities, with data, history, and assets they can use anywhere. It would be different from today's Internet, where customers and employees can have an identity just for a specific company, a particular platform, or a specific application. The assets and metaverse organisations will also have identities what belong to them and will travel through the platforms.

One way is to help consumers decide which aspects of their identity to share, allowing them to be anonymous or pseudonymous. Companies or third parties can also perform this role on their behalf. In the event of a lack of control over the key players' identities, it will probably be more difficult to trust them and protect them against phishing and other fraudulent activities.

- ***The metaverse experience: protecting against misinformation and abuse***

The customer experience and the 'employee' experience will change when offered through a VR or extended reality (XR) headset. Users can expect new sights, new sounds, new moves, and potentially new emotions. A breach of privacy or assault could be escalated, if it occurs when immersed in a three-dimensional world.

---

[2]A decentralised autonomous organisation (DAO) is an emerging form of legal structure that has no central governing body and whose members share a common goal to act in the best interest of the entity. Popularised through crypto-currency enthusiasts and blockchain technology, DAOs are used to make decisions in a bottoms-up management approach.

When stakeholders enter virtual spaces, they will expect to be protected by the organisation. If they suffer from abuse or misinformation in the metaverse environment of an organisation, its brand/reputation could pay a high price. A key way to instil trust in the metaverse is that the presence of the metaverse aligns with the values and purpose of the organisation.

- ***The persistent metaverse: building trust for when nobody's looking***

Even when there is no one, it is always there: it is true for the physical world, and it is assumed to be true for the metaverse as well. Even after customers or employees have withdrawn their VR or XR headsets, any activities they participated in will persist. The contract smart devices will continue to enforce business agreements and assets.

To ensure that virtual activities, investments, and company presence can work as intended in this persistent digital world, it may require rethinking digital services and reinforcing monitoring and controls.

What Are the Risks of Recreating Reality in the Metaverse?

Millennials already live online, from their digital representations hosted on social media platforms to online shopping for their hobbies or needs. The infrastructure is already there. But even as projects, start-ups, and large companies hope to cash in on the metaverse trend, all generations need to take the time to think and wonder about the risks to come.

- ***Is this real life or just a fantasy?***

South Korea is now experiencing a new phenomenon. With the rise of property prices, socio-economic inequalities, and dire career prospects following the devastating impact of the coronavirus pandemic, the MZ generation is racing towards the metaverse. In the metaverse, buying and selling parcels of land becomes suddenly a very real possibility and when combined with the monetary value of the real world, it serves as a levelling force in a society where the odds are not necessarily equal.

South Korea, as well as other markets like the Philippines, where citizens flock to virtual worlds like those offered by Axie Infinity, show how persistent structural inequalities cause people to look for alternatives.

- ***Is the digital divide widening?***

Similarly, when it comes to accessing the metaverse, what about the inequalities that could happen there? Much has been said about Facebook's foray into space, in large in part through its Oculus business unit. Critics were quick to point out that the entry of big tech into the metaverse only distracts from the principal fundamentals of the rise of Web 3.0, a more decentralised and fairer online ecosystem.

With so many aspects of life now being lived online, through education, career, and even dating, levelling these infrastructural access points to the metaverse will be critical.

- ***Is there a bug in the matrix?***

French philosopher and sociologist Jean Baudrillard coined the term hyperreality, the state in which reality and simulation are so intertwined that the distinctions between the two are lost sight of.

Eventually, if it turned out that the idea of the metaverse simply became reality in itself, whereupon should it be based? If 'Snow Crash' is to be taken as a warning, what the world finally knows is the rise of city-states governed by the interests of large corporations – inequality eventually prevails, and the metaverse serves more as a virtual escape, of idealistic distraction from the ruins of reality. Are we then really far from '1984'[3]?

There is no shortage of prophets of doom, and some believe that the metaverse generates 'terrifying dangers', and that we must figure out how to control it now before it is too late. While some observers are sceptical of how the metaverse could turn out to be revolutionary, other believe our lives will change immeasurably, in the same way the internet did.

How to Manage Risks in the Metaverse?

In risk management, AI must be analysed from the point of view of risk. How was the technology created? How is she exchanged? What basic data are used? As organisations resort to blockchain technologies, understanding the mechanics of the ecosystem is essential for businesses (crypto-currency still involves contracts!).

Identity is an important concept. With the ability of devices, every human being has multiple personas. Is it a self-dominant identity? Can everyone choose who has or does not have access to its data? It is essential to understand the relationship with business partners, third-party vendors, customers, and customers of customers. Who should be presented in these experiences and to which identity to attach?

Data protection is essential because immersive experiences and equipment generate more data. Analytics and social media are one thing, telemetry from headphones is another. Who gets the data of every minute of facial movement, composition, and expression of the pupil? Bioinformatics (technologies used to collect, store, analyse, and disseminate biological data and information) is subtle enough to diagnose early Parkinson's disease or dementia. These data could have serious consequences on the confidentiality of medical data.

One must be fully aware of terrorism acts that could be perpetrated by the metaverse. Terrorist regimes force children to become radicalised through games immersive. Children are sensitive to feelings of power and would be coerced into participating in in-person military games. The US Army also uses video games as training and recruiting tools.

It is essential to understand the speed at which the business is changing. You should check with the financial director who spent internally on equipment,

---

[3]Science fiction novel by Georges Orwell written between 1945 and 1949 and published in June 1949.

traces the money, and thus see who is investing in services or technologies to create a prototype and begin its journey in the metaverse.

The metaverse has stimulated the creative economy (a software-enabled economy that enables creators to derive income from their creations). Creators can digitally group their work and call it an asset, and that's an abstraction. As for the IP (Internet Protocol Address) of each business, including how it generates and nurtures its brand, is it a digital asset in this economy?

However, just like the Internet today, there are inherent risks and security issues that need to be addressed as the world moves into the age of digital connectivity. While the full potential of VR worlds is still unfolding, metaverse security consultants urge caution in listing the top 10 risks the metaverse traveller will be confronted with:

- ***Cyberbullying and harassment***

The issue of mental health and mental well-being in the metaverse has made the news before. Cyberbullying remains a serious threat to young adults and teenagers. The effects of cyberbullying are well documented and can include everything from low feelings of self-esteem to suicidal tendencies.

- ***Mental disorders***

Other threats are more difficult to avoid in a virtual world. For example, advertisements are used to stimulate the development of many free games. The individual malware could theoretically replace ads with images that can induce motion sickness or even epileptic seisures. Such images could be streamed to a person's VR headset.

- ***Identity theft***

Many experts are concerned about the possibility of identity theft becoming even easier in the metaverse if strict security measures are not implemented. The flight ID is already a multi-billion dollar industry in the real world; according to one study published last month, losses related to identity theft amount to approximately 24 billion dollars. The number of cases has increased by more than 50% compared to the figures of 2020, according to cyber security research.

- ***Unauthorised data collection by organisations***

Legitimate companies also collect personal information. However, VR has the potential to take information gathering to a point that can be at no limits for some people. For example, VR headset could allow third parties to collect more sensitive personal information, such as voiceprint data, biometric information, and even facial geometry.

- ***Ransomware attack***

Ransomware is a type of malware that can encrypt your personal information files and prevent you or anyone else from accessing them. It will then display a message urging you to pay a certain amount of money to get your data back, hence the name ransomware. You can probably imagine how problematic this could be in a metaverse parameter. Any metaverse profile contains much more information than a simple standard social media profile; it will also contain all kinds of sensitive information. Imagine not being able to access your bank accounts or even your data.

- ***Evolution of the perception of the real world***

A study by researchers at Stanford University[4] found that VR and AR, two of the cornerstones that will form the basis of the metaverse, can impact how people perceive the real world. For example, the participants in this study avoided sitting in a chair where they had seen an avatar generated by a computer sit in their AR environment.

- ***Deepfake videos***

In a world that thrives on the consumption of information, experts worry also false information campaigns disseminated by audio and video clips that threaten the security of our country. Deepfakes are video or audio clips that have been manipulated to look like someone else. Deepfaking works the same way as face swapping but uses sophisticated artificial intelligence algorithms to collect data on individuals from different angles so they can be overlaid with the existing video.

- ***Social engineering attacks***

Social engineering involves psychologically manipulating people into disclosing sensitive information. With the amount of personal data that will be stored in the metaverse, it could become a gold mine for hackers looking to sell personal information on the Dark Web. Ultimately, the basis of the security management metaverse will be education. Even with the best security system, if the operator does not know how to use the system or if he is irresponsible, it will not help the organisation.

- ***Risks specific to shared spaces***

The metaverse is driven by bringing people together. Although in some ways it may be a good thing, it can also present concerns. On today's Internet, you can find groups of like-minded people and create fantastic communities. In the metaverse, however, one must also interact with people who have opposing ideals. Studies have shown that people act differently in the virtual world versus the real world. This manifests rather strongly in the games world of massively multiplayer online role-playing game (MMORPG), where experienced players tend to denigrate players and even bully other players.

- ***Validation of new applications***

Just as on the Internet today, new applications have the potential to cause havoc in our digital lives. In a metaverse context, however, the damage can become even more disastrous with the sheer amount of sensitive data that will be preserved.

---

[4]For this development, see *New Stanford research examines how augmented reality affects people's behavior*. https://news.stanford.edu/press-releases/2019/05/14/augmented-realitavior-real-world/.

Therefore, measures should be developed to check whether all new applications contain malicious code.

The list will surely grow and evolve as we build our real virtual lives where almost everything will be gradually realised in the digital world[5] and it will become increasingly essential for the risk-management team to recruit millennials, likely the only ones with the skills to identify and assess risks in the metaverse!

How to Address Digital Security in the Metaverse?

Many are raising concerns on the subject of potential risks in an environment where the boundaries between the physical and virtual continue to fade. Therefore, it is necessary to build trusted ecosystems within the technologies developed for the metaverse. These trustworthy ecosystems will result from the integration of algorithms, structures, frameworks, regulations, and policies in hardware and software development cycles to address the distinct elements of security, privacy, and privacy security in the DNA of technology.

These trusted ecosystems will help create a stable, inclusive, and purposeful existence of a virtual and immersive existence.

- **How might these risks play out in the metaverse?**

At the heart of the concept of the metaverse is the idea that 3D virtual environment that is accessible and interactive in real-time will become the transformative medium of human engagement. For them to become practical, these environments will depend on the widespread adoption of XR.

Even if it's not a fully immersive existence, a lot of people are likely to spend more time mixing offline and virtual interactions, moving towards a mixed reality (MR). Privacy and security breaches can compromise security interactions and users. For example, it could take the form of a person who poses as a doctor to gain access to surgical room technology for digital surgeries.

- ***Where are we on digital risks today?***

By stepping back and observing the current digital environment, the risks of harm are already increasing. According to the latest Global Threats Assessment Report from WE Protect Global Alliance, 1 in 3 respondents (34%) to its global Economist Impact survey, was asked to online sexually explicit acts that he/she was uncomfortable with during his/her childhood. Additionally, the Internet Watch Foundation saw a 77% increase in content 'self-generated' sex of children between 2019 and 2020.

A comprehensive approach to security as the metaverse emerges will rest on public–private partnerships bringing together governmental, industrial, and academic experts, and private citizens. It is essential as digital hazards in the metaverse will be felt as more real depending on how our brains interpret the

[5]For more information, see the video Metaverse Security Center et la certification Certified Metaverse Security Consultant (CMSC). https://metaversesecuritycenter.org/.

immersive experience; Mary Anne Franks, president of the Cyber Civil Rights Initiative, in an article about VR and AR, mentions that research indicates that violence in VR is *'much more traumatic than in other digital worlds'*.

- ***How might the risks be exacerbated in the metaverse?***

Many current risks could be exacerbated in the metaverse. First, depending on how these digital spaces are governed, there are risks of unwanted contact in a more intrusive multimodal environment. Today, if someone we don't know or with whom we don't want to communicate contacts, he communicates by message, friendship or otherwise trying to communicate with us on platforms like Instagram, Facebook, etc. His ability to communicate is mostly limited to spreading text messages, photos, emojis, etc.

Harmful content that proliferates too quickly in today's digital lives can result in the metaverse to more graphic, 3D, and unwanted oral content that feels more intrusive and has a greater impact due to the multi-sensory nature of the environment in which it is propagated.

The rise of virtual currencies can often present another challenge in the proliferation of harmful content and activities online. For example, it is claimed that the children use their avatars to do lap dances in virtual strip clubs in exchange for virtual currency, 'Robux'. Cryptocurrencies are a popular option for those who buy child sexual exploitation material (CSAM) because their control is decentralised and their independence from financial institutions also ensures anonymity, according to an Active Fence report.

Given the role that digital currencies are supposed to play in the metaverse, financial incentives and payment structures that lead to the proliferation of harmful content are likely to increase in size and complexity with the transition to WEB 3.0.

- ***So, what can be done to contain these threats?***

Many companies, academics, experts from civil society, NGOs, and regulators, advocate enacting laws, and establishing new regulations for what is prohibited in the real world is also criminalised in online spaces. For example, Bumble is pushing to criminalise cyber-flashing. Their CEO, Whitney Wolfe Herd has asked lawmakers: *'If indecent exposure is a crime on the streets, then why is it not on your phone or computer?'* (World Economic Forum, 2022).

Human rights lawyer Akhila Kolisetty said India, Canada, Grenada, Britain, Pakistan, and Germany were among a small number of countries that banned image-based sexual abuse when private photos are shared without consent. Many countries do not have laws against emerging forms of digital abuse such as 'deepfakes', where the face of a woman or a man can be superimposed on a pornographic video and shared on messaging platforms (Louisot, 2023).

Many countries lag in these regulatory mechanisms and functions. The same is true for protecting children online. Updating laws to apply them in a digital context will be a key element of the governance of the metaverse.

We should become fully aware of how the software and hardware components of the technology are constructed to include the security elements to protect the integrity of the content developed.

- ***How would it be possible to ensure that this will not be a recurring occurrence in an essential virtual infrastructure?***

For Brittan Heller,[6] a specialist in technology and human rights:

> The platforms of virtual reality and augmented reality need specific terms of service for immersive environments, depending on how this technology interacts with our brain. We cannot simply apply existing social media rules to the Metaverse. This is important because the governance of platforms in the digital world must regulate behaviour, in addition to content.

Currently, one of the most common forms of governance in the virtual world is a reactive and punitive form of moderation. This does not prevent damage from occurring in the first place and often the consequences can be circumvented as bad actors become more sophisticated in how they toe the line policies. Finding ways to encourage better behaviours and perhaps rewarding positive interactions could become a bigger part of a safer digital future.

Who are Those Who Would Still Doubt the Strategic Importance of the Metaverse?

Many factors are driving investor enthusiasm, including continuous technologies progression of the infrastructure required to run the metaverse; favourable demographics actors; increasingly customer-focused marketing and engagement consumers; and increased market readiness as users explore the first version of the metaverse, largely powered by the game (some games with tens of millions of active gamers), with emerging apps encompassing the socialisation, physical fitness, commerce, virtual learning, and others.[7]

And for those who still doubt the reality of the metaverse, and especially its impact on the lives of organisations in all sectors, two illustrations in the insurance sector should convince them to reflect on its potential reality for their markets and their partners soon.

- ***Why does AXA choose to invest in the metaverse?***

AXA France takes its first steps in the metaverse thanks to the acquisition of a plot, from The Sandbox, a Hong Kong-based video game company. This is the first actor of the French financial sector (banking and insurance) to have

---

[6]*Technology and human rights specialist and founder of the Centre for Digital Civil Rights*. https://www.wired.com/story/what-mark-zuckerberg-gets-wrongand-rightabout-hate-speech.

[7]See *Value creation in the metaverse. The real business of the virtual world.* McKinsey. https://www.mckinsey.com/fr/our-insights/value-creation-in-the-metaverse-the-real-business-of-the-virtual-world.

established himself in this new virtual world. Through this initiative, the insurer puts into practice its ambition to better understand this universe and to animate its AXA Tech, Digital, and Data community of more than 2,000 people.

AXA France plans to create sharing spaces for its employees and customers on the metaverse and welcome hundreds of new talents. The French subsidiary of the insurance group will be accompanied by The Sandbox, Excelsior, and Metaverse Studio, for the development of his plot.

- ***Why does the Roam enter the metaverse?***

The Roam (Association of Mutual Insurance Bodies) announces the creation of its own pace in the metaverse. Called 'MetaRoam', developed in partnership with the start-up French Work Adventure. The space is accessible to its 71 members of mutual insurers since 4 July 2022. It is therefore for these mutual insurance companies a shared entry path in the metaverse.

Aware of the importance of the metaverse as a relational channel of the future, Roam is embarking on this universe to introduce its members to the web of tomorrow. Once familiar with this ecosystem, mutual companies will be able to think about how to exploit the potential of the virtual world.

So, What Can We Expect from the Metaverse and Will it Revolutionise Life?

With the metaverse, there are new building blocks in place, like the ability to host hundreds of people in a single instance of a server (the idealistic predictions of metaverse assume this will increase to thousands or even millions at a time, but that might be too optimistic), or motion tracking tools that can distinguish where a person is looking or where their hands are. These new technologies can be very exciting and futuristic.

Some limitations may be impossible to overcome. When technology companies like Microsoft or Meta show fictional videos of their visions of the future, they often tend to gloss over how people will interact with the metaverse. The VR headsets are still bulky, and most people suffer from motion sickness or physical pain if they wear them too long. AR glasses face a similar problem, in addition to the not-inconsiderable question of understanding how people can wear them around in public without looking like big boobies. And then there are the VR accessibility challenges that many companies turn a blind eye to.

Since Facebook's rebranding, the concept of the 'metaverse' has served as a powerful vehicle to repackage old technologies, overemphasise the benefits of new technologies and capture the imagination of speculative investors. But money pouring into a space does not necessarily mean a massive paradigm shift is just around the corner, as everything from 3D TVs to delivery of Amazon drones and Google Glass can testify to it. The history of technology is littered with the skeletons of failed investments.

Many companies have used already the cloud as their primary infrastructure and have allocated their workforce accordingly, so moving the desktop to a virtual world reality is a logical next step (even if the technology still has to evolve considerably to make the idea of being in RV 8 hours a day attractive).

The metaverse is still far from being a concrete, everyday reality, but when it enters daily life, not all brands will be able to grow in these competitive markets. Like the people who control them, avatars will have little time, opportunity, and energy to interact with companies. Brands that hope to thrive in tomorrow's metaverse must explore its limits and possibilities today and bet before there are no more virtual worlds to conquer as Nike and Gucci already did.

Our future digitised will be more interactive, more alive, more embodied, and more multimedia, thanks to the existence of powerful computing devices and smart wearables. Fundamental challenges and the research agenda are to shape the future of the metaverse in the next decades. There is an urgent need for, with the help of young millennials and the global community of risk managers to address these issues, as well as those relating to the climate, to justify and confirm their prospective role of the benefit for the economic and governmental actors to ensure a safer and fairer world.

Chapter 16

Rethinking the ERM for a New World

The evolution of ERM will lead to whole-of-government approaches to seize opportunities and contain threats. However, the success of ERM in a new normal depends on its ability to rest on a global philosophy and a fundamental objective ultimately summed up in respect for life.

As businesses struggled to adapt quickly, the crisis of the first part of the third decade of this century revealed three common sources of weaknesses in risk management:

1. Risk governance and oversight;
2. Business resilience; and
3. Cyber risk.

Governance, business resilience, and cyber-risk management are like the three feet of a stool; if one is weak, operations or even the entire enterprise can fall. Skills development in each area will become a competitive advantage as companies try to move forward in this decade.

Against the backdrop of infectious diseases (e.g. smallpox, cholera), the future of risk management will focus on the ability to move beyond past thresholds for collaboration and cooperation to meet the challenges of the day. Once this pandemic is behind us, there will be new pathogens threatening the future of the human species, especially if one takes into account the acceleration of the rate of deforestation and the increase in the number and concentration of domesticated animals from which new diseases often emerge.

Progress in risk management results from building institutional capacity to increase the likelihood and magnitude of opportunities (positive risk) while decreasing the likelihood and severity of threats (negative risk). These advances are both epistemological and cultural, which means that humanity:

→ increases his knowledge; and
→ uses this new knowledge in a way that serves the common good.

Enterprise Risk Management in Today's World: A Current and Futuristic View of the Complexity, Resilience, Responsibility and Tools in ERM, Part B, 185–196

doi:10.1108/978-1-83608-392-420241016

Rethinking ERM Implementation as a Socio-Technical Challenge[1]

ERM provides an integrated framework for all risk management activities, which facilitates the identification of such interdependencies. Proponents of an integrated risk management approach believe that ERM is more effective than traditional risk management (TRM) approaches thanks to the synergy induced by the consideration of interdependencies between individual risks. Indeed, while an individual approach to each risk reduces the volatility of benefits caused by a single source, an integrated approach reduces volatility at the corporate risk portfolio level.

The implementation of ERM is a complex and difficult project that involves both the technical and social systems of an organisation. ERM teams must therefore take into account not only technological issues but also social issues that can be under the radar. However, researchers and practitioners tend to approach ERM implementation as a technical problem; they evaluate, for example, the impact of ERM programmes on value, determine the organisation's risk appetite, and assess risk from an ERM perspective. This perception of the mechanism of change as purely technical prevents researchers and practitioners from taking into account the social issues related to ERM implementation.

Existing frameworks, such as ISO 31000:2018 or COSO-ERM 2017, implicitly assume that the organisation's employees are competent enough to collect, assess, and rationally use the information to make the right decisions for risk management within the organisation. As a result, they do not mention central concerns such as employee buy-in, the willingness of members of the organisation to invest the time and effort needed to acquire new knowledge about risk management. These frameworks do not take into account the organisational climate that promotes or hinders changes induced by the implementation of the MRA, nor the ability of the various functional services to adapt their structures to facilitate its implementation.

Due to the choice of ERM promoters to develop a strictly rational model, these frameworks oversimplify the complexities of human action and do not take into account human impulses or social meanings by which actors interpret and act on the behaviours of others.

In addition, ERM does not appear as a block, but as a set of distinct risk management approaches that must be integrated into an enterprise-wide implementation strategy. For this reason, successful implementation of ERM requires considerable effort to transform an organisation's work system to enable inter-organisational integration of data, business processes, and policies. Such a transformation involves two potential challenges:

- ***The first challenge is operational integration***: The ability of leaders to establish closer coordination between the distinct operational activities of different

[1]See Jean-Jules, J., & Vicente, R. *Rethinking the implementation of enterprise risk management (ERM) as a socio-technical challenge*. file:///d:/Users/LOUISOT/Downloads/RethinkingtheImplementationofEnterpriseRiskManagementERM.Accepted-1.pdf.

individuals and working groups within the organisation leading to a unified business process.

- ***The second challenge is social integration***: The ability and the willingness of different actors, working groups, or business units to work together to develop, establish, and implement integrated business processes.

Therefore, ERM can be described as comprising two interdependent subsystems: a technical subsystem and a social subsystem. The social subsystem concerns the attributes of people (e.g. attitudes, values, competencies), relationships between people, reward systems, and authority structures, while the technical subsystem deals with processes, tasks, and technology needed to transform inputs into outputs. Here, technology must be understood broadly as the body of knowledge about the relationship between machines and the process by which the organisation transforms inputs into outputs.

As a socio-technical system, the mechanism of change can also be considered as a practical system in which practical problems arise, a gap between the current state and the desired state, as perceived by the social group concerned. These are practical issues constituting challenges and barriers to ERM implementation.

ERM implementation requires a strategic direction that underpins it, a framework that specifies the vision and purpose of the project. The vision serves to set clear objectives and the overall direction of the project. It should be established at the design stage and be consistent with the project definition, scope, objectives, and strategy. A compelling strategic vision provides the criteria that support the implementation of ERM. And, it can only be effective with the support of leaders marked by the designation of a 'champion' member of top management.

With the implementation of ERM, the range of skills required for employees involved in risk management is broadened as they must collaborate with members of other functional units and provide access to their private garden, i.e. their information and expertise. The implementation of ERM results in significant changes in individual and collective behaviours, training and, learning. Therefore, simply adjusting the work system – organisational structure and work practices – is not enough; attitudes and behaviours also need to evolve.

As a result, employees involved are called to make a personal investment provided certain conditions are met. First of all, employees must feel involved in the ERM project, and cognitively engaged. Employees who are heavily involved in their work devote considerable effort to achieving organisational objectives. Therefore, they will make the necessary efforts to develop their competencies, skills, new attitudes and behaviours essential for the success of an efficient ERM.

In addition, the operational employees have an invaluable understanding and knowledge of the organisation. These resources must be leveraged through management practices that trigger and encourage employee active participation. The integration of procedures for all employees is essential to the success of any ERM programme.

Activities related to the development of ERM cross the boundary between the organisation and its external context since they cover both exogenous and endogenous risks. Indeed, many risks come from outside the organisation and the implementation of ERM includes the design of mechanisms to respond to changes in the external context. In summary, ERM involves complex interactions between functions and business entities, internally but also with external partners, and all influential stakeholders.

ERM processes are therefore integrated with other organisational processes, routines, resources, and capabilities to be implemented daily in all aspects of the organisation's life. While the success of ERM rested on in-house integration activities, existing specialised skills, databases, and technical and management systems, it also involves integrating the main components of logistics networks.

Therefore, the implementation of ERM requires a systemic approach at all levels, strategic, tactical, and operational. It is with this in mind that the development of cindynics systematically integrating socio-cultural factors through hyperspace of hazard analysis is now more relevant in this complex and volatile world where stakeholders' perceptions of risk have become a key factor of ERM.

Governance, Risk Management, and Strengthening Resilience

In the present world context, organisations must quickly assess the lessons learned since 2020, identify the most significant risks, and plan for new unknown or emerging risks. Organisations need to strengthen the role of risk management and pay more attention to risk governance within their board and their executive team.

Risk governance involves top management and the Board of Directors, and requires a governance framework that identifies the key risks executives and corporate officers must monitor. A company's financial health, the safety of its people, and its ability to be agile and maintain critical operations all depend on good risk management strategies and resilience plans.

Organisations should consider assigning risk management to one executive, a risk champion. Thus, the Risk Manager is directly involved in management and board-level discussions to ensure they have a full understanding of the organisation's risks. He/she also interacts more efficiently with business leaders to manage risk across the organisation and develop more mature risk strategies.

Risk management professionals can perform some of this work themselves by making an effort to work in different units of the organisation to develop greater visibility. If part of top management, risk management is in a better position to address all risks the business is confronted with, especially critical risks for the organisation's activities. Therefore, the risk champion/professional can:

→ Set priorities and quantifying risks;
→ Determine the risk tolerance of the enterprise;
→ Work with business units and senior management to reduce risk;
→ Ensure that appropriate tests are performed;
→ Developing risk transfer plans and providing risk reporting at the appropriate level.

The key objective is to strengthen the resilience of the organisation. Operational resilience includes crisis management, business continuity planning, and disaster recovery, including data backup and recovery. Enterprise Resilience Plans (ERP) help management teams and operational staff adapt business operations and strategies as needed in the event of a disruption requiring rapid operational change.

Despite warning signs of a possible global pandemic, very few organisations have developed resilience plans that have prepared response to the virus. Many companies had delays in decision-making at the beginning of the pandemic, causing significant operational disruptions. Cybersecurity risk management was a secondary element. Many businesses have struggled with managing remote work and new ways of doing business. The lesson for the rest of the decade and beyond is that companies can no longer defer managing resilience risks.

Operational resilience plans should:

→ Identify dependencies between business units, including business continuity plans and communication strategies;
→ Identify potential impacts on critical operations (including from third parties, partners, and customers); and
→ Integrate cyber-security requirements.

Testing resilience plans should be end-to-end and reporting should be provided to the organisation's top management, the Board of Directors, and the branch managers.

Resilience plans are important because they allow the company to pivot quickly, be agile in times of crisis, and remain competitive. Clients expect the organisation to be operational under all circumstances. Of course, workplace activities cannot stay the same after a crisis like the COVID-19, the war in Ukraine, the war in the Middle East, and the accelerating consequences of global warming. Companies must learn to manage their workforce remotely to get back on track and get started quickly.

Strengthening Cyber-Risk Management

Given the extent of organisations' reliance on technology, IT infrastructure deserves special attention in resilience plans. Technical disruptions can wreak havoc, destroy brands, result in regulatory fines and lawsuits, and have a significant impact on market share so integrating technology into resilience plans can be a decisive differentiator.

Most operational changes involve cyber risks. The pandemic has created an opportunity for cybercriminals who have found data centres and security operations centres without staff, staff working remotely (often unsecured), enterprise data transferred to online storage, and an increasingly vulnerable workforce.

When IT and cybersecurity personnel are not physically on-site and staff are working remotely from their homes using personal computers, this impacts the company's ability to respond to cyber incidents.

Cyber-risk management is about maintaining an enterprise security program aligned with best practices and standards and that tracks operational changes and the current threat environment. Cybersecurity programs include many activities that must be performed on an ongoing basis and reviewed regularly to ensure that they keep pace with evolving threats.

Large companies should conduct cyber-risk assessments every year, and small- and medium-sized businesses should do so at least every two or three years. In the event of a crisis, IT and cyber-security teams should be involved in planning the required operational changes. Modelling can be used to 'repeat' proposed changes and detect unintended consequences, including cyber risks.

Assessments based on the new environment and testing of response, backup, and recovery plans can help identify potential cyber risks and identify areas of the cyber-security programme that must be modified to maintain important risk controls in place and ensure the recovery of system activities.

Too often, IT managers do not participate in decision-making processes regarding operational changes. To be effective, it is necessary to ensure enterprise security programmes keep pace with operational changes, cyber-security teams work closely with Risk Management and Backup and Business Restart plans are aligned with the new threat environment.

Finally, technological developments require a robust and more coherent data protection framework, supported by rigorous enforcement, to ensure continued trade and economic development without imposing unnecessary barriers to the flow of information. Companies are required to introduce an integrated privacy policy and an effective data retention policy, as with GDPR in the European Union.

The reinsurer decided to share his risk expertise with CertX's expertise. This collaboration with the Swiss certification company – in which Munich Re has held a stake since 2021 – has created a unique solution: CertiAI.

CertiAI independently and objectively validates AI systems or AI solutions already used in production. For this, the program performs an analysis based on six different factors: fairness, autonomy and control, transparency, robustness, Cybersecurity, and, finally, data protection. This certification is a guarantee of quality for customers, investors and supervisory authorities (Oehrli, 2022).

Risk Management and Strategy[2]

The rise of risk management to the strategic level has been accelerated by the pandemic and global disruption since the beginning of the decade, but there is still a need to understand the interactions between the two activities. Strategy interacts with risk management at different levels, especially when diagnosing and defining the treatment programme with the objective of organisational resilience. There are several factors in considering these interactions:

---

[2]See *Stratégie et gestion de risques en entreprise*. Predica. https://www.institutdesactuaires.com/global/gene/link.php?doc_id=689&fg=1.

- Risk management is stimulated by increasing risk aversion, reinforced by new regulations. Systematic purchase of insurance covers must give way to approaches based on more mature risk management practices. The strategic approach proposes an effective approach by breaking down risk analysis into autonomous modules and by validating/invalidating hypotheses.
- Organisations are exposed to risks in many key directions. Analysing the cost and frequency of impacts makes it possible to rank risks from marginal to critical. Risks are split into three categories: transferable, controllable, and valuable. Each category determines management principles to be implemented.
- One risk can command treatments at 3 levels. Depending on the organisation's risk profile, the appropriate treatment tools to implement may differ. Risk transfer can take the form of contracts with partners, insurance contracts, financial engineering contracts, or the use of financial markets. For companies listed on the stock exchange, taking risks into account in the business model helps improve their financial valuation. Best practices help organisations assess their risk management maturity.
- The traditional purpose of risk management was to optimise the impact/cost ratio of the organisation's risk portfolio. However, the objectives of risk management are split to apply to each function. A strategic approach to risk leads to a combination of alignment, possible treatments, and dissemination of risk culture. Risk management is increasingly becoming a key function of corporate management.

Strategic analysis proceeds in steps:

- The first step consists of breaking down the problem into autonomous modules:
  - → A model identifies the factors and splits them into homogeneous groups. Thus, to analyse an insurance contract, a cash flow chart helps group together the factors related to various types of risks, those related to the macroeconomic and/or regulatory context, those related to the company itself, etc.
  - → Each of the identified modules must be autonomous, that is to say, lend itself to an analysis independently of the other modules; collectively they must be exhaustive, that is to say all the factors are taken into account, preferably each of them in a single module.
- The second step consists of applying an inductive and non-deductive approach. In other words, i.e. formulating hypotheses, then conducting the analyses (i.e. searching for information, constructing mathematical models, etc.) that will allow validating or invalidating the hypotheses. In this context, invalidating a hypothesis is as significant as validating it.
- Then, for the most complex problems, the general approach can be iterative. Before being able to formulate hypotheses for the resolution of autonomous modules, the strategic analysis must be used first to break down each module into sub-autonomous modules and ensure through validation/invalidation of hypotheses the validity of the scheme.

Innovations for ERM[3]

The discipline of ERM is still relatively young. Some organisations derive considerable strategic value from their ERM efforts, and they continue to improve their risk-monitoring processes over time. Unfortunately, other organisations have experienced 'adjustments' to their ERM processes, often struggling to achieve measurable results so that MRA is useful for decision-making within the organisation.

In an overview of practical next steps that business leaders can consider to strengthen the strategic value of their risk governance three elements are to be considered:

- ***ERM is still developing:*** The development of ERM concepts has helped organisations focus more on the risk-reward relationship. ERM is designed to help business leaders look to the future to better anticipate gaps in their organisation's processes that could impact the progress of their strategies and the optimisation of their goals.

In many organisations, leaders have not fully understood the importance and value that ERM can bring to strategic decision-making. The level of infrastructure investment to improve risk management processes remains relatively low compared to other infrastructure investments (such as investments in accounting and financial reporting systems).

- ***Risk governance must be reviewed:*** Business leaders need to innovate in their ERM programmes by strengthening risk governance processes. ERM processes that focus on the interconnection of elevators, engage business leaders, and take on greater leadership responsibilities concerning risk are likely to add value. The four key pillars of risk governance are:
  - → **R = Response**: Top Management should strive to proactively respond to the most important issues facing the organisation in a cross-functional manner (*rather than waiting to determine reactions to problems once they arise*).
  - → **E = Excellence**: Embracing excellence means accepting change as a constant in life and continually seeking opportunities for improvement. All functional areas should focus on changing conditions and assumptions that generate threats and opportunities.
  - → **R = Responsibility**: It is the heart of governance. Each risk category under each functional area represents a 'cornerstone' to link to ownership and accountability.
  - → **L = Leadership**: Decisions are made by leaders hence it is essential to:
    - choose connected leaders who are engaged with each other,
    - develop a leader's mindset regardless of position, and
    - ask leaders to adopt a mindset focused on the risks and issues facing the organisation.

---

[3]Seeking Innovations in ERM. (2021, August 3). *An interview with Jim Traut by Mark Beasley*. https://erm.ncsu.edu/library/article/seeking-innovations-in-erm?utm_campaign=ERM%20%7C%20Thought%20Papers&utm_medium=email&_hsmi=146173808&_hsenc=p2ANqtz-_m70GdoaXi-qLdZxwoEpVpHDDe9wSQFdX5kG4Pv5GZqu-sAsP3myf1o-j7BWN5KVCh2axh5WTBA4-lb0ZBljZbU-6K3Qw&utm_content=146173808&utm_source=hs_email.

- ***ERM value creation must be enhanced:*** The recent catastrophic events helped destroy silos within organisations. Leaders have been forced to 'look at' risks and this perspective should be maintained. Specifically, leaders came together to address the challenges of the pandemic, which brought confidence. This collective effort and trust have strengthened the culture of many organisations and fostered innovation in risk governance.

Directors and officers can take four practical actions to make the most of their efforts in ERM:

1. Engage functional managers with Board leadership and risk oversight responsibilities. Communicate this chart to all Chiefs;
2. Map risks by functional area category and link these categories to each functional area;
3. Update regularly the list of key risks for risk categories (risk register);
4. Identify current risk levels and actions to address gaps.

Rethinking Disturbance Impact on Risk Management Tools and Processes[4]

Now more than ever it is critical to understand the definition, sources, and economic, social, and operational impacts of disruption on an organisation. The ability to detect and recognise the sources and impacts of threats and disruptions, whether they result from technological innovation, changes in societal values, or unintended consequences of pandemic disease control, is essential to build resilience.

A 2018 study conducted by St. John's University found that most leaders believe that risks are increasing as well as disruptions. Even before COVID-19, there were significant disruptive factors that were primarily due to quantum improvements in hardware and software applications, which significantly reduced the 'cost of failure' when a particular application or approach did not meet the target level of commercial monetisation. Here are some of the key disruption factors:

- The cost of computer hardware has dropped sharply over the past 10 years, making it much more affordable to purchase or lease large computer capacities and processing, and faster, more powerful, and robust computer systems.
- Software running on more powerful computing equipment can process more robust and capable of processing large datasets and performing complex statistical analyses of 'big data'.
- The cost of default has been reduced to modest, otherwise negligible levels, allowing for the conduct of very complex computational experiments or the development of applications without worrying about the economic costs of the experiment or the commercial viability of the application.

[4] *Rethinking the impact of disruption on enterprise risk management tools and processes.* RIMS Executive Report. https://www.rims.org/about-us/newsroom/news/rims-executive-report-rethinking-the-impact-of-disruption-on-enterprise-risk-management-tools-and-processes.

With lower system hardware prices and robust enhancements and connectivity of analytics and machine learning software, there has been a trend towards the development of 'platforms' systems where a constellation of tools and capabilities are grouped to enable a broader user base. For platforms to succeed, they generally need to be open source to allow users to develop minimally viable products or tools that can be used in a specific product/service context. The platform may allow innovation or disruption, depending on the application.

Disruptions are increasingly becoming a business model. Echoing the link between high risk and disruption, a recent BRM summit at the Center for Excellence in ERM at St. John's University found that 95% of senior risk managers believe that digital disruption is one of their top risks in the immediate future.

These innovations generate disruptions; the world seems to have entered an entirely new era, the digital age. Risk managers must not only identify emerging and disruptive risks but also ensure that they fully understand the impact of these risks and disruptions on the business model.

As the speed and consequences of disruptions increase, risk managers will need to improve their awareness of disruptions, strategy, business model, and value creation. Risk managers must also review their risk awareness questions after rethinking or rebalancing the organisation's business model when the organisation has to go through disruptions or even ruptures.

Key risk indicators (KRIs) related to the impact of the business model can be very useful here. While it is true that other next-generation tools need to be developed to help companies and risk managers interpret and understand disruption risks. Some potential tools for risk managers in managing risks related to disruptions impacting strategic objectives are:

- Research and analysis of emerging risks;
- Disruptive risk research and analysis;
- Value chain analysis and calibration;
- Business model and value creation analysis;
- Adapt strategy to expected competitive and economic environment;
- Value analysis workshops;
- Black Swan workshops;
- Bow tie strategic analysis;
- Mind maps;
- Strategic framework;
- Engagement wheels;
- Thorough risk analysis;
- Analysis of pre-event situations;
- Scenario analysis;
- Workshops on game theory;
- Opportunities workshops.

An organisation may choose to respond strategically and innovate by creating its wave of disruption. The role of the risk manager is different in this case. For example, while Ford or GM may conduct black swan workshops on the future of thermal engines, Tesla, building electric cars, is probably not concerned. As a result, competencies and toolsets may also need to change. Here is a list of possible tools for this area:

- Build a disruptive culture of innovation;
- Ensure greater involvement in new strategic directions;
- Apply Ducker's business theory, challenge long-standing assumptions;
- Provide an overview of new strategic initiatives, become an agile organisation, or develop agile practices.

Since organisations have a limited amount of resources, they need to understand how innovation projects fit into an overall portfolio of innovation risks. An additional technique is to examine any unsuccessful project and understand what the risk assumptions were so that new projects can be rethought to better manage that risk.

A factor to consider is the extent to which a 'disruptive' entity would seek to displace or replace the current status quo of economic or commercial enterprises using risk management techniques. Organisations are facing an increasing range of risks in a world of increasing uncertainty. Risk managers play a key role in helping organisations identify not only emerging risks but also disruptive risks. Disruptive risks, carriers of ruptures, have a major impact and can threaten the whole organism in its very survival.

To identify these risks, organisations need to change their methods of detecting emerging and disruptive risks. They need also to modify their toolset to increase their ability to link these disruptive risks to the business model. Once the organisation reacts and builds its future or even a wave of disruption, the risk manager can become a valuable partner in helping it identify and manage the risks associated with plans, objectives, and initiatives, optimise resource allocation, increase the chances of success, in a word, build resilience.

Resilient, Dynamic, and Relevant: ERM in a New Risk Universe[5]

Every year, the CRO[6] Forum releases radar of emerging risks that took specific importance since 2022 as the world entered an era of renewed turbulences. Emerging risks are characterised by a high degree of uncertainty in terms of impacts and probability and have a significant potential impact on the Insurance businesses, investment categories, and/or operations.

Key trends are assessed and updated during the group working sessions. The 'digitisation of consumer behaviours' is merged with 'Demographic and Social Change'. 'Urbanization and social change' is merged into 'technological

---

[5]See Resilient, dynamic and relevant: ERM in a new risk environment. *Financier Worldwide Magazine,* November 2020. https://www.financierworldwide.com/resilient-dynamic-and-relevant-erm-in-a-new-risk-environment#.YvpLmRzP1PY.

[6]Emerging Risks Initiative. (2022). *Major trends and emerging risk radar*. https://www.thecroforum.org/wp-content/uploads/2022/08/ERI-Risk-Radar_2022_update.pdf.

developments and impacts on society'. Besides the in-depth examination of the description of all the risks on the radar including antibiotic-resistance, Artificial intelligence, Autonomous machines, Biodiversity loss, Climate (physical risk and transition risk), failure of critical infrastructure, cyber risks, crypto-currency, new infections, endocrine disrupters, pollution, terrorism, genetic engineering, international conflicts, etc., some new risks have also been added to the radar:

- ***Climate Engineering (including carbon storage):*** Climate engineering, also known as geoengineering, is the large-scale international response to climate change in the Earth's climate system.
- ***Lower Earth Orbit Space Risk:*** Lower Earth Orbit (LEO) is an essential space resource that depends on many aspects of our current lifestyle. Global communication systems – including satellite broadband coverage, earth observation systems, including satellite imagery and weather forecasting, and global positioning systems all rely on satellite infrastructure in LEO.

ERM rests on an extremely broad definition of risk that is not limited to risks that have purely negative consequences. This allows organisations to constantly review and revise their risk tolerances and risk appetite for various types of risks while considering how risks accumulate or interact.

With ERM, organisations can plan and implement policies and procedures that optimise their objectives for a given period and adjust them as they evolve to reflect changes in the context, for example, supporting dynamic growth. To curb threats and identify new opportunities for innovation, ERM programmes facilitate more effective coordinated risk management across various functional areas.

While the volume and types of risks (geopolitical, regulatory, cyber, and technological) have increased exponentially in recent years, the role of a CRO is still not recognised enough. As the upheavals continue, there is a consensus that ERM needs to become more involved and integrated into the day-to-day operations of organisations, it is no longer a secondary or separate function but is everyone's business.

Chapter 17

Managing Emerging Risk: An Ardent Obligation in a Complex and Volatile World

The recent collision between two major risks, black swans or grey rhinoceros requires the leaders of all economic and political actors to reconsider their register of emerging risks. This vital exercise must be conducted with all stakeholders' involvement, including their partners in fragile logistics networks.

The ISO planned standard on the subject will not be published and replaced by a technical document that should be published in 2023 or 2024. So it is up to other professionals to suggest a definition: emerging risks are new or changing risks that are difficult to quantify and that could have a major impact on society and the industry. Moreover, these are risks whose potential danger is not yet known reliably and whose implications are difficult to access. As a result, it would appear that emerging risks, by nature, do not lend themselves easily to modelling. Their uncertainty stems from a lack of data as all new risks, and also scientific, technological, or socio-political changes.

In this context, insurers and reinsurers are inevitably led to consider these risks as opportunities for growth. Emerging risks are classified into six main groups: economic, environmental, societal, technological, geopolitical, and, to a lesser extent, legal and regulatory risks; but some experts recognise only three categories: technological, crystallising, and aggravating:

- ***Technological risks***: they are truly new, emerging from new technologies and processes. This category would include risks associated with cyber-technology, genetically modified organisms, nanotechnology, e-cigarettes, driverless cars, etc.
- ***Crystallising risks:*** They are not new, but their manifestation and implications emerge. In this context, attention must be on emerging losses as well as emerging risks. This category would include asbestos, aluminium, nano-particles, and other health risks.
- ***Aggravating risks:*** They are relatively well known, but their impact has become potentially more severe. This category would include climate change, pandemics, antibiotic resistance, terrorism…

Enterprise Risk Management in Today's World: A Current and Futuristic View of the Complexity, Resilience, Responsibility and Tools in ERM, Part B, 197–210

doi:10.1108/978-1-83608-392-420241017

These categories are not sealed boxes; some emerging risks contain elements of the three categories. However, each category requires a different set of actions.

The main challenge with emerging risks lies in modelling and quantifying their potential impacts; they have become an essential component of any ERM programme in an increasingly complex and volatile world.

What Is an Emerging Risk?[1]

The concept of emergence explores processes of risk diagnosis that have sometimes comfortably settled in a formalism of periodic review. It is also indicative of a change in awareness of the issues of responsibility in the face of a risk appetite that must be chosen and assumed within the framework of ESG risks.

- ***Emerging risk definition***

For example, climate risk, is it an emerging risk? On a global scale, this is a risk that has been present for millions of years and has evolved significantly over many years. At the corporate level, is this an additional risk? For some, it may prove an additional threat or opportunity.

Comparing a company's register in 2010 and 2021 shows that new scenarios emerged with probability levels based on experience and/or risk perception. What are the origins of these new scenarios?

- ***Changes in risk exposure related to the environmental and operational context***

In the case of health risks in food chains, it is clear that the expression of risks in these processes is not the same as it was 30 years ago. The processes have evolved and some of the risks that existed in the past are no longer present and vice versa. In this case, the evolution of technologies makes cyber-risks significant.

Finally, an organisation can evolve, for example by developing in new geographical areas, and thus make new risks appear for it that are not emerging for all players. Thus, some risks disappear or decrease significantly and others appear in new ways.

- ***Strengthening regulation***

Any regulatory evolution is a potential source of risk even if it is meant to contain certain risks:

→ Which risk register for a data-sensitive company has not integrated data issues, including personal data under the influence of GDPR within the European Union?

→ Who has not systematised the risk of corruption, especially for organisations subject to specific legislations in the context of international activities, like SAPIN 2 in France?

[1]Bonmichel, B. *Qu'est-ce qu'un risque émergent?* https://blog.ifaci.com/quest-ce-quun-risque-emergent-par-beatrice-bonmichel/.

The normative framework generally follows changes in the environment (economic, social, societal, geopolitical, etc.), and new risks will have to be addressed in the future, driven by regulations. This is the case for CSR issues that are developing under the influence of regulatory developments but also under pressure from stakeholders.

- ***Interactions between risk and response(s)***

Actors' reactions to risk also contribute to the potential evolution of risks. The development of artificial intelligence, genetics, or the automation of processes, which are supposed to reduce certain risks related to manual processes or fraud, are also risk sources not yet completely identified. Complexity makes action-reaction chains harder to identify.

- ***Better understanding of causes and changing areas of vulnerability***

As the fourth industrial revolution is underway, there is increasing interconnectivity between systems and the use of new technologies in organisations; the stakes are significant and the 'threat' linked to a system interruption is identified. On the other hand, if the expression of causes evolves, the key concepts attached to the causes are generally already understood: lack of procedure, separation of tasks, competence, limit excesses, etc., remain classic risk exposures.

The causes may evolve in their modality of expression; the consequences nevertheless remain relatively identical, even if they are of varying magnitude: financial, legal, commercial, human, etc., they are generally correctly anticipated; of course, the main difficulty is to anticipate their importance and/or measure it.

- ***How can the emergence of new types of risk be managed?***

Monitoring of indicators remains the key point of the system as they allow to:

→ Understand significant strategic developments (business development, outsourcing, automation, etc.);
→ Understand changes in the external and external environment (risk factors);
→ Analyse losses and incidents (recurring or occasionally significant);
→ Manage the adequacy and effectiveness of key controls.

The emergence is the risk or the stakes of its steering to accompany the strategy? While the expression of risk may be emerging, the reasoning associated with risk reflections remains traditional, perhaps too!

- ***What are the emerging risks in healthcare?***[2]

Here are some of the factors that give rise to emerging risks:

→ Introduction of new substances or technologies into the living environment,
→ Unknown health effects *(lack of experience, unknown biological mechanisms, etc.)*;

---

[2]*Anticiper, la prise en compte des risques émergents.* https://territoire-environnement-sante.fr/thematiques/risques-emergents.

→ Cyclical increase in vectors of transmission of certain diseases *(potentially linked to a change in the environment)*;
→ Changes in populations at risk *(type, number)*.

Emerging risks are inherently highly evolutionary as scientific knowledge advances. Current issues include, but are not limited to:

→ **Endocrine disruptors (EP)**: substances capable of interfering with our hormonal system. Faced with multiple sources of exposure, the challenge is to understand the role played by these substances in the development of certain pathologies. Assessing their health effects is a scientific challenge and an important public health issue.
→ **Nano-particles, nano-materials**: particles or materials (natural or manufactured) containing a significant proportion of particles between 1 nm and 100 nm in size.
→ **Vectors**: these are, for example, insects or mites that can transmit certain infectious diseases (mosquitoes, ticks, etc.) by biting or biting. Their emerging character is linked in particular to changes in the environment and climate.

How Dynamic Risk Management Addresses Future Uncertainties?[3]

The digital revolution has increased the availability of data, the degree of connectivity, and the speed at which decisions are made. These changes offer a promise of evolution, but they could also lead to large-scale failures and security breaches, as well as rapid cascading consequences. At the same time, fuelled by digital connectivity and social media, reputational damage can trigger and spread rapidly.

Climate change is leading to massive structural changes in the risk-reward profiles of companies, which will accelerate non-linearity. Companies must take into account concerns about their immediate financial results and pressures from governments, investors, and society in general, not to mention the increasing frequency and severity of natural disasters.

Now, stakeholders expect organisations to take a stand on social issues, such as feminist and anti-racist movements. Employees are increasingly hearing about the company's policy choices and actions. The attention of regulators and authorities reflects the concerns of society in very broad areas, from data protection to climate.

The world is more interconnected than ever, from supply networks to information flows. But these links are at risk, due to geopolitical unrest, and most companies have not built strong enough links within the global system to allow them to continue to operate smoothly should connections be abruptly cut.

Businesses need dynamic and flexible risk management to deal with a rapidly changing world. The level of maturity of risk management varies depending on the sector and individual companies. Banks tend to have the most mature approach,

---

[3] *Meeting the future: Dynamic risk management for uncertain times*. McKinsey. https://www.reverso.net/traduction-texte#sl=eng&tl=fra&text=Meeting%2520the%2520future%253A%250ADynamic%2520risk%2520management%2520for%2520uncertain%2520times.

followed by companies in sectors where security is paramount, including fossil fuels, advanced technologies, and pharmaceutical specialties. However, beyond these key areas, virtually all organisations should update and strengthen their risk management approach with a dynamic approach to better prepare for the next normal.

- ***Detection of risks and weaknesses in controls:***

Organisations must both anticipate new threats and detect changes in existing threats. Today, many companies maintain a static, formulaic view of risk, with limited links to strategic or tactical decision-making.

They will need to anticipate, assess, and observe threats based on disparate internal and external data points. Dynamic risk management will therefore require them to answer the following three questions:

→ ***How will the risk landscape change over time?*** Some risks change slowly, while others can change and worsen rapidly. Regardless of speed, risks can be either cyclical and medium or structural and permanent. Most companies have focused on managing cyclical risks, i.e. back-to-normal risks, such as credit risk, that fluctuate with macroeconomic cycles.

→ ***How to prepare to meet the challenge of systemic risks?*** In today's world, the impact of risk can have long-term reputational or regulatory implications. Organisations must also determine whether the event that materialises the risk has an impact on their industry, the economy, and society in general, and the meaning for them.

For example, as companies host more personal data, risks associated with data breaches become more systemic and can impact millions of customers worldwide while taking into account the implications of GDPR within the EU.

→ ***What new risks will emerge in the future?*** Traditional risk identification approaches based on ex-post facts reviews and assessments will no longer be enough and new scenarios will be needed. Most organisations have not experienced historical losses from climate change, or significant reputation damages due to being on the wrong side of a social problem.

- ***Determination of risk appetite:***

Today, many organisations tend to think about their risk appetite in purely static and financial terms. They can fall into simultaneous traps of being both inflexible and reckless.

Going forward, they will need to establish a risk appetite aligned with values, strategies, capabilities, and the competitive environment. An effective ERM approach will contribute to dynamically delineate risk-taking, directly translating financial and non-financial principles and measures into a concrete vision of what the company will and will not do; for this they need to answer the following three questions:

→ ***What level of risk is acceptable?*** Organisations will need to adjust their risk appetite to reflect changing customer behaviours, digitalisation capabilities, competition, and global trends.

Geopolitical instability could increase consideration of counterparties and foreign exchange risk for the travel and infrastructure industries when considering engineering contracts, supply, and construction for multi-year megaprojects.

→ ***Should some risks be completely avoided?*** Companies need to draw clear lines about what is acceptable and what is not like crime, sexual harassment, etc. But for many risks, the frontiers are fuzzy, and every business needs a specific perspective based on a solid, objective evidence base. For example, will risk factors such as climate change make the risks of some businesses unsustainable?

On the contrary, a risk to reputation where there are environmental and social responsibility issues should lead to exit certain business lines. Companies will need to take positions on these issues and continually update them as contexts and databases evolve.

→ ***Does risk appetite adequately reflect the effectiveness of reduction measures?*** Companies are more comfortable taking risks when they have strong mitigation measures. However, the increased threat of new and serious non-financial risks challenges old assumptions about the effectiveness of these measures.

- ***Choosing a risk management approach:***

Today, many organisations rely on linear committee-based governance processes to make decisions about risk-taking, slowing down the process. In the next 'normal' world, organisations will need to make risk decisions quickly and flexibly, developing and implementing immediate or extended responses to avoid, control, or accept each risk.

Leadership should be actively engaged in decisions to determine which mitigating measures have proved effective, or not, in the past. Thus, the organisation can develop new approaches when needed to manage risk in today's world; the following questions need answers:

→ ***How to treat accepted risks?*** In the past, many companies have relied heavily on manual controls and human assessments of the effectiveness of risk reduction measures. This approach can generate excessive and costly levels of control in some areas while leaving gaps or insufficient controls in others.

→ ***How to respond in case of the occurrence of an event or failure of a risk reduction instrument?*** In the event of a major control failure, leading to a crisis, companies must be able to quickly switch to the human response mode supported by an action guide known to all. However, many companies have done little crisis preparation, based on the assumption that 'it won't happen here'.

Preparation includes the identification of potential negative scenarios and reduction strategies to be adopted before a crisis occurs, but also periodic simulations involving the Branch and the Board of Directors. Company strategies should specify when and how to escalate issues, crisis teams, resource plans and roadmaps for communications and stakeholder stabilisation, etc.

→ ***How to build resilience?*** Companies can learn from each event and each breach of control, thus refining processes and risk controls through a dynamic feedback loop. On a larger scale, companies have the opportunity to turn real crises into competitive advantages.

Business continuity, financial, and other plans can provide shock buffers. True resilience also comes from a diversity of skills and experiences, innovation, creative problem-solving, and basic psychological safety that allows maximum performance.

Five actions are needed to implement dynamic risk management:

- ***Reset risk appetite***: Shift risk from prevention and reduction to dynamic strategic enablement and value creation.
- ***Establish agile risk management practices***: Enable multi-functional teams to make quick business, innovation, and risk management decisions.
- ***Harness the power of data and analytics***: Using data to broaden the view of risk characteristics; Deploying algorithms to enable better error detection, more accurate forecasting, and micro-analysis segmentation.
- ***Develop risk management talent for the future***: Gain new skills and broad domain knowledge to foster a comprehensive understanding of the risk environment and strengthen risk management culture.
- ***Establish a true risk culture among operational employees***: Hold senior managers accountable for cultural gaps; link risk culture to day-to-day business activities and outcomes.

Risk levels are increasing, as are employees, customers, shareholders, governments, and all stakeholders' expectations and organisations need to rethink their approach to risk management to become a dynamic source of competitive advantage.

What Are the New Challenges for Hybrid (Combining Home and Office) Work?[4]

Agile measures have helped reduce operational disruptions. However, the urgency of implementation has significantly curtailed the normal audit process for information systems (IT) and data security policies and procedures, creating opportunities for new risks that need to be identified and addressed. The impact of recent crises has highlighted the potential for dramatic changes in how organisations assess, prioritise, reduce, and manage IT and information risks.

Organisations need to have a sense of how data is linked to processes, coupled with contextual measures aligned with business objectives. The resulting risk assessment allows for more informed decisions on how exposure affect business processes.

---

[4] *Navigating emerging IT risks in the hybrid work environment*. https://www.navex.com/en-us/resources/white-papers/navigating-emerging-it-risks-in-hybrid-work-environment/.

With a broader focus on business priorities and objectives, stakeholders can make informed decisions when allocating budget lines and resources to address potential vulnerabilities and understand how the operational implications of information-related risks can influence agile choices in the emerging hybrid environment.

- ***Understanding risk:***

The biggest challenge in an increasingly flexible hybrid work environment is its exposure to data exposure through 'permeable limits'. They are one of many risk vectors in a hybrid workplace, including:

→ ***Process awareness:*** When working on-site, employees can assume that their processes are governed by controls to generate alerts in the event of a potential incident. In a hybrid work environment, it is necessary to document the processes in place and determine how these processes are affected by remote or hybrid workers.

→ ***Asset awareness:*** It is the tracking and documentation of devices, such as computers, printers, etc., used in the office and those made available for remote work; it is important to know who is using these devices and whether they are configured to comply with protection policies.

→ ***Data awareness:*** It refers to data assets that are accessible in the office and remotely, identification of those that contain sensitive information, identification of existing data protection policies, and configuration of these policies for desktop and remote access.

→ ***Workplace awareness:*** In the rush to develop home workspaces, IT organisations may have overlooked some critical data protection protocols. For example, positioning screens prevent unauthorised persons from viewing sensitive data or implementing encapsulated virtual environments to prevent copying and pasting of text on the local desktop.

→ ***Role awareness:*** The organisation must have a clear idea of who has access to IT and data resources. Is access limited to internal staff? Are there third parties and other subcontracting partners? If so, do these external parties adequately protect data assets by following defined procedures and standards?

→ ***Attack surface:*** Focus on identifying areas through which a person can enter the network. Does the hybrid environment require new entry points that create new risks?

→ ***Compliance with agency policies:*** With a wide range of external guidance for the protection of information, organisations must ensure that the right data protection policies are defined and in place and are updated to reflect a hybrid environment.

→ ***Compliance training:*** No technological solution for risk management can eliminate the risks arising from the socio-technical impact of human input. Are people aware of data security issues and are they trained to process sensitive data when they are out of the office? Does the security training reflect the increased risks associated with phishing, malware, and ransomware?

Awareness of all employees is the foundation for an appropriate and effective ERM programme; keeping in mind, interactions between known and unknown risks can trigger major events.

- ***Guiding decision making:***

Awareness of exposures of all employees is the first step in prioritising investments and risk reduction efforts. Balancing the potential physical impact on the business with the cost of eliminating or mitigating these risks allows a risk analyst to prioritise efforts and optimise resource allocation.

Combine technology used to define operational actions with governance processes to produce reports and visualisations that can communicate value to all stakeholders.

- ***Solution criteria: How technology supports IT risk management?***

Organisations need to combine processes and technology to assess and prioritise IT risks. The complexity of this process requires developing criteria that may include, but not limited to:

→ ***Scope:*** Quantify the variety of IT, data, and environmental risks covered by a potential solution. Any offer must also allow the integration of several risk domains (third parties, business continuity) and understand how they affect global IT security.

→ ***Depth:*** The solution should capture the 'lineage' linking vulnerabilities and potential threats to the identified risks.

→ ***Relevance:*** To what extent does a given solution incorporate measures relevant to the company and provide insight into the most critical risks?

→ ***Historical perspective:*** Processes evolve and are affected by changes in the external environment. The risk management toolkit should examine how processes change over time as the organisation adapts to hybrid work arrangements.

→ ***Policy management:*** It is difficult to define and align enterprise data and IT policies – look for a product that helps manage, configure, and monitor policy compliance.

→ ***Training:*** Its importance cannot be overstated. A practical risk management solution will integrate monitoring methods and ensure the proper delivery of training.

→ ***'What if' planning:*** Given the complexity of the ever-changing risk environment, solutions should have the ability to understand how potential changes may impact different sectors, and explore how controls or risk management efforts can help address exposures.

→ ***Communication:*** Any IT risk management solution should allow the customisable presentation of aggregate parameters, adapted to different audiences, to facilitate the internalisation of the scope and scale of vulnerabilities and identified risks.

→ ***Answer:*** Once an incident has been identified, effective incident management solutions alert team members and facilitate investigations, root cause identification, and remediation.

→ ***Audit/Compliance:*** Finally, a solution should also facilitate the organisational development of compliance plans, the definition and implementation of controls, and the preparation of a control audit.

- ***Sustainable risk management in a hybrid work environment:***

The pandemic has also evidenced how quickly a company can transition to a home-based work environment, if necessary. Concerning the list of criteria and characteristics necessary for IT risk management, consideration should be given to adopting additional risk management solutions with four key characteristics:

→ ***Efficiency:*** Choose a solution that increases team and program efficiency by providing high-quality information and metrics leading to faster and more reliable decisions.
→ ***Effectiveness:*** Look for features that can increase effectiveness by integrating data from different systems and tools into the environment and visualise information in organisational contexts.
→ ***Agility:*** A comprehensive view of exposures to sensitive data allows teams to respond more quickly to adverse events.
→ ***Scalability:*** Seek a solution that can address the most critical challenges while laying the foundation for a broader Integrated Risk Management (IRM) programme.

In a hybrid work context, the organisations' resilience depends on strengthening their defences as part of an in-depth review of their cyber-risk management policies, including emerging risks.

Ten Critical Emerging and Market Risks to Consider[5]

Here are ten industrial sectors that could be faced with new and emerging risks in the medium range:

- ***Cyber complexity:***

It may take a long time for cyber risks to get off the list of emerging risks. While this is a well-known concern, cyber risk remains dynamic and complex.

Systemic risk will be subject to increased regulatory review soon, according to market participants. According to professional opinion, the focus will be on critical infrastructure industries such as financial services, energy, healthcare, and communications, and will spill over several other sectors.

- ***Trends linked to Cannabis:***

While concern about the use of cannabis, especially by employees, is becoming important in the United States, due to the gradual legalisation of its sale in different states, the problem has not yet touched the French market. However, large international operators should consider the issue before it becomes acute.

---

[5]Hemenway, C., Jergler, D., Simpson, A. G., & Wells, A. (2023, February 6). *10 emerging risks & markets to know about*. https://www.insurancejournal.com/magazines/mag-features/2023/02/06/705398.htm.

- ***Food network:***

The food supply system from farm to table is long, complex and, of course, extremely important. The network includes several trades. Their operations are different, but they depend on each other and insurance to manage some unprecedented risks.

Other risks facing the system include extreme weather conditions, labour shortages, transportation disruptions, material shortages, energy costs, import restrictions, safety requirements, wage pressures, government regulations, equipment failures, chemical exposures, liability issues, changing consumer tastes and cyber risks, not to mention human errors, mental stress, bad actors, the attitudes of employees and generous people's juries that grant broad compensation to victims in the sector.

Like businesses in other sectors, many also seek to reflect social responsibility in their operations. Insurers will need to know what monitoring and surveillance systems a company has in place and what changes it is making.

- ***Renewable energies:***

Solar and wind power outperform other forms of renewable energy deployed in North America, while the continent lags behind Europe and parts of Asia in developing offshore renewable energy sources.

Renewable energy, solar in particular, is on the rise because of its affordability and governmental incentives. In the United States with the Inflation Reduction Act, solar energy has grown at an average annual rate of 33% over the past decade, according to the Solar Industries Association, and this expansion leads to increased exposure to the risks of natural disasters.

The wind energy sector, the most widespread renewable electricity source in the United States, has also suffered many significant losses in recent years, including Hurricane Hanna in 2020 and Tropical Storm Nicholas in 2021.

The sector is expected to continue to grow in new sectors, such as offshore wind, clean hydrogen production, and low-income solar programs, and the report notes: Overall, there should be strong demand and attractive long-term incentives are creating strong headwinds, but there is still much turbulence to overcome.

- ***Environmental, Social & Governance (ESG):***

The ESG risk continue to be an important topic in all sectors, but being 'ESG and promoting a business as ESG' is not without risks. Moody's recently forecast an increase in ESG credit risk this year. The risks have been heightened by the current economic and political turbulence.

While ESG seems to be a hot topic, it may not be as important as some think. Bloomberg recently reported that the US ESG market is less than half the previously reported size. The US SIF Foundation reported sustainable assets totalling approximately $8.4 trillion in 2022, down from $17.1 trillion announced two years ago.

The European Union has started to remove ESG labels from funds under stricter rules in the region, and Asian regulators have also established stricter standards.

- ***Crypto-currencies markets:***

Months of turbulence in the crypto-currency sector have put down several major crypto investors, lenders, and exchanges that $1.3 trillion has been wiped out of the value of crypto tokens. Crypto Exchange FTX made the front page of bankruptcies after billions of dollars were withdrawn in three days, and fees were collected against its CEO (Reuters, 2023).

Recent developments have highlighted the cryptography market, which generally means increased regulation for the cryptography industry. The Securities and Exchange Commission is sharpening its teeth when it comes to cryptographic companies. Federal legislators have introduced bills to adjust the regulation of crypto-currencies.

The Federal Reserve, the Federal Deposit Insurance Corporation, and the Office of the Comptroller of Money (OCC) expressed concern about the safety and soundness of banking business models that are heavily concentrated in cryptography, and fraud and misrepresentation by cryptographic companies.

- ***Health – Home care and mental health services:***

In the healthcare sector, two subsectors in particular appear to offer opportunities: home health care and mental health care. The demand for these services is expected to increase even as they face challenges, particularly in staffing, to meet these expectations.

The mental wellness market will be fuelled by increased awareness of mental illness, more government initiatives supporting mental health services, the growing role of employers in the delivery of mental health services, the continued aging of the population, and a growing appreciation of the value of earlier intervention.

In terms of behavioural health, companies expect more newcomers to the field and established providers will expand beyond mild to moderate mental health conditions to address more severe conditions.

- ***Pet services:***

More and more owners like to pamper their pets with luxury items, gourmet foods, treats, and organic accessories, even Halloween costumes – pleasures facilitated by savvy online sellers and subscription services. They also buy supplements such as hemp sticks and fish oils for allergies. And, yes, there is such a thing as pet technology that includes self-cleaning litter boxes and collars with GPS trackers.

This labour-intensive industry faces its share of risks, including staff shortages and exhaustion, rising wages and rents, and increased competition. There are bites, scratches and kicks, strains, sprains, and back injuries. Liability proceedings are not so common and damages are limited.

- ***Political risk:***

Businesses are also concerned about the increase in disruptions caused by strikes, riots, and civil unrest, as the cost of living crisis affects many countries, according to the Allianz 2023 Risk Barometer. Overall in the United Kingdom and the United States, fewer business leaders feel well prepared to manage geopolitical risks and concerns about the possible consequences of war, including the risks of war and terrorism and economic unrest, compared to a year ago.

Inflation is a top concern according to the Beazley report, Spotlight on Geopolitical Risks, released in mid-2022. The report highlights that business leaders need to better understand their geopolitical risks and be prepared to mitigate them where possible. Insurers specialising in political risks, trade credit, and terrorism have a role to play in providing adequate coverage to provide the needed risk mitigation.

- ***Second-hand market:***

The second-hand market is expected to grow as a component of the Circular Economy.

The luxury resale fashion industry is gaining momentum, driven by consumer demand for second-hand luxury, the resilience of luxury buyers in an inflationary environment, and more affordable offers of luxury resale platforms. Luxury players like Balenciaga, Kering, Gucci, Valentino, and Coach have all stepped up their involvement in the resale space.

Many factors explain the growing popularity of second-hand according to the Professional Resale Association (NART); one of these growth factors in this sector is increased public awareness of recycling. The NART website explains: 'People prefer to ship, sell or give away their unwanted or unnecessary items rather than add them to the waste stream'.

What Lies Ahead for Emerging Risks in This Complex and Volatile World?

At the current pace of change, the world in the 21st century will experience 20,000 years of progress in just 100 years (World Economic Forum, 2023). This upsets the risk landscape and leads to an avalanche of new uncertainties and emerging risks that are essential for society to manage.

Emerging risks, whether unknown or not, can pose the greatest challenges to resilience, security, and business continuity. These 'new or increasing' risks may be related to different areas of activity, such as new processes, new technologies, new types of work environments, or social or organisational changes.

The development and implementation of ERM is a dynamic process in which each functional area experiments with new methods and procedures to establish integrated risk management routines and interacts with other functional areas. During this process, each functional area experiences new procedures locally, learns from other areas, and adapts to them. ERM is not a one-size-fits-all solution.

In each case, the Branch must decide on the content and configuration of an ERM solution based on the parameters of the internal and external context within which the organisation operates: the industrial sector and the competitive environment, and internal parameters, as the organisation's objectives and strategy. In addition, risks continually evolve as socio-economic and institutional environments evolve. The development and implementation of ERM result from a co-development process in which the identification, analysis, and assessment of risks follows a dynamic cycle of continuous improvement and change.

This provides a better understanding of the complexity of the adaptations to be made, including the type of dynamic capabilities that the organisation needs to leverage to achieve this in a proactive approach to managing emerging risks. Within this framework, it becomes essential to identify several socio-technical factors essential to the success of implementation, considered as a process of mutual adaptation between the mechanism of change and the organism.

By integrating these socio-technical factors, as well as other relevant factors as revealed by the organisational and technological innovation literature, more robust ERM models should be developed to explain and ensure the successful implementation of the ERM. The issue of leadership's involvement will always be the cornerstone of an ERM programme success.

Chapter 18

IAIS Provides Tools for Insurance Supervisors to Address Climate-Related Risks

> Rapid and far-reaching transitions across all sectors and systems are necessary to achieve deep and sustained emissions reductions and secure a liveable and sustainable future for all. These system transitions involve a significant up scaling of a wide portfolio of mitigation and adaptation options. Feasible, effective and low-cost options for mitigation and adaptation are already available, with differences across systems and regions.

This excerpt from *Synthesis Report of the IPCC Sixth Assessment Report (AR6)*[1] does not reflect the dire predictions of the scientists but stresses the urgency to act. However, these latest IPCC statements may be a wake-up call, citing 2026, just three years from now, as a pivotal year. Without a doubt, the pandemic has temporarily put the issue of global warming as the second most important concern of leaders. However, there seems to be a link between the two according to some theories.

Climate change is recognised as a global threat. It impacts human, societal, environmental, and economic systems due to rising temperatures and their consequences including rising sea levels and increasing the frequency and severity of natural disasters and extreme weather events. Climate change, as well as the global response to threats posed by climate change such as the reduction of greenhouse gas (GHG) emissions and adaptation programmes, can have a significant impact on the structure and functioning of the global economy and financial system.

Climate change and climate-induced risks are more and more recognised as a source of financial risks, with an impact on financial institutions' resilience, including insurers, and their financial stability. This is why the community of

[1]https://report.ipcc.ch/ar6syr/pdf/IPCC_AR6_SYR_SPM.pdf

Enterprise Risk Management in Today's World: A Current and Futuristic View of the Complexity, Resilience, Responsibility and Tools in ERM, Part B, 211–215

Published under exclusive licence by Emerald Publishing Limited
doi:10.1108/978-1-83608-392-420241018

insurers and reinsurers must carefully take into account not only this risk but also the impact of global warming on a range of risks, not just other natural hazards, but even fire and others that affect property and human beings.

In this environment, IAIS in partnership with the United Nations Forum on Sustainable Insurance (FIS), published a document that provides assurance controllers with concrete tools to strengthen their efforts to assess and manage climate change risks. The document is the first of its kind by a global standards body.

The document entitled *'Application Paper on the Supervision of Climate-related Risks in the Insurance Sector'*[2] provides recommendations and examples of good practices, in line with the AICA Fundamental Principles of Assurance (FPA), for assurance regulators to manage challenges arising from climate change. With this publication, IAIS[3] and SIF[4] aim to promote a globally consistent approach to climate risk oversight.

With the publication of the report, Vicky Saporta, President of the IAIS Executive Committee, said:

> IAIS is fully aware that failure to adequately manage the impact of climate change across the financial sector could jeopardize global financial stability and policyholders. The joint publication of this document by IAIS and SIF is intended to assist insurance controllers in their efforts to address climate change and other sustainability challenges.

For her part, SIF Chair Anna Sweeney said that 'through this publication, IAIS and SIF have developed an innovative partnership to increase oversight attention on the risks posed by climate change'.

Beyond the insurance supervisory bodies of most countries, since the IAIS comprises more than 200 jurisdictions, the document also proposes recommendations to insurers and reinsurers on how to manage their climate risks. It provides a framework for supervisors' investigation during their verification operations.

Finally, all risk management professionals should also become familiar with the new rules as they will have an impact on all insurance purchased by organisations, and not just those that cover climate risks. The implementation of the recommendations will have an impact on the allocation of assets in insurers' investment portfolios, and therefore their return; and their relations with the companies in which they are stakeholders will be impacted.

---

[2]Application paper on the supervision of climate-related risks in the insurance sector. https://www.sustainableinsuranceforum.org/view_pdf.php?pdf_file=wp-content/uploads/2021/05/210525-Application-Paper-on-the-Supervision-of-Climate-related-Risks-in-the-Insurance-Sector.pdf.

[3]IAIS – International Association of Insurance Supervisors, l'acronyme français est AICA.

[4]SIF – Sustainable Insurance Forum.

Only the main recommendations are outlined in this chapter, bearing in mind that they could become obligations in many countries if the members of the IAIS manage to convince their respective governments to implement them in their regulations.

Corporate Governance

When addressing climate-related risks, insurers and reinsurers are expected to integrate these risks into their overall corporate governance framework. For example, control functions (including risk management and actuarial functions) should give due consideration to climate-related risks and have the appropriate resources and expertise to manage them. To deal with changing risks, including climate risk, insurers' board's risk committee must identify the changing risk landscape and the possible ways to manage risk.

Insurers should include and assess climate-related risks as part of annual financial planning and short- and long-term strategic planning processes. Insurers should also ensure that climate change impacts are well represented in existing risk classes.

Insurers' strategic planning periods must be based on the risks of their insurance portfolio. There should be a good understanding and opportunity to discuss climate risks at the Board and Board level, including the Audit Committee and the Risk Committee.

Compensation can be used as one of many incentives to integrate climate-related risks into the risk management system. In this context, criteria used to calculate the amount of variable remuneration could include, among others, the management of climate-related risks within the insurer, for example through staff training or asset categorisation and performance. In addition, changes in the non-financial performance of investing companies could be a relevant indicator of the variable part of executive compensation.

Information Communication

Significant risks associated with climate change should be made public by insurers as required by regulation. Supervisors may use the framework of the Financial Stability Board (FSB) Working Group on Climate-Related Financial Information (CRFI) to develop best practices or set their supervisory objectives. Insurers should include in their reporting the extent to which their risk profile exposes them to the impacts of climate-related risks, as well as the measures or targets developed by the insurer.

The monitor requires insurers to disclose relevant and complete information promptly to provide policyholders and market participants with a clear picture of their business, risks, performance, and financial position. Public disclosures on emerging and emerging risks, including climate change risks, are of paramount importance to this objective.

By establishing disclosure requirements for climate change risks, the controller should take into account existing relevant requirements as well as proprietary and confidential information that could negatively influence an insurer's competitive position if made available to competitors. Controllers considering the introduction of mandatory climate change risk disclosure requirements could consider a range of approaches; and recognise the iterative nature of disclosure processes and the early stages of some aspects of climate risk assessment methodologies.

As the regulations allow controllers to meet requirements through general public financial reporting, supervisors may consider allowing insurers to add relevant climate information to these disclosures, where appropriate, rather than requiring duplicate disclosures for regulatory purposes. Insurers should describe the climate-related risks and opportunities they have identified in the short, medium, and long term, the impact of climate-related risks and opportunities on the company's business, strategy, and financial planning.

The information should include supporting quantitative data, where available and relevant, on their core activities, products, and services, including information at the business division level, area, or geography. Insurers should also indicate how the potential impacts of climate-related risks influence the policyholder, transferor, or broker selection, and whether specific climate-related products or skills are being developed, such as green infrastructure insurance, specialised climate risk advisory services, and policyholder engagement.

Insurers should provide information on the impacts of climate change on their operations and may be encouraged to provide information on the impacts of their operations on climate. This should allow stakeholders to understand the impact of climate-related risks on the insurer and vice versa.

Climate Risk Impact on Insurers, Reinsurers, and Insured

Climate-related risks are important to the insurance industry as they affect the insurability of the assets and assets of policyholders and the activities and investments of insurers.

But climate change also presents opportunities for the insurance sector: the insurance sector plays a crucial role in managing climate-related risks as an evaluator, manager and risk-bearer, and investor, and is particularly qualified to understand hedge pricing.

In particular, through risk-based pricing, insurers are sending critical economic signals about the changing risk environment. Insurers can also help build resilience through (inclusive) insurance.

This is why risk management professionals within organisations or in advisory positions, already in charge of the impact of global warming on all existing and emerging risks, should pay attention to the attached document published by IAIS and SIF. Of course, these elements are even more directly relevant for risk managers who manage captive insurance or reinsurance companies. Professionals directly involved in the subject should not hesitate to read the full document.

Indeed, it not only offers tools on climate risk management that beyond insurers could be implemented within organisations of all kinds as a guide of good practice, but even as jurisdictions adjust the tasks and competencies of their supervisory bodies to take this into account, it will have an impact on the very structure of the global insurance and reinsurance market, or the functioning of financial markets.

An adequate response by regulators to climate change risks and opportunities will support the insurance oversight objectives of protecting policyholders, contributing to financial stability, and promoting a fair, secure, stable, and sustainable insurance market.

Chapter 19

Key Risks for the Decade and Beyond

Heightened global risks[1] could reduce productivity levels as the cost-of-living crisis and challenging safety situation affect employees, according to the 2023 International SOS Risk Outlook and the global risk map.

Many of the findings in the report are based on a survey of 1,218 experienced risk management professionals in 108 countries and use data on the medical and safety environment from countries around the world with ratings ranging from risk 'insignificant' to 'extreme'.

The report warns that the Russia/Ukraine conflict will continue to have an impact beyond 2023, adding that geopolitical volatility will also spread beyond the region over the near future. Beyond the very visible Russia/West divide, and the war in the Middle East, Sino-American competition will increasingly dominate the geopolitical and economic landscape.

The lack of progress in addressing underlying economic or political problems will also likely lead to growing public dissatisfaction and cycles of unrest where the risk of violence increases over time, with high-risk locations such as Pakistan, Sri Lanka, Ecuador, Peru, and Iraq. Global polarisation will result in increased polarisation at the national level, resulting in social disorders that can increase local violence and criminal activity including in the United States and Western Europe.

The different challenges to which the world is confronted affect the European Union at the economic, environmental, demographic, and technological levels. The European Union has an opportunity to position itself as a strong global player, but will it be able to seize it with growing populism among the member states. Will the EU find the way to strengthen its capacity to play an international role?

Even before 2020, the megatrends observed at the EU and global level included, among others, fragmentation and external competitiveness, climate change, security and migration, and technological transformation. To turn challenges into opportunities, the European Union proposed and implemented solutions to stimulate investment, encourage international cooperation and development, and promote technological innovation, while addressing social challenges such as climate change.

[1] *Global risks could put firms into 'perma-crisis' mode – report*. https://cirmagazine.com/cir/c2022121401.php.

Enterprise Risk Management in Today's World: A Current and Futuristic View of the Complexity, Resilience, Responsibility and Tools in ERM, Part B, 217–227

Published under exclusive licence by Emerald Publishing Limited
doi:10.1108/978-1-83608-392-420241019

In an environment of constant economic disruption, excellence in risk management has become a competitive advantage in all branches. Organisations are looking to become more resilient. Through scenario-based foresight, early indicator monitoring, and crisis response capabilities, they become able to absorb shocks, pivot and, accelerate to new realities.

Ten Global Risks for the Decade[2]

The fact that most risks are interdependent means that reducing the risk for each will depend on many other risks that will decrease simultaneously. Similarly, the severity of any risk is linked to other risks and often exacerbates them. Nevertheless, it is useful to examine each risk individually, bearing in mind the interlocking nature of all risks, and foresee the direction that each will take in terms of probability – more or less high – even if no individual risk can completely disappear while the others have not been resolved.

1. Poly-crisis generated by the war in Ukraine and geopolitical risk:

The multi-crisis loop that flows from war in Ukraine, energy and food insecurity, inflation, the economic downturn, could lead to 'Ukraine fatigue' in the West, threatening vital support for that country.

The war is fraught with interdependent risks, including an ongoing and stalemate conflict; an escalation if the United States and NATO continue sending weapons to Kyiv in response to Putin's bombing; Russia's use of nuclear weapons if Kyiv attempted to retake Crimea; 'Ukraine's fatigue' in Europe as the recession took hold; and a rift between states-United States and the EU on the quantity and quality of military aid that should continue to flow to Kyiv, even if it is not yet in the making.

2. Increasing food shortages:

The World Food Programme (WFP) has highlighted a 'Ring of Fire' of hunger and malnutrition that extends around the world from Central America and Haiti to North Africa, the Sahel, Ghana, the Central African Republic, and South Sudan then east to the Horn of Africa, Syria, Yemen and Pakistan and Afghanistan. The number of people facing acute food insecurity has increased from 135 million to 345 million since 2019 (Burrows & Manning, 2022).

In addition to conflict, climate change, which causes more severe droughts and changes in precipitation patterns, is an important driver of food insecurity and is unlikely to be effectively mitigated rapidly. Soaring diesel fuel and fertiliser costs exacerbated by the war in Ukraine and supply chain issues *(getting crops to market and processing meat and poultry)*, increased food costs for livestock and dairy animals.

---

[2]Burrows, M., & Manning, R. A. *The top ten global risks of 2023*. https://nationalinterest.org/feature/top-ten-global-risks-2023-206027.

3. Popular movements in and confrontation with Iran:

The unprecedented popular uprising in 2022 could have turned Iran into a poly-crisis. The stars are already aligned for a new dangerous conflict between the United States and/or Israel and Iran. The nuclear deal with Iran, which was on the verge of success just a few months ago, is now on hold, if not dead. Iran is accelerating the production of bomb-grade highly enriched uranium (HEU, it has 60% of the 90% required for a bomb) and seems close to produce a bomb and could have a warhead available in two years or less.

Iran's supply of drones and missiles to Russia adds a new dimension to the confrontation and spurs further sanctions. The impoverished legitimacy of theocracy and the repression of the unprecedented popular uprising add to the uncertainty.

The current government in Israel and a Republican-dominated House of Representatives in the United States has intensified pressure to bomb or sabotage Tehran's enrichment plant as well as Iranian missile and drone installations. It did not happen and Iran seems to have given up attacking Saudi oil installations or oil tankers in the Gulf of Hormuz, due to its rapprochement with Saudi Arabia. A level of popular demonstrations that could bring down theocracy remains an unlikely event; should it happen, it could transform geopolitics in the presently troubled Middle East.

4. The worsening debt crisis in developing countries:

The United Nations Development Programme (UNDP) has warned that 54 low- and middle-income countries have 'serious debt problems'. These countries account for 18% of the world's population, more than 50% of people living in extreme poverty, and 28 of the 50 countries most vulnerable to climate change. Historically, debt relief has come 'too little too late' (Haque, 2022).

Solvency problems were often confused with liquidity problems, resulting in protracted debt crises with serious economic consequences. Low-income countries, such as Somalia and Zimbabwe, are at the top of the list of UNDP's economically troubled countries, but Oxford Economics estimates that many emerging economies will weather the storm, thanks to reduced spending early in the downward cycle.

The dire financial situation of many developing countries is a bad omen for achieving the UN sustainable development goals by 2030. The developing world will likely experience more poverty, slower improvement in education, and less capacity to fight climate change in 2023.

5. Soaring global debt:

The size of the debt is significantly larger than that of the 2007–2008 financial crises, and fiscal conditions in the major OECD countries are more problematic. Even more worrying is the decline in international cooperation, much less favourable than in 2008.

6. Worsening effects of global warming:

A warmer climate means more extensive droughts and floods, as well as dangerous changes in rainfall patterns that will disrupt agricultural yields. Western countries are already required to provide financial assistance to developing countries as they transition to a low-carbon world and have not kept their promises but the terms are not yet defined.

Beyond these threats, there are also unknown risks, the 'unknown-unknown' of the taxonomy of Donald Rumsfeld. If the 'unknown known' risks are discernible developments or trends whose possible trajectories can be assessed, there is also a range of unknown events – events that we cannot predict and that would have catastrophic consequences.

Among them: a super-volcano eruption (Yellowstone, Indonesia, Japan); a giant asteroid 6 miles wide, a magnitude that killed dinosaurs 66 million years ago; a solar storm – a coronal mass injection – that projects large amounts of magnetically charged particles onto the Earth that could disable grids for weeks or months, and bursts of radioactive gamma rays from deep space. On the other hand, thousands of viruses on our planet could trigger future pandemics, some harder to counter than the previous one.

Ten Major Threats on an Organisation for the Decade[3]

Contrary to the global risks above, Forbes has centred its approach on the top ten threats impacting organisations' strategic decisions from the point of view of CEOs.

1. ***Recession:*** While benefiting from a period of high inflation is not impossible, it is far from ideal when consumers have less purchasing power. The value of a currency is only as high as the number of goods or services a unit of money can buy.
2. ***Interest rate:*** Rising interest rates will continue to deplete the working capital of businesses across the economy. Given that retailers are concerned about consumer demand, they will likely be more cautious in purchasing inventory to avoid oversupply in the retail market. This will place a burden on small and medium-sized businesses, which are de facto warehouses for retailers since they hold products for longer periods.
3. ***Labour shortage:*** Current labour and skills shortages will continue in the foreseeable future as HR teams strengthen their recruitment and retention efforts to enrol and retain talent. HR teams will explore more diverse avenues, job boards, and organisations to find the common skills needed to support the business, tapping into all major and secondary markets as organisations are held accountable for their diversity spectrum, which has proven invaluable to existing and potential talent.
4. ***Rapidly changing market trends:*** Market trends are changing much more rapidly than before, and slow reactions can be detrimental. Companies will need to develop an ultra-fast reaction time to macroeconomic movements and use their data and technology to make quick decisions.
5. ***Procurement network:*** This problem will continue to hit businesses. Most supply networks are still configured manually. This means that a human adjusts

[3]Segal, E. *The 10 biggest risks and threats for businesses in 2023*. https://www.forbes.com/sites/edwardsegal/2023/01/01/the-10-biggest-risks-and-threats-for-businesses-in-2023/.

the parameters every time an interruption occurs. But it's a tedious task that people are simply too inefficient to achieve on a large scale.

6. ***Cyber security:*** This burden is no longer the IT department's sole responsibility. In a 2022 report, Gartner's research shows that 88% of board members view cyber security as a business risk rather than a technical IT problem. The same report indicates that by 2026, at least 50% of executives will have integrated performance requirements related to cyber security risk into their work contracts.
7. ***Damage to reputation:*** It continues to be a threat due to political extremism, social justice issues, environmental concerns, and more. As the media landscape and social media networks fracture, consumers do not always know what to believe. It is not easy to reverse or correct misinformation once it is released, and brands will need to remain vigilant and watch for threats, be proactive in their responses, and continue to have direct relationships with their audiences.
8. ***Inability to reach target audiences:*** It is increasingly difficult for organisations to reach their audiences, as consumers are inundated with information and many new ways to access content on screens. To reach consumers now, brands will continue to think outside the box to better understand and connect with their most important customers through relevant and personalised advertising that leverages creativity and new technologies.
9. ***Mental health issues in the workplace:*** Organisations do not have mandatory trauma-informed training to keep their environment safe. They have no psychological first-aid skills. There are no internal skills to help people manage their emotional problems. Leaders' expectations of employees wanting to return to the status quo as if the pandemic and other collective trauma were not happening will further contribute to global distress.
10. ***Lack of succession plan:*** As baby boomers leave the workforce, there is not enough succession planning or workforce replacement. More and more companies are likely to choose to hire foreigners. Successfully transferring ownership of a business to the next generation of family members or new external owners will require more time and dedication to train young leaders to take power.

What Are the Main Cyber Threats for the Current Decade?[4]

From spying on the nation-state to deep fake technology, these new threats are constantly evolving and can be difficult to defend against. If to know is to anticipate, in terms of cyber security to anticipate is to survive, or at least to give oneself more chances to get by. Also, the question of how the cyber threat will evolve arises more acutely as AI promises a new escalation.

---

[4]Pour cette partie voir:

→ Krim, M. (2022, December 23). *Cyber-sécurité: tandis que les entreprises augmentent leurs dépenses, les hackers misent sur l'IA pour améliorer leur efficacité*. http://itsocial.fr/enjeux-it/enjeux-metiers/direction-generale/cybersecurite-tandis-que-les-entreprises-augmentent-leurs-depenses-les-hackers-misent-sur-lia-pour-ameliorer-leur-efficacite/.

→ *The future is now: 2023's most dangerous emerging cyber threats*. https://www.linkedin.com/pulse/future-now-2023s-most-dangerous-emerging-cyber-joe/.

The cyber security market has experienced a strong acceleration in recent years. Entire ecosystems came together quickly to enrich their proposal and cover the needs of businesses. Spending on information security and risk management products and services has been on an upward trend and is expected to continue to increase.

Publishers faced a profound shift in the market as companies hastily completed the adoption of the distributed model. The generalisation of hybrid work had profound implications by accelerating the 'cloudification' of computer needs, and by spraying, once and for all, the boundaries of the famous perimeter to defend. Cyber security has undergone significant changes, migrating from the VPN model to the trusted zero model, or ZTNA (Zero trust network access).

Cybercriminals refine their business model: While businesses try to curb threats, especially those related to third parties, and worry about their compliance, cybercriminals refine their business model, based on ransomware, to make it more efficient and therefore more lucrative. Of course, the technological developments (AI, Blockchain, quantum, etc.) prompting the domain evolution do not vary. But on the side of adversity, it would be wise to seek answers on how to use it, particularly concerning AI.

It is feared that hackers should scale up their attacks through increased automation, and further target cloud and IoT (Internet of Things) environments. Their 'business model' should evolve in response to companies' defensive strategies and the cumulative effects of actions taken.

The cybercrime value chain should evolve: Actors specialised in ransomware could be forced to develop attacks on supply networks themselves to no longer depend on initial access brokers, use stolen data to manipulate transactions, sell more services to cybercriminal groups, merge with other criminal groups, or even working with government actors.

To address these threats, the Trend Micro experts propose a series of actions such as focusing defensive efforts on detection and incident response as well as initial access vectors, strengthening government sanctions against key threat actors and enablers, or regulating cryptocurrencies to increase transparency, protect consumers from fraud and make money laundering more difficult.

Emerging threats are new or rapidly evolving cyber threats that pose a significant risk to organisations. These threats can take many forms and can be difficult to predict or counter:

- ***Deepfake technology:*** It allows the creation of realistic videos or audio recordings that have been manipulated to show something that has not happened. This technology can be used to spread misinformation or conduct cyberattacks. For example, attackers may use deep counterfeit technology to create fake videos of executives making fraudulent statements or to impersonate a company's CEO in a phishing attack.
- ***Cloud security threats:*** Moving data and applications to the cloud introduces new security risks. These risks may include data breaches, unauthorised access to cloud accounts, and attacks on cloud infrastructure. It is critical for

organisations to carefully assess the security of their cloud service provider and implement appropriate controls to protect their data in the cloud.

- ***Cryptojacking:*** It refers to the practice of using someone's computer to mine crypto-currency without their knowledge or permission. This can be done by using malware or by manipulating a website to run the code that mines crypto-currency in the background. Cryptojacking can slow down a victim's computer but also lead to theft of sensitive data.
- ***Machine learning attacks:*** Machine learning algorithms can be used to automate and improve the effectiveness of cyber attacks. For example, machine learning algorithms can generate realistic phishing emails or escape detection by security systems. As machine learning technology becomes more advanced, there will likely be an increase in the use of machine learning in cyber-attacks.
- ***Attacks on quantum computing:*** Quantum computers are much more powerful than traditional computers and could break many of the encryption algorithms currently used to secure data. Quantum computers are still in the early development stages and organisations need to start looking at potential risks and looking for ways to protect their systems from possible quantum computing attacks.
- ***Cyber-espionage of nation-states:*** Some cyber attacks carried out by nation-states or state-sponsored hackers to collect intelligence or steal sensitive data. These attacks can be very sophisticated and may involve the use of advanced malware, zero-day exposures, and other tactics.
- ***Internet of Things (IoT) attacks:*** The IoT is the growing network of connected devices used in businesses and homes. These devices are often poorly secured, making them vulnerable to attacks. For example, attackers may be able to compromise an IoT device to access a network or to use the device to launch other attacks.
- ***Ransomware-as-a-service (RaaS):*** Ransomware is a type of malware that encrypts a victim's files and requires a ransom from the victim to restore access. RaaS refers to the practice of offering ransomware as a service, where anyone can buy and use ransomware to attack organisations. This made it easier for even unqualified attackers to launch ransomware attacks.
- ***Supply network attacks:*** They involve compromising a supplier to gain access to an organisation's networks or systems. This can be particularly difficult to detect and prevent, as the attack comes from outside the organisation. For example, an attacker may compromise a software vendor's update process to deliver malware to an organisation's systems.
- ***Social engineering attacks:*** They involve manipulating people rather than exploiting technical vulnerabilities. They can take many forms, such as phishing, pretence (impersonation to obtain sensitive information), and pretext (offering something to induce a victim to disclose sensitive information). Social engineering attacks are particularly effective because they exploit human weaknesses rather than technical exposures. For example, an attacker may send a phishing email that appears to come from a trusted source, to trick the victim into revealing their login credentials.

What Are the Main Human Resources Constraints for the Decade?[5]

When it comes to the workplace, COVID-19 has highlighted an important lesson: preparation is everything. In a new report, 'The Changing Nature of Work: 30 Signals for a Sustainable Future', the United Nations Development Programme (UNDP) examines how developments in the workplace are likely to influence the way society progresses.

Disruption planning is essential, not only to enable a rapid response to external shocks but also to ensure that any necessary adaptation includes marginalised populations. Here are five lessons from the report:

1. The pandemic has highlighted the importance of wellness:

Telework has blurred the line between work and personal life for many employees; it has intensified discussions about work-life balance and added stress to everyday life. This is particularly true for women, who experienced higher levels of anxiety during the pandemic, according to a multinational survey conducted by the French international development organisation Focus 2030.

Meanwhile, the pandemic has exacerbated existing social inequalities, making it harder for marginalised communities to access health care, education, and employment opportunities. In May 2021, the World Health Assembly recommended that governments integrate mental health support planning into emergency preparedness such as the pandemic. UNDP report suggests employers should also consider the impact of the pandemic on physical and mental health when rethinking future work models.

2. Digital technology will forever change the way we work:

The Fourth Industrial Revolution is underway, with cutting-edge technologies like robotics, artificial intelligence, and the Internet of Things changing the balance

---

[5]Pour cette partie voir:

→ *The changing nature of work: 30 signals to consider for a sustainable future*. https://www.undp.org/acceleratorlabs/blog/changing-nature-work-30-signals-consider-sustainable-future-22

→ *What are 'good work' goals and why should organizations care?* (2023, January 2). https://www.weforum.org/agenda/2023/01/what-are-good-work-goals-and-why-should-organizations-care-davos2023/?utm_source=sfmc&utm_medium=email&utm_campaign=2788732_Si-WeeklyNewsletterV5-Production-10-01-2022&utm_term=&emailType=Strategic%20Intelligence%20Weekly&ske=MDAxNjgwMDAwMDlyWGhNQUFV

→ *What are 'good work' goals and why should organizations care?* (2023, January 2). https://www.weforum.org/agenda/2023/01/what-are-good-work-goals-and-why-should-organizations-care-davos2023/?utm_source=sfmc&utm_medium=email&utm_campaign=2788732_Si-WeeklyNewsletterV5-Production-10-01-2022&utm_term=&emailType=Strategic%20Intelligence%20Weekly&ske=MDAxNjgwMDAwMDlyWGhNQUFV.

of how we work. By 2025, according to the World Economic Forum's Future of Jobs report, humans and machines will spend almost as much time on workplace tasks.

This is consistent with the UNDP report, which suggests that so-called 'super jobs' – roles that integrate human and mechanical skills – will require careful consideration of human-machine interaction protocols and ethics. An example of this is to ensure that AI systems are unbiased.

As process-based activities are increasingly supported by machines, there will be a demand for humans to develop new soft skills, such as empathy and creativity, to adapt to an increase in knowledge-intensive sectors such as financial services and product development.

3. Concerning new models of work, the world is still searching its way:

The world of work is no longer focused on traditional employment patterns. The Forum's Platform for the Digital Economy and New Value Creation estimates that 70% of the new value created in the economy over the next decade will be based on digital-enabled business models. Yet nearly half of the world's population is not connected to the Internet.

In the United States alone, the value of the on-demand economy is expected to reach more than $455 billion by the end 2023. This comes with its challenges, such as a lack of job security and social protection. UNDP believes that in the future we will see a mix of good practices from the private and public sectors, with new social safety nets adapted to new work models and improved digital infrastructure

4. Good working conditions can promote inclusion:

According to the UNDP report, technological advances could exacerbate inequalities. For example, the authors note that 'women have less time to retrain, upgrade, and look for work because they spend much more time than men on unpaid work'.

The report suggests that skills and innovation gaps should be addressed through a lifelong learning process, on-the-job experience, and the involvement of staff in developing how organisations create value alongside more formal qualifications. More inclusive workplaces – from wider corridors to areas designed for specific tasks and even virtual reality spaces to reduce isolation for remote workers – will also become common as we adapt to a new normal.

5. Entrepreneurship is transforming the way of doing business:

With technologies like crowdfunding, blockchain, and online banking that democratise access to investment, there are now more opportunities for disruptive ideas to take root, says UNDP. He predicts that start-ups will be at the forefront of adopting new organisational structures and practices, as they have already done with digital collaboration tools.

UNDP also sees a role for entrepreneurship within larger and more traditional companies, supporting a culture of innovation and integrating lateral thinking, autonomy, pro-activity, market awareness, and risk-taking.

Whatever the future of work, UNDP believes that one thing is non-negotiable: '*The interventions we create must focus on solving tomorrow's problems on a forward-looking basis, with humans at the centre of transformation*'.

Organisations need to reinvent their proposal and business model, focused on creating a workforce-based business and what is economically viable, to realise the future of work and remain attractive to employers.

Mid-century Horizon What: Challenges and Opportunities to Address with a Focus on the EU[6]

To turn challenges into opportunities, the European Union proposes and implements solutions to stimulate investment, encourage international cooperation and development, and promote technological innovation, while addressing social challenges such as climate change.

A centuries-old transformation is underway and the lack of political will could prevent the EU from becoming a major player in the world. The European Union has the opportunity to assume social and political responsibilities and to seize change as an opportunity to positively shape the future of humanity, both at the European and international levels.

At the EU level, many initiatives have been tabled and are under discussion, but others are needed to meet all the challenges ahead.

The acceleration of technological change, the emergence of new powers like China, demographic trends, and the importance of universal challenges such as climate change cast doubt on the effectiveness of a national approach in equipping our economies for the reality of the future

A constructive dialogue is the ultimate foundation for good governance, where the key issue is not so much securing the most resources, but how best to allocate them. The suggested approach for the EU to position itself as an assertive actor is to embrace change and see change as an opportunity, setting an example. Being virtuous in a world that is not is sometimes risky, hence the need to make school.

In the future, the challenges are likely to become increasingly acute.[7] Over the next two decades, competition for global influence is expected to reach its highest level since the Cold War, according to the US National Intelligence Council's Global Trends 2040 report.

While many world leaders may have an intuitive sense of where to start in building resilience, most are looking for a more rigorous and analytical approach

[6]See *HORIZON 2030 – Looking ahead to challenges and opportunities*. https://www2.deloitte.com/content/dam/Deloitte/lu/Documents/public-sector/lu-horizon-2030-looking-ahead-to-challenges-opportunities.pdf.

[7]See Grant, A., Haider, Z., & Mieszala, J.-C. *How to build geopolitical resilience amid a fragmenting global order*. https://www.mckinsey.com/~/media/mckinsey/business%20functions/risk/our%20insights/how%20to%20build%20geopolitical%20resilience%20amid%20a%20fragmenting%20global%20order/how-to-build-geopolitical-resilience-amidst-a-fragmenting-global-order_vfinal.pdf?shouldIndex=false.

to fostering geopolitical resilience and creating a 'resilience bonus' across the organisation. To address the geopolitical risks of the present and the future, leaders should challenge their organisations on six key dimensions of resilience: business model, reputation, organisation, operations, technology, and finance.

It is about building a resilient culture by aligning behaviour and performance management by investing in people to build loyalty and develop skills and talent. Beware of the need to align actions with values, especially at the level of key executives whose behaviour inconsistencies can damage the value of the company. In the age of instant information, it is essential to be attentive to the sociocultural factors that oppose uniform globalisation.

Chapter 20

How to Prepare for the Next Pandemic

To the extent that biologists are confident that new dangerous pathogens will emerge sooner or later, to avoid a repeat of the impacts of COVID-19, the world must start preparing now for the next pandemic. This is happening even in a challenging global context, with issues such as inflation and the Ukrainian crisis competing for attention.

To better prepare for future pandemics, the Group of 7, Canada, France, Germany, Italy, Japan, the United Kingdom, and the United States – announced the Pandemic Preparedness Compact at its annual summit in June 2022. The initiative aims to train scientists and healthcare workers from around the world with a standard set of pandemic response skills, creating a global network that can collaborate on outbreak detection and control.

The G7 compact suggests creating centres of excellence around the world that would teach virology and epidemiology skills needed to control pandemics, such as diagnostic testing and outbreak modelling. The centres would also provide laboratory equipment and links to industry partners.

Past experiences with H1N1 and other public health emergencies on campuses (bacterial meningitis, measles, tuberculosis, etc.) have provided invaluable information that has been applied to the COVID-19 response over the past three years. In turn, we need to learn from our collective experiences in managing COVID-19 on college and university campuses when planning for the next public health emergency.

In light of COVID-19, voices have been raised to ask the world to be better prepared for the next pandemic. Such calls have been made in the past and have resulted in concrete measures. Yet the world tends to move quickly, as new crises hold attention, resulting in the now familiar cycle of 'panic and neglect'. However, this is an ongoing concern because while the timing and nature of the next pandemic remain unknown, it is certain that it will occur.

Enterprise Risk Management in Today's World: A Current and Futuristic View of the Complexity, Resilience, Responsibility and Tools in ERM, Part B, 229–240

Published under exclusive licence by Emerald Publishing Limited
doi:10.1108/978-1-83608-392-420241020

Lessons Learned from the Pandemic in Universities?[1]

University leaders need to learn from their collective experiences managing COVID-19 on university campuses as they plan for the next public health emergency. Shared lessons will likely only be a starting point for the countless After Action Reports (AR) produced by International Health Regulations (IHRs) and various public health organisations in the United States. Of course, these 11 recommendations could apply to all sectors that receive from the public.

1. ***Building capacity before the pandemic:*** Public health services are critical partners, but in a global emergency, they will likely be overwhelmed and may not be able to provide support to universities. Many universities have quickly learned that they need to create their own internal contact and notification teams.
2. ***Plan, but keep in mind that this is just a plan:*** Continue to plan for the next pandemic with the full knowledge that the plan will only be a starting point. The plan must be flexible, adaptable, and extensible. While it should be comprehensive, it should be relatively simple and easy to implement.
3. ***Be proactive:*** Anticipate changes and resource shortages during a global pandemic. While it is important to take a balanced approach to having the necessary resources, anticipate shortages almost immediately when a public health emergency has been identified. Get ahead of the supply network and have multiple suppliers already in the procurement process. Meet early and plan for every eventuality a pandemic may bring.
4. ***Secure top management support:*** Like any business continuity plan or large-scale response, management support is essential, but it goes beyond a simple approval. Someone at the cabinet level has to take the lead in getting things done. Senior management needs to understand the need to make pandemic response a priority, especially in terms of staffing and funds.
5. ***Communicate often through multiple platforms:*** Employees, students, and families expect transparent and consistent communication. Information changes constantly during a crisis and it can be difficult to keep abreast of all the changes being implemented. Establishing a pace of communication is critical, especially with perpetual change occurring during a financial pandemic.
6. ***Leverage existing resources:*** Each university has resources that provide value during and after an emergency, including a pandemic. Some universities have medical schools or nursing schools, an extreme added value. The key to leveraging these resources is to plan and ensure that staff is trained and available as required.

Here are also some less operational lessons for the next pandemic:

1. ***Develop a family plan:*** Essential collaborators must have a family plan that will allow them to maintain essential functions within their department. This was

---

[1] *Preparing for the next pandemic: 11 Lessons learned from COVID-19 by universities.* https://www.campussafetymagazine.com/emergency/preparing-for-the-next-pandemic-11-lessons-learned-from-covid-19-by-universities/.

a challenge for family members who had children in school or who were the primary caregivers for seniors, dependents, and during such a long-term event. A plan for pets may be necessary if long absences from home are expected!

2. ***Expect mistakes:*** In non-public health emergencies, planning and responding to risks and active information are needed. With a new infectious disease, there is a need to 'follow the science', as science has changed quickly. Again, with a new illness, there will be mistakes that must be tolerated. Don't blame employees for taking initiative or thinking outside the box.
3. ***Build partnerships:*** Build early relationships with internal campus partners (e.g. police, housing, and catering) and external partners (local health services, hospitals, and providers).
4. ***Identify essential employers:*** Review policies, procedures, and job descriptions so that essential individuals that may be required to report to work in the event of a public health emergency are identified. A generic list of essential collaborators may not work for emergency response, especially in public health emergencies.
5. ***Avoid burnout:*** Front-line employees and those in critical support roles – such as IT teams that have developed tools to manage daily health checks, contact tracing, and monitoring tests – may be absent from work. Employees should be encouraged to take regular breaks, walk away, and adopt relaxation techniques.

Planning may not provide all the answers and all the situations that may arise, but it does provide a framework for action, describes employees' expectations for their potential duties and responsibilities, and frames the potential severity of a response concerning human, financial, and operational impacts. Planning and readiness enable an effective and efficient response.

Five Strategies to Prepare Now for the Next Pandemic, the US Experience[2]

Texas public health researchers who are interested in both conducting health disaster responses and evaluating emergency management have developed five strategies that reflect the situation in the United States that will give the world a head start – and perhaps even help prevent the next outbreak from turning into a pandemic:

1. Strengthening existing systems:

The process generally works as follows: Once a clinician diagnoses a disease on the World Health Organisation and Centers for Disease Control and Prevention's watch list, she reports the case to local health authorities for investigation. Information is transmitted at the state, federal, and international levels.

If a pathogen goes beyond local control and begins to spread, governments have emergency management systems in place to respond. These incident

---

[2]See *5 Strategies to prepare now for the next pandemic*. https://today.tamu.edu/2021/03/08/5-strategies-to-prepare-now-for-the-next-pandemic/.

command structures provide a framework for responding to crises ranging from infectious diseases to natural disasters to terrorist attacks.

A practical way to prepare for a future pandemic is to ensure that all these systems and structures remain stable. This means maintaining funding, training, and personnel for a rapid global response, even when no pandemic threat is visible on the horizon.

2. Prepare the public for participation:

Effective pandemic response requires a clear and consistent voice and a concrete message that reflects best practices based on sound science. Messages and data that clearly explain how each person plays an important role in the pandemic – and that could evolve – are critical.

Advice is more effective if adapted to different audiences. In the South, distrust of government and healthcare provider screening and vaccination efforts is directly linked to language barriers and immigration concerns. A strategy for reaching diverse and often underserved populations is to rely on local faith community leaders to help spread public health messages.

Preparation requires a 'comprehensive community approach' that engages everyone in the planning stages, particularly those of underserved or vulnerable populations. Building relationships now can improve access to information and resources when the next disaster strikes.

3. Coordinate and conduct exercises:

Emergency managers and health care leaders have long recognised that a coordinated response by various teams is essential to public health emergencies. Real-world emergency simulation exercises help public servants prepare for crises of all kinds. Like a fire drill, they bring community stakeholders together to examine a hypothetical disaster scenario and define roles and responsibilities. These practice sessions include individuals working in public health, emergency management, and healthcare, as well as federal, tribal (Indian Nations), state, and local front-line responders.

Practice scenarios must also include the reality of previous disasters, such as a hurricane or winter storm that puts even more stress on the disaster response system. These exercises allow a community to test parts of the overall emergency management plan and identify gaps or areas for improvement. Plan testing and ongoing training ensure everyone's readiness.

4. Update the manual:

After each major disaster response, all the different groups involved (law enforcement, EMS, fire, emergency management, public health, search and rescue, etc.) conduct what are called 'after-action reviews'. They can improve their plans for next time.

A thorough review of the response to the current COVID-19 pandemic at all levels will help identify gaps, challenges, and successes. These 'after-action' findings need to be integrated into future planning to improve preparedness and response to the next pandemic.

5. Build a new normal:

At the time of the 1918 Spanish Flu pandemic (H1IN1), few Americans had a telephone. Quarantine rules have led to more households using the telephone and accelerated research that has reduced reliance on human telephone operators. Similarly, there is no doubt that COVID-19 has led to the rapid change that will last and help nations prepare for future events.

Some of the sudden and dramatic changes in norms and behaviours, such as the use of face masks in public, may be among the easiest strategies to keep in place to deal with a future respiratory virus pandemic. Just as telephone systems have continued to improve over the past 100 years, continued innovation is building on the rapid adoption of COVID-19 related technologies that will help people adapt to sudden lifestyle changes when the next pandemic hits.

Why it Is Necessary to Prepare Now for the Next Pandemic?[3]

As the war in Ukraine has exacerbated the situation in the world emerging from COVID-19, it is relevant to question the military response and national defence strategy in this context. This is a doctrinal reflection developed by a retired United States general, but its implications could extend to the entire free world, particularly due to the significant contribution of the United States to NATO's defense, as illustrated daily by the war in Ukraine. The Joint Forces and the military-industrial complex are at a turning point during what will be a decisive decade.

The current environment requires the joint force to strengthen and integrate deterrence in all areas, theatres, and spectrum of conflict; modernise the nuclear enterprise; secure allies and partners; and prepare to triumph in high-power conflicts. The United States must rise to this challenge with enthusiasm, discipline, and strength. Now is the time for strategic initiatives.

Today, military power is increasingly projected through early access to data at all levels, through software, computer and networking infrastructure, artificial intelligence, and autonomous systems. The infrastructure, technology, and data architecture that enable senior managers to make timely, informed decisions and apply the required forces when and where the need arises are the real enablers of victory and success.

A data view that aggregates, deciphers, and provides a holistic perspective of information to support the President and Secretary of Defence supports decision-making in response to incidents that impact the Department's resources and capabilities. Joint data sharing within the defence community and with allies and partners allows for a coordinated response. Rapidly implemented, action plans can be assessed; risk calculations of low-density, high-demand critical capabilities analysed, and pre-positioning and deployment of personnel and equipment can mitigate the loss of life, goods, and natural resources.

[3] *The time to prepare for next pandemic is upon us.* https://www.nationaldefensemagazine.org/articles/2022/9/19/the-time-to-prepare-for-next-pandemic-is-upon-us.

Technical advances in all military domains will threaten American territory and interests in unpredictable ways. The time lag between the indications and the tactical and strategic attack threat warning will be shortened, and our actions and our lack of tactical actions will play out on the global stage and have strategic and long-term implications and effects.

Future wars will include protracted conflicts in contested environments – what we call the competitive phase of operations. We are living and living this phase today and, in my opinion, we are not dominating the enemy.

The pandemic has exposed the threat of infectious diseases to economic growth, social programmes, political stability, and global security. Even before the emergence of COVID-19, global experts in health and biological defence encouraged a greater focus on pandemic preparedness.

While the full spectrum of threats related to weapons of mass destruction requires and is beginning to receive attention and concern, there is growing concern about new infectious diseases and chemical threats, and their potential impact on US national security and defence interests.

This includes the health and operational readiness of US forces, allies, and partners abroad; undermining national security partnerships by producing long-term economic, political, and security destabilisation; and diverting attention, resources, and capabilities to define strategic defence objectives to meet the immediate needs of an incident.

Biological threats increase, whether natural, accidental, or deliberate, and the likelihood of a catastrophic biological event also increases. For the first time in our history, we have an opportunity – thanks to advances in science and technology – not only to fill our inventory but also to transform our capabilities.

An effective programme to ensure that the United States is prepared for future pandemics and other major biological threats will require a significant annual investment over a sustained period. However, the investment required is modest compared to other efforts to build capacity to protect the country from significant threats.

Pooling resources and achieving common objectives for our common defence are critical to ensuring that security and defence interests are met. Continuing to deepen the level of cooperation between partner and allied countries on these new threat reduction activities is essential to achieving long-term goals.

Could the Next Pandemic Come Soon and Be More Deadly?[4]

Pandemic risk is vastly underestimated and outbreak preparedness measures are significantly under-invested. A careful analysis suggests that future pandemic risks are important.

---

[4]See Smitham, E., & Glassman, A. *The next pandemic could come soon and be deadlier*. https://www.cgdev.org/blog/the-next-pandemic-could-come-soon-and-be-deadlier.

Here are three key takeaways from the event:

- ***The next pandemic could be much closer and more severe than generally envisioned:***

COVID-19 is generally seen as a 'one in a lifetime' or 'one in a century' pandemic. Historical modelling shows that this may not be the case.

Using a model, based on catalogues of simulated epidemics and pandemics, the Metabiota team also estimated the likelihood of another event as damaging as COVID-19. The Metabiota approach is important, stressed Dean Jamison, because it applies epidemiological and disaster modelling techniques to estimate the expected impact of future outbreaks, and assesses long-term pandemic risk in a way that the previous epidemiological literature did not.

Their results are worrisome and put the risk much higher than many seem to expect. They estimate that the annual probability of a pandemic of the magnitude of COVID-19 in any given year is between 2.5% and 3.3%, which means a 47% to 57% probability of another global pandemic as deadly as COVID-19 over the next 25 years. These numbers illustrate the importance of immediately preparing for future outbreaks. Outbreaks will occur – just knowing when and where.

- ***The most vulnerable countries are at higher risk of overflow events and are less equipped to respond:***

Aware of both this increased risk and the need to react, the African Risk Capacity (ARC), a specialised agency of the African Union, is working on financing options for the response to epidemics through risk profiling, emergency planning, parametric insurance, and risk transfer, and epidemic modelling. Previous ARC modelling work has shown that the probability of an annual occurrence of an outbreak with more than 6 Ebola cases is 10% each year in Uganda for example. Robert Agyarko of the ARC emphasised the need for rapid containment to control spread and reduce impact.

Robert Agyarko reminded us that we need short-term access to vaccines now, in addition to building long-term capacity for all regions to respond to COVID-19 and anticipate future pandemic threats. The African continent continues to grapple with the COVID-19 pandemic amid a rapidly changing third wave – with just over 1% of Africans fully vaccinated. The most important thing we can do as a global community is to ensure equity in global access to vaccines.

- ***What is spent and done now to contain the impacts can mitigate the risks:***

®To rapidly contain epidemics, countries and global health institutions need resilient health systems and effective mechanisms for outbreak preparedness and response. Comprehensive documentation of pandemic events with complete data is essential to ensure that decision-makers recognize the clear and present risks.

Early response and effective preparedness are critical to mitigating risk. And mitigation works. Metabiota analysis, based on simulated event catalogues, estimates that preventing only 1% of overflow events could prevent a significant number of deaths in the future – 100 times fewer deaths over 10 years.

- ***Outbreak Preparedness Index:***

Robert Agyarko and Cristina Stefan shared the Epidemic Preparedness Index (EPI) of the African Risk Management Capacity, a comprehensive measurement based on simulated disease behaviour and response capacity to determine levels of preparedness for outbreaks. The EPI assesses the ability to detect, communicate, and respond to an epidemic, tailored to national and sub-national formats, and thus what countries and regional organisations can do to prepare for and mitigate the risk of an epidemic.

- ***Conclusion:***

Modelling shows that the next pandemic could be much closer than we think, and early action and preparation, and funding for these mitigation strategies, is critical to ensure the current pandemic does not happen again.

More and smarter funds are essential for the world to prevent, detect, and respond to future pandemic threats, and clearer governance is urgently needed to make the global system work better to save lives and economies. It is time for new global funds to protect the world from pandemics.

Better pandemic risk science will lead to better predictions in the future; the world could use a scientific body to systematically assess and build consensus on what drives pandemic risk and how it evolves, or an intergovernmental group on pandemic risk.

According to Infectious Disease Experts, There Will Be Another Pandemic. Here Are Six Ways to Prepare[5]

The panic-neglect cycle is the habit of under-investing or giving insufficient attention to the public health infrastructure and functions needed to prevent, identify, contain, and respond to infectious disease outbreaks.

Another pandemic seems inevitable, with more than six in ten infectious diseases occurring in animals and affecting humans. It remains to be seen whether we will apply the lessons of the current pandemic, but it is essential to do so to end this cycle so that outbreaks do not become pandemics with innumerable consequences, including millions of lives lost and drastic impacts on healthcare, mental health, the economy, education, relationships, and careers.

While much of the burden of preparation falls on public health facilities, the public can play a critical role. Here's what some of the best infectious disease experts think both can do to help:

1. Increase the amount of public funding:

More funding is needed for commodities, such as enough testing when the time comes so we are not behind as in the case of the COVID-19.

[5]Rogers, K. *There will be another pandemic, infectious disease experts say. Here are 6 ways we can prepare for it. CNN.* https://edition.cnn.com/2022/06/01/health/prepare-for-next-pandemic-life-itself-wellness/index.html.

More needs to be invested in global health. WHO's budget is less than that of some of the big cities in the United States, even though they have to take care of the pandemic risk for 200 countries and all the other things that WHO does.

Pandemic preparedness should be seen as a real strengthening of the global public health system. Currently, in Canada, it is unclear whether Parliament will be able to allocate reasonable budgets when 80% of Canadians feel that their COVID-19 risk is over.

2. Protect nature:

Interacting with or eating stressed or diseased animals exposes humans to a greater likelihood of catching a virus. The risk of spreading the virus is also higher between humans and animal species that have similar DNA or have lived together over time, such as pigs or cattle.

Environmental health is part of our health to reduce the impact of the virus. Everyone must do their part to slow down climate change. Due to rising temperatures, animals migrate from the south to the north. When animals migrate and change territory, they come into contact with other animals with which they have never been in contact before. And they exchange viruses, just as they exchange viruses with men.

3. Act early and decisively:

Infectious disease experts who quickly detect outbreaks of a new disease and address them quickly while they are small are essential to preventing a larger emergency.

The group, Resolve to Save Lives, has suggested a global galvanising goal it calls 7-1-7: that every outbreak around the world be detected within seven days of its emergence, reported within one day, and controls implemented within seven days.

4. Improve public health communication:

Communication about the pandemic has been 'difficult as people have been divided against a common enemy, this pandemic virus' (Walensky, 2022). Dr Rochelle Walensky, Director of the CDC in the USA, said: '*We had to make decisions with imperfect data and imperfect times, but if we had not made a decision at that time, it would have been a decision in itself. We need to track and understand the best science we have at the time the decision is made*'. The CDC plans to spend much of its time finding ways to make public awareness part of pandemic surveillance. And Dr Fauci confirms: '*You have to be consistent, always stick to facts, evidence and data. That was one of the problems, of course, when I was on the coronavirus working group under the previous administration*'.

5. Fighting disinformation:

There's a saying that a lie can travel halfway around the world before the truth even puts its boots on. It has been very difficult for health, doctors, and others to cope with viral disinformation, which is spreading even faster than Omicron according to specialists. Pandemic-related misinformation can influence people's motivations, beliefs, and decisions about their health, politics, environment, and more.

Some social media apps, such as Instagram and TikTok, have launched features that help people get accurate information from credible health organisations when they view content about the coronavirus or vaccines. It's not easy to confront loved ones about their misleading or false social media messages, but there are ways to do it skilfully with empathy.

6. Keeping healthy:

Individual resilience is another key factor in preventing serious illness and death during pandemics. One of the reasons COVID killed so many people was that there were a significant number of people who had preexisting conditions.

Healthy lifestyles that promote immunity can make a big difference. Everyone needs to take the medications prescribed to them, find healthy foods they love, and not smoke or be exposed to other people's smoke. To be healthy is not a matter of depriving ourselves, but rather of determining what we like to do healthier.

What Cost to Prepare the World for the Next Pandemic?[6]

Preparation begins at the country level and includes five components:

→ First, it requires strong and resilient health systems, particularly primary care, to help detect epidemics, provide essential care, and support the deployment of vaccines and other medical countermeasures.
→ Second, it requires surveillance systems and laboratory capacity to detect outbreaks of human and zoonotic diseases.
→ Third, there needs to be coordination mechanisms across sectors for prevention and preparedness.
→ Fourth, preparedness requires legal frameworks and regulatory instruments to support outbreak prevention and the deployment of countermeasures.
→ Fifth, we need well-functioning supply chains and adequate inventories of essential goods and equipment.

Many countries, especially low- and middle-income countries, have longstanding weaknesses in these areas of preparedness, which also translate into regional weaknesses. Even better prepared countries were deeply challenged by the COVID-19 pandemic, highlighting the vulnerabilities associated with the collapse of global supply networks and the role of lack of trust and mechanisms of government coordination impacting the quality of the response.

The World Bank, although the International Development Association (DA) and the International Bank for Reconstruction and Development (BIRD), has a strong track record of providing the long-term, predictable, and sustainable financing countries need to prepare for pandemics, often requiring multi-sectoral interventions. The World Bank's suite of financing mechanisms and instruments,

[6]See *How much will it cost to prepare the world for the next pandemic?* World Economic Forum. https://www.weforum.org/agenda/2021/11/preparing-for-next-pandemic-covid-19/.

its global footprint, its strong presence in countries, its multi-sectoral expertise, and broad reach with decision-makers position us well to increase global support for country and regional preparedness.

Global financing needs are diverse and complex. A key priority is to increase R&D funding for therapeutics and vaccines. This sector receives significant public, private, and philanthropic funding, particularly in support of the Coalition for Epidemic Preparedness Innovations (CEPI), created by the World Bank. It has supported the IFF and seeks to positively disrupt funding models for vaccines against epidemic diseases.

Funding medical countermeasures is equally important to ensure timely and equitable access to all countries. On the demand side, this will require leveraging our collective experience of common procurement mechanisms such as COVAX and the African Vaccine Acquisition Trust (AVAT). On the supply side, there is a need to strengthen distributed manufacturing capacity to ensure equitable access to low-cost vaccines. Perhaps it is time to consider a new 'global compact on pandemic preparedness', similar to the one on climate, to ensure a common commitment and collective responsibility for pandemic preparedness.

The Next Pandemic, When and How?[7]

Infectious disease outbreaks are more likely to occur when a range of risk factors combine. An El Niño weather event in 1998 caused flooding in Kenya, Somalia, Sudan, and Tanzania, forcing livestock and humans to live closer together on the remaining dry lands. This increased the risk of cross-transmission of pathogens. Due to a shortage of vaccines, cattle have not been vaccinated against the Rift Valley fever virus, a common infection among ruminants in the region.

Floods have created more mosquito breeding sites, leading to a rapid increase in mosquito populations. Mosquitoes are a means of transmitting the Rift Valley fever virus from animals to humans, and from humans to humans. This facilitated the emergence of the virus in human populations, which was then transmitted from human to human. The alignment of all these risk factors, such as Reason plates, has led to a significant outbreak of Rift Valley fever among the human population in the region.

Respiratory infections are one of the highest risks of an epidemic or pandemic after emergence and spread between humans, as infected humans often create aerosols when they cough, sneeze, or speak loudly.

The main causes of climate change can also increase the risk of pandemics. Deforestation, urbanisation, and the huge livestock needed for a growing meat production industry are bringing more and more animals into contact with humans. This increases the likelihood that pathogens will 'jump' from animal to animal.

It is widely accepted that there will be another pandemic and that, through many of the same activities that fuel climate change, humans are creating more

[7]See Heymann, D., Ross, E., & Wallace, J. *The next pandemic – When could it be?* https://www.chathamhouse.org/2022/02/next-pandemic-when-could-it-be.

opportunities for pandemics. The most important task for all countries is to strengthen their capacity to identify and respond to epidemics where and when they occur. This includes gene sequencing pathogens and sharing sequence data in global databases.

The biggest challenges in preparing for the next pandemic may well be political. As with the current pandemic, national sovereignty must be respected, but the challenge is to ensure that these concerns do not outweigh the solidarity required for an adequate global response. A COVID-19 becomes endemic, politicians may lose the will to fund and take the necessary steps to maintain and improve the world's preparedness for another pandemic.

As with climate change, pandemic preparedness is based on solidarity between developed and developing countries, as well as a political focus on problem-solving rather than blaming it. Implementing collaborative surveillance to detect new diseases is essential; emergency coordination such as national action plans for prevention preparedness; access to countermeasures such as accelerated research and development; community protection; and safe and scalable care. These efforts must also be supported by a strong workforce and funding.

Part 5

ERM Specific Domains & Tools

Chapter 21

Managing Legal Risk

Boards of directors and top management, especially CFOs are confronted with an ever-changing legal and regulatory environment with exposure to financial and reputational losses if legal risks are not properly managed. Therefore, in-house legal teams, supported by their risk managers, are expected to do more to identify, manage, and mitigate legal risks within their organisation. In the financial services sector in particular, there is an increased interest in regulation, particularly in examining how the Legal Department fits into the overall corporate risk framework.

Society and stakeholders' pressures lead organisations to identify and manage overlaps and gaps between legal services and operations more effectively. Legal risk includes all uncertainties that businesses may face as a result of fraudulent activity. Legal risks usually relate to losses that organisations may incur as a result of their activities and that may cause conflicts and disputes with third parties.

For example, businesses face legal risks due to defective transactions. Similarly, failure to take appropriate measures to protect its assets, whether physical, or intangible, can lead to legal risks. Legal risks may also refer to the risks that organisations face as a result of changing and diverse legal and regulatory contexts.

Managing legal risk as a discipline is a relatively new way of thinking for many legal teams. Awareness of the need for a specific approach to legal risk, distinct from compliance management, has led ISO to develop a specific standard published recently.

Legal Risk Taxonomy

The ISO 31022:2020 standard does not propose a taxonomy for the approach of legal risks but a definition reproduced below which does not differ from the common definitions mentioned above; it is directly derived from that of risk in ISO 31000:2018: 'the impact of risk on the organisation's objectives' and therefore implicitly covers both threats and opportunities, while most authors only consider the negative side (Fig. 21.1).

Enterprise Risk Management in Today's World: A Current and Futuristic View of the Complexity, Resilience, Responsibility and Tools in ERM, Part B, 243–255

Published under exclusive licence by Emerald Publishing Limited
doi:10.1108/978-1-83608-392-420241021

Impact on the objectives of uncertainty in relation to legal, regulatory, and contractual issues, or with non-contractual rights and obligations.

Fig. 21.1. Legal Risk Definition in ISO 31022 Project Coupled with Risk in ISO 31000.

Legal risk comes from a variety of sources but usually from legislation and regulations that apply to an organisation. For example, it can be the labour code, safety laws, tax laws, insurance code, etc. Therefore, each type of legal risk can have a different impact on an organisation and its operations. The sources of risk, both internal and external, are detailed in the standard but are limited to the following taxonomy:

- ***Assets***: Legal risk arises from a company's inability to protect all its assets, tangible assets, such as buildings and equipment, as well as intangible assets, such as human capital and intellectual property. To protect the rights and obligations of legal assets held by a company, the General Counsel must have a clear picture of them to identify and manage risks and avoid adverse consequences in collaboration with the Risk Director. Thanks to a good knowledge of these assets, together they can protect the rights and obligations related to all their legal assets.
- ***Regulation***: Regulatory risk refers to all risks that organisations are confronted with as a result of changes in the regulations governing the organisation's activities in the various jurisdictions in which it operates. This is a killer risk for an organisation depending on an operating authorisation from a supervisory body; it could lose it or to have conditions applied (retrospectively or potentially) impacting its economic value.[1]

It is crucial to identify and follow all applicable rules. Each body may be subject to regulations prescribed by institutions, committees, or public administrations. It is therefore essential to know which ones apply specifically to its activities and the associated rules, such as the specifications, policies, standards, or laws that it must comply with to avoid penalties and litigation. It is also important to know what changes are being made to avoid any risk of non-compliance.

Proactive regulatory risk management requires implementation specific policies, procedures, and protocols, including legal watch to ensure your company's compliance long before regulatory changes are enforced.

- ***Contracts***: Contractual risk refers to the risks associated with the contracts with partners; it consists mainly of the failure of one of the parties failed to meet its obligations, i.e. an organisation suffers financial loss due to a partner not honouring a contract or the organisation itself not properly managing its contractual obligations and benefits.

[1]PwC Definition.

Therefore, contractual risks have legal and financial implications. Since it concerns the operations and legal issues of an organisation, contractual risks are part of legal risks. When considering contract risks, the contract management process should also be analysed to fully understand the organisation's risk exposure.

Faulty processes, resulting from manual errors, non-compliant provisions, and/or inability to conclude the contract on time, can put the company at risk. On the other hand, the use of automated systems and contract management software can standardise these processes and allow managers to draft contract clauses using templates, reducing the organisation's vulnerability to this type of risk.

- ***Litigation***: Working in a business environment creates many responsibilities that may result in various disputes. Legal disputes are situation in which a legally founded complaint is filed by the organisation or by a third party. This is particularly the case for professional misconduct, accidents, product liability, etc.

To reduce the risk of litigation, the legal department can take proactive measures. In particular, it can set up risk transfer agreements, ensure compliance, maintain accurate records, and use legal management software that alerts it to potential risks in this area.

Despite the presence of a regulatory class, ISO was able to distinguish between compliance management and legal risk management. The ISO 37301:2021[2] standard on compliance management systems specifies the requirements and provides guidelines for the establishment, development, implementation, evaluation, maintenance, and improvement of an effective compliance management system within an organisation.

Legal departments must manage proactively legal risks to protect their organisations and the interests of key stakeholders. Therefore, professionals need a structured way of identifying, assessing, and mitigating risks, and also collecting legal data to recognise, track, and report these risks in a way that allows owners of these risks to be informed.

Measuring and Managing Legal Risk[3]

Legal risks must be defined and classified for organisations to develop an effective strategy for managing these risks that are hard to assess. The informal notion of risk as the possibility that something bad might happen already mentioned is not a bad place to start to define risk but it lends itself poorly to measurement and management. This is why it is necessary to divide the risk into measurable parts.

[2]Replaces the previous one **ISO** 19600:2014.
[3]See Mark Little. (2018, March 8). *How to measure and manage legal risk*. https://www.berkmansolutions.com/articles/risk/how-to-measure-and-manage-legal-risk.

- ***Risk is the probability of loss due to the occurrence of an event:***

Accurate quantification is desirable under certain circumstances where it is possible. Large companies, financial in particular, have sufficient data on operational claims to build predictive models based on experience to measure risk. But there are exceptions.

To illustrate how risk could be defined in statistical terms, the classic formula is $R = P \times S$, where P is the probability of occurrence of an event and S for severity, the significance of the impact of its occurrence. The impact is essentially financial, but it can take into account the non-financial consequences as long as they lend themselves to an appropriate risk quantification formula.

However, most organisations do not have the necessary data or resources, or confidence in abstract risk models. Even organisations that do not have strong claims histories can still measure and manage risk, particularly legal risk, by simply taking a few steps towards quantification, moving away from the concept of a harmful event.

- ***Risk according to ISO 31000 & ISO 31022 lends itself to a different approach:***

Following ISO 31000 risk definition, risk management begins by identifying uncertainty and then assessing the effects (positive and negative) of both threats and opportunities. Legal risk is difficult to measure and has specificities. However, with the help of the ISO 31000 risk definition, the experts recognised that it was possible to express and measure legal uncertainties and their potential effects and developed ISO 31022.

- ***Legal Risk Taxonomy:***

Structural legal risk is rare for most organisations because it arises from the uncertainty surrounding the foundations of a particular industry, technology, or business method. When an industry is regulated, for example, there was a structural legal risk that this industry would be deregulated. The scope of a structural legal risk is broad and usually changes the competitive landscape.

The potential effects are varied, some positive, and some negative, depending on the positioning of a given organism. Structural change can benefit one organisation while harming another.

Structural legal risks may arise from sources other than legislation. Antitrust litigation can significantly change prices in a key industry or business relationship. Consumer protection enforcement measures can also change the fundamental assumptions of an industry, but make marketing practices unacceptable (multi-level marketing, for example).

- ***Efficient Identification of Legal Risk:***

It rests on the practical definition of risks proposed in ISO 31022, hence it includes both 'positive risks' and 'negative risks'. Therefore, it offers the right perspective to identify legal risks and ultimately manage legal risks as both threats and opportunities.

A risk can only be managed if the scope and components of uncertainty are well understood. It is only with this that a legal risk management strategy can be developed, a component of the ERM strategy and a pillar of the overall resilience strategy.

- ***Risk criteria, treatment cost, and mapping:***

For risk identification and assessment to prioritise risks, it is still necessary to establish risk criteria. They lead to consistency in how an organisation identifies and measures each component of risk. There are often only three risk criteria:

1. Likelihood is measured as a percentage probability;
2. Impact limited to negative consequences of the occurrence; and
3. Risk is measured by the product of both without further consideration (*see the risk equation above).*

Legal risk mapping is a tool for the ranking of all types of risks in increasing order of importance for the organisation. It provides a representation of the prioritisation based on the consequences of the legal risks identified in terms of value destruction on three distinct factors (strategic value, financial value, and institutional value).

The value chain of the activity is taken as the starting point for assessing the degree of uncertainty in the legal standards involved at each stage, to identify the events that will be able to cross these standards, and to assess the degree of uncertainty associated with these events, to finally assess the impact of the legal risk and thus position it on the legal risk mapping of the company.

The frequency and severity approach is not sufficient as organisations take into account other dimensions. The cost of risk treatment is assessed against the level of risk following the risk criteria. The cost is also to be considered in relation to risk tolerance.

- ***Tolerance/appetite for legal risk:***

A legal risk tolerance policy is an explicit recognition of the level of risk and the types of risks an organisation will accept with reasonable treatment (residual risk). The impact of legal risks on the organisation's objectives can be significant. The ISO standards 31000 and 31022 invite consideration of a set of consequences when assessing the impact of risk.

While some important consequences are not financial, in particular the issue of reputation stakeholders' trust, it is essential to focus on the financial aspects of legal risk as the people responsible for managing legal risk on the front lines, lawyers, contract managers, and others, have often difficulty communicating to the organisation's leaders the value of preventive legal risk management.

It is important to develop an explicit legal risk tolerance policy that achieves two objectives:

→ It allows the organisation to optimise the cost of risk treatment; the organisation cannot know how much to spend on preventive risk management if it does not have a target to determine what risks are acceptable; and

→ It improves organisational efficiency; for example, it is not unusual for sales managers to complain about blocked transactions in a legal quagmire. If both parties, commercial and legal, understand the organisation's risk tolerance, then sales executives and lawyers can work together meaningfully to finalise a contract.

Concerning legal risk, it is essential to measure the financial implications of risk, cultural and political factors must be considered.

- ***Legal risks in the context of global and financial strategies:***

Legal risks are rarely addressed in a collective approach, let alone in the context of the organisation's financial objectives. Risk managers, contract managers, and lawyers often consider that only zero legal risk is acceptable. Sales managers and business leaders often just want to see all transactions complete. How can an organisation balance these conflicting viewpoints? A risk tolerance policy is essential; but how to select a number (assuming for now that the focus is on finances)?

Organisations, departments, and teams all have objectives. The discussion should start with the strategic plan, in particular the financial aspect, and should take into account the following:

→ Price increases occur despite contract terms because no one monitors the contract efficiently;
→ The supervisory bodies consider guarantee contracts to be insurance contracts that impose regulatory fines; and
→ A key supplier is failing and a backup provider to replace it in the emergency is more expensive.

Six Steps for Managing Legal Risk[4]

All too often the heads of legal or compliance of an organisation react with surprise when it is challenged in a court of law or it receives regulatory sanction of whatever nature; this results from the fact that the organisation does not systematically manage legal risks as it should. Legal risk remains one of the most difficult and least understood risks to manage. To improve the management of legal risks within any organisation, the six-step process proposed here is aligned with ISO 31000 & ISO 31022 suggestions:

1. Choose or develop a framework:

There are different reference frameworks and large organisations can also design a specific framework that fits their management system. It should also be stressed that it is not always possible to establish ex nihilo a framework for

[4]See Mark Little. (2018, March 8). *6 Steps to legal risk management*. Risk Management. https://www.berkmansolutions.com/articles/risk/6-steps-to-legal-risk-management.

rigorous quantification and that certain risks are better suited to a qualitative or semi-quantitative approach as described above. Of course, ISO 31000 or COSO-ERM frameworks can be used as a guide in paving the way for both threats and opportunities. Four imperatives should be kept in mind for a legal risk management framework:

→ Remain simple, without being simplistic;
→ Be scalable, without being overly restrictive;
→ Be adaptable but with specific instructions; and
→ Be practical, to be rigid.

2. Secure management support:

Most operational functions are faced with legal acts and therefore risks, whether in purchasing, sales, or even production. This means that beyond the commitment of top management, it is essential to obtain the support of the chain of command. Four keys to winning membership:

→ What is the scope of the Legal Risk Management Initiative *(i.e. departments, divisions, or business)*?
→ What types of legal risks will be tracked as part of the initiative *(contracts, settlements, litigation, etc.)*?
→ Who are the recipients of legal risk reports *(management level, corporate functions, etc.)*?
→ What is the budget available to monitor and address legal risks in terms of time, finance, and personnel?

Answers to these questions will guide the organisational commitment to initiate the process.

3. Legal risk identification:

The identification process comprises three steps:

→ **Finding sources of legal risk:** The main sources already mentioned above are assets, contracts, regulation, litigation, and structure.
→ **Identify current and potential risks:** Uncertainties with legal consequences can arise from hazards (personal injury), events (one occurrence), situations (entry into a new international market), and scenarios (the counterparty does X, Y, or Z).
→ **Recording risks in a risk register:** A risk register is essentially a list that also includes certain attributes of each risk. To start, follow the risk title, the probability on a simple scale as an estimate, the consequence rating on a simple scale as an estimate, and the combined risk rating on a simple scale.

At this stage, risk analysis should be undertaken to make informed decisions on how to manage legal risk.

4. Legal Risk Analysis:

Risk analysis helps understand the content of the risk register. Legal risks analysis starts with the assessment of the existing controls. Risk controls can take various forms depending on the risk, the sector, and the organisation. To manage contractual risk, an organisation may use a requirements tracking system to ensure that individual obligations are met.

Once the effectiveness of risk controls has been assessed, the likelihood and consequences of each risk should be analysed. The likelihood of a legal risk is the combination of the possibility of discovery *(will the applicant or control body determine the problem)* and the possibility of an adverse decision. Similarly, the consequences are the product of damage (usually in financial terms) and frequency (the number of incidents).

Risk analysis is an iterative process. Some risks will be removed from the register, some will be merged, and new risks will emerge from an iteration of the analysis.

5. Legal risk evaluation and reduction:

The purpose of a legal risk evaluation is to prioritise them. The organisation's risk tolerance is at the heart of risk evaluation. Legal risks that exceed the limit and are deemed 'intolerable' must be addressed. The idea behind risk treatment is simple: change the risk so that it becomes tolerable. The risk need not be eliminated, it is sufficient to reduce it to a tolerable level. Risk treatment options are as diverse as the risks to be managed:

→ **Avoidance:** Not starting or continuing the activity that may create an unbearable level of uncertainty;
→ **Exploitation:** Increase the activity that creates the risk, if the consequence is beneficial (opportunity);
→ **Prevention:** Remove the source of risk (in case of threat);
→ **Protection:** Modify the likelihood and/or consequences of the risk (risk reduction);
→ **Transfer:** Share risk through contracts (transfer for reduction) or insurance (transfer for financing).

Adapting these instruments to legal risk brings legal professionals closer to the different activities within the organisation to reduce costs and impacts of uncertainty.

6. Communicate and consult:

To have a meaningful and lasting impact on the organisation, thinking holistically and communicating clearly to everyone according to their interests and expectations are essential. Risk management is essentially multidisciplinary, at the border of the fields of in-house lawyers, compliance officers, contract managers, and all operational employees contributing to the creation of value.

Managing Legal Risk in Time of Crisis[5]

In a crisis context, legal analysis and assessment of legal rights, obligations, and responsibilities are essential to the proper functioning of compliance, risk management, and strategic decision-making of organisations, particularly financial institutions.

Agile management of legal risks is needed to contain risks threatening the sustainability of the organisation so as not to miss significant opportunities, to manage or reduce threats and avoid unnecessary expenses. Four fundamental factors must be taken into account for effective legal risk management:

1. Ensure appropriate management interactions between all control functions:

Control functions, legal, compliance, risk management, and internal audit, are all essential to the proper functioning of the organisation. That's why they have to interact at different levels, and everyone has to have direct access to report to the board or a committee of that board; that helps to ensure their independence.

Directors should establish a trusting relationship with control functions based on fairly regular personal contact between control functions and an independent (non-executive) director in particular the chair of the risk or audit committee. This is the opportunity for directors to continuously assess the quality of the management of control functions.

In addition, the heads of control functions should meet regularly to share important issues managed on an interdisciplinary basis from the outset.

These meetings should be encouraged at all levels, especially at the top. However, line workers can identify potential problems at an early stage. Such an approach provides the legal service with various points of contact, since it:

→ Must be represented in the various risk forums within companies.

→ Must be actively involved in the work of compliance departments and their associated risk assessments; although there are some unique legal risks in any institution (e.g. litigation, contractual interpretation), most of the risks attributed to compliance have a legal flavour and so do many other risks related to control functions. The legal department needs to participate in risk assessments that would facilitate direct investigation and discussion with control groups by focusing on current risks and horizon analysis to identify emerging risks.

→ Be able to ensure a holistic approach that takes into account a practical understanding of the organisation's transactions, as well as relevant legal areas. Organisations should avoid an overly specialised approach that ignores levels of understanding of the feasibility of a company's operations.

---

[5]See *Legal risk management in a crisis.* https://www.shearman.com/perspectives/2020/04/legal-risk-management-in-a-crisis.

In heavily regulated professions and activities, such as financial institutions, directors' impression for legal security may have been reinforced by the apparent satisfaction of the supervisory bodies with the overall architecture of the bodies' current arrangements and by the adoption of certain regulations that reinforce it.

2. Managing overlap between legal and compliance:

Through the compliance function, organisations aim to meet the requirements imposed by oversight bodies on how they conduct their activities. The mission of compliance is to provide advice on regulatory requirements, design and develop processes and procedures to ensure that the organisation complies with those requirements, and test the operational effectiveness of these processes and procedures. It would be a mistake to try to make a clear distinction between legal and compliance, leaving the responsibility for a particular case to one or the other; on the contrary, they must work together on all files to achieve common objectives.

The rules and regulations enforced by compliance services have the force of law through first and second lines of defence, which means, among other things, that financial regulation is ultimately a form of law, and legal analysis is essential. Legal analysis plays a central role in interpreting the meaning of regulations and how best to apply them, and on a day-to-day basis, legal analysis is an area where the legal function should play a central role.

Legal analysis is not only relevant in a litigation context. Of course, if a matter turns into litigation, it is resolved in a court proceeding, where the rights or harms of the situation would be defended by lawyers before a judge. Even in this case, the compliance department will likely have a role to play in providing the relevant counsel with a full understanding of the organisation's practices; therefore, even in these more prominent 'legal' areas, it should not make sense for one function to claim competence or dominance to the exclusion of others.

Legal analysis is also essential to the development of appropriate frameworks and processes, the review of risks, and the resolution of issues that arise. Legal interpretations are essential to understanding regulation and achieving desired outcomes most efficiently and effectively. Any failure to fully integrate the legal analysis is likely to result in unnecessary risk, inefficiency, and expense.

The necessary reasoning is subtle and based on a specific vocabulary. It is taught and teachable – it is the same reasoning that makes it possible to understand and apply the concepts and rules contained in the applicable underlying legal systems – but it requires application and practical experience in complex situations.

3. Develop adequate legal thinking on 'risk':

Legal risk arises in all the activities of any business, as the law underpins almost all the relationships, products, contracts, goods, and behaviours that are involved in any organisation, especially financial institutions. The involvement of legal expertise is therefore necessary to reduce risks, at least as a general business proposition, and also under the Basel Rules for financial institutions. In any bank, its assets and liabilities are legal constructions. This is also true for many sectors because they owe their existence, nature, and essence to the law. They include the following considerations, how:

→ Have been drafted provisions relating to the company's relations, assets, and liabilities?
→ Do they comply with applicable laws and regulations?
→ Do we enforce laws, regulations, and court decisions around the world?

Risk management policies involve many assumptions about how contracts work and how the organisation behaves. More importantly, it is generally assumed that contracts must be executed according to their terms.

Jurists trained in countries of Roman-Germanic tradition, countries of the code, must bear in mind that in the systems of 'Common Law', the law allows the choice of action of the parties: the freedom of contract is generally respected, subject to certain fairness exceptions, which are applicable only in the context of consumer relations, although such exceptions are sometimes even accepted in institutional relations, especially in the United States. Clarity in the thinking and drafting of contracts is therefore essential.

Types of situations in which the involvement of in-house lawyers reduces risk in the risk function include:

→ Collateral management issues that may arise when addressing leverage and/or liquidity issues. With a sound legal structure that contains risks, the company can get a better overlap, a reduction in customer warranty requirements (creating a competitive advantage), reduced costs of exposure to clearing houses, and greater flexibility in the use of collateral:
    ✓ the use and enforceability of collateral to mitigate counterparty risks;
    ✓ legal opinions on termination clauses;
    ✓ optimisation of the capital structure and how the relevant instruments are drafted to comply with the applicable capital eligibility rules (in particular for financial institutions);
    ✓ structuring around bankruptcy issues;
    ✓ validity and risks associated with the use of different types of collateral, such as the transfer of securities as opposed to the mortgage, lien, or pledge; and
    ✓ Legal structuring of off-balance sheet assets.
→ Clearing opportunities, which may result from cross-guarantee structures and consolidation of exposures in the smallest number of entities in an enterprise, and could dissociate exposures from other legal and documentary aspects of transactions;
→ Regulatory accounting, where consideration of the most cost-effective capital arrangement for business lines, such as derivative accounting activities, involves an analysis of the differences between capital and tax rules in different jurisdictions; and
→ Modalities, streamlining legal and regulatory exposures through standardisation and careful elaboration of modalities.

4. Manage feedback loop with internal control:

Internal audit control risks and compliance, and critical business processes – a 'third line of defence' after business processes, then risks and compliance. The process is to do an audit and generally should not be interpretive, so there is no immediate connection to the legal department.

Ongoing interactions between internal audit and legal are important for identifying significant or recurring issues, the risks they may point to, and the steps an institution should take to mitigate those risks and avoid future liability for failure to do so. A thorough understanding of internal audit processes can help the company to develop plans and adopt practices that make the overall legal, regulatory, and compliance environment more effective.

Legal Department's Role in Managing Legal Risks[6]

Gradually, the comprehensive and integrated approach to risk, also known as ERM, has been extended to all industrial and commercial sectors.

Today, each company has its own, more or less extensive, risk culture. Thus, organisations are accustomed to operationally treating risk, and complying with the standards of their trade. In the IT world, risk management is also highly developed and is part of the service provided to customers. The function of the Risk Manager is to identify, understand and manage the risks to which the organisation may be exposed.

As organisations become more mature in legal risk management, legal risks are identified separately and included in an organisation's risk management register. This change in approach and mindset will allow legal services to more effectively meet increased expectations and contribute to competitive advantage by controlling all legal risks arising from the organisation's operations.

It is therefore up to the legal function to map the organisation's legal in cooperation with the risk management function for inclusion in the global risk register, to implement the compliance policy required in particular by membership in a group, to put in place rules of integrity and ethics that apply to everyone.

Once identified, the risks must be prioritised according to their potential impact on the company and the stakes involved. Then, the leader makes decisions, and determines which risks deserve more attention than others and the attitude to be held against them (reduction, circumvention, confrontation, etc.).

The legal counsel is not to turn into a risk manager; however, risks are an ideal way for lawyers to add value and acquire a transversal dimension by participating in the development of practical solutions. Thus, they become facilitators where they were too often seen as obstacles to development. By becoming proactive rather than reactive, they position themselves in prevention, rather than confining themselves to a curative role.

---

[6]See Laurent, M.-P., Raggl, A., Rougeaux, C., & Tejada, M. (2021). *A strategic vision for model risk management*. McKinsey & Company.

In this monitoring role, the legal function must pay particular attention to the cost of risk, which is complex to determine: between notions of damage to the company's image, and actual litigation. As regards the other departments, the legal function must therefore be proactive and take part in the discussions on the concept of risk. Without positioning itself as a brake, but rather as a vector of enrichment and progress, it shares the views of its peers: financial director, production director, purchasing director, sales director, etc.

When a crisis breaks out, organisations still too often neglect to make systematic feedback preferring to leave this bad moment buried in their past. Here too, lawyers have every right to bring their colleagues together to provoke and analyse feedback.

Through risk, the legal function therefore has the enormous opportunity to position itself as a vehicle for questioning, dialogue, and knowledge enrichment, in a pragmatic manner.

Legal Risk in Strategic and Tactical Thinking

Risk is inherent to all activities of the company. Managing them relies on law as well as management science. Each of these disciplines will enable it to seek a form of the effectiveness of identification actions, risk reduction, and financing. Hence, the concept of risk must be analysed under the cross-examination of legal and management sciences.

Hence, the need to mobilise the sources of law and management to identify the notion of risk as it is currently considered, used, interpreted, and declined in the organisational context – and more generally – in management. It is a question of knowing how to organise the convergence of these areas of knowledge to better understand the notion of risk, to better anticipate it, and to better manage it.

From the inability to identify, anticipate, or manage risk to the definition of relevant actions, the risk is a major concern that every organisation must integrate into the daily life of its activity. The risk, the uncertainty inherent in any action, may indeed inhibit its development or constitute a stimulus to action.

Both law and management sciences are open to interdisciplinarity. The judge is even sometimes asked to seek extrinsic knowledge before deciding. The obstacles to the convergent analysis of law and management sciences are therefore more academic constraints than the reality of practice. On the contrary, mobilising managerial and legal knowledge dynamically through company practices appears to be a legitimate empirical approach.

Thus, this dialogue between law and management leads to better risk management through the development of management tools based on anticipation and mapping of potential risks. The combination of law and management sciences has paved the way to an optimised management of legal risks in any organisation.

Chapter 22

Managing Risk in Procurement Network

Over the past three years, multinational organisations have experienced significant disruptions in their supply networks. The coronavirus has wreaked havoc on multinational corporations and has highlighted the interdependencies and complexities inherent in many supply networks, not to mention the still difficult-to-measure consequences of the war in Ukraine and now the war in the Middle East.

While there is no simple answer to mitigate potential disruptions to the supply system, organisations can follow certain basic principles to reduce their risks and ensure business continuity. Investing in resilience should be at the heart of any strategy to take steps to reduce the risks of any supply networks. One of the keys is to back up any decision with reliable data and a risk assessment. If there is one lesson from recent events, it is that resilient organisations succeed best.

Embed Resilience in Supply Network Security Design[1]

By 2020, companies had already begun to rethink their distant supply networks in response to changing labour costs, advances in automation, rising protectionism, and external shocks, such as natural disasters. However, the disruptions in the early 20s have highlighted the structural gaps that prompted organisations to rethink their approach to global manufacturing and procurement.

Plant lockdowns, transportation disruptions, and panicked purchases have resulted in shortages of everything from medical supplies to household items to essential components of the automobile and electronics. The crisis has also exacerbated geopolitical tensions, trade restrictions, and nationalist policies to promote a domestic industry; they are likely to continue reshaping the global economic landscape.

[1]See *5 Strategies to Manage Procurement Risk*. (2022, June 13). https://www.rmmagazine.com/articles/article/2022/06/13/5-strategies-to-manage-procurement-risk?utm_source=magnetmail&utm_medium=email&utm_term=jplouisot@aol.com&utm_content=TWR%5F07022022%5FNM&utm_campaign=ESG%20report%2C%20Pride%20%2B%20DE%26I.

Enterprise Risk Management in Today's World: A Current and Futuristic View of the Complexity, Resilience, Responsibility and Tools in ERM, Part B, 257–269

Published under exclusive licence by Emerald Publishing Limited
doi:10.1108/978-1-83608-392-420241022

With massive value at stake, multinational companies seek to reduce risks and ensure better access to supplies and markets. They are exploring opportunities to diversify and regionalise their manufacturing and supply networks, add backup production and distribution capabilities, and reorganise inventories. Executive decisions will be heavily influenced by two key factors:

→ ***'impetus for change'***, such as economic and political pressures; and
→ ***'ease of adaptation'***, i.e. the difficulty of replacing some suppliers and the capital costs associated with moving to new locations.

The main elements to be taken into account in the current situation for the security of procurement networks:

- ***Changing global procurement landscape:***

Manufacturing channels and supply networks have been established largely to take advantage of differences in cost factors, such as labour, materials, and energy, as well as the ability to meet client needs within a given time frame and a specific quality standard in given markets. In recent years, concerns about market access, resilience, and environmental sustainability have become more important.

Significant production changes have been announced since the development of the pandemic. Taiwan Semiconductor Manufacturing, the world's largest silicon wafer smelter, said it plans to build a $12 billion plant in Arizona to deliver its many American customers, for example, and Mazda has moved the manufacture of some automotive components from China to Mexico.

As a result of these geopolitical, economic, and technological forces, as well as different shocks, resilience and access to critical supplies and markets, are becoming priorities.

- ***High-risk sectors:***

To understand which supply networks are likely to experience the most significant change, a matrix was generated that traces 16 industrial sectors on two axes:

→ ***The first is the impetus for change,*** an indicator of supply network risk. Factors include high dependence on imports, reliability of major supplier countries, exposure to potential government trade restrictions; and
→ ***The second is the ease of adaptation***, a measure of how easily companies can adapt their supply networks. Factors include the sector's capital intensity, the level of regulatory challenges that could limit adjustments, and the availability of other suppliers. In some sectors and product categories, China is virtually irreplaceable because it has an overwhelming advantage in terms of the size and depth of its capabilities, or because of limited capacity in other countries.

When individual companies and products within each industry segment are encouraged to change or facilitate adjustment, the matrix will, of course, vary depending on the markets they serve or the configuration of their supply chain.

The risks of supply disruption for industries and national security in developed countries are high, and pressure to increase domestic production is increasing. The impetus for change is also strong in China, where manufacturers import 86% of the semiconductors they use to manufacture electronic devices, at a time when the Governments in the USA and the EU are exploring stricter trade restrictions on technology.

In other industries where countries are heavily dependent on imports, supply networks are less likely to undergo significant changes because the impetus for change is weak. For example, the US imports most of its luxury goods and clothing from the EU and Asia. However, governments do not see these sectors as strategically important, and overconcentration is not a major risk because supply networks are fairly simple with many potential source countries for products.

- ***Definition and measure of resilience:***

Companies should measure their exposure to disruptions in absolute terms and relative to their competitors. Supply resilience should be measured for all three parts of the value chain:

→ ***Sourcing:*** Key measures to assess the resilience of a company's supply ecosystem include the degree of importation of goods, the percentage of suppliers that are concentrated in certain countries, the share of supplies that are supplied regionally and that are close to end-customers, and availability of spare suppliers for critical components and inventory levels of key inputs.

→ ***Manufacturing:*** Companies can assess their manufacturing resilience by looking at the percentage of capacity concentrated in certain countries, the amount of outsourced production, and if they have backup production capacity on existing sites in the event of an emergency or qualified backup facilities on different sites.

→ ***Delivery***: Downstream channel resiliency measures that deliver products to customers include the share of market revenue that could be impacted by significant price increases, the share of the distribution network that is covered by a single partner the average transport time of a product from a factory to a customer, and the stock levels in the final market.

- ***Option to reinforce resilience:***

When supply chain risk is deemed high, companies have a range of remedies to improve their resilience all along the value chain. When a particular line of business and product are in a matrix of change and easy of adjust, it is likely that the levers that companies deploy to improve the configuration of their supply network. A company may conclude that it can best achieve its strategic objectives by revising, migrating, or regionalising its supply network.

In terms of procurement, to improve resilience, they can reduce the risk of geographic overconcentration of their supply base by reallocating procurement within their existing global supplier networks to bring them closer to final markets.

They can also convince suppliers to move all or part of their production to other locations. Manufacturing networks can be made more resilient by expanding the capacities of existing factories and adopting a contingency strategy that preserves other factories within their networks and manufacturers under safeguard contracts that can quickly accept work if some facilities have experience in managing disturbances. To improve delivery resilience, companies can relocate their finished product inventories closer to final markets.

To assess and adjust their supply networks, organisations can take the following seven-step approach is expected to allow them to adapt supply networks and establish a competitive advantage:

1. ***Align design principles with the new reality:*** Begin by assessing whether the supply network is adequate in light of new economic and geopolitical realities. Identify the high-level risk exposure and trade-offs involved in optimising the supply network.
2. ***Segment the portfolio by supply chain risk and understand performance drivers:*** Define key segments of your business portfolio and assess supply network risks based on multiple factors, including products, geographic footprint, technology, and exposure to potential policy changes. Evaluate the current performance of suppliers and manufacturing networks on cost and service levels, etc.
3. ***Identify the levers and options at the segment level:*** Assess all levers applicable to supply network optimisation based on the profile of each segment and the most significant risks in the supply network. Determine the level of effort required for each action and its likely impact on the capabilities of the supply network.
4. ***Evaluate supply chain design options for each segment:*** For each potential action, analyse trade-offs between geopolitical risk and factors such as production costs, logistics, tariffs, market access, and resilience; select the appropriate approach to optimise supply networks.
5. ***Identify key performance indicators (KPIs) for resilience:*** A company could choose to supply at least 30% of major products or inputs from three or more qualified manufacturing sites in different geographic regions and to keep its capacity utilisation below 85%.
6. ***Enterprise-Wide Pressure Testing Design Choices:*** Consolidate the proposed changes at the segment level and assess the resulting internal and external network at the enterprise level. Then analyse the redesigned supply network under a set of scenarios that could cause market disruptions such as an escalation of the US–China trade war, conflict in Ukraine, financial crisis leading to the failure of key suppliers, or another pandemic.
7. ***Implement network redesign and monitor performance:*** Develop an implementation plan for the new supply network and a system for monitoring its performance and the quality of relations with economic partners during macroeconomic and geopolitical environment evolution.

To prosper and succeed in the existing global economy, supply networks will be redrafted to enhance resilience to disruptions, and flexible enough to take advantage of new sources of competitive advantage.

Formalise IT Service Provider Risk Management to Reduce Business Disruptions[2]

IT Supplier Risk Management (ITRM) ensures the use of external service providers, IT providers, and other providers does not create an unacceptable risk of disruption of activities, or a negative impact on the organisation's performance. It aims to specifically identify third parties who are responsible for the management, access, or provision of data to information assets. This includes third parties that execute or control critical business processes and IT systems.

With the development of the fourth industrial revolution, organisations are becoming increasingly dependent on third parties. Many ITRM programmes are being developed as tactical responses to ensure compliance with a growing list of data protection and cyber-security regulations. The approach to manage supplier risks is often labour-intensive, inefficient, and only marginally productive. However, capabilities can be developed and improved through a comprehensive approach to reduce the residual risk of IT providers and, increasingly, an ecosystem of other parties.

Highly regulated industries, such as financial services, have always been at the forefront of this activity, creating detailed guidance on establishing a supplier risk discipline.

A risk management framework for information systems should operate as part of an ERM programme and not in isolation.

- ***Identify and prioritise major risks:***

The first steps in ITRM are to identify relevant risks to the organisation, which typically depend on the industrial sector, as well as the applicable legislative and regulatory framework. Applying a risk prioritisation approach distinguishes between the level of risk that should concern the company. This allows suppliers to be segmented based on risk relevance for the organisation. Risks can be grouped by potential impacts and exposure. These risks fall under the following taxonomy:

→ ***Financial risks:*** They determine the financial viability of a supplier and any financial problems the supplier may have that will affect its performance obligations. Factors that may influence a supplier's financial risk include market dynamics, economic climate, competition, and suppliers' business and operational models.
→ ***Operational risks:*** They determine the organisation's risk for its key operational functions due to the supplier's inability to perform all or part of the function. This can result from a supplier's inability to provide adequate resources, poor processes, inability to respond to a pandemic, or failure to

[2]See *5 Strategies to Manage Procurement Risk*. (2022, June 13). https://www.rmmagazine.com/articles/article/2022/06/13/5-strategies-to-manage-procurement-risk?utm_source=magnetmail&utm_medium=email&utm_term=jplouisot@aol.com&utm_content=TWR%5F07022022%5FNM&utm_campaign=ESG%20report%2C%20Pride%20%2B%20DE%26I.

defend against a cyber attack. This should also include an assessment of the supplier's Business Continuity Management (BCP) program and IT Disaster Recovery (Restart) Plan.

→ ***Cyber risks:*** They refer to technologies and processes that defend digital assets from malicious attacks or threats and respond to these events to minimise damage. Risks include the detention or threat of your data for ransom, sabotage, espionage, and political motives. As organisations digitise processes, and adopt cloud services, cyber security risks need to be assessed to determine if controls are appropriate given the nature of the services.

→ ***Legal risk***: Related to regulation and compliance, the company needs to examine a range of regulatory, industry, process, and geographic requirements that suppliers must meet, and that customers must assess and follow. These risks may be related to areas such as accounting, reporting, user rights, data privacy and security, business resumption, and business continuity.

→ ***Strategy risks:*** They analyse the risks associated with changing supplier strategy about the products or services a client has acquired. Sudden changes in strategy, or inability to adapt to a change in strategy. This may include changing the supplier's supply network and subcontractors, which may be the result of leadership changes.

→ ***Geographic risks:*** These include risks related primarily to the provision of services or products outside the customer's home country or region. These risks may be geopolitical or caused by climatic or natural disasters, currency fluctuations, legal, and resource or infrastructure risks.

Risks can also impact business and organisation, such as brand, reputation, revenue, profitability, growth, or even survival. All supplier risks are assessed based on their threat or impact, likelihood of occurrence, and exposure to the business.

The risk taxonomy allows focusing on the riskier suppliers. Thus, resources can be appropriately allocated to assess high-risk suppliers. It can also be used to evaluate third-party vendors like when the primary vendor uses a third-party to store customer data. Many control bodies have identified these relationships with third parties as critical risks.

The taxonomy is also used to determine the level of authority within the organisation that can accept risk on behalf of the company, for example, a vice president for high residual risks.

- ***Work with Information Security and ERM to manage risks:***

ITRM must be aligned with an organisation's ERM programmes, operations, and IT systems to ensure end-to-end process continuity and effective risk governance. ITRM's activities are conducted within the limits of the organisation and its processes but must be examined as part of the overall risk portfolio and risk reduction strategies. Such activities and responsibilities include:

→ Procurement – Demonstrates financial due diligence by providing supplier credit risk data;

→ Information Safety – Review security controls, certifications, questionnaire responses, and data confidentiality controls provided by vendors;

→ Legal – Review contractual clauses and sources of information on ongoing litigation or potential mergers or acquisitions;
→ Commercial – Review Business Continuity Plans for suppliers or businesses to assess processes.

ITRM should collect risk data from these disparate sources and provide a complete picture of a given supplier's overall risk posture, and then define risk and assign risk responsibilities. Ultimately, responsibility for supplier risks rests with the business owner of the supplier relationship.

Any IT risk management programme should include:

→ Lay the foundation for supplier business continuity and contingency planning as required;
→ Link information security risks to financial sustainability risks and goods and services posing the greatest potential threat;
→ Identify governance requirements to develop transparency and visibility with suppliers and their third parties.

Mitigation measures should be documented in the risk register, with a primary owner and a date for completion or review of mitigation measures. Experience shows that those who identify a risk owner see a significant improvement in risk outcomes. If the reduction obligation is the responsibility of the technology provider, then this should also be documented in the contract, with termination rights if the reduction is not implemented within the agreed time frame.

If a risk is accepted, it must also be recorded in the risk register with the risk owner within the company. Risk Acceptance Authorisations should be aligned with ERM frameworks, including accountability to Board Risk Committees.

The final step in ITRM is to track the risks of change. Assign automated resources or processes to perform monitoring and facilitate reconciliation and risk reduction. In principle, the following actions and events take place:

→ ***Update risk register*** – Review agreed mitigation measures and ensure they are implemented. If the supplier has not met the requirements of the contract, escalate. If the contract is significant, seek legal advice to report a breach of the contract.
→ ***Risk factors*** – Monitor underlying risk factors at least annually and preferably on an ongoing basis, leveraging external data sources. They may include the financial stability of the supplier, legal action against the supplier, or cybersecurity risks. When the supplier's risk rating changes, escalate those risks to the company manager.
→ ***Contract review*** – Review contracts annually or more frequently for critical suppliers to ensure all risk due diligence is completed, such as updated financial sustainability reports, relevant certifications, and confirmation of employee history and due diligence checks.
→ ***Changes to Terms of Use*** – Review procurement, vendor management, legal services, IT, ERM, and information security with key business stakeholders regularly. These reviews should examine current and future risks and identify

gaps in ITRM policies or processes. If the use case has changed, are more sensitive data now being processed?

→ ***Risk Reporting*** – Develop and review IT supplier risk registers on an ongoing basis. At a minimum, the supplier risk register should identify the risks, the responsible body, the potential impact of the risks, and the reduction efforts undertaken. This should be presented to the risk committee of the company concerned.

To summarise, here are the three main conclusions concerning ITRM:

- Risk management responsibilities related to IT service providers often lack consistent and integrated practices to diagnose, track, reduce, and record supplier risks;
- Cyber-security and data protection regulations increase the need for comprehensive approaches to manage supplier risks and ensure compliance;
- Failure to track vendor risks and the organisation's evolving use of cloud solutions increases the threat of cyber and operational risks that may threaten business continuity.

Key recommendations for procurement and vendor management to manage partner risks are:

- Identify and prioritise the most important risks to their business and operations by working with enterprise risk teams and relevant stakeholders to define their supplier risk management frameworks;
- Cooperate with Information Security and Enterprise Risk Managers to manage risk through risk assessments, risk analysis and mitigation options offered to suppliers and business owners;
- Implement a supplier risk monitoring plan by allocating resources to manage the risk register, respond to changing risk factors or events, and report on risk compliance.

Risk, Resilience, and Rebalancing in Global Value Chains[3]

Companies that have successfully implemented a global 'lean' manufacturing model have improved their performance indexes such as inventory levels, timeliness of full deliveries, and shorter lead times. However, these business model choices have sometimes had unintended consequences if they did not consider the associated risks. Complex production networks have been designed to maximise efficiency, cost, and proximity to markets, but not necessarily to ensure transparency or resilience.

Shifting the physical footprint of production is just one of many options for building resilience. The latest advances offer new solutions for scenario execution,

[3]See *Risk, resilience, and rebalancing in global value chains*. McKinsey. https://www.mckinsey.com/~/media/McKinsey/Business%20Functions/Operations/Our%20Insights/Risk%20resilience%20and%20rebalancing%20in%20global%20value%20chains/Risk-resilience-and-rebalancing-in-global-value-chains-full-report-vH.pdf.

monitoring multiple layers of supplier networks, accelerating response times, and even changing the production economy. Some manufacturing companies will likely use these tools and develop new strategies to address the pandemic as more agile and innovative organisations.

Companies face a range of hazards, from natural disasters to geopolitical uncertainties and cyber attacks on their digital systems. Global flows and networks offer more 'surface' for impacts to penetrate and damage to propagation. Shocks are distinguished by their predictability, the frequency with which they occur, the magnitude of the impact on industries and regions, and the magnitude of the impact on supply and demand.

Value chains are exposed to different types of shocks based on their geographic footprint, production factors, and other variables. Those with the highest trade intensity and export concentration in a few countries are more exposed than others. They include some of the most valued and valuable industries, such as communications equipment, computers, electrons, and semiconductors and components. Many labour-intensive value chains, such as clothing, are highly exposed to pandemics, heat stress, and flood risk.

Increasing the resilience of supply networks includes strengthening risk management capacity and improving transparency; enhancing redundancy in supplier and transportation networks; maintaining more inventory; reducing product complexity; creating flexible production capacity between sites; and improving financial and operational capacity to respond to and recover from shocks quickly.

Seven Strategies to Strengthen the Resilience of Supply Networks[4]

Procurement professionals should explore new technologies and strategies to manage the core functions of the supply network. A strong procurement risk management plan can help the organisation contain costs, avoid unpleasant surprises and operate effectively.

---

[4]See Kaplan, D. A. *4 strategies to improve supply chain resilience.* https://www.servicenow.com/workflow/it-transformation/4-strategies-to-improve-supply-chain-resilience/?campid=88038&cid=e:EM-eDM-Workflow-Newsletter-08DEC20-Global&utm_source=marketo-workflownewsletter&utm_medium=email&utm_campaign=EM-eDM-Workflow-Newsletter-08DEC20-Global&mkt_tok=MDg5LUFOUy02NzMAAAGEEBo4dRxh_MuCphh4VjdYx1X0NwR-T2nUebZdG-pC9nB5rRJEbWyoZ7SxPvAnY7AlN_UD9E9WERQgwhypuT2PEGdyQtgT5x-h6l-q396I77kC3ZjaLj; *5 Strategies to Manage Procurement Risk.* (2022, June 13). https://www.rmmagazine.com/articles/article/2022/06/13/5-strategies-to-manage-procurement-risk?utm_source=magnetmail&utm_medium=email&utm_term=jplouisot@aol.com&utm_content=TWR%5F07022022%5FNM&utm_campaign=ESG%20report%2C%20Pride%20%2B%20DE%26I; Galer, D. (2021, October 1). *Managing supply chain disruption.* https://www.rmmagazine.com/articles/article/2021/10/01/managing-supply-chain-disruption.

The traditional just-in-time model relied on stability and predictability in an interconnected global network; it no longer is the case today. Experts believe there is a need for more resilient supply networks that can respond more quickly to unexpected fluctuations in supply and demand.

Today, digitalisation has become the foundation of any resilient supply network, but it needs to be integrated into a broader strategy. This can mean the use of tools that provide real-time visibility of stocks, blockchain adaptation to track a product from raw material to delivery, or the use of predictive algorithms that model how delays ripple through a supply network. Here are seven strategies that can help your organisation mitigate procurement risks:

- ***First strategy: Cost analysis, transparency, and compliance***

Expense data analysis provides valuable information on procurement cost errors such as unidentified payments, redundancies, duplicate invoices, fraudulent or non-compliant expenses, and specific suppliers that could be renegotiated.

Reviewing past spending can also help avoid risks such as inadequate internal needs analysis. For example, it is possible to identify over-evaluation or under-evaluation of needs, if the work is over a limited period, or if an insufficient budget has been programmed.

Relying on a single supplier for essential goods and services could pose a huge risk. Should he not deliver on time, the entire supply network could be disrupted. Expense analysis can also help determine if some suppliers are too expensive or if there are too many suppliers.

Implementing a transparent procurement policy helps reduce duplication in purchased products. Due to increased visibility, duplicate requests will be closely monitored and therefore avoided. Focusing on compliance also helps to control internal processes and regulate spending within the organisation. The higher the compliance rate, the less waste generated by the purchasing process.

- ***Second strategy: Monitoring inventory level***

Just-in-time inventory management has reduced storage costs and waste, and improved cash flows. When in the case of a disruption to the supply network, this policy severely curtails the company's ability to deliver final products to customers. Just-in-time inventory management can prove problematic in other situations, such as when a large shipment contains damaged or incorrect goods. Businesses must assess whether the benefits of these inventory strategies outweigh the risks to their operations.

- ***Third strategy: Managing suppliers' relationships***

In a stable environment, economic efficiency led to the consolidation of supplies; however, for key products and services that are crucial to the company, it was already recommended to have more than one supplier. Indeed, with several suppliers, an organisation avoids dependence on a single supplier who could make or break the business and unnecessary bottlenecks when demand takes off. Thus, an organisation is more agile when confronted with unforeseen events thanks to a multi-suppliers approach.

One reduction tactic is to have suppliers located in different regions. If a major problem occurs in one part of the world, the materials or services may still come from suppliers located elsewhere. It can be useful to help companies in countries that are not exploited or less exploited develop their expertise or access their resources so that they can become reliable alternatives.

On the other hand, working with several suppliers can give the company more leverage with each supplier and reduce the risk of one being unable to deliver. A careful and objective assessment should reveal the number of additional or 'next-level' suppliers used for each type of product or service provided. In all cases, it is necessary to build strong relationships with suppliers that guarantee long-term success.

Effective supplier management can significantly reduce the risk of disrupting the supply network, particularly late deliveries or poor-quality products.

- ***Fourth strategy: Vertical integration***

Vertical integration consists in owning and managing one's supply network or much of it. Vertical supply integration can also result from strategic investments and guarantee the security of supply. Companies with large investment portfolios could choose to buy shares or take an interest in companies that are part of its supply network. As an investor, the company tends to be better informed about its supplier's business. If the investment is significant enough, it could even give the company a seat on the board of directors thus providing some influence on the provider's resilience management.

To assess the benefits of vertical integration, long-term macro-trends must be assessed. Should climatic, political, social, or other conditions over the next decade encourage greater control of the supply chain? Many sources of information can help with these considerations.

- ***Fifth strategy: Product recalls***

Food product recalls due to bacterial contamination can be extremely costly for supermarkets and suppliers. For example, BrightFarms found that by recording data from each stage of the growth and delivery process, they could identify issues such as storage temperature changes. Because green lettuces are sold at higher prices than conventionally grown lettuces, this technology can help them track KPIs to determine the highest yield products.

- ***Sixth strategy: Montreal versus Toronto – Labour unrest***

Even before the pandemic, the Port of Montreal was facing supply pressures from labour strikes, while Vancouver was experiencing disruptions from climate-related flooding. While the port used to measure the performance of its supply network based on transit time, reliability, and vessel weight, its new measures aim to predict the behaviour of the entire supply chain.

Initially implemented for medical supplies, the Port plans to use the technology for other products such as microchips or auto parts, charging a surcharge for priority service.

- ***Seventh strategy: Overcoming spreadsheets limitations***

The pandemic has also highlighted the limitations of using spreadsheets to manage supply networks. The tool, which has long been an essential component of supply chain management, does not meet the real-time information needs of manufacturers and data providers.

Cooperating with top management, procurement managers, and all relevant functions, risk managers should explore possible strategies to mitigate the impact of a supply disruption, including purchasing insurance covers, which, while not preventing the occurrence and extent of disruptions, may offset the associated financial losses.

Some strategies may need to be modified to meet specific needs, and multiple methods may be required. There are many ways to reduce risks associated with uncertainty in the supply system; whatever the objective, it is essential to take proactive action and set up the optimal cocktail based on the seven strategies suggested.

The Future of Procurement Networks and the Importance of ESG[5]

From climate change litigation to diversity and inclusion, environmental, social, and governance (ESG) issues are an important source of emerging responsibility for directors and executives. Investors, employees, and consumers will increasingly expect companies to actively consider ESG factors while companies face a growing range of legal and regulatory requirements for ESG transparency as developed in earlier topics in this book.

Publicly traded companies are already required to manage and report on their sustainability, and there is a move to require them to investigate their procurement partners' ESG practices. The impact of their activities on the environment and society as a whole is now regularly measured and assessed through ESG ratings, scrutinised by investors and the press.

The level of risk that lurks in supply networks is not always evident based on a company's ESG current rating. To further complicate matters, research suggests that many companies do not fully understand their threat level. The European Union has introduced a new supply chain due diligence regulation which incorporates mandatory human rights and environmental due diligence.

As building sustainable supply networks becomes essential, there is a lack of reliable data to compare suppliers and third parties. In many cases, there is no formal contractual obligation to encourage sustainable business practices within supply chains.

The lack of data is compounded by the fact that much of the supply network is made up of private companies. Large companies that want to better understand

[5]See Minutella, C. *The road to future-proofing your supply chain*. https://www.strategic-risk-europe.com/home/the-road-to-future-proofing-your-supply-chain/1437276.article?utm_source=adestra&utm_term=Read%20more&utm_medium=email&utm_campaign=24388.

their suppliers often find less emphasis on ESG policy awareness, procedures, and policies as they progress through the supplier network.

Supply network risk management was traditionally focused on geopolitical and logistical threats. Today, it is likely to be linked to cyber risks, data protection, and information security, allowing senior management to stay awake at night.

A new legal and regulatory environment implies aligning the priorities of third parties in the supply network with the sustainability objectives of the customer. By focusing on ESG factors in the management of their supply system, organisations reinforce their role as reliable service providers in a competitive marketplace and ultimately create value.

Security of Supply Networks at the Heart of Resilience

Many companies still focus too much on short-term financial performance relative to their long-term development and sustainability aspects. Rainer Baumann, Managing Director of the Swiss distribution group Migros, identifies three areas of vulnerability for organisations' supply network interruption:

- Disruption of raw materials *(often as a result of extreme weather and natural disasters)*;
- Transportation disruption *(e.g. when the Rhine reached dangerously low levels in 2018)*;
- Production disruption *(e.g. Parmesan shortage due to Italian lockdown)*.

Rayner Baumann pointed out that during the pandemic businesses often had to fight simultaneously all three forms of interruptions. For example, companies that had raw materials were not able to produce finished products because the factories were confined. In the meantime, ships, railways, and trucks were forced to stop or slowed down considerably. In the UK, reports have highlighted that some raw materials were affected due to a lack of seasonal workers and fruit pickers although this lack was a combined consequence of the pandemic and Brexit.

There will be more disruptions in the future as extreme weather events appear to be on the rise as evidenced by summer 2023. Climate disruptions to supply networks will become more frequent and severe. Due to the expected risk of weather events, political risks, socio-economic risks, and emerging risks still poorly identified, and the complex nature of supply networks – companies, especially multinationals, need to broaden the scope of their procurement risk assessment.

Chapter 23

Marketing, Demarketing, and Risk Management

While there may still be debates and controversies, they tend to become confined to economists from the same theoretical mind frame. The dominant thought framework does not allow taking into account what does not exist... until it happens! The crisis caused by subprimes was such a case in point; if there were then other economists, coming from other currents, practicing other methods, convinced of the impending disaster, such as Cassandra, they were inaudible.

The economists who practice economics differently are often called 'heterodox'. John Maynard Keynes called them, and himself 'heretics', to point out that they were banished from the mainstream. Their common characteristic is to recognise the crucial importance of institutions in the face of the idea that economic relations obey natural and universal laws. For this reason, and without denying their great diversity (and divergences) of analyses, it is probably preferable to describe them with the more positive term of 'non-institutional' economists. Their approach seeing economy as part of social sciences makes it possible to raise debates and make visible problems that can only be outlined by the standard approach.

Today, more than ever, the world needs a diversity of approaches in economics and, therefore, the 'institution' movement. Precisely, global and integrated risk management is an illustration of the need for a diversity of thinking in economics since it is a question of knowing how to challenge certainties to cope with an increasingly volatile and complex world, hence an ever-changing risk landscape.

It is important to prepare for the challenges ahead, but no one knows where the next stage of our journey will take us. While most economic actors spend time trying to increase the demand for their products and/or services, others try to decrease it; hence, the needs for a new approach labelled 'demarketing'.

Enterprise Risk Management in Today's World: A Current and Futuristic View of the Complexity, Resilience, Responsibility and Tools in ERM, Part B, 271–281

Published under exclusive licence by Emerald Publishing Limited
doi:10.1108/978-1-83608-392-420241023

What Are the Five Major Marketing Risks for an Organisation?[1]

Learning to manage marketing risks can help create more effective campaigns, reach a wider audience, and drive engagement and relevance in the company's marketing programmes.

A marketing risk is an event or perspective that could threaten the success of a marketing campaign. Because of the number of elements involved in marketing, such as product, strategy, budget, image, competition, and consumer opinion, the field is a source of considerable uncertainty.

Risks can take many forms and must be addressed through a structured and proactive marketing plan. Here are five key marketing risks that could affect a business and strategies to treat them:

- ***Risk to reputation:***

A reputational risk is a risk that can affect stakeholders' perception of a brand and/or business. Negative public reactions, bad publicity, or uncontrollable events can hurt an organisation's reputation. Several factors that can compromise his reputation, including:

→ Customers service;
→ Organisational efficiency;
→ Product accessibility; and
→ Product/service reliability and quality.

To mitigate this risk, it is necessary to find tools to maintain a level of favourable brand perception among stakeholders. Perception can be assessed using tools such as surveys and consumer feedback. Responding to customer concerns directly and quickly can improve perception and help better understand customer needs.

Their input can also guide efforts. For example, if consumers seem frustrated by the quality of the product or the efficiency of the ordering process, it is possible to use feedback information to design and implement beneficial improvements.

- ***Minimal marketing strategy:***

Limited marketing reach or lack of diversification could result in a limitation of engagement and the number of leads. Marketing strategy can profoundly influence the success of a product or service launch. A diversified marketing strategy can reach broader audiences and increase reach and engagement.

An organisation can overcome this risk with dynamic leadership, well-communicated goals, and strong collaboration among team members. By diversifying the approach and creating a marketing plan that encompasses multiple

---

[1]*5 Common marketing risks that can affect your business.* https://www.indeed.com/career-advice/career-development/marketing-risks.

communication channels, such as blogs, forums, social media, videos, and emails, it is possible to effectively expand the strategy and broaden the customer base.

- ***Lack of specific brand messages:***

It is important to review and refine brand messages to ensure reaching the ideal customer. To avoid missing targets, core demographic data should be regularly re-evaluated thus ensuring marketing efforts maximum efficiency. When the 'ideal' client is defined, the entire team's involvement ensures the multiple perspectives and angles of the selected target are considered.

Analytical tools help identify the highest levels of client engagement. Using these strategies jointly can give leaders and the entire team the most complete picture of their targets. The important factors to consider when establishing the ideal customer profile are:

→ Demographics such as age, sex, and average annual income.
→ Where to find the ideal customer (target)?
→ What unique selling points the products/services can have for target customers? and
→ The best way to communicate with target customers.

- ***Pricing strategy:***

Pricing strategy is essential for a company's success. They are company-specific, and are an essential component of a robust marketing strategy. Pricing strategies often fall into one of four categories: high, moderate, low, or reduced.

Each price level has its unique advantages and disadvantages. The marketing team should work with management and operations to determine an effective pricing strategy. An organisation can change its pricing strategy if necessary, using techniques such as price increases, flash sales, and online promotions. Marketers can overcome this risk by learning how to effectively market changes to their target demographic and taking action on the information they receive about their current pricing approach.

- ***Partnerships and franchises:***

Partnerships and franchise can prove powerful tools in a business and can drive sales, grow the customer base, and increase business volumes. The use of partnerships can also increase brand awareness and engagement within the target community.

However, they carry specific risks as partners and/or franchisees' actions can influence brand perception. For example, if partners or franchisees take action that does not align with the company's values, they risk adopting behaviours that tarnish the company's image. This is why it is essential to nurture relationships with companies that adhere to the company's fundamental values and transparently present themselves. In this way, successful partnerships can be established to represent the company.

How Can Risk Management Enhance Marketing Strategies?[2]

A marketing risk is the risk of failure or loss during any marketing activity, from production to distribution; it may include one of the following:

→ Incorrect pricing of a product;
→ Choosing the wrong advertising channel for a target audience;
→ Distribution delays;
→ Negative comments on social media or review sites;
→ Staff turnover; and
→ Operational changes.

Without being exhaustive, this list makes it clear that marketing departments are exposed to any of these types of issues that can cause financial losses and harm a company's brand.

A marketing risk management plan is a comprehensive risk reduction system that anticipates, prepares for, circumvents, or overcomes potential challenges. Some threats have been outlined in the previous section but the following is also to be examined:

- ***Risk linked to the brand:***

Any business can see its brand devalued as a result of fierce competition or poor marketing. If the strength of a brand is overestimated, it may result in misuse of marketing techniques. It may already be too late when the company realises that it needs to double its efforts or spend more resources to promote its brand. So, regardless of the brand, investing resources in marketing tactics, such as referencing and content marketing, is critical to staying strong in the competitive marketplace.

- ***Wrong target market calculation:***

Not conducting extensive market research, collecting data in the wrong place, and using the data inappropriately can pose risks to the marketing plan. If the market is not understood, the ensuing strategy may target the wrong people or portray an inadequate image of the product being sold. To create a marketing message that appeals to the desired target audience, thorough research beforehand is needed.

- ***Trends evolution:***

In today's digital world, marketing trends are changing daily. If marketing strategies are not up to date, business outcomes will be at risk. Always keep an eye out for the latest promotional messages from your niche, price changes, and marketing automation technology, and constantly track what competitors are doing.

---

[2]Lynch, K. (2022, February 21). *4 ways risk management plans can help your marketing strategy*. http://www.ranky.co/growth-hacking-and-inbound-marketing-blog/4-ways-a-risk-management-plan-can-help-your-marketing-strategy.

- ***Promotional risk:***

If a poorly calculated approach is used to promote the goods and services, efforts will be in vain. False, misleading, and exaggerated messages can also hinder marketing efforts. In addition to ensuring that the promotional techniques used are compelling, powerful, and effective, it is essential to ensure that advertising practices are ethical.

The essential issue is whether the message will reach the intended target, whether potential customers will react positively, or even if the brand will be recognised. A marketing risk management plan aims to contain these risks. By following a risk management process suggested in the ISO 31000, it is possible to better understand why such a plan is important:

- ***Risk identification:***

The most important role of a marketing risk management plan is to identify and define any barriers that the marketing team may encounter. Knowing what is in the future, team members can make the right decisions to avoid the threat and/or minimise negative impacts. With this in mind, it is possible to be more confident in developing and implementing a marketing strategy.

- ***Risk analysis and evaluation:***

The risk management plan provides important information about the risks to be considered during the planning phase and after the implementation of marketing efforts. The analysis of each potential risk determines the likelihood, magnitude, and frequency of the risk. It is then possible to modify the marketing strategy to overcome all the challenges that arise along the way. Analysing all the risks before launching marketing efforts will enhance success chances.

- ***Selecting and implementing necessary treatments:***

The risk management plan must address all challenges in the best possible way by developing mitigating measures in advance. Sometimes it is possible to attack the risk at the root, to remove its causes, and to avoid it completely, sometimes it is only possible to reduce its severity or frequency. For example, if the marketing messages are deemed to not generate traffic, adopting a more effective strategy is possible.

- ***Risk monitoring and review:***

It is possible to predict when the threat will become a serious problem and put measures in place to address it. In today's marketing landscape, there are ongoing challenges. Competitors may find better innovations, customer preferences may change or sales may start to drop. A risk management plan helps to monitor and be prepared for most new and existing challenges.

Marketing departments often focus their energy on the planning and execution phases of marketing activities, but they must go further to succeed; with the support of risk management and within the framework of the ERM strategies, they can engage in marketing risk management to ensure that risky marketing activities are managed pro-actively. While all team members need to be aware of potential risks, one team member should be assigned to assess risks regularly throughout the planning process.

What Is Demarketing and How to Use it?[3]

Organisations are developing marketing strategy that are increasingly aggressive, and demarketing may seem like a bad practice for some companies. However, this technique is sometimes extremely effective and useful for a company in particular for managing ESG risk (Fig. 23.1).

The concept is not new since it was forged in 1971 by Philip Kotler and Sidney J. Levy, professors of marketing, and researchers at the Kellogg School of Business but it had not experienced any real 'commercialisation' until global warming and the depletion of natural resources give it new visibility in association with the circular economy.

This approach can be adopted to protect consumers from potential harm *(alcohol, tobacco, etc.)* because demand is higher than the supply that cannot satisfy it or because of the very high cost of advertising the product. A good example of demarketing is that of the five-star hotels which, to preserve an elite status, do not hesitate to offer a pricy menu, create car parks at a distance, etc. anything that could dissuade average persons from using their services.

Demarketing strategies fall into three main categories: general demarketing (marketing a product for all with the aim to reduce the overall demand for this product), selective demarketing (operating on a class of consumers to protect the most loyal consumers), and ostensible demarketing (creating an artificial shortage to stimulate the appetite of the public). There are different strategies for demarketing:

> Composed of the word 'marketing' and the prefix 'de' which gives a word the opposite meaning, refers to the strategy, adopted by a public or private organisation, to discourage purchases from certain segments or all consumers, temporarily or permanently. For a company, there is demarketing if the marketing strategy chosen does not maximise demand, even though there are alternative growth-oriented strategies.

Fig. 23.1. Demarketing Definition.

---

[3]See two articles:

→ *5 efficaces stratégies de démarketing à exploiter.* https://www.lebusinessjournal.com/management/5-efficaces-strategies-de-demarketing-exploiter

→ *Démarketing: un drôle de concept, non?* https://novelus.fr/demarketing.un.drole.de.concept.non-33-434.php

- ***Bait marketing:***

It consists of marketing a product to attract consumers who can then be induced to acquire through the same structure another product much more profitable. Some consider this strategy to be based on deception; however, it works and even proves to be devilishly effective.

- ***Demarketing based on pricing strategy:***

For example, price discrimination is practiced when two units from the same property are sold on the market at different prices to persons under identical conditions. When companies develop such a strategy, they deliberately create costs that are primarily aimed at discouraging consumers from seeking a lower price. In this way, active consumers pay a much higher price while those who make small transactions pay a lower price without more. Low-cost airlines regularly use this strategy by offering products and services simultaneously to different segments of the market.

- ***Demarketing based on shortages:***

Companies cause false shortages for some of their products, creating a sense of urgency for buyers to quickly get a product without thinking too much because they don't want to miss an opportunity. To get quick results, companies accompany this fictitious shortage of products with a proposal for deliveries at a later date. An artificial shortage forces consumers to buy more units of a product when it is available again to prevent another shortage.

- ***Demarketing based on differentiation:***

Concerning the traditional four Ps of marketing (product, price, place, and promotion), some companies try to adopt demarketing strategies by focusing on these four Ps. Some increase the price of a product, and discourage price-conscious consumers from buying it, while others focus on a second P, the product and thus remove all warranties or accessories that accompany their product. Concerning the third 'P', namely place, companies sometimes restrict the availability of a product in certain places and therefore use a demarketing strategy. The last 'P', the promotion, applies by reducing promotions made on a product.

- ***Demarketing of mass costs:***

This strategy is used when a huge crowd is expected at a specific time such as Black Friday or the first day of sales. Then, a crazy world of consumers is rushing into stores, which pushes away other consumers who prefer to pay more and buy from companies that do not offer Black Friday.

In everyday life, consumers and even organisations are faced with this approach almost regardless of their habits. For example, when buying a pack of cigarettes, what are the messages conveyed? The messages of deterrence aim at preserving health. The same goes for wine and spirits with health messages such as 'the consumption of alcoholic beverages during pregnancy, even in small quantities, can have serious consequences on the child's health' or advertising for certain foods: fat, sweet, etc.

Recently, several demarketing campaigns have emerged for destinations victims of their success: the arrival of too many tourists generating impacts on the local population and the environment. This is the case for Iceland following an influx of visitors that is five times greater than the number of inhabitants, or for New Zealand which wants to avoid an increase of visitors on some 'spots' touted on my social media.

What Is 'Counter-Marketing'?[4]

Changes in market dynamics bring about changes in the marketing function. While many marketing changes have already begun before the onset of COVID-19, the pandemic has accelerated these trends and in many cases has left a unique footprint.

Brands rely on the marketing function to generate the message internally and externally. Purpose-based marketing, the mission, was a growing trend at the beginning of the year that only got worse when the pandemic hit. When empathy is critical and it's easy to say and do the wrong thing to alienate stakeholders, marketing needs to be at the centre of the action to ensure that all messages are authentic, brand-consistent, and relevant. It is clear, however, that a tone of support and empathy must also be accompanied by concrete actions that are consistent with the message. To quote the English saying often cited in risk management: *'Talk the talk, and walk the walk.'*

In this context, many citizens and consumers have been confronted daily with counter-marketing strategies without having any idea of the concept. Counter-marketing involves advertising techniques that try to reduce the demand for a product used. Counter-marketing usually uses negative messages to prevent people from using a product and in this sense it is one of the possible forms of demarketing.

Further analysis could include the pharmaceutical industry in the same category since more and more drugs are being avoided to treat certain symptoms if these specialties can easily be replaced by natural remedies. Fundamentally, the counter-marketing strategy puts into perspective the explanations of the hazard linked to using a specific product or service. It communicates social costs and can use multiple pathways and strategies. In general, the counter-marketing strategy should work with other tactics to change social norms.

Often used to take an opposing position on a controversial topic or to counter an impression that could be made by advertising from another party, the counter-marketing strategy tends to introduce brand substitution. This is therefore a risk to be considered in the context of reputational damage since a counter-marketing campaign could undermine stakeholders' trust. Therefore, brand strength is the key factor in the effectiveness of a counter-marketing tactic.

To be effective, counter-marketing programs must be assessed and have explicit objectives associated with performance measures, while aspects such as time, money, and political context are important variables for the performance of the strategy.

---

[4]Bhasin, H. (2020, January 25). *Counter marketing – A demarketing tactic*. https://www.marketing91.com/counter-marketing/.

With change sweeping through work and life, brands rely on marketing to stay connected with consumers during turbulent times. Brands will live and die based on their ability to withstand current changes in consumer beliefs and behaviours.

Demarketing, Communication, and Brand-Building Campaigns in the 'New' World[5]

In the past, 'demarketing' was applied to situations to control demand in times of low production. In the same sense, downsizing the economy was an environmental movement in the 1960s, discussed by many important scientists, but more related to the cultural agenda and confronted by many economists and entrepreneurs. Nowadays, the subject is related to the complexity of studies such as extra-activism and anti-colonialist movements and is part of the post-humanist agenda.

Philip Kotler and Sarkar explained in 'Brand Activism' how for a brand creating value for a segment of the population is not enough if it creates threats for everyone and the planet. In 2017, in 'Welcome to the Age of Demarketing', recalling an article from the 1970s, Kotler explained the new strategic importance of this expression in our time. In 2021, during this global pandemic, he explained that we need to understand that there are no more solutions, 'we need to use demarketing tools' immediately.

In the economic field, many specialists initiated these discussions a long time ago, building the ecological economy, as is the case of Professor Alier, who published since the 1970s and explains how GDP (Gross Domestic Product) is no longer enough and keep in mind Nepal, where the government instituted the GHI (Global Happiness Index).

The connection between demarketing and sustainable development results from the fact that demarketing, or decay, and other expressions used in this sense to reduce something, does not exactly mean to get a drop in production of something or even to get lower profits necessarily. In other words, delivering a lot of products on a global scale, on time, for a good cost, can be considered efficiency, provided it is achieved with a small overall footprint, and respect for diversity and human rights.

Other crucial elements of this process are the campaigns of demarketing and communication for the right positioning of the brand, the education of consumers and stakeholders, are the following:

1. Choose the right approach, which is not necessarily attractive or compelling to sell to clients and partners;
2. Decide on the right tools, in the case communication actions are important because strong integrated marketing communication planning makes a huge difference;

[5]Forni, D. F. F., & Romanini, A. V. *Demarketing and the role of communication and branding campaigns in a post-Covid world: Who will pay the bill?* file:///d:/Users/LOUISOT/Downloads/Demarketing_and_the_role_of_communicatio-2.pdf.

3. Understand the link between these elements and the ESG (Environmental, Social, and Governance) programme, which deserves methodologies to compare global objectives with equities and establish the best measures in line with new broad public policies.

Socially responsible values have been the main concern in recent years; the current flow of crises from which the world has not yet emerged will likely accelerate this trend. For example, recent research on Australian households shows a growing culture of doing the right thing, caring for society, and 'being all in the same boat'. And the recent wave of activism should give consumers a better idea of their power to hold large organisations to account. Many say brand reactions during the crisis will have a significant impact on whether they will continue to buy it in a new normal for the world.

More importantly, brands must support their bold statements with concrete actions. Some brands perceived to benefit from a given cause or situations have already been impacted. Brands need to make clear commitments to the causes they believe in and act on them, or risk newly empowered consumers denouncing them.

What Lies Ahead with Marketing Emerging Risks in this Complex and Volatile World?

The founding principle of sustainability is that a generation should not exploit existing resources – oil, water, air, wood, and fish – so intensely that the next generation is doomed to accept a lower standard of living. As the earth's resources decline, we may need to move from the age of marketing to the age of demarketing.

How does that affect business decision-making? Companies that embrace sustainability must make fundamental changes to their production and marketing strategies and practices. Paul Polman, CEO of Unilever, said, *'Our ambitions are to double our turnover, but to do so while reducing our environmental footprint… This must be done through more responsible consumption…'*

Sustainable companies need to introduce clear criteria to guide their new product development programs, invest more in reuse and recycling, and convince their stakeholders, employees, channels, suppliers, and investors, to fight waste and accept certain limits to growth. Businesses will need to adjust their compensation regimes to better balance growth and sustainability objectives. Executives should be compensated based on achieving the expected growth rate while reducing impact on the environment.

There are precautions when trying to reduce the demand for a desired object. First, the demarketing campaign could make the product or service more desirable: a ban on a book or film often has that effect. Second, it can create a criminal class that will thrive during the induced shortage, as was the case during the 'prohibition' era in the United States, when alcohol was banned. Third, human rights defenders could complain about the government's interference in what they consider to be citizens' rights, particularly the right to bear arms in the United States (Second Amendment to the Constitution).

The interface role of demarketing is particularly important in the field of environmental protection and invites those who develop it not to ignore the multiplication of forms of resistance against ecological issues. To evolve with society and/or make society evolve, it is necessary to respond more concretely to the responsible demands of certain prospects and to promote the emergence of more sustainable lifestyles. We must reflect on the devaluation or restriction of trade based on the principles of sustainable development.

Environmental demarketing invites a comparative analysis of the commercial policies of firms and the pressures exerted on them by stakeholders. Societal and environmental challenges are increasingly important:

- population growth, emergence;
- economies of developing and emerging countries;
- population, limited stocks of natural resources;
- management of high-risk waste…

These challenges are taking on a special dimension today in the post-Covid world where the geopolitical situation has further blurred the lines. Then the role of marketing is to evolve. Even if technical and technological advances make it possible to consume less and meet increasingly demanding environmental standards, it now seems inevitable to change some traditional consumption patterns.

Messages against the trend of explicit demarketing may weaken the firm's competitive position in certain markets. Making a product less attractive for environmental reasons may, if consumers are not sufficiently prepared, act against the company involved. Repositioning, based on the use of an inverted mix, can destabilise customers and cloud the company's reputation.

Beyond the recovery and/or defence of the ecological theme, environmental demarketing is presented as a way to reorient the commercial policy of the company. This reorientation is all the stronger as it is partly the result of increasing pressure from different stakeholders. The typology of environmental demarketing shows that the actors are plural. The different messages they carry thus link the market, social, and political spheres in an unusual and innovative fashion.

Risk managers need to prepare for the future by simultaneously leading much long-term efforts. They must ensure that they deepen and accelerate the digital transformation of the function, win the talent war, and acquire cutting-edge expertise in regulation, cyber security, analytics, and digital innovation. Moving to Reasoned Growth requires understanding the risks associated with marketing and demarketing, an essential component of the periscope to scrutinise the horizon to identify emerging risks related to new marketing practices.

Chapter 24

Human Resources Risk Management

Human resources (HR) management reflects the strength of corporate governance and organisational resilience capabilities. The new HR issues have become significant concerns for organisations and have made a risk management approach to this function even more urgent at all levels.

New HR issues can be very diverse in the current context, where commonly discussed issues have been exacerbated by crises that have collided since the beginning of the decade. Although this list is not exhaustive, these problems include adjustment to the performance and well-being of employees; the struggle of organisations to improve wages; the difficulty of instilling confidence in employees; the increase of internal and external conflicts during an unexpected public crisis on a large scale. Effective HR practices are essential for organisations, especially during a crisis, so they must prepare contingency plans to address the risks associated with emerging HR issues and their impacts on their overall operations.

The development of next-generation communications technologies such as artificial intelligence (AI), machine learning, cloud computing, and the Internet of Things has fostered innovation in HR practices, especially during the pandemic. The ability to continually optimise potential HR practices indicates an organisation's ability to dynamically allocate HR, which has the most direct impact on emergency management outcomes.

Regardless of the industry and profession, the decision-making process is important for all managers. Soft skills like critical thinking and problem-solving can be strengthened by analysing risk. Risk analysis is therefore an important tool to control, assess risk impact on HR.

Today, Human resource risk issues are fundamentally related to the hiring and retention of talents essential to the organisation when populations are aging and millennial expectations are very different from those of Generation X.

Enterprise Risk Management in Today's World: A Current and Futuristic View of the Complexity, Resilience, Responsibility and Tools in ERM, Part B, 283–294

Published under exclusive licence by Emerald Publishing Limited
doi:10.1108/978-1-83608-392-420241024

Risk Analysis for HR[1]

As in any field, the HR risk analysis must allow them to be prioritised to manage them effectively and:

→ Mitigate the consequences of a damaging incident;
→ Determine if the benefits outweigh the risk, in any HR project;
→ Decide how the employees and the company will respond to emergencies; and
→ Eliminate risks whenever possible.

Taking risks is not an option but taking too much risk can lead to failure. Risk analysis is the foundation for efficient risk-taking. An HR manager must work with top management to resolve critical management issues regarding talents and competencies in a rapidly changing internal and external context; this has led to an increased role for operational HR.

Change is one of the most frequent challenges confronting today's organisations. Transitioning is always risky as human beings tend to dislike changes in their work environment. Strong cooperation between HR and RM professionals is required: HR managers must be aware of these hazards while risk managers are increasingly conscious of the importance of HR in managing risk.

But how do HR professionals contribute to risk management? For example, if there is a steady decline in production noticed by senior management. Once the risk is identified, the HR manager is called upon to determine the human part of the issue. A gap between what should be done operationally and what is done operationally could be the source of the risk.

However, a company's performance rests also on the relationship between the HR manager and operational and strategic managers especially on performance criteria. Therefore, HR's main responsibility is to cooperate with operational managers and earn their trust, that is, to foster relationships of trust between managers to validate criteria. These partnerships are established at all levels: senior managers, line managers and supervisors, as well as specialists in various functions. This cooperation must be open to the extended enterprise, i.e. encourage customers and suppliers to participate.

If HR management plays an important role in risk management, but HR managers only deal with the human side of risk and HR risk control strategies would include succession planning, executive coaching, and talent development, all aimed at ensuring that a company and its entire staff are well prepared to manage risk.

In addition, the HR executive plays a critical role in risk management by defining the characteristics of key positions or leaders within the organisation. Staff turnover is also a potential risk from an HR perspective; training, development,

---

[1]Talent Management Essentials. (2019, January 15). *Future risk management in human resources*. https://www.tmi.org/blog/future-risk-management-in-human-resources-talent-management-essentials.

and mentoring of employees within the organisation to increase employee participation and morale for future positions.

Are Talents at the Heart of HR Risk Management in the Future?[2]

For any HR executive, managing future risks in the talent pool is critical; beyond succession plans, further analyse of the complexities of employees' departure is needed to address the talent issue through appropriate systems and processes to ensure the adequacy of a future pool of talent. Here are the five pillars of talent management:

- ***Talent focus:***

The first pillar is developing and understanding the talents that will be needed in the future to fulfil the vision and the mission of the organisation, and ensure all employees embrace it. This is achieved when all understand where they 'fit' into the entire contribution process for organisational objectives. Constant communication is required so that the hierarchy of decision-making and the strategic objectives of the organisation are integrated into individual KPIs and KRIs.

- ***Talent gap analysis:***

The second pillar is the specific analysis of existing talent gaps within the organisation. Technical skills, soft skills, communication skills and a willingness to outperform are coveted traits and must be identified in all departments, teams, and functions.

With appropriate mapping of current talent availability, and expected attrition, it is possible to identify talent gaps in the future based on future needs. Then the situation can be visualised and presented to the branches for further review, and consolidated for the Board and Top Management so that they can endorse the recommendations to close the gap.

- ***Talent acquisition:***

The third pillar consists of the five essential factors of talent acquisition in the 21st century: job branding, attraction, candidate experience, constant device-based awareness, and bias-free assessment. Employer branding and social media awareness will make the organisation a buzzword in the workplace culture and potential talent must be ready to line up for consideration.

Constant communication based on media, including social media, where prospects can exchange, encourages communication, expression, and careful listening. Thus, potential candidates will remain engaged until their assessment process begins, when potential bias must be monitored from the top.

---

[2]Talent Management Essentials. (2019, January 15). *Future risk management in human resources*. https://www.tmi.org/blog/future-risk-management-in-human-resources-talent-management-essentials.

- ***Prejudices elimination:***

The fourth pillar is concerned with diversity and inclusion which have become top priorities, but it may not be for the manager directly in charge of the hiring. Therefore, at the strategic talent manager's level, a conscious effort must be made to educate hiring managers not to allow common hiring biases to influence their choices.

The hiring process must be tailored to add the exact skills needed by the organisation as previously identified in the talent gap without forgetting the aspirations of the prospective candidate. In the digital age, it is possible to integrate into an ongoing bilateral feedback mechanism that provides a balanced view of the interaction and allows top management to identify if the hiring process has been biased.

- ***Skills development and succession plans:***

Once the talent gap is identified and employees understand the organisation's vision and mission clearly and commit to making every effort to achieve the company's objectives, there remains to act internally as needed.

Before an external search, skills that are lacking may be found internally through appropriate training and adequate succession plans. These should rest on ongoing performance assessments, stakeholders' relations, leadership qualities, and personality traits to develop an organisational structure including contingency plans ready to be implemented as soon as an employee signals his/her intention to leave the organisation. Detailed and well-designed orientation tracks, knowledge transfers, and, when needed, minimal external coaching to prepare for the new position, should be enough in most situations.

Sound risk management, motivated employees, successors in place, and skills development in progress, are the foundations of the work of the 'talent manager' implementing the HR strategy with the main objective of employee satisfaction.

What Are the Main Sources of Risk in HR?[3]

Employees perform work for which they receive a salary. However, the total cost of an employee's compensation is not limited to the salary, even including social security contributions. Here are the top eight HR risks an organisation faces and their causes.

- ***Worksite culture:***

Experience shows that there are two main types of workplace culture:

→ ***Team culture***: It unites all members of the organisation to achieve the desired goals of the organisation's leadership. This culture is typically embodied in the way business is conducted, what kind of camaraderie is shared by all, how efforts are unified, and how communication flows from one side of the organisation chart to the other (and everywhere in between).

---

[3] *HR Risk Management – Top 8 Sources of Human Resource Risk*. https://treadstonerisk.com/blog/hr-risk-management-top-8-sources-of-human-resource-risk/.

This type of culture calls for a specific building process for each organisation. Sometimes very charismatic leadership can set the tone, and everyone agrees. In very 'flat' organisations, a common rallying cry or a common goal or cause binds everyone together. Regardless of the source, it is necessary to cultivate and hire staff that will fit in with this culture to maintain or improve it.

→ ***Security and risk management culture***: An organisation's partners, clients, and suppliers in particular, care more about why an organisation does something before they even think about how they do it. Well, today the 'how' has become very important.

The way of operating any organisation must include a huge dose of a culture of safety and risk management at the corporate level. Why? Because the way to operate has to take risk into account in terms of performance and opportunity cost.

Recently researchers with a psychoanalysis background have revived the Marxist concept of 'living work'[4] for which living work constitutes the event heart of human activity. They point out that the work involves, in many respects, damage to the physical and mental health of individuals while at the same time recognising the structuring character of the work from a social and individual point of view.

The approach is based on communication, exchanges, and discussions between researcher and worker that emerge a large part of the iceberg hidden in the depth of collective strategies about the organisation of work to highlight the emergence of the psycho-dynamics of work. The 'living work', the new theoretical base of which was laid at the turn of the 1980s, marks a turning point in the psychopathology of work, which until then was mainly concerned with how psychosomatic diseases and the mentally ill are described.

Recovering occupational health most often comes up against the impossible transgression of prescriptions, which block the 'man-organisation relationship of work'. The clinician therefore has to assess the individual's scope for action in defining the organisation of his work. So there are ways out of the pain in the workplace, which includes recognition and self-esteem. Perhaps the most logical conclusion is that for harmony in the workplace, the two cultures mentioned above must be combined.

Therefore, it is necessary to consider how the safety management and team culture could collapse and harm the organisation losing the trust of internal and external stakeholders:

→ ***Social unrest*** – caused either by the perception of unfair treatment or concerns about the direction of the organisation. The consequences can be an increase in staff turnover, a decrease in morale, a decrease in productivity, and a slowdown in overall growth.

→ ***Lack of leadership*** – most organisational failures are related to a lack of leadership, which is never more evident than cultural failures. Leaders must accept

---

[4]Dejours, C. *Situations du travail*, Paris, Puf, 2016.

and practice what they preach in both areas. 'Do as I say, not as I do' is a recipe for disaster.

→ ***Uncontrollable circumstances*** – from disaster to economic crisis. In these situations, a robust culture can save the body. However, a weak culture is very rarely improved by an external crisis. Typically, even average organisational cultures fail in chaos.

- ***Workplace accidents, medical expenses, and loss of productivity:***

Some work accidents are the result of unusual and exceptional circumstances, but others are the result of unsafe workspace, improper procedure, or external influence (think of the consequences of being struck by a reckless driver). Potential impacts on an organisation may include:

→ Loss of productivity;
→ Increased labour costs *(anyone who can work overtime?)*;
→ Lower employee morale;
→ Medical expenses and disability awards;
→ Fines and regulatory sanctions *(beware of labour inspection)*; and
→ Staff turnover costs.

- ***Employment-related legal proceedings:***

Sometimes, a poorly executed HR process can not only fail to meet expectations but also discriminate against one or more employees. This can happen inadvertently or intentionally. A strong organisational culture is about holding these people accountable for their actions and the potential to undermine that culture.

An organisation also needs processes in place to ensure that employees feel that their complaints and comments are heard and taken seriously. Employment-related litigation is one of the fastest-growing HR expenses (excluding medical expenses). Here are some effects:

→ Several lawsuits will cost significant amounts for legal defence, damages and even the employee's legal fees in states that allow the transfer of costs;
→ Employee morale will fall if the collective opinion is that the organisation is not doing enough or nothing to protect them from discriminatory treatment or a dangerous workplace;
→ Reduced employee productivity and increased absenteeism – if employees don't feel safe at work, they don't hesitate to take a sick leave;
→ Reputational damage – if the situation deteriorates sufficiently, a toxic work environment can generate negative stakeholders' opinion and limit the pool of potential new employees. It can result in the inability to hire the best talent and the loss of business streams due to reputation deterioration. With social media, this type of information spreads rapidly and can be registered forever on the Internet.

- ***Liability for employee benefits:***

Employee benefits programmes are a cost for organisations, but they are also part of the package to attract the best talents and keep them as part of RSE management. It is a complex issue that must be reviewed with the help of specialised consultants. In all cases, these specific causes and effects need to be considered:

→ Poor communication can result in employees or their dependants having a poor understanding of the benefits to which they are eligible, eligibility deadlines, or extreme disappointment when employee expectations are not met. This may lead to lower morale, higher staff turnover, and potential legal action (legal fees and damages).
→ Programme design issues may be unintentional or intentional; inadvertently exclude from eligibility an employee or group of employees; or intentionally exclude from eligibility where regulations or legislation, including terms of collective agreements, are misunderstood or ignored… This may result in very costly litigations (legal fees and damages) and the possibility of fines.

- ***Network and data security risks:***

Hackers often use channels related to employees' behaviour. From opening suspicious emails to volunteering login credentials or financial information, staffs are on the front lines fighting the intrusion or perhaps opening the door so that a hacker can enter directly. The key here is training and awareness because the causes are primarily related to poorly followed procedures with the following potential costs:

→ Data loss;
→ Network and business disruption;
→ Loss of income during periods of inactivity;
→ Data repair or replacement costs;
→ Forensic audits; and
→ Regulatory fines and penalties *(like GDPR within the EU).*

- ***Theft and embezzlement:***

Every year, there are stories about employees who are unhappy or short of money and who have embezzled money from their employers. The causes may vary, but often involve an employee who has gone through difficult times, has a behavioural problem (e.g. gambling habit), or is unhappy and wants revenge for what he/she feels is an injustice. The ultimate losses here are all the unrecoverable assets, the loss of an employee (who is often really creating value), and the impact on the reputation of the event disclosure.

- ***Training and competencies:***

Training and skills failures are generally the results of a poorly designed programme that does not prepare employees for success. The causes are usually apathy or ignorance of training gaps. These may result in liability litigations brought by customers or third parties, piracy, claims on professional liability, repeated work accidents, and possibly the death of an employee.

- ***Turnover rate:***

Staff turnover is a common theme in HR risk management. The costs of high turnover rates can be very high for an organisation. Some studies show that a single lost employee incurs expenses amounting to several times his annual salary.

HR risks are present at every stage of employment from hiring to termination or retirement. A proactive approach is needed to ensure that planning for HR is always a priority. When developing a risk management plan for HR activities, there are several areas to focus on. This generic taxonomy can serve as a starting point, but all organisations must identify and assess their specific risks (Table 24.1).

HR risks are a major challenge for organisations. Their consequences can directly impact their functioning, development, image, and income statement. However, interest in HR risk mapping remains limited for a majority of actors even though they recognise the importance of taking into account risks related to HR.

The role of an HR risk management professional involves examining all the possible consequences of risks for employees, which may be related to employee behaviour, management styles, or wages, for example. A fundamental aspect of HR risk management is ensuring that the organisational structure supports its employees. By ensuring that a company's systems effectively serve its employees, incidents become less likely. An engaged and attentive workforce is a strong ally in the risk management process.

Table 24.1. HR and Risk Management.

HR Activity	**Potential Risk**	**Elements to Consider**
Compensation and employee benefits	• Financial exploitation	• Who has signing authority? • How many signatures are required? • Are there controls?
Recruitment	• Discriminatory practices	• Have potential candidates been fully screened? • Have local human rights laws been respected? • Is there a fixed trial period? • Can promises made to the candidate not be honoured? • Did the employee sign the policies and contract of employment before being hired?
Worksite Health and safety	• Hiring unqualified or dangerous candidates	Are safe working conditions provided and safety checks regularly performed? Does staff receive adequate training?

(*continued*)

Table 24.1. (*Continued*)

HR Activity	Potential Risk	Elements to Consider
		• Is there assurance that proper clothing and safety equipment are used? • Are adequate policies, procedures, and committees in place?
Employees supervision	• Abuse • Reputation with stakeholders • Disclosure of personal information	• Are adequate guidance and training provided? • Is adequate supervision (especially for off-site or after-hours activities) provided? • Is there an effective performance management system? • Are privacy guidelines being followed?
Employees attitudes	• Abuse • Reputation with stakeholders	• Are there written job descriptions for all positions? • Is there a follow-up when work description parameters are not met? • Is extensive orientation and training provided? • Is an employee guide provided to all? • Are there comprehensive policies and procedures in place? • Is ongoing training provided on policies and procedures? • Are written records kept of performance issues? • Is there assurance that the organisation's valuables are safe? • Are robust cash management procedures in place? • Are adequate harassment policies and procedures enforced?
Employees departure	• Appropriate • Reputation with stakeholders • Compensation	• Are organisational information and equipment retrieved from a laid-off employee used (mostly from home)? • Is there assurance that all access codes, passwords, etc. are disabled? • Are exit interviews conducted? • Is there a proper record of compensatory leave and vacation balances?

How to Stop Wasting the Most Valuable Resource: Middle Managers?[5]

Middle management has a vital role within organisations but often feels undervalued. Local managers and supervisors face pressures from above and below, they tend to be both underdeveloped and powerless; and they face increasing pressure to offer flatter, faster, and leaner organisational structures, which leads to being underutilised and not appreciated. The results of a new McKinsey global survey of middle managers suggest that many companies could unintentionally impair the ability of middle managers to play their role.

Companies treat middle managers as a centre of attraction, requiring managers to devote a large portion of their time to non-administrative tasks and navigating the organisational bureaucracy rather than allowing them to focus on the most important role of an organisation: fostering talent.

Despite the importance of these relationships between middle managers and supervisors and the employees they supervise, these report spending almost three-quarters of their time on tasks not directly related to talent management. In their survey, Mc Kinsey identified three areas where organisations can better help their managers deliver more value:

- → ***Spend more time on talent***. Organisations can help managers who need to devote time to planning and lower-value tasks focus on priority talent needs.
- → ***Eliminate organisational barriers***. Many managers report challenges from above and below, and responses suggest that any reduction in excessive bureaucracy could improve the work of managers.
- → ***Customise incentives***. Understanding what motivates middle managers can help organisations provide the best environment for their managers to succeed.

Organisations should reward community coaching, often rewarding managers in the way that matters most to them. New responsibilities are the most commonly reported reward: nearly six in ten respondents say they have received new responsibilities as a result of their efforts in their current role. In addition, about half of respondents say their work has been rewarded with increased autonomy and bonuses.

Understanding Human Resource Risks in the New 'Normal' World?

Although it is not clear if the world is on its way to a new normal or if constant change will prove the norm in the future, the evidence is that Flexible working arrangements already frequent universities, high-tech enterprises are increasingly

[5]*Stop wasting your most precious resource: Middle management*. McKinsey & Company. https://www.mckinsey.com/capabilities/people-and-organisational-performance/our-insights/stop-wasting-your-most-precious-resource-middle-managers.

being promoted by enterprises, and units in other industries and induce transformations in working methods.

Flexible working arrangements have created new challenges such as increasing inequality, personal exhaustion, and reducing work efficiency. Although teleworking, or working from home, which are flexible work arrangements, are effective in ensuring the health and safety of employees, self-control becomes an important factor and has caused negative emotions. In addition, distance learning technology for students in underdeveloped regions is difficult to implement. When organisations shift their workforce to digital platforms, they weaken regions with poor digital infrastructure.

Organisational flexibility that became a central measure for coping with the epidemic remains a work in the current volatile and complex context; however, it is difficult to improve organisational flexibility in HR because of the double heterogeneity of industry and business.

Leadership practices also lead to issues of gender, discrimination, safety management, and education. Limited performance management practices were adopted during the outbreak, making it more difficult for employers to distinguish contributions from employees and to provide career development opportunities tailored to their needs.

Experienced with widespread social distancing policies in various countries during the pandemic, remote and flexible work continues to be embraced in many countries, resulting in communication and transmission issues within the organisation and especially with extended supply networks.

HR risk management is strongly associated with managerial practices and corporate culture. In the absence of management support and committed leadership within the company, RM and HR teams cannot develop robust actions, or compliance with social law, nor implement internal controls or audits to rely on real HR risk measurement indicators.

Cyber risk has become an HR issue and four key risks that HR teams need to consider when developing a specific cyber risk management plan are:

- ***Staff's technological competence:***

The rate of technological change means that the technical complexity of the work sometimes exceeds the competence of the workforce. For example, the American leader GE has discovered that the importance of technology in its industrial processes and the speed with which it has evolved have overwhelmed its employees.

When workers have time to learn a few technologies in depth, they can follow the new iterations, threats, and uses of this technology. HR leaders know that when employees take on a manageable workload, they can master the technology they need to use, which makes them feel strong and capable in the labour market.

- ***Ineffective or non-existent integration strategies:***

In this volatile economy, many companies are unable to attract or recruit talent that meets their quality standards. When they recruit these candidates, they may not take full advantage of their skills and knowledge due to poor integration strategies.

Integration impacts retention, which impacts recruitment. To provide a world-class on-boarding experience for new employees, keep it simple, interesting, and personal, and make sure you start even before the new employee steps into his job.

- ***Non-compliant record keeping with data regulations:***

Regulators are tracking the type of data companies can collect, where and how they store it, who can see it, and how they can highlight and use it. If HR teams do not keep the appropriate records or if these records are lost or destroyed, they may face financial and legal penalties.

It is also important to stay abreast of changes to requirements. Recently, for example, the GDPR has changed the rules on how international companies doing business in Europe can communicate with potential employees. As data becomes more valuable and vulnerable, laws are expected to continue to tighten.

- ***Employees training:***

In some organisations, employees may be partially or completely trained for their current role. In other cases, employees can get a good initial training, but no refresher is offered. According to some experts, the best time to train employees is about three months after their start. Most of the information provided in the early days of a new job is passed on to employees because of the volume and scope of the change. It is best to give instructions on company technology and updates on company policy after new employees have had time to adapt.

To overcome proximity bias and other issues related to hybrid and remote work innovation, HR professionals need to encourage and educate leaders and work to establish objective performance metrics to establish fair pay and promotion strategies. With talent shortages ahead more strategic training of the workforce is expected on the competencies and talents required for an organisation's ability to strengthen its competitive advantages and ultimately achieve robust resilience.

Chapter 25

Cyber-risk and Ransomware

> One difference between the French-style appeasement and the American-style appeasement is that France pays a ransom in cash and gets its hostages back while the United States pays a ransom in arms and is taken more hostages. (William Safire[1])

This declaration is half a century old and refers to the taking of human hostages by terrorist groups; already then the issue of ransom payment was on the table as decision-makers had to cope with the fact that hostages' lives were at stake. Then, the main issue was payments by the states but some private organisations were also involved, as well as their insurers. Covers wording required that the contract be kept secret and, in most cases, the insurer appointed a team of specialised negotiators to deal with kidnappers.

With the growing importance of advanced technologies in organisations' daily life, cyber-risk management has become a specific programme, an essential component of ERM; and ransomware is a major issue. With cybercrime, most often the motive is money, and some criminal organisations are setting themselves up as for-profit enterprises, and refuting the very notion of political or humanitarian engagement. The ransomware concept was first introduced at an international medical conference on AIDS in 1989 and was known as the Trojan Horse AIDS.

Today, ransomware is much more pernicious and produces significant economic and social costs. The effects of ransomware go beyond data loss. A recent university study showed a striking impact on hospitals in particular, showing 36 deaths per 10,000 heart attacks that could have been prevented had the systems not been infected (PBS NewsHour, 2019).

In England, WannaCry's attack on the National Health Service (NHS) resulted in the cancellation of thousands of appointments and surgeries in five regional hospitals (Collier, 2017). It took almost a year to fully assess the damage and costs caused by the attack on individual health systems.

---

[1]William Safire is an Anglo-American columnist, journalist, and specialist from New York. He was advisor to Richard Nixon for whom he wrote many speeches.

Enterprise Risk Management in Today's World: A Current and Futuristic View of the Complexity, Resilience, Responsibility and Tools in ERM, Part B, 295–303

Published under exclusive licence by Emerald Publishing Limited
doi:10.1108/978-1-83608-392-420241025

Ransomware attacks have increased regularly in the last 10 years, and more rapidly so during the COVID-19 pandemic, which has resulted in more online services while making critical infrastructure more vulnerable to cybercriminals. According to Cyber-security Ventures, ransomware has cost organisations around the world more than $20 billion in 2021, and it is expected that global cybercrime will have an impact of $6 trillion before the end of the decade. These estimates include the costs associated with restoring data and infrastructure, as well as the often significant costs associated with hidden expenses to mitigate the social damage of an attack.

Ransomware can kill when it attacks healthcare facilities. Tragically, the first ransomware death occurred in 2020. The event occurred on September 10 when the Düsseldorf University Hospital, the closest facility to a woman in need of urgent medical care, was closed due to a ransomware attack: the patient had to be transferred to another hospital 30 km away; unfortunately, it was too late when she was admitted.

Such consequences are more than sufficient to justify that top management devotes the time and resources essential to find solutions to implement a global cyber-security policy to strengthen cyber-resilience for the extended organisation.

What Are the Steps of a Ransomware Attack?[2]

Experts agree that the development of a ransomware attack takes place in five phases:

- ***Step 1 – Infection:***

Initial entry into the system is through spam, phishing attacks, or an operating kit – easily accessible on the Dark Web. During this step, system and user vulnerabilities are exploited. Gaps in user awareness and training, as well as breaches of corporate security policies, provide ransomware input into IT infrastructure.

- ***Step 2 – Administration:***

Mechanisms for continuous service are established. These mechanisms modify the registry keys to protect the ransomware, hide it, and allow auto-start-up even after a system shutdown. This phase allows ransomware to encrypt files at a later date without requiring additional actions by the user or the ransomware control centre.

- ***Step 3 – Rescue attack:***

This is a self-defence mechanism for ransomware to ensure its effectiveness and facilitate payment. CryptoLocker and Locky, two ransomware variants, include commands to remove all shadow copies of infected systems. Other variants search for folders containing backup files to delete them.

- ***Step 4 – Encryption:***

Encryption keys are installed at the heart of the local system. Early forms of ransomware included encryption keys in the application, allowing security teams

[2]The anatomy of a ransomware attack – September 07, 2022 – https://www.jpmorgan.com/insights/cybersecurity/ransomware/the-anatomy-of-a-ransomware-attack

to easily identify unencrypted keys and information. Today, encryption keys are not provided with the application, and file recovery time varies depending on the characteristics of the IT infrastructure such as file size, network characteristics, and number of connected devices.

- ***Step 5 – Ransom payment, corrective action, and advice to users/regulators:***

The ransomware notifies the user of the infection, requires payment, and provides instructions for payment. In general, the user has a deadline for payment, with penalties or increased ransom for not having paid on time. After payment of the ransom, the ransomware frequently tries to remove evidence of its presence that can be identified by forensic investigators.

Typically, organisations victims of ransomware face huge financial, resource, and time losses to restore operations and access their pirated systems; as a result, they prefer to pay the ransom money instead of pouring huge resources into repairing the damaged system. However, sometimes criminals do not provide systems restoration despite payment of ransom.

Does Giving in to Blackmail Not Set a Dangerous Precedent?[3]

Ransomware has become a common weapon in the arsenal of cybercriminals who regularly attack individuals and organisations. In these attacks, their victims suffer at least financial damage either by ending up paying the ransom or by bearing the cost of repairing the damage caused by the attacks. It is now all too clear that becoming a ransomware target is no longer about 'if', but rather about 'when'.

Reliable data on ransomware is not readily available as most victims choose to remain silent. Ransoms demanded by pirates vary considerably but can reach tens of millions of dollars. However, according to cyber security experts, the initial demand is often substantially reduced during negotiations.

Criminals have three preferred target industries: industry, professional services, and public administration. They target 'prospects' that have a low tolerance for downtime. Organisations that rely on near-permanent availability can lose millions of dollars every day in the event of an interruption: their leaders are more likely to pay the ransom to restart operations quickly.

IBM Security X-Force has noted also an increase in ransomware attacks on educational institutions; the development of virtual courses or experimentation with hybrid environments has accelerated since the pandemic and these developments make them an attractive target for hackers (IBM, 2022).

A victim who gives in and pays a ransom contributes to the development of crime as it fuels a security racket. But victims make purely economic decisions: paying the ransom is cheaper than losing data. When declining to pay, the victim

---

[3]See Riley, M., & Mehrotra, K. (May 14, 2021). *Paying cyber ransoms sets a bad precedent but happens often*. https://www.bloomberg.com/news/articles/2021-05-14/paying-cyber-ransoms-sets-a-bad-precedent-but-happens-often.

is likely not to recover their data – sometimes there is an effective free descriptor available, but most of the time, the security industry cannot provide one – and the damage may be so severe that the victim goes bankrupt. Who could blame individuals or corporations who decide to pay rather than commit financial suicide? In fact, for businesses, it may seem responsible to pay rather than destroy the livelihoods of staff, including those in the lower salary range less likely than managers to survive the damage to their finances.

Of course, for victims who do not pay, ransomware attacks may shrink their bottom line; however, crime would not go away, but scammers would explore other avenues – or perhaps dark, sinister alleyways. However, attacks will remain economically viable until potential victims are willing or able to proactively defend their data. Of course, both public and private bodies should implement such defences. However, too many CEOs consider it less expensive to pay ransoms than to finance a rescue strategy; this is probably a mistake because the robust backup practice protects against all kinds of cyber misfortunes, not just ransomware.

However, in the end, victims must always weigh the pros and cons of the payment bearing in mind that they:

- have no guarantee that all its data will be decrypted;
- will never know if their data has ever been sold on the Dark Web or not; and
- fuel future attacks.

Are Insurers Funding Criminal Activity?[4]

Some say that insurers inadvertently fund organised crime by reimbursing companies for the ransom they paid to regain access to data and systems after a hack attack. Ciaran Martin, who ran the National Cyber Security Centre of Great Britain until August 2020, expressed concern that so-called ransomware was 'on the verge of becoming out of control' and that there was a risk that the NHS (National Health Service) systems would be infected during the pandemic.

The issue is fuelled by the lack of legal barriers preventing companies from paying ransoms to cyber-gangs, typically from Russia and other former Soviet states, and then seeking reimbursement from their insurer. Victims pay criminals in Bitcoin and claim cash from their insurers.

Ransomware criminals hold organisations hostage and demand large payments with greater frequency and scale. To restore victim systems, the common practice is that the hacker requires to be paid in crypto-currency, which cannot be traced by the victim or the police.

'Explosion of ransomware cases has been fuelled by the rise of cyber insurance': this is the common wisdom for commentators, but also by political leaders.

---

[4]See *Insurers 'funding organised crime' by paying ransomware* claims – Exclusive: former cyber-security chief calls for a law change and warns situation is 'close to getting out of control'. https://www.theguardian.com/technology/2021/jan/24/insurers-funding-organised-by-paying-ransomware-claims.

However, the importance given to cyber insurance seems to be contradicted by its still low level of penetration: despite several years of rapid growth, policies dedicated to cyber-risk, including ransomware, are purchased by relatively few organisations (33% in the US, according to a survey), and globally only a 'small minority' of cyber risk is assured.

Each major cyber attack reveals new facets of the challenge of securing the world's digital economies. The lesson of recent attacks should be that ransomware is a strategic threat that requires diversified, multi-layered defences accessible to all parts of the economy. Insurance can be one of these defences, as it has been for centuries in other risk categories. It can encourage risk management, through policy requirements and pricing risks; Insurance is particularly important for small and medium-sized enterprises, as it can provide specialised resources to help businesses prepare for and recover from cyber events.

Ransomware has grown to become the most serious form of cybercrime, developing into an industry with the 'ransomware-as-a-service' model. Despite their freedom of operation, it seems that organised cybercriminal groups can be constrained and ultimately deterred by a combination of negative publicity and drastic responses. However, it is essential to quantify cyber risks to critical infrastructure and develop risk management tools at the level of sophistication of criminal activities.

Insurance companies themselves are a target of choice for criminal groups. Insurers should therefore carefully examine their approach to ensure that their products promote better e-risk management by, for example, tightening the conditions under which a ransom can be paid. Uncertainty in the availability of cyber insurance has broader impacts on resilience.

Organisations' level of preparation for cyber events varies widely, and even the most sophisticated can be compromised by weaknesses in their digital supply network. This knowledge imbalance puts initiative in the hands of cyber-aggressors and means that disruptive cyber-attacks can have significant and unexpected consequences. The patchwork of mechanisms to encourage good practice and share intelligence needs to be strengthened by a collective 'nervous system'.

Beyond the legislative and regulatory environment, more education on preventive measures is essential. Proper backups and other proactive techniques could put an end to this without forgetting that the problem of paying ransoms is that it does not guarantee that recovery across their entire functionality will be effective. In addition, claims usually increase over time.

Will Governments Ever Ban Ransom Payments?[5]

Ransomware has become an increasingly visible threat in the United States and abroad. Cybercriminals have long used the software to plunder their victims. Some countries, including North Korea, Russia, or even Iran or China, are also accused of using ransomware to make money and/or for spying activities. For instance, several

[5]See *The insurance business in the post-Covid-19 era*. https://www.atlas-mag.net/en/issue/insurance-in-the-aftermath-of-covid-19.

criminal hacking groups are based in Russia and states formerly members of the Soviet Union, except the Baltic region; it seems that the Kremlin and other governments in the region are turning a blind eye to their activities, despite their denials.

As far as Britain is concerned, British extortion laws prohibit the payment of ransoms to terrorists; they have been enacted largely in response to the threat of kidnapping. But cyber-attacks are generally not conducted by terrorist groups, so there is no ban on paying ransom demands; moreover, it is possible to claim compensation from your insurer, if no personal data has been involved.

Regarding the United States, the US Treasury reminds us that 'facilitating ransomware payments to sanctioned hackers can be illegal', by announcing a crackdown on the rapidly growing market for consultants who assist organisations with settlements to cyber-criminals. In two notices, the Foreign Asset Control Office (OCFA) of the Treasury, and its law enforcement network warned that facilitators could be prosecuted even if they or the victims did not know that the ransom pirates were under American sanctions, especially hacker groups in countries like Iran, North Korea, and Russia.

In addition, OCFA and its armed arm have also warned that cyber security companies may have to register as money services businesses if they help make ransom payments. This would impose a new regulatory reporting requirement on the cyber security industry, a sector so far largely unregulated. However, financial institutions are required to produce reports that identify suspicious transactions, including those that could involve ransomware or other criminal activity.

However, in a country like the United States, it seems incredible that all law enforcement organizations, including the Cybersecurity and Infrastructure Security Agency (CISA), Federal Bureau of Investigation (FBI), police, and other cybersecurity authorities, have been unable to block such cyberattacks. This has led victims to prefer paying a ransom to minimize their losses rather than cooperating with police in the hope of identifying and convicting the criminals. In the EU, there are calls to consider imposing restrictions on the payment of ransoms.

What Lessons to Learn from Pandemic Events?[6]

Hackers have taken advantage of the climate of uncertainty and instability exacerbated by the 2020 pandemic while being amplified by the tele-work movement adopted by businesses that are not ready to face remote implementations.

---

[6]See:

→ *This Year in Ransomware Payouts (2020 Edition)*. https://heimdalsecurity.com/blog/ransomware-payouts-of-2020/.

→ *Colonial Pipeline paid ransomware hackers $5 million, U.S. official says*. https://www.nbcnews.com/tech/security/colonial-pipeline-paid-ransomware-hackers-5-million-u-s-official-n1267286.

→ *Colonial Pipeline paid $5 million ransom to hackers* – Published Thu, May 13 20212:05 PM EDTUp dated Thu, May 13 20216:38 PM EDT – Eamon Javers@EamonJavers & Amanda Macias@amanda_m_macias – https://www.cnbc.com/2021/05/13/colonial-pipeline-paid-ransom-to-hackers-source-says.html.

Naturally, as people wanted to ease their confusion, Web searches related to the coronavirus increased. As a result, cybercriminals have begun to hide ransomware and disguise it as COVID-19-related documents, seeking to entice victims to access fake websites or download malicious apps. During this time, researchers have found that the COVID-19 pandemic has led to a 72% growth in ransomware attacks.

Also, security researchers discovered a phishing document targeting University of British Columbia (UBC) staff with a fake COVID-19 survey.19, which used model injection to download and execute a remote model that included a malicious macro. When the macro was executed, it released the Vaggen ransomware and demanded a Bitcoin payment, the equivalent of $80 for each student and teacher.

- ***Top attacks in the USA in 2020***[7]

The list of the most important ransomware payments in 2020 in the United States makes it possible to notice how easily organisations of all sizes can become victims of cyber-paralysing attacks; it's not just for large multinationals or even the competitive private sector.

- ***Cyber attack on a French hospital***[8]

Pirates have paralysed a French hospital in Oloron-Sainte-Marie, demanding a ransom to restore its network in the third cyber attack on a hospital in less than a month. On 8 March 2021, the entire hospital was paralysed by the attack. The ransomware made the hospital's computer system completely inoperative and a €40,000 Bitcoin ransom was requested to unlock the systems.

To prevent the spread of malicious code, all computer devices were disconnected from hospital networks. The attack was reported to the cybercrime department of the gendarmerie, which visited the scene, as well as to the French National Agency for Security of Information Systems (ANSSI).

The health facility can accommodate more than 300 patients and has approximately 600 employees. However, his normal operations were reduced due to the computer attack. This attack on a French hospital illustrates how healthcare facilities have become a high-profile target for cybercriminals, particularly due to the coronavirus pandemic.

According to Anssi, hospitals are more likely to pay the ransom given the critical need for continuity of care for inpatients. A few weeks before the hospitals of Dax, in the Landes, and Villefranche-sur-Saône, in the Rhône, were also attacked by hackers; and several new attacks took place since then.

- ***Colonial Pipeline Attack in the United States***[9]

Colonial Pipeline paid the pirates who shut down some of its networks the ransom demanded. The news was made public by Bloomberg but the American authorities refused to confirm.

---

[7]See reference in the previous note.

[8]*Third French hospital immobilised by a cyberattack and ransom demand.* https://www.rfi.fr/en/france/20210311-third-french-hospital-immobilised-by-cyberattack-and-ransom-demand.

[9]See 2nd and 3rd reference in note #6.

Colonial, which operates the country's largest fuel pipeline, informed that it had been hacked on 7 May 2021, and had shut down the four major pipelines serving the Eastern and South-eastern United States as a precautionary measure. Petrol prices went up, and some stations ran out of fuel. The Department of Transport issued an emergency order allowing truck drivers delivering fuel in affected states to work more hours than would normally be possible under federal regulations.

A week after the attack, the company announced that it would resume operations. However, the company indicated that some markets served by Colonial Pipeline may experience or continue to experience intermittent service interruptions during the start-up period.

Hackers, known as DarkSide, are part of several ransomware groups that hold agency records and demand payment, either by locking their records and making them unusable or by threatening to make them public. DarkSide, like many ransomware gangs, are supposed to operate from Russia, and their ransomware programme is designed to shut down if they infect computers that run in the Russian language.

In a statement, the group said it was an apolitical group simply trying to make money by paralysing fuel distribution in the United States. Also, DarkSide is known to provide victims who pay for a decryption programme that works painfully slowly.

What is in the Future for Ransomware and Its Victims?[10]

Ransomware is the fastest-growing malware threat with a catastrophic impact on an organisation. It could disrupt all organisations, both public and private, that use IT infrastructure, whether it's on-site, managed by a third party, virtual, or in the cloud.

Typical attack vectors include email phishing schemes, negative advertising, and untreated vulnerabilities. Once ransomware has penetrated an organisation's computer network, it can propagate and corrupt data on networked systems. Data at risk can include daily transactional information and operating systems, system configurations, and even backup and cloud-based data. When systems are infected and storage encrypted as a result of ransomware, organisations have the choice to pay the ransom, hoping that their data will be preserved, or to recover and rebuild.

The digital 'extortion pandemic' is showing no signs of abating, however, and as ransomware attacks are taking more and more lives in all parts of the United States, and more generally, in the Western world, there is mounting evidence that the next two years could bring more concerted pressure for specific legislation.

While some may view backup and recovery as the last line of defence against ransomware, it may be more effective to design it as a meaningful part of proactive strategic planning.

Fortunately, properly protected and secure backup systems can be used to restore data and infrastructure to a well-known state before a ransomware event and provide the confidence to thrive in the face of a ransomware attack, ensuring data availability and business continuity. Leaders of all organisations need

---

[10]See *The insurance business in the post-Covid-19 era.* https://www.atlas-mag.net/en/issue/insurance-in-the-aftermath-of-covid-19.

to make sure that this describes their organisation by following best practices to protect computer systems is probably the safest path to cyber resilience.

In general, prevention is always better and easier than the cure. Fortunately, there are many measures to prevent ransomware, such as keeping backups, making regular patches, using multi-factor authentication and strong passwords, presenting training programmes for your employees, and using appropriate cyber security tools (Fig. 25.1).

In addition, the protection of an organisation must be designed in lines, from bottom to top. The first line of protection against ransomware should be employee awareness through training in cyber security. This training does not stop at understanding how to recognise an attack but includes a rigorous and continuous cycle. All staff needs to understand the motivations behind a ransomware attack, what they need to do if they believe the organisation has been targeted, how their actions will influence the final result, and what the restart process should incorporate the assumption that an attack could turn into an epidemic, or even a pandemic.

The best way to avoid being exposed to ransomware – or any type of malware – is to be a careful and conscientious user of a computer. Malware distributors have gotten smarter and smarter, and you have to be careful what is downloaded and before clicking. In addition, it is recommended to:

- Maintain operating systems, software, and applications;
- Ensure anti-virus and anti-malware solutions are configured to automatically update and run regular scans;
- Back up data regularly and verify that these backups have been performed;
- Secure backups, and ensure they are not connected to the computers and networks they backup; and
- Develop and implement continuity plan exercises if that the company or organisation is the victim of a ransomware attack.

'Do not become obsolete as an old technology, by continuing to innovate'[11]

Fig. 25.1. Tips to Avoid Ransomware.

[11]Sukant Ratnakar, Indian business man, speaker and motivator.

References

Barberis, N. (2013). Thirty years of prospect theory in economics: A review and assessment. *The Journal of Economic Perspectives*, *27*(1), 173–196. https://doi.org/10.1257/jep.27.1.173

BCI. (n.d.). *Integrating crisis management & business continuity for a successful response*. BCI. https://www.thebci.org/news/integrating-crisis-management-business-continuity-for-a-successful-response.html

Berman, J. (2014, April 20). The three essential Warren Buffett quotes to live by. *Forbes*. https://www.forbes.com/sites/jamesberman/2014/04/20/the-three-essential-warren-buffett-quotes-to-live-by/

Bertoncelj, D. D. B. (2019, August 7). *What is risk perception and how can we improve it?* SilverBulletRisk. https://silverbulletrisk.com/en/blog-what-is-risk-perception-and-how-can-we-improve-it/

Britannica. (2024). *mind. Encyclopedia Britannica*. https://www.britannica.com/topic/mind

Burrows, M., & Manning, R. A. (2022). The top ten global risks of 2023. *The National Interest*. https://nationalinterest.org/feature/top-ten-global-risks-2023-206027

Collectivegreen. (n.d.). What's the difference between circular economy and sustainability? *Collective Green*. https://www.collectivegreen.de/whats-the-difference-between-circular-economy-and-sustainability/

Collier, R. (2017). NHS ransomware attack spreads worldwide. *Canadian Medical Association Journal*, *189*(22), E786–E787. https://doi.org/10.1503/cmaj.1095434

Cynefin Framework. (2021, September 30). *The Cynefin Co*. https://thecynefin.co/about-us/about-cynefin-framework/

Esanum. (n.d.). *Coronavirus – Les apports de la cindynique, « science du danger »*. https://www.esanum.fr/today/posts/coronavirus-les-apports-de-la-cindynique-science-du-danger

EU Monitor. (n.d.). *Circular economy: Definition, importance and benefits*. https://www.eumonitor.eu/9353000/1/j9vvik7m1c3gyxp/vknegugz7hwu?d=30-10-2018

Evans, S. (2023, April 18). *UK regulatory approach to ILS deemed 'not fit for purpose'* Artemis.bm – the Catastrophe Bond, Insurance Linked Securities & Investment, Reinsurance Capital, Alternative Risk Transfer and Weather Risk Management Site. https://www.artemis.bm/news/uk-regulatory-approach-to-ils-deemed-not-fit-for-purpose/

Griffin, R., & Moorhead, G. (2007). *Organizational behavior: Managing people and organizations* (18th ed.). Houghton Mifflin Company.

Haque, T. (2022). Serious debt crisis unfolding in the poorest part of the world: A way forward. *Modern Diplomacy*. https://moderndiplomacy.eu/2022/10/24/serious-debt-crisis-unfolding-in-the-poorest-part-of-the-world-a-way-forward/

Heckerman, D. (2008). A tutorial on learning with Bayesian networks. In *Studies in computational intelligence (Print)* (pp. 33–82). https://doi.org/10.1007/978-3-540-85066-3_3

IBM. (2022). *X-Force Threat Intelligence Index 2022*. https://www.ibm.com/downloads/cas/ADLMYLAZ

IMdR. (n.d.). *Cindynics – IMDR*. https://www.imdr.eu/818_p_52253/cindynics.html

IRM India. (2022). *Complexity and risk: The 4 principles*. https://www.theirmindia.org/blog/complexity-and-risk-the-4-principles/

Knight, F. H. (1921). *Risk, uncertainty and profit*. https://fraser.stlouisfed.org/files/docs/publications/books/risk/riskuncertaintyprofit.pdf

Lombardi, M., Fargnoli, M., & Parise, G. (2019). Risk profiling from the European Statistics on Accidents at Work (ESAW) accidents' databases: A case study in construction sites. *International Journal of Environmental Research and Public Health (Online)*, *16*(23), 4748. https://doi.org/10.3390/ijerph16234748

Louisot, J. (2023). *Comprendre et mettre en œuvre le diagnostic des risques: développer les comptétences ERM d'un organisme*.

Louisot, J. (2023). Metaverse & risk management. *International Journal of Research Studies in Science, Engineering and Technology*, *10*(2), 1–21. https://doi.org/10.22259/2349-476X.1002001

McNally, D. (1990). Political economy and the rise of capitalism: A reinterpretation. *The American Political Science Review*, *84*(1), 284–285. https://doi.org/10.2307/1963654

Meyer, E. (2014). *The culture map: Breaking through the invisible boundaries of global business*. Public Affairs.

Nickerson, C. (2023, October 10). *Prospect theory in psychology: Loss aversion bias*. Simply Psychology. https://www.simplypsychology.org/prospect-theory.html

Norouzi, N. (2021). Learning economy: A new hope to achieve a sustainable economic system. *Circular Economy and Sustainability/Circular Economy and Sustainability*, *2*(2), 535–555. https://doi.org/10.1007/s43615-021-00107-z

Oehrli, P. (2022). *CertX launches its CertAI validation platform after being acquired by Munich Re*. Switzerland Global Enterprise. https://www.s-ge.com/en/article/news/20222-cybersecurity-certx-launches-its-certai-validation-platform-after-being-acquired

PBS NewsHour. (2019, October 24). *Ransomware and data breaches linked to uptick in fatal heart attacks*. https://www.pbs.org/newshour/science/ransomware-and-other-data-breaches-linked-to-uptick-in-fatal-heart-attacks

Quantivate. (2022, August 9). *The state of ERM: Risk management maturity needed | Quantivate blog*. Quantivate. https://quantivate.com/erm-risk-management-maturity-benchmarks/

Reuters. (2023). Crypto's string of bankruptcies. *Future of Money*. https://www.reuters.com/business/finance/cryptos-string-bankruptcies-2023-01-20/

Soudi, N., & Mokhlis, C. E. (2021). The impact of CSR communication on the company's reputation. *Estudios De Economía Aplicada*, *38*(4). https://doi.org/10.25115/eea.v38i4.3983

Sue, V. a. P. B. (2010, June 14). *'It takes many good deeds to build a good reputation, and only one bad one to lose it.' Benjamin Franklin – Penn & Beyond*. https://ulife.vpul.upenn.edu/careerservices/blog/2010/06/14/it-takes-many-good-deeds-to-build-a-good-reputation-and-only-one-bad-one-to-lose-it-benjamin-franklin/

The Nobel Prize. (n.d.). *Daniel Kahneman: Facts*. https://www.nobelprize.org/prizes/economic-sciences/2002/kahneman/facts/

UIS. (2010). *The 2009 UNESCO Framework for Cultural Statistics (FCS)*. https://unstats.un.org/unsd/statcom/doc10/Bg-FCS-e.pdf

Walensky, R. (2022, July 16). COVID Federal Response Hearing on Capitol Hill, June 16, 2022, Washington, DC.

World Economic Forum. (2022, May 20). *How to address digital safety in the metaverse*. https://www.weforum.org/agenda/2022/01/metaverse-risks-challenges-digital-safety/

World Economic Forum. (2023, October 06). *This timeline charts the fast pace of tech transformation across centuries*. https://www.weforum.org/agenda/2023/02/this-timeline-charts-the-fast-pace-of-tech-transformation-across-centuries

Bibliography

A System to Managing Legal Risk – Interview with Yota Kremmida (2021, May 26). https://ceeinhousematters.com/ceeihm-issue-1-3/14404-a-system-to-managing-legal-risk

Abouki, Y. (2018, February 28). *Understanding the role of threat modelling in risk management*. https://resources.infosecinstitute.com/topic/understanding-role-threat-modelling-risk-management/

AI Risk Management Framework: Initial Draft. (2022, March 17). https://www.nist.gov/system/files/documents/2022/03/17/AI-RMF-1stdraft.pdf

Amadeo, K. (2022, January 29). *The causes of the subprime mortgage crisis*. https://www.thebalancemoney.com/what-caused-the-subprime-mortgage-crisis-3305696

ASHRM. *Enterprise risk management for boards and trustees: Leveraging the value*. https://www.ashrm.org/sites/default/files/ashrm/ERM-for-Boards-and-Trustees.pdf

Avetta. *Supply chain ESG strategy – How to get started or advance in maturity*. https://www.avetta.com/fr/node/8616

Bakertilly. (2020, May 26). *Enterprise risk management to support crisis response – a process, not a project*. https://www.bakertilly.com/insights/enterprise-risk-management-to-support-crisis-response

Barberis, N. C. (2013). Thirty years of prospect theory in economics: A review and assessment. *Journal of Economic Perspectives*, *27*(1, Winter), 173–196. http://dx.doi.org/10.1257/jep.27.1.173

BCI Crisis Management Report 2021. https://www.thebci.org/uploads/assets/a9bfc1b4-9dce-440b-9fce248a049862d2/5834ae75-93b8-4c81-a7d67b6d8bc594bb/BCI-0007l-Crisis-Management-ReportSinglesLow.pdf

Behavioral economics for sustainability and circular economy. https://www.frontiersin.org/research-topics/21449/behavioral-economics-for-sustainability-and-circular-economy

Benomar, J. *Culture d'entreprise et gestion des risques*. https://livre.fnac.com/a8762479/Julien-Benomar-Culture-d-entreprise-et-gestion-des-risques

Benwell, S. (2021, September 20). *Governance: Why culture matters*. https://www.strategic-risk-europe.com/home/governance-why-culture-matters/1438881.article?utm_source=adestra&utm_term=Read%20more&utm_medium=email&utm_campaign=24948

Bertoncelj, B. *What is risk perception and how can we improve it?* https://silverbulletrisk.com/en/blog-what-is-risk-perception-and-how-can-we-improve-it/

Bodenheimer, R. (2021, June 11). *What is critical race theory? Definition, principles, and applications – A challenge to the rhetoric of colour-blindness*. https://www.thoughtco.com/critical-race-theory-4685094

Bonfiglioli, E. (2021, April 6). *What is model risk management?* https://www.yields.io/blog/what-is-model-risk-management/

Bonneau, C. (2018). Histoire des théories et paradigmes économiques depuis 1945 – La Découverte. *Regards croisés sur l'économie*, *1*(22), 156–162. https://www.cairn.info/revue-regards-croises-sur-l-economie-2018-1-page-156.htm

Boult, M. (2022, July 14). *Where risk meets sustainability*. https://www.strategic-risk-europe.com/home/where-risk-meets-sustainability/1441768.paper?utm_source=adestra&utm_term=Read%20more&utm_medium=email&utm_campaign=26149

Boyden Executive Monitor. (2018). *Regulation and the role of the board* (N° 14). https://www.boyden.com/media/regulation-and-the-role-of-boards-5441813/regulation-and-the-role-of-boards.pdf

Bradley, C., Hirt, M., & Smit, S. *Strategy to beat the odds*-https://www.mckinsey.com/capabilities/strategy-and-corporate-finance/our-insights/strategy-to-beat-the-odds

Businesswire. (2022, mai 18). *RMS améliore la modélisation des risques climatiques et transpose de nouveaux modèles en haute définition*. https://www.silicon.fr/press-release/rms-ameliore-la-modelisation-des-risques-climatiques-et-transpose-de-nouveaux-modeles-en-haute-definition

Central Bank of Nigeria. *Guidelines for the management of reputational risk*. https://www.cbn.gov.ng/Out/2019/BSD/Guidelines%20on%20the%20Management%20of%20Reputational%20Risk.pdf

Chambers. *Crisis and Risk Management 2022 – The leading Crisis and Risk Management Providers worldwide*. https://chambers.com/legal-guide/crisis-risk-management-108/download

Chen, J. *Prospect theory: What it is and how it works, with examples*. https://www.investopedia.com/terms/p/prospecttheory.asp

CIPD. *Managing multicultural teams*. https://www.cipd.co.uk/knowledge/fundamentals/relations/diversity/managing-multicultural-teams

Circular economy & sustainability. https://www.gs1.org/public-policy/priorities/circular-economy-sustainability

Circular economy and sustainability – Insight from the research: Italian entrepreneurship. Successful trend analysis for the country's economic recovery. https://romebusinessschool.com/blog/circular-economy-and-sustainability/

Circular economy: How it can contribute to sustainable development. https://earth5r.org/circular-economy-can-contribute-sustainable-development/

Clever Technologies. *Les 8 étapes du cycle de gestion des risques*. https://gestion-risques.solutions/

Conn, C., & McLean, R. *Six problem-solving mindsets for very uncertain times*. https://www.mckinsey.com/~/media/McKinsey/Business%20Functions/Strategy%20and%20Corporate%20Finance/Our%20Insights/Six%20problem%20solving%20mindsets%20for%20very%20uncertain%20times/Six-problem-solving-mindsets-for-very-uncertain-times-vF.pdf

Cornilliet, M. (2017, février 16). *ECE: maîtriser la théorie économique en 7 points*. https://major-prepa.com/economie/ece-maitriser-theorie-economique-7-points/

Coso. *Effective enterprise risk oversight – The role of the board of directors*. https://www.coso.org/documents/COSOBoardsERM4pager-FINALRELEASEVERSION82409_001.pdf

Crespo, I., Kumar, P., Noteboom, P., & Taymans, M. *The evolution of model risk management – An increasing reliance on models, regulatory challenges, and talent scarcity is driving banks toward a model risk management organisation that is both more effective and value-centric*. https://www.mckinsey.com/capabilities/risk-and-resilience/our-insights/the-evolution-of-model-risk-management

Darsa, J.-D. *La gestion du risque est un tremplin pour la direction juridique*. https://www.editions-legislatives.fr/actualite/-la-gestion-du-risque-est-un-tremplin-pour-la-direction-juridique-selon-jean-david-darsa

Dash, S. N. (2021, April 4). *Enterprise Risk Management (ERM) and risk governance*. https://www.mpug.com/enterprise-risk-management-erm-and-risk-governance/

Deharo, G., Point, S., & Madanamoothoo, A. (2014). Les risques en entreprise: dialogues entre la gestion et le droit. *Management & Avenir*, *8*(N° 74), 135–143. https://www.cairn.info/revue-management-et-avenir-2014-8-page-135.htm

Deloitte. *Sustainability and the board: What do directors need to know in 2018?* https://www2.deloitte.com/content/dam/Deloitte/global/Documents/Risk/gx-sustainability-and-the-board.pdf

Deloitte. *Tying the knot: Integrating ERM and BCM to improve resiliency.* https://www2.deloitte.com/id/en/pages/risk/articles/integrating-erm-bcm.html

Deloitte Legal. *Legal Risk Management – A heightened focus for the General Counsel.* https://www2.deloitte.com/global/en/pages/legal/articles/legal-risk-management.html

Deutz, P., Cecchin, A., & Salomone, R. (2022). Circular economy and sustainability: View from the International Sustainable Development Research Society 2020 Conference. *Circular Economy and Sustainability, 2*, 665–668. https://link.springer.com/paper/10.1007/s43615-022-00178-6

Dietz, M., Henke, N., Moon, J., Backes, J., Pautasso, L., & Sadeque, Z. (2020, December). *How quantum computing could change financial services.* https://nebash.ngontinh24.com/article/how-quantum-computing-could-change-financial-services

Difference between crisis management and risk management. www.differencebetween.com

Disentangling circular economy, sustainability and waste management principles. https://www.bakerinstitute.org/research/disentangling-circular-economy-sustainability-and-waste-management-principles

Donaire, N. (2019, February 26). *Enterprise Risk Management (ERM) and the board: What you need to know.* https://www.diligent.com/au/enterprise-risk-management-erm-and-the-board-what-you-need-to-know/

Dowd, B. (2021, September 23). *Ensuring an effective CEO-risk manager partnership.* http://www.rmmagazine.com/articles/article/2021/09/23/ensuring-an-effective-ceo-risk-manager-partnership

Enterprise Risk Management (ERM). *Luciano Fantin: This article deals with Enterprise Risk Management and its increased importance in times of crisis.* https://www.risk-fence.com/en/erm-enterprise-risk-management/

Enterprise risk management and the value of a centralized, consistent approach to managing risk. https://acuityrm.com/blog/erm-and-the-value-of-a-centralized-approach-to-managing-risk/

Enterprise risk management framework. Deposit Insurance Corporation of Ontario. https://www.dico.com/design/Publications/En/ERM%202011/ERM_Framework_September_2011.pdf

Epstein, C. (2014, June 6). *How exotic financial strategies created the perfect storm for the 2008 recession.* https://theprogressiveinvestor.org/how-exotic-financial-strategies-created-the-perfect-storm-for-the-2008-recession/

ERIC ED020696: Cross-cultural testing – What to test. https://archive.org/stream/ERIC_ED020696/ERIC_ED020696_djvu.txt

ERM Initiative Faculty. (2011, September 1). *Cyber crisis management: A new philosophy and approach to incident response.* https://erm.ncsu.edu/library/article/Cyber-Crisis-Management

ERM Initiative Faculty and Erika Baker, Class of 2019 Master of Accounting Student. (2019, January 29). *Trends in crisis management & strategies to survive a crisis.* https://erm.ncsu.edu/library/article/trends-in-crisis-management-strategies-to-survive-a-crisis

Evans, D. *Risk intelligence: How to live with uncertainty.* https://www.mindtherisk.com/literature/71-risk-intelligence-how-to-live-with-uncertainty-by-dylan-evans

FERMA position paper on the European Commission's proposal for a Corporate Sustainability Due Diligence Directive (CSDD). https://www.ferma.eu/app/uploads/2022/05/FERMA-position-paper-on-Corporate-Sustainability-Due-Diligence.pdf

Financial Stability Board. *Principles for an effective risk appetite framework.* https://www.fsb.org/wp-content/uploads/r_131118.pdf

Fisic, I. (2022, March 28). *How to overcome cultural and language barriers in the workplace.* https://clockify.me/blog/managing-teams/cultural-and-language-barriers-at-work/

Frías, J. Y. *Interculturality, multiculturalism and transculturality in social translation and interpretation*. Universidade de Vigo. https://cedille.webs.ull.es/M4/07yuste.pdf

Full circle: The importance of sustainability and the circular economy. https://www.canon-europe.com/business/insights/papers/circular-economy-sustainability-importance/

Gauth, G. *La modélisation des risques, peut-on dompter le hasard?* http://biblos.hec.ca/biblio/lecons/Cahier_Gauthier_Genevieve_2011_11_15.pdf

Gerhard, F., Silva, P. J., Tejada, M., & Wallace, T. (2021, January). *The next S-curve in model risk management: How banks can drive transformations of the model life cycle in a highly uncertain business landscape*. https://www.mckinsey.com/capabilities/risk-and-resilience/our-insights/the-next-s-curve-in-model-risk-management

Gestion des risques de catastrophe et guerre de territoire. https://www.nouvelles-du-monde.com/gestion-des-risques-de-catastrophe-et-guerre-de-territoire/

GFIA – IAIS approach to resolution powers and planning must reflect insurers' business model. https://www.asiainsurancereview.com/News/View-NewsLetter-Article/id/75616/Type/eDaily/Global-IAIS-approach-to-resolution-powers-and-planning-must-reflect-insurers-business-model-per-GFIA

Ghețe, A. *Cross-cultural management and organisational performance*. https://www.performancemagazine.org/cross-cultural-management/

Gilbert, S., & Nolop, B. *Risk in the C-suite – Aligning risk communication between the board and management*. https://www.oliverwyman.com/content/dam/oliver-wyman/global/en/files/archive/2013/CH_2_Risk_in_the_C-Suite.pdf

Grabisch, M. (2000). A graphical interpretation of the Choquet integral. *IEEE Transactions on Fuzzy Systems*, *8*(5), 627–631. https://doi.org/10.1109/91.873585

Harbourfront Technologies. (2021, February 24). *What is legal risk?* https://harbourfront technologies.wordpress.com/2021/02/24/what-is-legal-risk/

Hayes, A. (2021, June 02). *Enterprise Risk Management (ERM)*. [Reviewed by Amy Drury]. https://www.investopedia.com/terms/e/enterprise-risk-management.asp

Hazan, E., Kelly, G., Khan, H., Spillecke, D., & Yee, L. *Marketing in the metaverse: An opportunity for innovation and experimentation*. https://www.mckinsey.com/business-functions/growth-marketing-and-sales/our-insights/marketing-in-the-metaverse-an-opportunity-for-innovation-and-experimentation

Head, C. L. *How to address digital safety in the metaverse?* https://www.weforum.org/agenda/2022/01/metaverse-risks-challenges-digital-safety/

Honey-Rosés, J., Anguelovski, I., Bohigas, J., Chireh, V., Daher, C., Konijnendijk, C., Litt, J., Mawani, V., McCall, M., Orellana, A., Oscilowicz, E., Sánchez, U., Senbel, M., Tan, X., Villagomez, E., Zapata, O., & Nieuwenhuijsen, M. *The impact of COVID-19 on public space: A review of the emerging questions*. https://www.academia.edu/42955741/The_Impact_of_COVID_19_on_Public_Space_A_Review_of_the_Emerging_Questions

How a circular economy could help businesses turn waste into resources. https://topicinsights.com/sustainability/circular-economy-economic-model/

Hult, H., & Lindskog, F. (2007). *Mathematical modelling and statistical methods – For risk management lecture notes*. https://people.kth.se/~lindskog/papers/RMlecturenotes07B.pdf

Integrating balanced scorecard and enterprise risk – Ascendant. https://www.ascendantsmg.com/enclosures/ERM%20and%20the%20Balanced%20Scorecard%20-%20Ascendant%20Strategy%20Management%20Group.pdf

Integrating crisis management & business continuity for a successful response. https://www.thebci.org/news/integrating-crisis-management-business-continuity-for-a-successful-response.html

Intégrer la gestion des risques au sein de son activité. https://www.leaderinfo.com/integrer-gestion-des-risques-activite/

Islam, M. *Data driven economy urges global leaders to ensure right to privacy*. https://www.academia.edu/45649647/Data_Driven_Economy_Urges_Global_Leaders_to_Ensure_Right_to_Privacy

Jean-Jules, J., & Vicente, R. *Rethinking the implementation of enterprise risk management (ERM) as a socio-technical challenge.* https://www.tandfonline.com/doi/abs/10.1080/13669877.2020.1750462?journalCode=rjrr20

Kahneman, D., & Ostversk, A. (1979, March). Prospect theory: An analysis of decision under risk. – *ECONOMETRICA ICI*, *47*(2). http://web.mit.edu/curhan/www/docs/Articles/15341_Readings/Behavioral_Decision_Theory/Kahneman_Tversky_1979_Prospect_theory.pdf

Kasia Bogadkowska. (2021, December 6). *Race to the Metaverse opportunities and risks for brands and IP rights.* https://www.webtms.com/race-to-the-metaverse-opportunities-and-risks-for-brands-and-ip-rights/

Ken Tysiac. (2022, March 3). *How ERM and concentric circles can help manage crisis-related risk – Considering emerging risks and interconnected risks can aid in strategic decisions.* https://www.fm-magazine.com/news/2022/mar/how-erm-concentric-circles-can-help-manage-crisis-related-risk.html

Kumar, A. *Security risks associated with metaverse in 2022.* https://www.detoxtechnologies.com/security-risks-associated-with-metaverse/

La théorie des perspectives ou le choix orienté. https://www.andlil.com/theorie-des-perspectives-153648.html

Landini, M. *La gestion des risques interculturels: un enjeu stratégique pour les entreprises.* https://portail-ie.fr/analysis/2082/jdr-la-gestion-des-risques-interculturels-un-enjeu-strategique-pour-les-entreprises

Lee, L.-H., Braud, T., Zhou, P., Wang, L., Xu, D., Lin, Z., Kumar, A., Bermejo, C., & Hui, P. *All one needs to know about metaverse: A complete survey on technological singularity, virtual ecosystem, and research agenda.* https://www.researchgate.net/publication/355172308_All_One_Needs_to_Know_about_Metaverse_A_Complete_Survey_on_Technological_Singularity_Virtual_Ecosystem_and_Research_Agenda

Lee, S. *The meta risks of the metaverse.* https://cio.economictimes.indiatimes.com/tech-talk/the-meta-risks-of-the-metaverse/5228?redirect=1

Legal risk management in a crisis. https://www.shearman.com/perspectives/2020/04/legal-risk-management-in-a-crisis

Liverpool Hope University. *The metaverse poses terrifying dangers academic warns.* https://techxplore.com/news/2021-11-metaverse-poses-dangers-academic.html

Lucas Boncourt. (2022, septembre 16). Gestion de crise: l'information géographique à l'épreuve du feu. In *Localtis – Données, Environnement, gestion données, Numérique, Sécurité.* https://www.banquedesterritoires.fr/gestion-de-crise-linformation-geographique-lepreuve-du-feu

Managing an organisation of different culture: Concepts of international human resource management. https://studycorgi.com/managing-an-organisation-of-different-culture-concepts-of-international-human-resource-management/

Managing risks across UNDP programming and operation. https://info.undp.org/sites/ERM/Shared%20Documents/UNDP%20ERM%20Guide_Sept2019.pdf

Mark Little. (2018, March 8). *6 Steps to legal risk management.* Risk Management. https://www.berkmansolutions.com/articles/risk/6-steps-to-legal-risk-management

Mark Little. (2018, March 8). *How to measure and manage legal risk.* https://www.berkmansolutions.com/articles/risk/how-to-measure-and-manage-legal-risk

McKinsey. *The future of business: Reimagining 2020 and beyond.* https://www.mckinsey.com/~/media/McKinsey/Featured%20Insights/The%20Next%20Normal/The-future-of-business-Reimagining-2020-and-beyond-vF

McKinsey. *Value creation in the metaverse. The real business of the virtual world.* https://www.mckinsey.com/fr/our-insights/value-creation-in-the-metaverse-the-real-business-of-the-virtual-world

Meidl, R. *A circular economy does not necessarily translate to sustainability.* https://www.forbes.com/sites/thebakersinstitute/2021/08/03/a-circular-economy-does-not-necessarily-translate-to-sustainability/

Metaverse definition what exactly is it? https://cryptogamingarea.com/en/faq/metaverse-definition/

Model risk management: A practical approach – Four essential building blocks. https://www2.deloitte.com/us/en/pages/financial-services/articles/model-risk-management.html

Model risk management: A practical approach for addressing common issues. https://www2.deloitte.com/content/dam/Deloitte/us/Documents/financial-services/us-fsi-model-risk-management.pdf

Model risk. https://corporatefinanceinstitute.com/resources/knowledge/modelling/model-risk/

Munich Re develops a tool to certify IA. https://www.youtube.com/watch?v=BMw6ZYBFn9o

Mustafa, S. *Inculcating sustainability and circular economy – Perspectives in institutions of higher education*. https://www.academia.edu/45666306/Inculcating_Sustainability_and_Circular_Economy_Perspectives_in_Institutions_of_Higher_Education

Naim, P. (2022, May 12). *Les réseaux Bayésiens pour la modélisation du risque*. Risques. https://variances.eu/?p=6672

Nickerson, C. (2022, May 11). *Prospect theory: How users make decisions*. https://www.simplypsychology.org/prospect-theory.html

Norouzi, N. (2022). Learning economy: A new hope to achieve a sustainable economic system. *Circular Economy and Sustainability*, *2*, 535–555. https://link.springer.com/paper/10.1007/s43615-021-00107-z

Oyster: The Global Employment Report. (2022). https://www.oysterhr.com/global-employment-report-2022

Pan, Z. *A review of prospect theory*. School of Management, Jinan University. https://www.scirp.org/journal/paperinformation.aspx?paperid=91480

Pelletier, B. *Travailler avec les Français: témoignages de 22 étrangers venant de 19 pays*. https://gestion-des-risques-interculturels.com/pays/europe/france/travailler-avec-les-francais-temoignages-de-22-etrangers-venant-de-19-pays/

Prospect theory. https://www.britannica.com/print/article/1939431

Prospect theory. https://www.economicshelp.org/blog/glossary/prospect-theory/

Prospect theory: Applications in political science. https://www.britannica.com/topic/prospect-theory/Applications-in-political-science

Quantitative. (2022, July 22). *The state of ERM: Research reveals need for risk management maturity*. https://quantivate.com/erm-risk-management-maturity-benchmarks/

Quinn, S., Ivy, N., Barrett, M., Witte, G., Gardner, R. K. *NIST Internal Report – NIST IR 8286C – Staging cyber-security risks for enterprise risk management and governance oversight*. https://doi.org/10.6028/NIST.IR.8286C

Rebooting your culture for hybrid work. https://www.servicenow.com/workflow/wp-content/uploads/2022/01/Workflow_hybrid-work-culture-report_final-1.14.pdf

Renn, O. *Risk perception and risk management: A review Part 2: Lessons for risk management*. Center for Environment, Technology, and Development, Carle University. https://www.researchgate.net/publication/279396833_Risk_perception_and_risk_management_A_review

Resilient, dynamic and relevant: ERM in a new risk environment. *Financier Worldwide Magazine*, November 2020. https://www.financierworldwide.com/resilient-dynamic-and-relevant-erm-in-a-new-risk-environment#.YvpLmRzP1PY

Rethinking risk in a post-pandemic world. https://www2.erm-academy.org/publication/risk-management-article/rethinking-risk-in-a-post-pandemic-world/

RIMS Executive Report. *Rethinking the impact of disruption on enterprise risk management tools and processes*. https://www.rims.org/about-us/newsroom/news/rims-executive-report-rethinking-the-impact-of-disruption-on-enterprise-risk-management-tools-and-processes

Risk & crisis management. https://tuckerhall.com/specialties/risk-management-crisis-management/

Risk and crisis management: The Northern Rock Case. https://graduateway.com/risk-and-crisis-management-northern-rock-case-study/

Risk management and modelling – Measure what Matters, Make better decisions. https://hubbardresearch.com/risk-management-modelling/

Risk management versus crisis management explained. https://pm-alliance.com/risk-management-versus-crisis-management-explained/

Role of data analytics in risk management. https://www.ey.com/en_in/risk/role-of-data-analytics-in-risk-management

Roy, S. M. *Life of tribals during COVID-19 times*. https://www.academia.edu/49918068/Life_of_Tribals_during_COVID_19_times

Sabine Zimmer. (2022, May 18). *Managing risk in the metaverse*. Big Data, Data & Cybersecurity. https://sharedassessments.org/blog/managing-risk-in-the-metaverse/#

Sagar, K. (2022, 11 April). *The metaverse explained everything you need to know*. https://www.linkedin.com/pulse/metaverse-explained-everything-you-need-know-sagar-khurana/

Sand Run Risk Blog. (2021, March 19). *Rethinking ERM in the age of pandemics and cyber crime: Part X - Reverence for life is the bedrock of total engagement*. https://www.sandrunrisk.com/blog/rethinking-erm-in-the-age-of-pandemics-and-cyber-crime-part-x-reverence-for-life-is-the-bedrock-of-total-engagement

Sandra Helou of Zilliqa. *What are the risks of recreating reality in the metaverse?* https://forkast.news/what-are-risks-recreating-reality-metaverse/

SAS. *From crisis to opportunity: Redefining risk management*. https://www.sas.com/en/whitepapers/from-crisis-to-opportunity-112141.html

Seeking Innovations in ERM – August 3, 2021 | An interview with Jim Traut by Mark Beasley. https://erm.ncsu.edu/library/article/seeking-innovations-in-erm?utm_campaign=ERM%20%7C%20Thought%20Papers&utm_medium=email&_hsmi=146173808&_hsenc=p2ANqtz-_m70GdoaXi-qLdZxwoEpVpHDDe9wSQFdX5kG4Pv5GZqu-sAsP3myf1oj7BWN5KVCh2axh5WTBA4-lb0ZBljZbU-6K3Qw&utm_content=146173808&utm_source=hs_email

Sennara, M., & Hartman, F. T. (2002, October 3). Managing cultural risks on international projects. In *Conference paper risk management, organisational culture*. https://www.pmi.org/learning/library/managing-cultural-risks-international-projects-1044

Shorthose, S. (2020, June 30). *Managing risks and C-suite expectations during a crisis*. https://www.kyriba.com/blog/managing-risks-and-expectations/

SIGMA. *Maintaining resilience: The role of P&C insurers in a new world order*. https://www.swissre.com/dam/jcr:f4657ae2-412c-40b9-a6af-d84c7282b735/2022-09-09-sri-sigma5-maintenance-resilience-en.pdf

Simonfy, Z. Les usages de la notion de transculturel dans le discours médiatique. Revue d'Etudes Canadiennes en Europe Centrale.

Slovic, P. *Perception of risk*. https://www.researchgate.net/publication/325954197_The_perception_of_risk

Stratégie et gestion des risques en entreprise. https://www.institutdesactuaires.com/global/gene/link.php?doc_id=689&fg=1

Stronger, fitter, better: Crisis management for the resilient enterprise. https://www2.deloitte.com/za/en/pages/risk/articles/crisis_management_for_the_resilient_enterprise.html

Terms of reference for board oversight of enterprise risk management ('ERM') – Capstone Mining Corp. https://s25.q4cdn.com/701614211/files/doc_downloads/board_documents/Board-Risk-Terms-of-Reference.pdf

The ERM Foundation Annual Review 2021. https://www.erm.com/globalassets/documents/erm-foundation/erm-foundation-annual-review-2021.pdf (ERM means here Environmental Resources Management)

The key to managing across cultures in 2022 and beyond. https://www.oysterhr.com/library/the-key-to-managing-across-cultures-in-2022-and-beyond

The metaverse explained: Examples. https://www.brisklogic.co/the-metaverse-explained-examples/

The state of risk oversight 2021 – An overview of enterprise risk management practices. https://fr.search.yahoo.com/yhs/search?hspart=trp&hsimp=yhs-001&type=Y61_F1_148993_102720&p=the+sate+of+risk+overview+2021+NC+University

The University of Vermont. *ERM roles and responsibilities*. https://www.uvm.edu/erm

Top 10 metaverse risks. Blog. https://identitymanagementinstitute.org/top-10-metaverse-risks

Transforming risk management into risk intelligence. https://globalriskcommunity.com/profiles/blogs/transforming-risk-management-into-risk-intelligence

True or false? 10 myths about hiring global employees. https://www.oysterhr.com/library/myths-about-hiring-global-employees?utm_campaign=22-06-14%20CD%20Global%20Employment%20Report&utm_medium=email&_hsmi=216755048&_hsenc=p2ANqtz-_IQU474JUhcWxXyg6z19eUVRNZaV9SRGYfpJ5p0haMpt6HT9Tt2ShoPKDerAmMZtx1IqKTzlVhPkZKacoHNtE1jIAaqw&utm_content=216755048&utm_source=hs_automation

Trust and risks in the metaverse: 6 key considerations. https://www.pwc.com/us/en/tech-effect/emerging-tech/metaverse-trust-and-risk-considerations.html

What is metaverse, how can I be in the *metaverse*? [*metaverse explained*]. Publié le 19 mai 2022. https://www.linkedin.com/pulse/what-metaverse-how-can-i-explained-samuel-abayomi/

What is prospect theory? Definition, theory and an example. https://www.toolshero.com/decision-making/prospect-theory/

What is the difference between Circular Economy and Sustainability? – Sustainable Living – Stefan Simon for Collective Green. https://www.collectivegreen.de/whats-the-difference-between-circular-economy-and-sustainability/

What is the metaverse and how it works – Metaverse explained. https://blog.portion.io/what-is-the-metaverse-and-how-it-works-metaverse-explained/

What is the metaverse exactly? https://www.wired.com/story/what-is-the-metaverse/

What makes or breaks predictive modelling for risk management? https://maritime-executive.com/features/what-makes-or-breaks-predictive-modelling-for-risk-management

Williams, C. *3 Easy to use tips to understanding why executives want ERM*. https://www.erminsightsbycarol.com/understanding-why-executives-want-erm/

Williams, C. *3 Factors to consider before escalating risk issues to the board*. https://www.erminsightsbycarol.com/escalating-risk-issues-board/

Williams, C. *5 Tips to making board risk reports meaningful tools for decision-making*. https://www.erminsightsbycarol.com/board-risk-reports/

Williams, C. *The board's role in risk oversight and why it's important*. https://www.erminsightsbycarol.com/boards-role-risk-oversight/

Winning the ESG race – Walking the talk on ESG has gone from a stroll around the block to a rigorous fitness regime – DILIGENT. https://www.diligent.com/wp-content/uploads/sites/8/2021/09/Whitepaper-Winning-the-environmental-social-and-governance-race.pdf

Xilu. (2021, January 7). *Risk management committee: Role and responsibility assignment matrix*. https://tmqresearch.com/risk-management-committee-role-and-responsibility-assignment-matrix/

Yang, B. W., & Hurtado, G. H. (2022, March 09). *Nouvelles méthodes de travail: comment les outils numériques optimisent la gestion des sinistres complexes*. https://axaxl.com/fr/fast-fast-forward/articles/comment-les-outils-numeriques-optimisent-la-gestion-des-sinistres-complexes?utm_campaign=INTE_FRA_RSNA_FNA_INA_NEWS_FFF_Email_March_2022&utm_medium=email&utm_source=Eloqua

Index

Printed and bound by CPI Group (UK) Ltd, Croydon, CR0 4YY

13/09/2026

14961063-0005